WITHDRAWN
UTSA LIB

RENEWALS 458-

PUMP *and Dump*

PUMP

and *Dump*

The Rancid Rules of the New Economy

Robert H. Tillman
and Michael L. Indergaard

RUTGERS UNIVERSITY PRESS
NEW BRUNSWICK, NEW JERSEY, AND LONDON

A volume in the Critical Issues in Crime and Society series,
edited by Raymond J. Michalowski Jr.

Library of Congress Cataloging-in-Publication Data
Tillman, Robert.
 Pump and dump : the rancid rules of the new economy / Robert H. Tillman and
Michael L. Indergaard.
 p. cm.
 Includes bibliographical references and index.
 ISBN-13: 978–0–8135–3680–4 (hardcover : alk. paper)
 1. Securities fraud—United States.   2. Corporations—Corrupt practices—United
States.   3. Energy industries—Corrupt practices—United States.   4. Telecommunica-
tion—Corrupt practices—United States.   5. Electronic commerce—Corrupt prac-
tices—United States.   I. Indergaard, Michael, 1956–   II. Title.
 HV6769.T554 2005
 364.16′8′0973—dc22

                                                                    2005004409

A British Cataloging-in-Publication record for this book is available from the British Library.

Copyright © 2005 by Robert H. Tillman and Michael L. Indergaard
All rights reserved
No part of this book may be reproduced or utilized in any form or by any means, electronic or mechanical, or by any information storage and retrieval system, without written
permission from the publisher. Please contact Rutgers University Press, 100 Joyce Kilmer
Avenue, Piscataway, NJ 08854-8099. The only exception to this prohibition is "fair use" as
defined by U.S. copyright law.

Manufactured in the United States of America

**Library
University of Texas
at San Antonio**

[A] certain class of dishonesty, dishonesty magnificent in its proportions, and climbing into high places, has become at the same time so rampant and so splendid that there seems to be reason for fearing that men and women will be taught to feel that dishonesty, if it can become splendid, will cease to be abominable. If dishonesty can live in a gorgeous palace with pictures on all its walls, and gems in all its cupboards, with marble and ivory in all its corners, and can give Apician dinners, and get into Parliament, and deal in millions, then dishonesty is not disgraceful, and the man dishonest after such a fashion is not a low scoundrel.

—Anthony Trollope, *An Autobiography* (1883),
on the social context of mid-nineteenth-century London

CONTENTS

PUMP *and Dump*

Introduction

In a decade of corporate makeovers, few firms could match Enron when it came to reinvention. Little more than a week after the roaring nineties came to an end, Enron was at it again, using its annual analysts meeting on January 11, 2000, to trumpet a new "Broadband strategy." A rapt audience of two hundred analysts and institutional investors listened to Enron's latest rendition of a story that Wall Street loved—the saga of a company transforming itself—this time into a bona fide New Economy firm. Enron executives proclaimed that its new proprietary software would allow it to become "the world's largest buyer and seller of bandwidth" and "the world's largest provider of premium broadband delivery services."[1]

In truth, Enron had yet to solve the formidable technical problems involved, and the markets for neither broadband nor digital content were wanting for suppliers. However, it did have some high-powered business

1

stars to back up the story. Enron chairman and CEO Ken Lay—widely seen as a free market visionary because of Enron's success in trading natural gas and electrical power—announced that broadband trading would overshadow these previous accomplishments. Scott McNealy, the CEO of Sun Microsystems, made a surprise appearance to announce that he would be selling eighteen thousand routers to Enron that could be used to build its ambitious network. Jeffrey Skilling, Enron's intimidating chief operating officer, delivered the punch line concerning the bottom line: Enron would soon capture 20 percent of the U.S. market for bandwidth "intermediation," which would bring in $1 billion in operating income to the firm by 2004; content services would create global revenues of $11.7 billion by 2008, generating another $3.5 billion in operating income. These two new parts of Enron, he avowed, were worth $29 billion—or $37 a share more than Enron's existing stock price. After the speeches the analysts were ushered through Enron's broadband offices, where they marveled at the flat-screen TVs and glass-enclosed servers—unaware that these were props, added for just this occasion. They duly phoned in the good news about "the last undiscovered technology play," and Enron's stock shot up 26 percent before the day ended (p. 244). In the next few weeks a chorus of analysts sang praises for Enron's latest makeover bid: "impressive story. . . . We see validation in the sheer technical excellence that was obvious from our walk-through of Enron's facilities. . . . The risk is staggeringly low and the potential reward is staggeringly high. . . . Although this is still an energy company, in our view, Enron fits the description of a 'New Economy' stock" (p. 244).

Enron's New Economy launch propelled it through the April 2000 meltdown of dot-com stocks. In July, when Enron and Blockbuster formed a partnership to deliver videos online, Ken Lay announced that Enron had put together "the killer-ap for the entertainment industry" (p. 292). Nothing ever came of the deal, but Enron's stock kept rising until August, when it peaked at $90 a share, giving the company a total market valuation of $70 billion (p. 244).

The New Economy Pump and Dump

Although Enron's coming-out party as a New Economy concern occurred near the end of the era, the firm had long embodied many of the trends that came together under the "New Economy" moniker in the later half of the 1990s. Enron presented itself as the kind of innovative firm that remade the rules. In the words of its auditor, Arthur Andersen, Enron "is a first mover, and expects to push the edges of established convention, and where they can, create new conventions . . . often in very gray areas" (p. 147). And the manner in which Enron went about remaking the rules drew on disparate notions that would later become loosely bound together as New Economy doctrine.

First and foremost, Enron embraced free market ideals with a fundamentalist fervor that gave the firm an air of "irrational exuberance" several years before the bull market took off. Like firms in several other New Economy sectors, Enron used the free market mantra as it lobbied to alter its regulatory environment. In his role as Enron's ambassador to Washington, Ken Lay labored to clear out the regulatory rules with the same vigor that his friend President George W. Bush used to clear out the underbrush at the ranch; moreover, the free market convictions of Lay—a former undersecretary in the Department of Energy—did not stop him from requesting public resources for his firm.

Market fundamentalism, in combination with the sensibilities of a former McKenzie consultant, fueled Skilling's effort to use the lure of vast monetary gain to harness the firm's intellectual capital to the agenda of bold risk-taking. Skilling was the point man in the effort to convince analysts, the financial media, and institutional investors that Enron was a new kind of firm—a first mover that could achieve high growth because of its fearless embrace of free markets and state-of-the-art risk management. He also brought two other typical New Economy practices to Enron: a resolve to pump up the firm's stock value and the kind of aggressive accounting that helped firms show high quarterly earnings. Skilling also espoused the kind of cultural superiority that was *de rigueur* at dotcom firms, dividing the world into those who "got it" (the new reality) and the hapless souls who toiled in the "butt crack" economy.

Finally, the dark side of the New Economy predominated in the less visible bowels of Enron—a realm commanded by Andy Fastow, the chief financial officer. Like "Scotty" in the engine room of the Starship *Enterprise,* Fastow continually struggled to keep it all from blowing. Fastow helped the firm "make" its numbers by putting together teams of financial engineers that drew on not only his financial staff but also collaborating investment bankers, accountants, and lawyers. By hiding self-dealing between Enron units and disguising bank loans, the financial engineers created the appearance of revenues that helped the firm meet its quarterly earnings targets—and allowed it to show only $13 billion of its $38 billion in debt on its balance sheets.

By the time this debt had sunk the firm, several dozen insiders had cashed in hundreds of millions in stock, leaving most investors (and Enron's workers) to see their holdings go down with the ship. Here then was one last area where Enron proved to be a New Economy standard bearer: dumping of stock by the well-connected at the expense of everyone else.

Considering just Enron's workers, there are some twenty thousand epilogues to Enron's New Economy story. Take, for instance, Janice F. After working for Enron for sixteen years, she thought she had realized her lifelong dream of financial security when she retired in late 2000 with $700,000 in her 401(k) savings plan account. The following year, Janice grew nervous as the value of Enron's stock began to decline, and in October 2001 she tried to get her money out of the account. Janice was shocked to learn that the company had imposed a lockdown on the plan that prohibited current and former employees from transferring funds out of their accounts. When the lockdown was finally lifted, her shares had lost so much value that all she received was a check for $20,418. This reversal of fortune had a devastating effect. Instead of a comfortable retirement, the sixty-one-year-old was forced to live primarily off $500 a month in Social Security benefits. In order to reduce her expenses, she turned off her electricity at night, stopped using her air conditioner, reduced her phone calls to a minimum, and shopped at thrift stores.[2]

The fate that befell Janice and millions of other holders of New Economy stock is not all that different than that experienced by victims of what securities regulators call "pump and dump" schemes. In "classic" pump and dump schemes, employees of small securities brokerage firms make cold calls to potential investors from "boiler rooms," pitching stock in small companies without revealing that insiders at the brokerage firm hold stock in the companies being pitched. Their forceful marketing often produces a buying frenzy that drives the stock value up; when the stock peaks, the insiders sell their holdings at a fat profit while outsider investors are left holding the bag as the value of their investments plummet. For regulators, these schemes are straightforward violations of law and there is little hand-wringing about sending perpetrators to jail.

We propose that by the late 1990s, conditions in much of the U.S. corporate economy—and in the energy trading, telecom, and dot-com sectors in particular—had become criminogenic, in that they facilitated criminal behavior and that this behavior, stripped to its essentials, resembled the classic pump and dump schemes. We argue that the pump and dump analogy captures two core tendencies of New Economy enterprises during the rise and fall of the 1990s boom. The pump side stems from efforts of firms and their backers to follow a key tenet of New Economy doctrine: boost your share prices so you can turn the stock into a "currency" that will allow you to acquire other assets at less cost—fueling a spiral of growth that will, in turn, reinforce the stocks' standing. To this end, firms and assorted confederates (business intermediaries) used various mechanisms to boost the value of stock—and more desperate measures to maintain its value when the positions of firms began to deteriorate. On the dump side, insiders cashed in (usually surreptitiously) before the stock collapsed—selling their holdings for fantastic profits—while employees and other investors ended up with stocks that were worth a fraction of what they paid for them, or nothing at all.

Yet the analogy is obviously limited—the phenomenon we explain is much broader and more complex—intertwined with legitimate entrepreneurship and historic shifts in state regulations, markets, and technologies. The challenge we take on in this book is to do justice to the systemic character of New Economy frauds as well as its human dimensions; we want to capture the full range of motivations and social circumstances involved and the damage done to individual lives and the larger society. The lead participants in New Economy frauds stand in marked contrast to the shadowy characters who inhabit boiler rooms. They included entrepreneurs who were celebrated as New Economy heroes, reputable professionals, prestigious financial institutions, and business notables with the highest of political connections—ranging from new "friends of Bill" to old buddies of "W." A broad swath of American institutions served as their boiler room; their modus operandi was to exploit normal institutional mechanisms for gaining expert approval and public notice. And, to an extraordinary extent, they came to see even the most egregious organized deceptions to be "normal" practice in their line of business. It is the seeming normality of the New Economy scandals that warrants special scrutiny and concern. How was it that such a broad spectrum of corporate America ended up a "field of schemes" where many a reputable business could resemble a two-bit securities scam?

In trying to account for the scandals, most economists have extended a stylized portrait of individual rationality to explain the behavior of entire social segments. In contrast, we draw on economic sociology to show that rationality is "instituted"—framed by "rules," in their various guises.

We argue that the New Economy scandals resulted from the interaction of rules nested at three levels of corporate governance: (1) Congress, under the influence of corporate contributors and free market ideologues, set the general tone by promoting "market" rules while gutting protections for ordinary investors; (2) business professionals, who were supposed to monitor corporations, cashed in on their positions of institutionalized trust by joining executives in propagating New Economy business rules in particular sectors; and (3) smaller circles that controlled access to the "deal flow," in effect, made their own rules as they developed norms and routines that helped organize (and normalize) collective corruption. Rationality was also structured by one's position within webs of fraud. Those with centrality had much more knowledge about the nature of schemes (and power) than their accomplices—and victims.

A Thousand Points of Blight

Talk of a New Economy reached a crescendo in the last few years of the 1990s, but waves of economic change had been transforming the American landscape for a quarter century. The federal government's retreat from the Keynesian welfare state, seemingly endless corporate restructuring, a new round of globalization, financialization, and the advance of digital technology all had roots in the 1970s. As these trends accelerated in the 1980s, they produced excitement about new forms of collaboration (teams, networks) and innovative work, but also considerable anxiety about what all the change meant for the general well-being. A decade that began with the excruciating decline of manufacturing ended with painful bouts of corporate downsizing that cut deep into the white-collar ranks—and a devastating stock market crash that stopped (temporarily, it turns out) a new breed of Wall Street financial players. The severe recession that ushered the United States into the 1990s sapped all sense of momentum in the American economy. It also dashed hopes for the future of a new generation, as was apparent in the "slacker" persona. When President George H. W. Bush tried to lift the gloom (in a manner that would not commit the government to do much of anything), his tribute to volunteerism—a "thousand points of light"—drew ridicule.

And then it all seemed to turn around within a few years and the different elements of change seemed to interact in magnificent fashion to spur entrepreneurship, innovation, and increases in productivity. The longest sustained economic expansion in U.S. history took off and was punctuated by resounding booms in the stock market, particularly in the technology segment. The Dow Jones Industrial Average reached 12,000, while the NASDAQ hit 5,000; by the end of the decade it seemed that the wealth was trickling down to the lower levels. Income began to increase and poverty rates declined. The celebration of American technology and financial "innovation" became intertwined with post–Cold War triumphalism, and our leaders announced to the world that unfettered capitalism was "real" capitalism. And then everything seemed to change again. Our New Economy champions fell hard with the spring 2000 market crash or were disgraced by the ensuing scandals.

Over the last three years, a startling series of corporate scandals has shaken the economy to it its core as high-flying firms such as Enron, Global Crossing, and WorldCom crashed amid allegations of accounting fraud and insider dealing. Coming in the wake of the dot-com bust, the crisis in corporate governance confirms that the New Economy as we knew it circa 1999 was propped up by illusions. Each day seems to bring new revelations about misdeeds at some of the country's largest and seemingly most successful firms. The Bush administration has publicly stated that these incidents represent the actions of a "few bad apples" whose rooting out with swift prosecutions can set the economy right again. In this book we take a different view: that these scandals are evidence of systemic problems; that they are not limited to a few individuals and a few companies, but instead are widespread; and that the matter cannot be resolved with a few indictments, but requires fundamental changes in the way that corporate America is governed.

2002: Year of the (Corporate) Rat

As 2002 began, a bankrupt Enron Corporation was at the center of a growing controversy after the public learned that executives had dumped their stock while prohibiting employees from selling theirs. The telecom giant Global Crossing declared bankruptcy, and the SEC and FBI began investigations into the firm's accounting practices.[3] At nearly the same time, the powerhouse investment bank Credit Suisse First Boston (CSFB) agreed to pay $100 million to settle charges leveled by the SEC that the firm had made shares in "hot" IPOs available to favored clients before the public had access, and that those clients then "flipped" the stock, making enormous profits.[4] The chilling revelations continued through the spring and summer. Arthur Andersen, the accounting firm for both Enron and Global Crossing, was indicted for destroying documents related to Enron.[5] The SEC filed suit against Waste Management, Inc., for massive fraud involving overstatements of profits.[6] New York Attorney General Eliot Spitzer made public damning evidence of bias and conflicts of interest among highly regarded stock analysts at firms such as Merrill Lynch.[7] Xerox Corporation agreed to pay a large fine to settle charges that it had used accounting tricks to boost earnings and revenues by over $4.5 billion.[8] A number of energy trading companies admitted they had engaged in "round-trip" transactions with each other so as to inflate revenues.[9] WorldCom revealed massive accounting "irregularities," was charged with a massive fraud by the SEC, and soon filed for the largest corporate bankruptcy in history.[10] The Justice Department announced it had begun a criminal investigation of another telecom giant, Qwest, regarding the use of "swap" transactions to boost earnings,[11] a Senate panel discovered evidence that bankers at Citigroup, J. P. Morgan, and Merrill Lynch had assisted Enron in setting up sham deals to avoid taxes and hide debt,[12] and the media giant AOL Time Warner announced that it was under investigation by the SEC for possible accounting abuses during the period leading up to the historic merger.[13] The second half of the year saw revelations and charges of misdeeds concerning Salomon Smith Barney, Tyco, Inc., more telecom firms, Enron, and CSFB. A *Business Week* cover story succinctly summed up the question on the mind of the public: "How Corrupt Is Wall Street?"[14]

A number of business leaders and conservative apologists have argued that the "corporate crime wave" that surfaced in 2002 was overblown by the media. In order to counter this critique, one must, in the words of eminent sociologist Robert Merton, "establish the phenomenon"—ensure that "the phenomena be shown to exist or to occur before one explains why they exist or how they come to be."[15]

Hard data on corporate crime are difficult to come by since federal authorities, who spend billions of dollars collecting and disseminating vast reams of data on street crime, do not systematically collect any data on white-collar crime. One can, however, get a sense of the dimension of the problem by examining two sets of trend data: (1) statistics on the number of financial restatements filed by corporations; and (2) data on class action lawsuits filed against companies alleging securities fraud.

Financial Restatements

All publicly traded companies are required to submit annual financial statements to the SEC. These statements are meant to provide investors with basic information about the companies' structure and performance and include information on things such as assets, liabilities, revenues, and earnings. If information is discovered after the statements are filed that alters those numbers, companies are required to submit revised statements, or "restatements." While a restatement can occur for a number of reasons, many of the companies involved recently in accounting scandals were forced to file restatements because of "accounting irregularities." Thus, financial restatements can be seen as one indirect measure of corporate misconduct, specifically, intentional efforts to mislead investors.

In 2002, the General Accounting Office (GAO), the research wing of the U.S. Congress, conducted a study that put together information on 845 public companies that had filed a total of 919 restatements between January 1, 1997, and June 30, 2002. One might deem these, with a bit of poetic license, the New Economy's "thousand points of blight," as they all involved "accounting irregularities," defined as: "an instance in which a company restates its financial statements because they were not fairly presented in accordance with generally accepted accounting principles (GAAP)," including "material errors and fraud."[16] The yearly counts, along with projections for the second half of 2002, are presented in Figure I.1. The data revealed clear trends: this six-year period saw an increase of 170 percent in the number of restatements, growing from 92 in 1997 to an estimated 250 in 2002. The 845 companies that filed restatements in the 1997–2002 period represent some 10 percent of all companies listed on the three major stock exchanges: The New York Stock Exchange, the American Stock Exchange, and NASDAQ.[17]

Several other findings in the study are noteworthy. First, the GAO found that by far the most common reason (38 percent) for restatement was "revenue recognition," that is, the amount of revenue claimed. This is significant because, as we will see in later chapters, many corporations inflated revenues in order to pump their stock values. Second, the study also showed that restatements had a very negative impact on investors. The researchers found that restating companies lost an average of 10 percent in stock price the day after restatement, producing a total loss in market capitalization of over $100 billion.[18] This point is underscored by a third finding: The size of companies (in terms of the total value of

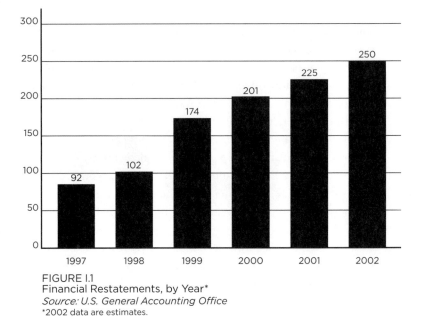

FIGURE I.1
Financial Restatements, by Year*
Source: U.S. General Accounting Office
*2002 data are estimates.

their stock) that filed restatements increased by more than 300 percent during the period, from a median market capitalization of $143 million in 1997 to $351 million in 2002. This means that in the late nineties investor losses were accelerating as a result of restatements.

Class Action Securities Fraud Lawsuits

One recourse available to shareholders is to file a class action lawsuit alleging that they suffered monetary damages, typically resulting from a decline in the value of their shares, because of the fraudulent actions of executives, managers, or other corporate insiders. The ability to bring these suits was significantly restricted in 1995 when a Republican-controlled Congress passed (over the veto of President Clinton) the Private Securities Litigation Reform Act as part of House Speaker Newt Gingrich's conservative agenda. The law was ostensibly intended to reduce frivolous lawsuits, but had the effect of raising the bar on all securities lawsuits, and helped shield executives and corporate "advisers" (e.g., lawyers and accountants). The law's impact was evident in 1996 when the number of class action securities fraud lawsuits filed in federal courts dropped by 43 percent from the previous year. Despite these restrictions, the number of shareholder lawsuits swelled in the late 1990s.

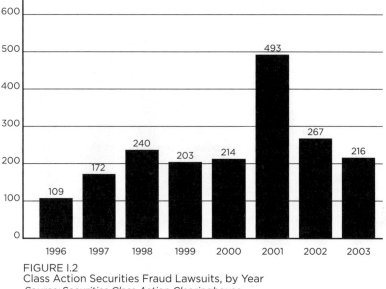

FIGURE I.2
Class Action Securities Fraud Lawsuits, by Year
Source: Securities Class Action Clearinghouse.

The data in Figure I.2—collected by researchers at Stanford University—show trends in class action securities lawsuits alleging fraudulent behavior on the part of company insiders.[19] The yearly counts show a dramatic increase in the number of suits, rising from 109 in 1996 to a peak of 493 in 2001. Significantly, a large number (312) of the 2001 suits involve IPO (initial public offering) allocations, in which shareholders typically alleged that company insiders, investment banks, and analysts conspired to drive up stock prices in IPOs in order to profit from pre-market allocations of the stock at below-market prices to insiders—leaving non-insiders to pay inflated prices for their stock. The great majority of the IPO-allocation suits involved high-tech firms, particularly dot-coms (see chapter 3). The data also reveal that 40 of the 267 suits filed in 2002 involved allegations of misconduct by stock analysts, based on public disclosures concerning their role in hyping stocks. Like the re-statement trends, the data on class action lawsuits indicate that the scope of corporate frauds involving securities increased dramatically in the latter half of the 1990s. These suits, for the most part, were large cases involving hundreds—if not thousands—of shareholders and allegations of many millions of dollars in losses.

Two studies provide a basis for determining the broader impact of corporate corruption on the economy and on ordinary individuals. The Brookings Institution estimated that corporate scandals occurring in the period beginning with Enron's bankruptcy in December 2001 and ending with WorldCom's bankruptcy announcement in July 2002 caused a loss of $35 billion in the gross domestic product in the year following the WorldCom announcement.[20] Using the Brookings Institution methodology, the New York State Office of the Comptroller estimated that the scandals cost that state's economy $2.9 billion in fiscal year 2002–2003 and cost the state retirement fund for state and municipal employees $9 billion. And it estimated that in the period from mid-March 2002 through mid-July 2002, corporate scandals caused the average 401(k) plan participants who were in their sixties to lose $10,450 from their accounts.[21]

While these studies are open to criticism, they do begin to give us a sense of the macro- and micro-level costs of the corporate scandals in the late 1990s. Among other things, they confirm the fact—often noted by criminologists but rarely by politicians—that the monetary costs of white-collar crimes, including corporate crime, dwarf those of street crimes. The costs of many corporate crimes are often diffused over large numbers of victims, shareholders, for example. It is only when the brunt of these costs are felt by identifiable individuals—people like Janice F.—that the public fully grasps the harm that these crimes can inflict.

The Rules Thing (Partnoy's Complaint)

One of the most perplexing and frustrating puzzles of the New Economy scandals is the failure of the rules; neither old laws nor the "new rules" touted by New Economy advocates seemed to deter wrongdoing. A second question concerns the rationality of those involved. What were they thinking? What made them think that they could get away with it? Surprise has given way to dismay as we hear that in case after case elaborate accounting deceptions were probably legal, which raises questions about the rationality of the system of corporate governance itself. A host of books has emerged to explain some pieces of the puzzle. Most have focused on a single firm (usually Enron) or some strategic issue (accounting, regulation). Several have tried to show how a variety of elements interacted in a perverse manner so as to subvert regulations and laws.

Could it actually be that the rules were so watered down by the late 1990s that it was nearly impossible for business to be convicted of a financial crime? Frank Partnoy—a law professor and ex–Wall Street trader—comes close to making this conclusion in his book *Infectious*

Greed. He argues that the financial machinations of firms such as Enron were not illegal as much as they were "alegal"—the result of "15 years of changes in law and culture that had converted reprehensible actions into behaviors that were outside the law, and, therefore, seemingly perfectly appropriate."[22] One factor is the increasing complexity of financial instruments, such as derivatives, which, Partnoy argues, has caused employers to lose control over subordinates. In this "new world," it was difficult for boards of directors—let alone ordinary shareholders—"to decipher their company's financial statements" (p. 35). A second factor is the sagging of regulatory oversight as a result of ill-advised deregulation and anemic enforcement. Together, these developments created a "loss-of-control daisy chain": "Regulators had lost what limited control they had over market intermediaries, market intermediaries had lost what limited control they had over corporate managers, and corporate managers had lost what limited control they had over employees" (p. 3).

The scenario Partnoy sketches suggests a network of actors, each of whom suffered from what organizational theorists refer to as "bounded rationality." The ability of each actor to make decisions was impaired by a lack of information concerning what the other actors were thinking and actually doing. This led to "exponential risk-taking at many companies, largely hidden from public view" (p. 3).

Of course, the impairment in question was moral as well as rational in nature, involving the spread of dubious sensibilities and practices. Partnoy repeatedly refers to the spread of a culture (within and between firms) that he vaguely characterizes as "greedy," "mercenary," or "selfish"—imprinted by the "morals of the market," where personal gain is the prime value. Yet, *Infectious Greed* depends on biological metaphors to try to capture the process through which the rancid sensibilities and actions spread "like a virus." He speaks of a "financial virus" that went through the stages of "incubation" and "infection" until it was distributed widely through "propagation mechanisms," such as the financial media, and resulted in an "investing epidemic" (p. 275) that came to a head in the dot-com stock bubble. And he—like most post-boom commentators—draws on nineteenth-century conceptions of the "maddened crowd" to explain the boom as a matter of "herd thinking." At the same time, he argues that the predators who made a killing among the hapless herd (bankers, executives, and institutional investors) were "rational actors" pursuing their individual interests in an understandable manner, given the structure of "incentives" and the "messages" generated by regulatory action (and inaction).

Partnoy rightly stresses the linkages between rules and rationality, but his assumption that rationality is only present in the form of individual calculation prevents him from answering the question, "What were they thinking?" Research shows that white-collar criminals usually embrace or develop some set of norms that condone or even mandate misdeeds. As one scholar puts it, "white collar criminals should be viewed as conformists rather than deviants."[23] In fact, it is not difficult to identify myriad "rules that mattered" during the New Economy period.

Rules That Mattered

We argue that the continuing neoliberal push to change laws and regulations in accordance with "market rules" interacted with an emerging set of guidelines—New Economy business doctrines—to turn a large spectrum of corporate America into a criminogenic landscape. In other words, the dominant sets of rules in the 1990s combined with structural forces to make the economy vulnerable to frauds. Moreover, the small groups of executives and business intermediaries that actually organized frauds and other misdeeds developed their own sets of rules.

The Market Rules

At the broadest levels, some of the rules that mattered were derivative of the continuing neoliberal political movement. This was the domain of neoclassical economists, corporate diplomats (e.g., Ken Lay), industry lobbyists (e.g., Silicon Valley tech firms, the big accounting firms), and their political allies (e.g., assorted senators and representatives) who single-mindedly invoked the "free market" while pressing legislators and regulators to loosen regulations—and to gain favorable rules (or public resources) to aid particular interests. John Campbell, a leading sociological observer of neoliberalism, has shown that the movement has produced a broad and diverse outpouring of formal and informal guidelines and sensibilities—a bricolage of economic ideologies, paradigms, programs, and rhetoric for public debates.[24] Importantly, neoliberals introduced "rules" regarding matters of corporate governance for both government and corporations.

The prime directive to government, derived from Austrian philosopher Fredrick Hayek, was to reduce regulation so as to unleash the "spontaneous order" of the market, based on the innovative risk-taking of actors freed up to pursue their individual interests.[25] Very concrete changes in the formal rules resulted during the 1990s: various sectors were deregulated (e.g., the telecom sector), a 1994 Supreme Court decision and 1995 congressional legislation greatly reduced the liability of "corporate advisors" (e.g., accountants, investment banks, lawyers) for frauds committed by their corporate clients, and new sectors were left unregulated, or "self-regulated" (e.g., energy trading, financial derivatives). Implicit in the first injunction to government was a second: its priority should be the promotion of economic growth. Analysts detected a more activist stance in neoliberal policy by the federal government in the 1990s.[26] For example, Joesph Stiglitz, from his vantage point as former head of President Clinton's Council of Economic Advisors, noted that the administration's original intent in the 1996 Telecommunications Act was to "cause a flood of new investment and innovation that would wash away the advantages of the incumbents—and erode away their market capitalizations."[27]

In general, the informal policy of the Clinton administration was to promote the financial and technology sectors as twin engines of the U.S. economy. This strategy was reinforced by the privileging of the financial sector by two high-ranking federal officials: Federal Reserve chairman Allan Greenspan and Treasury secretary Robert Ruben. Stiglitz reports that the administration considered it imperative to win and keep the confidence of Wall Street—there were to be no public criticisms of the sector nor musings about new regulations. Greenspan used his Federal Reserve position to manage financial crises (e.g., 1987 Wall Street crash, Mexican Crisis, Asian Crisis, Long-Term Capital Management bankruptcy) through the use of interest rates and/or by coordinating (formally or informally) groups of financial institutions. However, he resisted using the Federal Reserve to actively intervene to control the growing stock market bubble of the late 1990s. In fact, Greenspan—a former acolyte of market fundamentalist Ayn Rand—is an apt symbol of the permissive regulatory posture of the 1990s. Partnoy reveals that Greenspan held an astounding conviction for someone who was one of the nation's top regulators: "Although Greenspan publicly mouthed support for laws prohibiting financial fraud, in private he was willing to disclose his true opinion—that he believed that there was no need for anti-fraud rules."[28] Greenspan, as befit his Randian roots, believed that market competition by itself would resolve problems such as fraud. No one will do business with someone who has a reputation for financial deceptions. And business actors will generally refrain from misdeeds because of their concern for their reputation among their peers.

Importantly, neoliberal theorists (especially economists from the University of Chicago) were nearly as aggressive in presenting corporate managers with guidelines—particularly, injunctions to manage corporate capital and other assets in the manner of a financial entrepreneur. Sociologist Paul DiMaggio notes that, in effect, what was being advocated was "a compelling new image of the firm" that "quickly shaped the thinking of investors, legal scholars, and managers alike."[29] On the eve of the 1990s, managers were issued their own prime directive: Their only legitimate obligation was to shareholders and they should strive to maximize the value of their holdings. Several guidelines were presented that complemented this "shareholder" conception of the firm.

Economists advised that providing executives with stock options was a desirable way to align their interests with those of shareholders. And the convention developed that quarterly financial results (e.g., earnings) provided an accurate indicator of how well managers were doing in performing their duties to shareholders.

The new conception of the manager's duty to actively evaluate and manage a firm's financial assets reflected the emergence of a more general sensibility—a hyper-rational fascination with the prospects for managing risk scientifically, particularly through the use of complex financial derivatives to hedge risk. Moreover, Partnoy reports that some economists advised that derivatives were also a tool that could be used to avoid regulations that "didn't make sense"—that is, were not rational from the business point of view.[30]

New Economy Doctrine

A fixation with stock values and quarterly financial results certainly dominated the decade, but as it progressed, fewer executives, entrepreneurs, and business intermediaries were likely to think of their activities in relation to the shareholder model. Instead, they increasingly embraced narratives, norms, values, and sensibilities that came together as New Economy doctrine in the later half of the 1990s. This realm, animated by the narrative of the rise of a New Economy and a new type of firm, was the domain of top executives, such as WorldCom's Bernie Ebbers, Enron's Jeffrey Skilling, hundreds of dot-com notables, and a multitude of "experts" (e.g., financial analysts and commentators) who publicly vouched for the New Economy status of individual firms.

The core idea calls to mind the new firm and financial emphasis of the shareholder model, but New Economy doctrine drew on all sorts of ideas about organizational forms and practices (e.g., teams, networks, knowledge work) that complemented digital technology and unfettered markets. Much of the rhetoric asserted that the arrival of new economic conditions had made the old rules obsolete—just as they were pushing old economy hierarchies toward the dustbin of history. Moreover, it was claimed that the business cycle had been overturned and that high growth and low unemployment could exist indefinitely without generating inflation. New rules about investment styles were presented to investors: they should shift from the "value" strategy of holding shares in old established corporations to a "growth" strategy of investing in companies with potential for achieving high rates of growth—in the manner of tech industry "gazelles." A whole spate of rules were presented concerning the new business model that was appropriate for those who hoped to exploit new technologies and markets.

The new firm was said to be one that possessed few material assets but did have the kind of talent and technology that could transform markets. This model drew heavily on the example of tech firms such as Sun Microsystems, Microsoft, and Cisco Systems. Neil Fligstein, an economic sociologist, argues that firms such as Cisco (often cited as the paradigmatic New Economy firm) maintain dominance in their markets through buying up relevant innovations or by building the insights of others into their own products. Cisco makes great use of networks and the Internet to minimize its own physical operations. And it also uses its own highly valued stock to acquire small firms that possess special workers or technologies. Fligstein proposes that the lead of firms such as Cisco leaves would-be New Economy players with several options. If they want to maximize their potential for financial gain by being "innovators who take risks," they can "go 'public' and sell stock, sell out to one of the industry giants, or try to become one of the giants themselves."[31]

A whole body of practical knowledge evolved in the last half of the 1990s, advising would-be New Economy firms to: be a "first mover" that dominates a new market niche; line up a chain of high-status business intermediaries to help the firm gain credibility—and have a high-profile IPO; and boost the share price so the stock could be used as a currency, allowing one to acquire talent, capital, and other firms at less cost, fueling a spiral of growth that would, in turn, reinforce the stock's standing. This model was complemented by another model with roots in West Coast tech culture—a model for lawyers, accountants, and investment bankers who serve tech firms.[32] These business intermediaries were advised to become New Economy players by accepting equity in their clients or to otherwise position themselves as insiders near the "deal flow."[33]

(Im)moral Economies

Unlike a rose, a "gift" by any other name is not as sweet—especially if the name is "bribe," "kickback," or "pay-off." Thus, overseas Chinese entrepreneurs often present "gifts" when they seek to establish access to the mammoth markets of the Chinese mainland, as do electronic components salespersons in the United States trying to establish or maintain "relationships" with employees of prospective customers. So, too, did would-be players trying to secure access to the sweet spots of the New Economy. These disparate economic actors exchanged "gifts" or "favors" so as to create or manage business relationships, generate trust, and—most importantly—forge a sense of obligation on the part of prospective partners. Social scientists often use the term "moral economy" to refer to forms of exchange that are guided by relationships and norms of reciprocity.[34] But while conventional cases like that of the Chinese entrepreneurs or electronics salesmen typically are constrained by rules against gifting in situations where it seems a blatant bribe, in the less ethical small worlds of the New Economy, questionable forms of assistance were not shunned as much as they were cited as bases for "special" forms of reciprocation. Moreover, central actors in stock promotion and financial engineering networks generally had the power to make the gifting rules because they controlled access to the deal flow.

Most of the dubious forms of reciprocity in the New Economy involved some sort of business intermediary and linkages to the financial sector. Frank Quattrone, an investment banker who pioneered ties between Wall Street and Silicon Valley, also reportedly pioneered the "secret rules"[35] that became commonplace by the late 1990s: investment banks that were underwriters for IPOs by high-tech start-ups allocated "hot" (but under-priced) IPO stocks to institutional investors or tech firms in return for other sorts of investment banking deals (often at unusually high fees). His staff at CSFB aggressively reminded recipients of IPO allotments of their obligations. Jack Grubman—an analyst at Citibank's Salomon unit—used much the same methodology to organize would-be New Economy players in the telecom sector (e.g., WorldCom). Managers of mutual funds allowed institutional investors to engage in illicit trades in return for securing their business. The New York Stock Exchange—a major regulatory body but also a powerful showcase for firms doing IPOs—was said to resemble an old-time political machine in that it operated as a "favors" system and followed "Grasso's Rules"—the personal dictates of its director, Richard Grasso.[36] Grasso's compensation package of some $140 million from the board of directors (heavily laden with investment banks) seemed to be the biggest favor of all.

Enron's CFO, Andy Fastow, turned the tables on the bankers by organizing an elaborate tier system to broker access by some seventy financial institutions to the firm's robust investment banking business. Fastow's financial engineers saw themselves as "reinventing corporate finance, rewriting the rules."[37] In the case of "relationships" with investment banks, the rules were codified in a fifty-eight-page document prepared for a "relationship review" meeting in 2000. As reported by *Fortune* magazine, "Tier 1 banks had to be willing to lend large sums to Enron 'when needed,' be willing to 'underwrite $1 billion in short period of time,' 'give Fastow ready access to their top executives,' and have a relationship officer 'capable of delivering institution.'"[38] Every year, Fastow invited Tier 1 bankers to join him and his staff on expensive junkets to exotic locales. For example, as a side trip during a Las Vegas get-together, Enron rented a fleet of fifteen helicopters to fly the bankers to the Grand Canyon for a picnic (p. 88). For their part, the bankers cited the special "relationship" with Enron in asking superiors to approve their participation in deceptive (and sometimes illegal) deals. One memo at Citibank remarked, "given the importance of this relationship . . . it is difficult if not impossible to deny this request" (p. 90). Banks were no more shy than Enron in bringing up the issue of reciprocity—especially when a bank had ignored the rules to assist Enron. For instance, one Citibank memo noted, "Sounds like we made a lot of exceptions to our standard policies. I am sure we have gone out of our way to let them know that we are bending over backwards for them . . . let's remember to collect this IOU when it really counts" (p. 90).

Field of Schemes

Economic sociology helps us understand the nature of the different sorts of rules that mattered during the New Economy and provides basic insights on the social processes through which these rules spread across segments of the U.S. economy—ranging from the system of corporate governance to the smaller domains that it encompasses: specific sectors (e.g., the telecom industry) and the small groups that directly engaged in misdeeds. Neoclassical economics fails here on the basis of the notion that it holds most dear—that rationality is mainly a matter of individual calculation. This idea forces conventional economists to cling to the dubious assumption that "information" can be treated as "datum, whose meaning is self-evident."[39] In contrast, sociologists provide a rich inventory of assorted kinds of "rules" that not only supply guidelines for action, but also frameworks for interpreting information—typically a group (rather than an individual) project that inherently is shaped by social circumstances. We propose that the first two sets of rules that mattered—the market rules and New Economy doctrine—contributed to the rise of criminogenic conditions in the U.S. system of corporate governance—turning it into a "field of schemes" pocketed with immoral economies.

Instituted Rationalities

The sort of rules of interest here are institutional webs of meaning— "socially constructed systems of norms, values, beliefs, and definitions."[40] Economic sociologists propose that the system, or "field," of corporate governance is ordered by three types of institutional guidelines: (1) regulatory (or coercive), (2) normative, and (3) cognitive (or interpretative).[41] The U.S. field of corporate governance has traditionally depended more on external constraints to exert control over corporate managers than is the case in most other nations. Paradoxically, the U.S. system is increasingly relying on the normative and cognitive sorts of guidelines enacted by business professionals instead of the coercive rules of the state—a trend that accelerated under the "market rules" of the 1990s. In the best of times, the state's use of coercive force vis-à-vis business has been problematic—especially where the financial sector is concerned. Financial regulations need to be regularly revised to respond to novel sorts of deceptions that emerge as businesses develop new practices and norms.[42] A glaring inadequacy of regulation in the thoroughly neoliberal 1990s was that political allies of various business interests succeeded in blocking attempts by regulators to respond to emerging problems (e.g., accounting, derivatives). The power of state regulators was also weakened in particular sectors where representatives of the industry to be regulated were allowed to strongly influence, or even write, new legislation. When a law is weakly enforced (or vaguely written), groups of firms commonly develop their own models for compliance with regulations, which courts, in turn, may "legitimate or delegitimate."[43] But anemic regulatory enforcement and prosecutorial actions (especially in complex financial cases) meant that little such testing was done.[44]

Institutional analysts often stress the role of professionals who have jurisdiction over some particular area of law; to the degree to which they are committed to their professional norms—a critical example of the normative type of guidelines—they try to ensure that firms are in compliance. Professionals and their presumed normative commitments became increasingly important for corporate governance in the 1990s as key monitoring functions were delegated (intentionally or by default) to "reputational intermediaries"—accountants, investment bankers, financial analysts, credit rating services, and lawyers. Outside accountants were pivotal to the system, as their audits were the main sources of financial information on firms for the other reputational intermediaries—and for regulators, such as the SEC.[45]

Importantly, many of these same business intermediaries often play key roles in carrying a third type of institutional guideline—cognitive (interpretive) frameworks—for they supply firms with commercial services or even perform their roles as independent monitors. During the New Economy, commercial sensibilities increasingly overshadowed professional norms, as court decisions and new laws greatly reduced their liability for fraud, while the financial stakes soared and New Economy doctrine itself advised business professionals to become entrepreneurial players in the deal flow. Thus, their commercial services included delivery of specialized technical "products"—some of which were dubious schemes for tax avoidance or "swapping" of assets to boost revenues—as well as business models (which tended to draw on New Economy doctrines). Related to the latter, these business intermediaries played core roles in social movement–like mobilizations of groups of firms that embraced/promoted new business recipes in the cause of challenging incumbent firms and business models. Over the last thirty years, these models have tended to involve some sort of financial conception of the firm; a novel neoliberal version—the shareholder value model—was ascendant on the eve of the 1990s.

Normalized Corruption

Insights from the application of institutional analysis of white-collar crime at the organizational level shed much light on the third domain of "rules that mattered"—the immoral economies. Blake E. Ashforth and Vikas Anand have offered a particularly relevant account of how *social* dynamics are set in motion when corruption is collective in nature, involving "cooperation within a group such as a workgroup, department or organization."[46] In such situations, corruption becomes "normalized"—a "way of doing business" (p. 11)—that is, incorporated into the group's stock of knowledge, its routines, and the processes through which it socializes newcomers; moreover, the group culture tends to develop rationalizations of corrupt practices. Once corrupt practices are no longer "idiosyncratic" but have been "institutionalized" in a business structure and culture, they may often be implemented without much conscious reflection.

Ashforth and Anand suggest that participants in corruption are likely to differ in their degree of involvement, their knowledge of the whole, and the means by which they become involved. Once embedded in routines, corrupt practices are likely to be broken down and parceled out as "specialized tasks" for different individuals. Thus, many participants may not know that they are contributing "to the enactment of a corrupt practice" and it may be "difficult for any one individual to comprehend (and easy to deny) the 'big picture'" (p. 12). However, the implications are that *organizational leaders are likely to have a high degree of culpability.* They are the ones who usually initiate suspect practices; they are potent role models and can stress the imperative of getting results while indicating a disinterest in the means; and they control many of the "levers" through which practices are institutionalized. Managers are the "legitimate agents of the organization" who "authorize" corruption through informal encouragement or tacit condoning. However, they typically retain "plausible deniability," as responsibility for corrupt practices becomes diffused and corruption may be insulated in particular units.

Group dynamics also help explain a common finding in white-collar crime studies that "corrupt individuals tend not to view themselves as corrupt" (p. 15). The culture that such a group develops draws on self-serving rationalizations to depict suspect acts in ways that "reconcile" them "with societal norms" (p. 17). These may include arguments that activities are actually legal or that deny responsibility or blame the victim (e.g., for inadequacies or greed); or they may attack regulations as flawed or appeal to higher loyalties (e.g., efficiency, free markets, innovation).

The rationalities generated in collective corruption also help us see why people participate in "unsustainable fictions" even to the point of "suicidal corruption" (p. 23) that seems sure to bring them down, if not the enterprise. They may develop "illusions of control and invulnerability . . . credit themselves with more power over events and others' perceptions than is warranted" or have an "illusion of morality—an unquestioned belief that one's group is inherently ethical . . . on the side of the angels" (p. 24). However, Ashforth and Anand note that the tendency of participants in collective corruption to "hide their activities" makes it evident that they "usually remain aware of the fact that outsiders would view their behavior as corrupt" (p. 16).

A final point suggests key connections between the "market rules" of neoliberalism and those of the immoral economies that engage in organized corruption: corruption is abetted by factors in the larger environment, such as lax regulation/law enforcement, heightened competition, and a "constellation" of business values such as "free enterprise (minimal regulation), individualism, competitive achievement, profitability, efficiency" (p. 5). The "perspective for making sense of the group's role in the wider organization or society" (p. 16)—and that serves to "neutralize the stigma of corruption" (p. 9)—may well draw on these broader business values.

The Road to Perdition (A Map)

Attempts to interpret the significance of the New Economy scandals often refer to previous episodes in American history in which a cycle of innovation became blighted by speculation and swindle. The conventional view is that these eras demonstrate that great waves of innovations are usually intertwined with some amount of illicit activities and that the undeniable progress made in such eras suggests that the misdeeds are both inevitable and relatively unimportant. The classic example is the corruption-ridden stock booms associated with the organization of the railroads in the nineteenth century—a basic progression in technology that set the stage for the second industrial revolution.

We draw on an alternative view of the relationship of corruption and economic change offered by Charles Perrow, a leading organizational theorist. His recent account of the railroad industry in his book *Organizing America*[47] shows that fraud, swindle, and other forms of corruption can actually be constitutive forces in major episodes of economic change—and generate great costs for society. This work also suggests that the institutional environment forged in that era to support a new kind of firm—the corporation—contained deep criminogenic structures that abetted financial deceptions; we propose that institutional changes of the last few decades—especially those that removed checks on corporate power—returned us to a similar set of conditions in the 1990s.

Rules of the (Rail) Road

Perrow's story begins early in the nineteenth century, when an assortment of elite interests began to mobilize around the project of creating a new kind of establishment—a large firm largely unfettered by the law, which could serve as an instrument for concentrating power and wealth. As this effort mushroomed over the course of the century, it altered the basic legal rules governing business and promoted new ideologies about the virtues of the new form of enterprise, the corporation. This movement succeeded in reducing the rights of individual states to regulate firms and established legal provisions for special features, such as "limited liability." The movement came to a head during the high point of railroad development, when corporate interests succeeded in changing the legal definition of the corporation so that it had the same standing as an individual person—and thus could own other firms. Subsequently, this legal fiction permitted the great merger movements at the turn of the century that produced several hundred great firms that dominate to this day.

Standard accounts of the era by economists typically cite efficiency as the causal factor behind the rise of corporations—a benign development that blessed society with unprecedented prosperity and wealth. However, Perrow shows the rise of the corporation to pivot on the exercise of power—in the political as well as the economic realm—by a coalition of elite organization interests (or what other observers refer to as "corporate capitalists"). This exercise of power entailed not only efforts to change the law but also blatant corruption of government officials, financial fraud, and the marshaling of market monopolies. The new institutional environment that supported corporations also established a basic structural contradiction—a separation of control from ownership. Moreover, while "ownership was widely dispersed . . . control was centralized in the hands of three groups which often overlapped: owners of large blocks of stock, top managers, or investment banks" (p. 198).

These three interests were advantaged in terms of the power and inside information to which they had access. Conversely, ordinary investors and creditors were disadvantaged, as their ability to act as an interest group were hindered by their lack of ties to each other and by their lack of inside information. Finally, Perrow observes that the financing system that developed around corporate capitalism provided managers with a flexibility that has "opened a large door for inefficiency, and for corruption" (p. 198): "if the return from revenues is insufficient, the firm can go into the stock or bond market and obtain funds to keep going. . . . This may allow an inefficient firm to survive for years, especially if bondholders have little information about its performance, or are given, as was common, deceptive information" (p. 200).

Interestingly, the new institutional environment not only resulted in a tidal wave of fraud and speculative overbuilding involving railroads, but also novel sorts of malfeasance whose legal standing was unclear. Perrow notes, "many activities only subsequently were declared illegal," adding that "we do not pass laws against unimagined behavior" (p. 141). Still, he stresses that these deceptive actions were "unethical" exercises of elite power that represented corruption in an institutional sense, if not a legal one. Finally, he stresses that the wave of corruption which blighted the railroad industry generated economic injustice and social costs on a staggering scale. "The railroads were immensely profitable, but corruption meant that the profits were not returned to either the government that subsidized so much of it, or even to many of the private investors (shareholders and bond holders), but to a small group of executives and financiers" (p. 144). And the course of American society was changed. Immense resources were wasted, laws protecting workers and communities were eroded, and legal restraints were removed, clearing "the path that enabled large organizations to concentrate wealth and power" (p. 142).

The (Investor) Revolution Betrayed

In one important respect, the institutional environment changed dramatically during the New Deal. Perrow comments that what had previously been a weak federal state gained considerable capacities as a regulatory apparatus. Agencies such as the SEC were formed to protect small investors from a swarm of financial frauds that had plagued the 1920s. This regulatory system was far from airtight and constantly had to adjust to new conditions, but it did place real checks on corporate power. Over the last quarter century, a host of economic developments, in combination with the neoliberal political mobilization, has produced a sustained reworking of the institutional environment, leaving few checks intact on financial entrepreneurs in particular.

Initially, taking advantage of a sequence of crises (stagflation, foreign competition in manufacturing, global instability of currencies) to establish itself as *the* alternative to the Keynesian welfare state, neoliberalism subsequently became intertwined with a number of defining changes: the rise of the tech sector, the flow of middle-class savings into equities, and the financial reorganization of corporations.[48] The Silicon Valley tech industry, originally dependent on Cold War defense expenditures, became thoroughly embedded in the liberalized system of financial regulation during the 1980s, taking advantage of laws on stock listing, options, financing, bankruptcy, and taxation that abetted "risky investments."[49] Lax antitrust policy and tax cuts, along with the rise of junk bonds and institutional investors, helped stimulate the financialization of corporations. Corporate raiders, fueled by junk bonds, challenged managerial prerogative in the 1980s, creating an opening for a coalition of institutional investors and investment banks who, claiming to represent investor interests, pressured managers to embrace the shareholder model.[50]

On the eve of the 1990s, the conventional wisdom was that the rise of institutional investors (pension funds, mutual funds, insurance companies) had concentrated the power of ordinary investors, allowing them to mount an insurgency against the entrenched power of managers—an "Investor Revolution."[51] This renewed battle for control of the firm was marked by a new activism on the part of institutional investors and by the introduction of new governance mechanisms to protect shareholder interests. Led by CalPERS, the manager of the mammoth pension fund for California state employees, a number of activist institutional investors waged a high-profile campaign to shake up corporate leaders and boards at stagnant firms; they succeeded in spurring the removal of CEOs at several major corporations in the early 1990s, including General Motors. Observers proclaimed that the boards had been duly disciplined. Stock options were introduced to harness executives to shareholders' interests—a move that economists argued would allow them to act as robust entrepreneurs rather than as bureaucrats.[52] Financial analysts joined in, using quarterly results to evaluate firm performance.

However, the New Economy scandals suggest that the Investor Revolution was quietly suppressed rather early on. Executives conducted a decade-long march through the institutions, waving banners of a free market and singing psalms in praise of investors, when, in fact, they were waging aggressive lobbying campaigns (with their investors' money) to change the rules in ways that would buffer them from scrutiny. The promiscuous deregulation that resulted increased the role of reputational intermediaries in monitoring corporations. Yet, the success of these intermediaries in limiting their own liability—in combination with other facts—completed the subversion of the shareholder movement. The flood of capital in the 1990s into equities and venture capital raised the stakes. There is growing evidence that many institutional investors—in reality, yet another sort of intermediary—were co-opted; managers had the golden touch in the stock market and were willing to share (e.g., IPO allotments). And though the New Economy mobilization promoted a financial conception of the firm, it also stressed timely exits by insiders. Reputational intermediaries were drawn by the rewards to be reaped as carriers of New Economy recipes and also were encouraged to become insider players.[53] Rather than acting as objective monitors, they helped managers pump the stock values of firms or assisted in financial engineering that indirectly had the same effect. Attempts by regulators to develop responses to emerging problems were blocked by powerful interests who justified their efforts with free market or New Economy rhetoric—as did members of the corrupt networks that wound through the guts of the corporate economy like a mass of tapeworms.

The Most Rancid Rule of All

One does not have to dig very deep into the New Economy scandals before you encounter a pair of riddles that are nearly as intricate—in a sociological sense—as the financial machinations were in a technical sense: What were the perpetrators thinking? and What happened to the rules? Here conventional economics, with it rigid and sterile conception of the human actor, can only flounder about with wooden caricatures. From a sociological point of view, the answer lies in examining the social and cultural fabric that was used to organize suspect activities—particularly the webs of ties and sensibilities that extended beyond the boundaries of individual firms.

By taking an approach that is institutional and relational, this book will show that what specific participants were thinking depended on the particular set of business sensibilities (or culture) that guided their cooperative efforts, which, in turn, depended on the positions they held in networks of stock promotion and/or financial engineering. This approach allows us to distinguish between types of participants in terms of their centrality—the scope of activities they were involved with and/or had knowledge of as well as the power they exercised vis-à-vis accomplices. And we can show how multiple rules (and rationalities) interacted in the course of the New Economy scandals.

We argue that the formal rules of law and regulation were, intentionally as well as unintentionally, eroded. In some cases the lines between legal and illegal activities were made faint, if not erased. In areas where state power was marginalized, so too were the sort of institutional rules that guide professionals; in this vacuum a third sort of institutional guideline often rose to the fore—business sensibilities that ranged from publicly promoted New Economy doctrines to the shared understandings of shadowy networks of financial engineers. As an alternative to the stylized portrait that economics offers of individual rogues who rationally act on their self-interest as they sidestep legal rules—or operate in a legal vacuum—our exploration of the New Economy's "rancid rules" turns the spotlight on the political ideologies and business doctrines that subverted the formal rules of law and regulations—and the shared understandings that clusters of actors developed about how they could collectively exploit the particular opportunities for illicit gain that resulted.

What is at stake in trying to solve the riddles of the New Economy? If history is a guide, the sequence of innovation, swindle, boom, and bust that marked the 1990s has taken us to the cycle's all-important endgame stage. What is yet to be finalized are institutional frameworks for regulating an economy that is being restructured around flexible forms of organization (especially networks), digital technology, and globalization. Kevin Philips reports that when previous cycles of economic and technological change were marred by scandal and swindle, reformers responded by challenging free market doctrines and by developing forms of regulations appropriate to new conditions.[54] This is the point that the United States has reached. However, Philips fears that the financialization that has transpired in this cycle may be more deeply rooted and that the political corruption that it promotes may block the reform impulse. If that is the case, the endgame we face may concern the kind of fall from prominence that the Netherlands and Great Britain took after financialization (and foreign military expenditures) compromised the integrity of their economies.

The immediate threat is that a shallow reform impulse may normalize financial predators—leaving us believing that it is to be expected that entrepreneurial types will deceive, cheat, and thieve—and that we are dependent on such a mentality to sustain our economy. Finally, there is the possibility that we largely will be left on our own—somehow charged with ferreting out financial shams as we earn our daily bread and try to save up for our retirements. More is at stake than our financial security. Historical analysis of eras when free market boosters dominated government shows that free market growth comes at the expense of the social and cultural fabric[55] and that the victims of business predators end up being blamed—as inferior judges of risk—for the injuries and deceptions they suffer.[56] Our study suggests that unregulated markets spur the formation of packs of rogue entrepreneurs who feed on moral society—cashing in on social resources, such as relationships, reputation, and trust. *Caveat emptor* is a sensible guideline in any era, but when it is the only norm that stands between ordinary investors and predatory insiders, "buyer beware" is the most rancid rule of all.

CHAPTER ONE

The Classic Pump and Dump

I n the early morning hours of October 26, 1999, police in Colts Neck, New Jersey, received a call reporting a possible murder. The call took them to an unlikely site for a homicide investigation: a white-brick mansion set on a ten-acre wooded lot, with an ornate Italian fountain in the middle of a circular drive. When the police arrived, they discovered a grisly scene: two men in their late thirties and early forties sprawled out on the dining room floor, the victims of an execution-style slaying with gunshot wounds in the head and chest.[1] Had the two been drug dealers or Mafia lieutenants, the manner of their deaths might not have been unusual. But they were neither. Albert Alain Chalem and Maier Lehmann worked in the securities industry, operating as what the newspapers would later refer to as "stock promoters," aggressively marketing penny stocks from an Internet site. Both men had checkered histories involving numerous run-ins with regulators and law enforcement agencies. Still, their deaths, with all the earmarks of a Mafia-style assassination, shocked many inside and outside the securities industry, and prompted the press to speculate about the role of organized crime in the once-staid stock market, including a *Business Week* article on the killings entitled: "A Message from the Mob?"[2] As of this writing, the murders of Chalem and Lehmann remain unsolved, but more significant is what the case tells us about the murky world of the penny stock, or microcap stock, industry and particularly that segment of the industry which specializes in pump and dump schemes.

The routes traveled by Chalem and Lehmann to arrive at the New Jersey mansion that fateful evening were different in many ways, but were similar in that both involved prolonged excursions to the fringes of the securities industry. By all accounts, Chalem was the more mysterious and flamboyant of the pair. From 1994 to the end of 1996, Chalem worked as a broker—despite not having a broker's license—for a Tampa-based brokerage firm, A. S. Goldmen, whose principals would later be indicted for stock fraud, amid allegations of ties to organized crime groups. (One of the theories floated after Chalem's death was that he was killed by a Mob group after they learned he was acting as a government witness in the Goldmen case.) Chalem liked living in the fast lane, or at least liked to give that appearance. He lived in the New Jersey mansion where he met his death (although the house was actually owned by his girlfriend's father), owned a condominium in Fort Lauderdale, maintained two boats—one docked in Florida and one on the Hudson River—and drove a Hummer, the massive sport-utility vehicle made popular by Arnold Schwarzenegger.

Lehmann, by contrast, lived a relatively quiet life on Long Island with his wife and five children. Despite his unassuming lifestyle, Lehmann had a history of problems with the law. In 1994, he plead guilty to charges that he defrauded an insurance company by faking two robberies at a video store he owned.[3] In 1998, Lehmann was fined $630,000 by the SEC for his involvement in a firm, Electro-Optical Systems Corp., whose principals claimed to be developing a new fingerprint identification technique, but who a federal judge claimed were operating the company simply to "line their pockets" by manipulating the firm's stock. Lehmann's role in the scam was to help pump the stock's value by doing things like bribing an Internet newsletter publisher to make the company its "pick of the year." For his role in the scheme, Lehmann received one hundred thousand shares in Electro-Optical, which he sold for a profit of nearly half a million dollars.[4]

In the late nineties, during the height of the stock market frenzy and the feverish surge in the popularity of day trading, Chalem and Lehmann teamed up to create an Internet site, Stockinvestor.com, that was registered in Panama and managed out of Hungary, on which they dispensed stock tips to investors on penny stocks, which sold for less than $10 a share. The site offered free stock research to anyone who signed up for their service—all they had to do was provide their e-mail address. Even before their deaths, many suspected that Chalem and Lehmann were simply using the Internet to operate an updated version of the classic pump and dump scheme. The real purpose of the site was to gain access to millions of e-mail addresses from potential investors, whom they would then barrage with "stock tips." In the small-scale, penny stock market, buy orders from even a relatively small group of investors can cause the value of a stock to surge, resulting in significant profits to those who had purchased stock earlier at much lower prices. For example, in the same month that the pair was murdered, Stockinvestor.com sent out a "buy" recommendation for stock in a London-based Internet service provider, resulting in a surge in orders for the shares. Prior to the recommendation, the stock was selling at around $5 per share. After the recommendation went out over the Internet, the price shot up to $8.75 for a few days.[5] For his efforts, Lehmann received one hundred thousand shares in the company—which he sold, after the price peaked, for a profit of half a million dollars. All told, company insiders made $12 million by dumping their shares in the inflated stock that would eventually sell for ten cents a share.[6]

While technically working in the securities industry, Chalem and Lehmann inhabited a world that was, on the surface at least, very different from the world of Wall Street investment bankers. In the words of an article that appeared in the *New York Times* shortly after Chalem's and Lehmann's deaths,

> [T]here are really two Wall Streets. One is the Wall Street of the New York Stock Exchange closing bell, of brash stockbrokers and hair-trigger traders, of big deals and big fortunes, of Microsoft and mutual funds. But in the crooked alleys of Lower Manhattan flourishes another Wall Street. This is a world of low-priced stocks and high-priced dreams, of grimy offices and sham companies, of swindlers and touts who prey on average people trying to grab the brass ring in the greatest bull market in American history. Like the world of organized crime, with which it increasingly overlaps, it is a vio-

lent place full of colorful characters and arcane lingo, of "naked shorts" and "pump 'n' dumps."[7]

There is considerable truth in this "two Wall Streets" perspective. Outwardly, Lehmann and Chalem did indeed inhabit a world that was very different from the one experienced by the traders, analysts, and brokers at the big investment houses. But, a reevaluation of this perspective in light of recent events suggests that these differences may have been more superficial than substantive and that these "two Wall Streets" may have met and converged at a certain point. What we will see in this chapter, and throughout this book, is that in the 1990s both the denizens of boiler rooms—people like Maier Lehmann and Albert Alain Chalem— and the well-heeled occupants of mahogany-paneled corporate boardrooms arrived at the same conclusion: during a period of ever-rising stock values, there are millions, indeed billions, of dollars to be made, not in developing a better product or in providing a more efficient service, but in convincing investors that they too can be winners in the giant casino known as the American stock market.

In this chapter we take a closer look at the world of penny stock fraud artists. We hope to show that despite their differences, the schemes hatched by Chalem and Lehmann and their colleagues were, in their essential features, strikingly similar to those orchestrated by top executives at Enron, Global Crossing, WorldCom, and many other fast-moving corporations.

The Penny Stock Industry

Many people may think of the "stock market" as consisting of the stocks whose values stream across the bottom of the screen on CNBC, not realizing that those are only stocks listed on the major exchanges, like the New York Stock Exchange. In the shadow of these markets are thousands of stocks issued by companies not listed on any of the major exchanges and whose share price is low, generally less than $5. These stocks are known as penny stocks (sometimes referred to as microcap stocks because of their company's low capitalization) and are traded on what is known as the Over the Counter (OTC) market. Unlike stocks traded on the major exchanges, many companies issuing penny stocks are not required to submit financial data to the SEC. Nor are they covered by the same federal and state regulations as stocks listed on the exchanges.

Instead of governmental regulation, the OTC market is overseen by the National Association of Securities Dealers (NASD), a private association representing securities brokers.

One of the major differences in penny stocks and other stocks is how their value is established and made known to the public. For stocks trading on the major exchanges, their trading price is posted and made available to the public by the exchange on which the stock is traded. By contrast, OTC stocks' quotes are listed on a Bulletin Board maintained by the NASD. Importantly, stocks listed on the Bulletin Board are not the same as those listed on NASDAQ, an ambiguous situation that crooks often exploit in misleading investors into thinking that the OTC stocks they are buying are listed on NASDAQ, when they are not. Stock quotes on the Bulletin Board are made known to the public only through certain brokers, known as market makers, who buy and sell stocks listed on the Board. The end result of these differences is that the OTC market offers fewer safeguards to investors, who are much more vulnerable to fraud and deceit than those who trade in stocks listed on the major exchanges.

Until the 1980s, penny stock sales were mainly regional. In 1985, there were only fifty-five firms specializing in penny stocks, and all were headquartered in five western states. By 1990, that number had increased to 325 firms that operated across the country.[8] Despite their relatively small numbers, suspect firms specializing in penny stocks, referred to in the vernacular as "bucket shops," were causing major problems for investors and regulators in the early 1980s. In a remarkable foreshadowing of things to come in the next decade, the biggest problem these bucket shops posed for regulators was in the area of initial public offerings, or what were referred to in those days as "Hot New Issues." The early eighties was another period of "irrational exuberance," a time when the gross national product, the stock market, and the number of initial public offerings were growing at unprecedented rates. It was a particularly euphoric time for new issues, as many investors seemed to be following what is known as the "Greater Fool Theory," in which "the prices of securities are often buoyed not by a rational evaluation of the issuer's business prospects, but by the expectation that other buyers will be willing to pay a higher price for the stock"—that is, that there is always a greater fool who is willing to pay more for a stock than one paid for it.[9]

The willingness of the investing public to place money in firms that produced little or no evidence of their economic viability was an open invitation to con artists. A good example was a company called the Lezak

Corp., whose IPO was described by a congressman in the following way: "The company was incorporated in January 1983. It has engaged in no business whatsoever and has no plan of operation other than it will not engage in exploration for oil or gas, fuel distribution, or mineral extraction business. It has no operating history and it is embarking upon a novel type of enterprise. The company has no plan of operation and can provide the investor with no information whatsoever as to its intentions. Now that's incredible."[10] Despite all this, the firm took in over $3 million in its initial public offering.

In one of the more ironic twists in the history of penny stock fraud, the congressman who made the above statement while he was chairing a Senate committee investigating penny stock fraud in 1983 was none other than Alfonse D'Amato, who, a decade later, would himself be implicated in a penny stock IPO scheme involving the notorious boiler room brokers at Stratton Oakmont, whose exploits are described later in this chapter.

In retrospect, the schemes of "hot new issues" promoters in the early 1980s provided a virtual blueprint for the "hot IPO" hustlers of the late 1990s. As an SEC report outlined in 1983, promoters would engage in "gun jumping." They would attempt to "attract publicity to an offering and 'condition the market'" before the stock was even registered, and they would hold "road show" sales meetings in which they would use misleading statements by the issuers and underwriters to whip up demand for the stock. Once the stock was issued, promoters would engage in a number of illegal practices, including "tie-in arrangements" in which either underwriters or customers, in exchange for the ability to purchase stock at the below-market initial price, were required to place bids in the "after-market" (when the shares are offered to the public) at higher prices, or were required to purchase shares in another offering. In another clear violation of SEC regulations, underwriters would conspire to "park" shares they had purchased in IPOs in offshore accounts, in an attempt to disguise their true ownership.[11]

Despite the public attention these fraudulent schemes were generating, by the late 1980s, problems in the penny stock market were, if anything, worse than ever. In response Congress passed the Penny Stock Reform Act of 1990, which, among other things, required brokers to obtain signed releases from new penny stock buyers indicating they were aware of the risks. While the early evidence suggested that the new law helped to curb problems in the industry, after a few years it was clear that the crooks had figured out ways to work around the new rules and were defrauding investors with new and more costly schemes.[12] Regulators estimated that by 1997 penny stock fraud was costing consumers $6 billion a year, three times the $2 billion price tag they had placed on these scams in the 1980s.[13]

Many regulators and law enforcement officials realized that what they were witnessing was one of the negative consequences of the democratization of the stock market. In the past, investing in securities was restricted to a relatively small, well-to-do segment of society. Individuals would make investment decisions after consulting with a broker, whom they often knew well and with whom they had a long-term relationship. In this not-so-distant past, brokers functioned more as personal financial advisors, looking over an individual's assets and goals and making investment recommendations accordingly, in face-to-face meetings with their clients. This scenario had been radically changed by the 1990s. In 1998, 84 million Americans were invested in the stock market, either through direct ownership of securities or through participation in a mutual fund or pension plans.[14] It was the age of telemarketing, and securities were being sold the same way as Florida condominiums and magazine subscriptions were: over the phone. As a New York attorney general's report put it: "In the telemarketing of securities . . . brokerage firms do not sit in their offices waiting for business to walk through the door. They hire aggressive, unregistered, unskilled broker trainees to make hundreds of telephone calls to total strangers every day in order to identify a few prospects who can then be called back by a registered broker for further massaging. This army of the untrained is motivated by greed and will engage in any artifice to get past a defensive perimeter, whether a secretary or expression of disinterest."[15] These "brokers" resembled less the sincere, somber, "one investor at a time" advisors pictured in commercials than the desperate real estate salesmen portrayed so vividly in the movie *Glengarry Glen Ross*.

The daily operations of boiler rooms were well described in the New York attorney general's report:

> There is an appealing ad in the newspaper for a "Broker Trainee" position at an impressive Wall Street address. You respond to the ad and the very next day the firm schedules you for an appointment with a dozen other people. The job requires aggressiveness, determination and commitment, but is also very tedious. A broker (not the firm) pays the initial salary of $250.00 a week directly to you. You are told that a broker, on average, can earn $150,000.00 a

year. Desiring to become a broker, you are lured with the promise of unlimited earning potential if you just tap into your resources, put in the time and work hard.

You are now on the job. Fast-paced meetings are held before the market opens and after the market closes. They are a blend of motivational speeches and constant criticism that not enough leads were obtained. Training is nothing more than learning cold-calling tactics. Be aggressive and do not let people off the phone. Stay on the phone and get the information. No matter what, get the lead. Supplied with a script, you engage in rehearsing and role playing to find out what the problem is. Why can't you keep people on the phone? Why are you not getting leads? You practice rebuttals to maintain people on the line. You are never instructed on proper sales practices and risk disclosure, but you are told that you cannot say anything about stock on the phone. This is despite the fact that the script and solicitation materials you use contain many references to stock.

The firm keeps you cold calling for long hours by publicly berating you about not producing enough client leads because you do not stay late enough and you are not dedicated and aggressive enough. Accommodations are less than ideal. You sit in a packed room of more than forty people. You dutifully use the script and you make at least three hundred phone calls a day. People walk the aisles and monitor you and your progress constantly. Ever vigilant, they question you whenever you are not actually on the phone cold calling for clients. As a firm tactic to motivate you to work harder and commit more, the firm partner will yell and curse at you, and you, in turn, will yell and curse in order to produce client leads. At the end of the day, you write up your leads and give them to a broker. At the end of the week you are paid $250.00.[16]

Pump and Dump

While boiler room operators use a variety of illegal schemes to make money, their scam of choice is the pump and dump. Stripped down to its essentials, the scheme works like this: stock promoters buy a significant portion of the thinly traded shares in a relatively small company, usually a new company whose shares are being sold on the OTC market for the first time. Typically, the company is not required to register its stock offering with the SEC because it falls into one of the categories that are exempt from registration. The SEC exempts from registration companies: (1) with less than $10 million in assets; (2) that raise less than $5 million in a twelve-month period (Regulation A Offerings); (3) "seeking to raise up to $5 million, as long as the companies sell only to 35 or fewer individuals or any number of 'accredited investors' who meet high net worth or income standards" (Regulation D Offerings); (4) that sell their stock only to foreign or offshore investors (Regulation S).[17]

Next, boiler room "brokers" relentlessly hype the stock through cold calls to prospective investors, promising them that the company is the next Microsoft or Netscape, but failing to inform them about their employer's position in the stock. Investors are forced to take the word of the broker about the growth potential of the stock because there is little published information on the company, such as a prospectus filed with the SEC. The resultant buying frenzy causes the value of the stock to shoot up, and when it reaches its peak the insiders quickly sell their stock, causing its value to plummet. The hapless investor is left with near worthless stock in a company that bears little resemblance to the dynamic firm that brokers described.

The key to the "pump" is the ability of the cold callers to convince prospective buyers on the other end of a telephone to gamble on an unknown quantity. Lists of prospective customers, particularly those with enough assets to qualify as what federal regulators refer to as "accredited investors" (individuals who "meet high net worth or income standards"),[18] are obtained by simply reading Yellow Pages listing of doctors and other professionals, or purchasing "lead cards" that identify small business owners from Dun & Bradstreet, or by obtaining listings of the occupants of high-rent office buildings.[19] Boiler room brokers are given scripts that guide them through their pitches and are rigorously trained to be aggressive, intimidate customers, and never take no for an answer—as revealed in the following recorded conversation between a broker and a customer:

> BROKER: The stock is going to do something for us in the profitable area on a short-term buy. Let me at least pick up 500 shares [a step-down from the 1,000 shares he was initially trying to sell].
> CUSTOMER: I have to find where I'm going to get the money [$1,500].
> BROKER: I'll let you have 7 days to do that. I mean, in 7 days you can build a mountain. The bottom line is, Robert, for today we

need to own the stock. . . . I'm not worried about funds. I know you are good for the money. You know, the bottom line is that you need to own the stock though. . . . Please do the 500 with me. Let's let the ball roll here.

CUSTOMER: Well . . . I'm going to have to look for the money first.

BROKER: I am asking you to make a commitment of $1,500.

CUSTOMER: You don't want me to commit for something if I don't find the money first.

BROKER: You cannot tell me that you can't commit yourself to $1,500, and you have 7 days to raise that kind of money, selling stock or whatever you have to do. Stretch yourself Robert. All I am asking you is to be involved.

CUSTOMER: Let me think about it.

BROKER: Robert, the only thing you are going to think about is what you are eating for lunch today.

CUSTOMER: I guess you are right about that, but I still don't want to move right now. Let's wait a bit.

BROKER: How can we wait Robert? The money doesn't work around your time. The money works around its own time. . . . You know just as well as I do that you have the money. All that is, is that you are holding yourself back from making money.[20]

One of the favored techniques of boiler room stock hustlers involves luring in prospective customers with promises of access to "hot IPOs." Many members of the public have heard of "IPOs" but know little about them other than that they are a good thing to get in on. Dishonest brokers exploit this incomplete knowledge by convincing clients to purchase stock in a little-known start-up company, assuring them that the stock value will skyrocket after opening day. The key, however, is to prevent the buyer from selling on opening day, either with assurances that the value will continue to rise or by simply refusing to execute their sell orders, thereby allowing insiders to sell their stock in the company at the inflated price.

Goodfellas in the Boiler Room

In spring 1997, federal and state authorities initiated a crackdown on penny stock scam artists.[21] Armed with search warrants and arrest warrants, agents fanned out across the nation, shutting down boiler rooms, seizing records, and hauling stock hustlers off in handcuffs. In total, authorities shut down fourteen firms in twenty states. One of the factors that prompted this renewed focus on boiler rooms was mounting evidence of the involvement of organized crime groups in these operations. For several years, white-collar crime investigators had been running across the names of known mobsters, while agents focusing on organized crime groups had begun noticing that their subjects were increasingly involved in nontraditional areas of crime, such as stock fraud. Many experts believed that as a result of several decades of relentless pressure by law enforcement agencies, organized crime groups were being forced out of their traditional economic strongholds—the construction industry, garbage hauling cartels, and food and produce markets—and were moving into more white-collar industries, such as health care and securities. As one FBI official put it, "They are analogous to companies in Chapter 11 bankruptcy. They are still in business but many of their old moneymaking bases have dried up and they are moving into new industries to fill the cash void."[22]

One of the Mob-linked boiler room operations caught in law enforcement's net was a Brooklyn-based brokerage firm run by a financier and Rolls-Royce collector named David Houge. Along with a motley crew of associates, Houge was running classic pump and dump schemes selling penny stocks, in which they secretly held a significant position, listed on the OTC Bulletin Board. One of those stocks was issued by Legend Sports, a Florida company that claimed to be building a chain of golf courses and entertainment centers across the country. Legend's principals had run into trouble in Florida for running a Ponzi scheme in which they marketed promissory notes to primarily elderly investors via a network of insurance agents, who promised them that their investments were "guaranteed" by surety bonds written by offshore insurance companies. Regulators shut the operation down after they discovered that less than 6 percent of the $16.8 million raised with the sale of the notes had been returned to the investors and that the surety bonds were worthless pieces of paper written by shell companies.

In an effort to erase this shortfall, Legend's principals turned to David Houge and his associates in New York to sell stock in the beleaguered company. Legend's stock was hyped heavily by Houge's cold callers, who claimed to be licensed brokers but in fact were simply hired thugs reading from scripts. What they did not tell prospective investors was that Houge and his confederates had used an offshore shell company to purchase large shares of the stock, thereby hiding their stake in the company from regulators. Once the stock price reached an artificially high level, they sold off their stock, causing the values to plummet and leaving outside investors with losses of more than $5 million.

Among the cold callers employed by Houge were members of the Colombo Mob organization and members of the Bor Russian crime family. A confidential informant told investigators that Houge had claimed he was working for the five organized crime families in New York and that in this operation he was the "brains" while his organized crime partners provided the "brawn."[23] On the day of his arrest, the scene at the Brooklyn courthouse where he and his partners were arraigned could have been taken from the *Sopranos* television show. One observer described it as "a bunch of young guys in muscle suits with very well-put-together girlfriends."[24]

The Houge ring was just one of over a dozen corrupt securities firms that authorities identified as having organized crime connections. A 1996 *Business Week* article sounded one of the first alarms about the Mob's presence on Wall Street, warning: "The Mob has established a network of stock promoters, securities dealers, and the all-important 'boiler rooms'—a crucial part of Mob manipulation schemes—that sell stocks nationwide through hard-sell cold-calling . . . [and] Wall Street has become so lucrative for the Mob that it is allegedly a major source of income for high-level members of organized crime."[25] According to the article, mobsters had made their own contributions to securities fraud by adding to traditional pump and dump schemes a practice known as "boxing" a stock—intimidating other brokers (often through threats of violence) into refraining from trading in a stock in order to keep the price artificially high while insiders sold their shares. The tactic was reportedly employed by a brokerage firm underwriting a "hot IPO" in which one of the principals was none other than John Gotti Jr., son of the imprisoned head of the Gambino organized crime family.[26]

Among the companies cited by authorities as having Mob connections was Stratton Oakmont, a Long Island brokerage firm that specialized in microcap IPOs and which also had an extensive record of trouble with regulators and law enforcement officials. In many ways, Stratton Oakmont symbolized all that was wrong with the penny stock industry; the president of the North American Securities Administrators Association (NASAA) referred to Stratton Oakmont as "the poster child for microcap stock fraud."[27] The men behind Stratton devised a sophisticated pump and dump scheme that tenaciously remained in operation for many years, despite repeated efforts of authorities to shut them down. For these reasons, the firm, its principals, and their associates present an ideal opportunity for an extended case study of fraud in the microcap industry.

The Princes of Pump and Dump

On a September day in 1998, thirty-six-year-old Jordan Belfort was pulling out of his driveway at his home on Long Island with his daughter for a trip to a local video store when he was stopped by two FBI agents and arrested on charges of money laundering and securities fraud.[28] The next day, Belfort's business partner, Daniel Porush, was arrested near his home in Palm Beach, Florida. With these arrests the FBI had caught two of the biggest fish in the murky pond of crooked securities operations. Dubbed the "princes of pump and dump," Belfort and Porush ran a boiler room on Long Island that had bilked thousands of investors out of $250 million. The story of how two guys from Long Island, one a former meat salesman and the other a drug-addicted college dropout, could have created a financial empire that brought them millions of dollars in ill-gotten gains and enabled them to associate with fashion celebrities, dot-com entrepreneurs, senators, and gangsters is an interesting tale in itself. More importantly for our purposes, it is a story that illuminates the darker recesses of the financial infrastructure that lie behind corporate America.

Stratton Oakmont's origins can be traced to a chance encounter between Jordan Belfort and Daniel Porush on a playground in Bayside, Queens, in December 1988. Belfort, who until recently had been selling meat on Long Island, told Porush, who was running an ambulette service at the time, that he could make a lot more money doing what he was doing: selling stocks.[29] A few months later the pair, along with twenty-three-year-old Kenneth Greene, who had previously worked with Belfort selling meat, opened an office of what would later become Stratton Oakmont at a friend's car dealership.

The venture was an immediate success. Belfort adapted some of his meat-selling techniques to cold-calling tactics for selling stocks, including what became known as the "Kodak pitch": offering prospective customers blue chip stocks, like Kodak, and then, after gaining their confidence, pitching them a highly risky microcap stock. It was a version of the old bait-and-switch sales tactic and it was very effective and lucrative. Just a few years after he had stopped driving a meat truck for a living, Belfort was driving a $175,000 Ferrari Testarossa.[30]

Belfort and Porush moved Stratton Oakmont's office from the car lot to a corporate park in Lake Success, New York, and hired scores of young "trainees" to work for them as salespeople. Stratton brokers could make a lot of money, but they also faced grueling workdays and rigorous demands on their performance:

> The brokers sat "cheek by jowl" in a room the size of a basketball court. All of their desks were lined up side by side in rows. The firm held mandatory sales meetings every day at 8:30 a.m. at which time sales techniques were demonstrated and scripts for the firm's "house stocks" (i.e., those in which the firm made a market) were distributed. Brokers were expected to follow the scripts and only give customers the information they contained. Brokers were discouraged from doing any outside research, and told to rely on the firm's research and representations. Aside from training in high pressure sales techniques, brokers received no instructions from Stratton management.
>
> After the morning sales meeting, brokers were expected to spend the entire day (except for a lunch break) on the telephone.
>
> The firm expected a high volume of sales, and if brokers did not stay on the phone, they were fired. Stratton was run like a "bootcamp," with all of the brokers' activities closely monitored and scripted by the firm's principals. At the end of the day, a second sales meeting was held at which time each broker was required to report his production for the day.[31]

The "boot camp" regimen worked. Stratton brokers were earning $300,000 to $400,000 a year. In 1994, the firm reportedly grossed $100 million.[32]

Unfortunately, Stratton Oakmont's success did not extend to its clients. Over the years in which the firm was in business, a number of journalists pointed out a disturbing pattern in the stocks the firm promoted: they tended to lose their value quickly. Between 1990 and 1996, Stratton Oakmont underwrote thirty-four IPOs. In many if not all of these, an initial spike in the value of the stock was followed by a sharp decline.[33]

One Stratton IPO that caught the attention of regulators, journalists, and eventually prosecutors was a stock issued by a company called the Solomon-Page Group, an executive recruiting firm that Stratton took public in 1993. In June of that year, Belfort, Porush, and Greene paid $250,000 for 700,000 shares of Solomon-Page, which eventually turned into a little over a million shares after a stock split. In September 1994, NASDAQ refused to list the stock because of the high proportion of shares owned by the Stratton executives. In order to meet NASDAQ's demands, Belfort and Porush sold all of their shares to a subsidiary of Solomon-Page, which then sold the shares to a number of Stratton-connected individuals, including nine Stratton brokers. The stock opened at $6.50 a share on October 20, 1994, and two weeks later reached a high of $7 a share.

The day after the IPO, the company's largest customer announced that it was taking its business elsewhere. Not long after, the stock value began to plummet, so that by November 23 it was trading at under $4 per share and by July 1995 was selling for under $2 a share.[34] By this time, of course, all of the insiders had sold their shares for fat profits.

One should not get the impression that all of Stratton Oakmont's clients were victims. Indeed, some of them did very well with their investments with the firm. One of those was U.S. senator Al D'Amato. As noted earlier, D'Amato—nicknamed "Senator Pothole" because of his ability to get things done for his constituents (e.g., fixing a pothole)—had chaired a congressional committee in the early 1980s in which he expressed his outrage at boiler room abuses. In the spring of 1994, D'Amato was once again expressing his outrage on the Senate floor. This time his target was President Bill Clinton and First Lady Hilary Rodham Clinton, whose investment of $1,000 in cattle futures that returned a $5,300 profit was under investigation. According to D'Amato, a profit of this magnitude would have required trades in $374,000 worth of futures. D'Amato strongly implied that the Clinton's had abused their power when he stated: "If you or I tried to trade $374,000 worth of commodity contracts with only a thousand dollars to back up the trade, it could not be done."[35]

Actually, D'Amato probably could have; just two months after making this statement, the senator was forced to admit that the previous year he had opened an account with Stratton Oakmont and had made a number of trades involving "hot IPOs" underwritten by Stratton, including one in which he bought and sold shares in a computer firm on opening day, earning a profit of $37,125 in less than twenty-four hours. Coincidentally, D'Amato at the time was the ranking Republican on the powerful Senate Banking Committee whose responsibilities included overseeing the Securities and Exchange Commission, which was then investigating Stratton Oakmont. It was probably also a coincidence that in 1992 Belfort had contributed $11,000 to D'Amato's election campaign (though the senator later returned it) and $100,000 to the Republican

National Committee.[36] D'Amato turns out to be the Forrest Gump of securities fraud, appearing over the years in one financial scandal after another. In the late nineties, he served on the audit committee of Long Island software maker Computer Associates, where he approved spectacular bonuses for some of the company's executives, who would later be indicted on charges related to a massive accounting fraud.[37] The former senator, who walked away from the scandal unscathed, symbolizes the links between the traditional and the New Economy pump and dump schemes.

The early nineties were heady times for Porush and Belfort. They were making money hand over fist at Stratton, and they displayed it in their increasingly ostentatious lifestyles. Belfort owned two homes on Long Island with a combined value of over $11 million and a fleet of cars that included a Mercedes-Benz, a Ferrari, and a Porsche, although he preferred to be chauffeured to work in a limousine equipped with a bar and television. For fun he liked to sail his 166-foot yacht—complete with a helicopter, seaplane, and kayaks. When the yacht sank in the Mediterranean under suspicious circumstances, Lloyds of London paid Belfort between $6 and $7 million. The slightly less flamboyant Porush used some of the roughly $30 million he made at Stratton to purchase homes in Westhampton and Palm Beach and a fleet of expensive cars that included a Bentley. The pair liked to take lavish trips, including a trip to Scotland aboard a chartered jet to play golf at two premiere courses.[38] The money was flowing so freely and the scams so easy that in 1990, when he was stopped by a police officer for speeding, Belfort told the officer his line of business and got the cop to agree to drop the ticket in exchange for being cut in on an IPO deal. The officer eventually convinced four of his fellow policemen to start accounts with Stratton.[39]

Yet, despite their affluence, there was a darker side to Porush and Belfort's lives. Both had long histories of drug and alcohol abuse. According to court documents, Belfort was addicted to quaaludes throughout most of the nineties and regularly used cocaine and other drugs.[40] In 1996, while under the influence of quaaludes, he was in a traffic accident in which a woman was injured. He finally hit rock bottom the next year when—after a three-day binge of quaaludes, cocaine, and Xanax— he pushed his four-year-old daughter into his car, determined to drive to Florida, and immediately ran the car into the garage door. His partner, Porush, also had his own struggles, later admitting that by 1995 he was using quaaludes three or four times a day. Over the next several years he was arrested three times for driving under the influence.[41]

From Footwear to Flipper: The Steve Madden Connection

A number of Porush and Belfort's pump and dump schemes involved high-fliers from the world of fashion. One of those was Steve Madden, a shoe mogul and boyhood friend of Porush. In the summer of 2000, at the height of his career in the shoe industry, Madden was indicted by federal prosecutors on charges related to his role in stock manipulations orchestrated at Stratton Oakmont and other brokerage firms. Although he was eventually convicted and sentenced to prison, it took prosecutors nearly ten years to put an end to Madden's criminal career.

The first question that comes to mind in looking at Madden is: Why did he do it? Here was a man who had started his career selling shoes in the early 1980s at a small store on Long Island and by 1999 was the head of a fashion empire that included sixty retail stores and nationwide sales of $163 million.[42] All of it was perfectly legal, so why would he have turned to crime? The answer probably has more to do with Madden's personality and connections made in his early years than it does with economic rationality.

Madden and Daniel Porush grew up together, having first met when they were both second graders at P.S. 1 in Lawrence, Long Island, in the 1960s. They stayed friends over the next several decades and in the 1990s became business partners. The two also showed an early propensity for crime. According to court documents, in the late 1970s Porush and Madden placed bets through an illegal sports betting operation run by Madden, and in 1980, when they were in their early twenties, the two friends burglarized the home of a friend's neighbor, stealing a television and a fur coat.[43]

Madden got his start in the shoe industry in the late 1970s when—having dropped out of college—he went to work as a salesman in a Long Island shoe store. By 1989, he had moved to Manhattan and had begun designing his own shoes, selling his designs from the back of his car. His 1970s-revival platform shoes for women caught on, and by the early 1990s he was selling his designs out of his own store in the trendy SoHo section of New York to customers who included a number of celebrities.[44] His shoes were featured in surrealistic ads combining traditional and punk-inspired imagery that appeared in malls, on billboards, and in subway cars.

In the midst of this rise to success, Madden launched a second, less-public career in stock fraud. In 1990, he joined his childhood pal Porush, who was by then starting to make serious money at Stratton Oakmont, to take part in a series of IPO scams. As described later by prosecutors and securities regulators, between 1991 and 1997, Madden participated in at least twenty-two IPO scams with Stratton Oakmont and with a Stratton-spin-off firm, Monroe Parker. In most of these schemes he took on the role of a "flipper"; he would purchase a substantial number of shares in an IPO, at a prearranged price, before they were sold in the aftermarket, and then, almost immediately, sell them (or "flip" them) for slightly more than he paid for them back to the underwriters—Stratton Oakmont or Monroe Parker. The firms' principals were thus able to gain control of the company's outstanding stock at a below-market price. Then their boiler room operations would go into high gear selling the stock at a much higher price to the public, while Belfort, Porush, and the other insiders secretly sold their shares to the unsuspecting public.

In the Solomon-Page IPO described earlier, Madden acted as a flipper, purchasing 50,000 shares at $4.00 a share on October 27, 1994, and then selling them the same day for $6.375 back to Stratton Oakmont, resulting in a $118,750 profit. However, in a prearranged agreement, he returned much of these profits to Stratton by buying 700,000 shares in another Stratton IPO at $0.4375 and selling them back the next day to the firm for $0.34375 per share, resulting in over $65,000 going back to Stratton. These and other IPO manipulations proved very profitable to both Stratton Oakmont and Madden, who pocketed over $1 million as his cut in these transactions.

Madden's biggest payday came when he, Belfort, and Porush orchestrated an IPO scam involving Madden's own company. Despite Madden's overall success, in 1993 his company, Steve Madden Ltd., was not doing so well financially. In that year, the company lost $895,000 on sales of $6 million.[45] Madden and his pals at Stratton Oakmont came up with a scheme that guaranteed they would make a lot of money from the company regardless of its future fiscal health. In doing so they were guided by the same logic that executives at Enron and other corporations would soon discover: deceptive schemes that artificially inflate the value of one's company's stock while at the same time disguising one's position in those same stocks can serve as a counter to the uncertainties of the marketplace.

Early in 1993, Madden, Belfort, and Porush began planning to take Steve Madden Ltd. (SML) public. In essence, they were going to use the same techniques that they had used in other IPOs that Stratton Oakmont had underwritten to enrich themselves at the investors' expense, by transferring large blocks of the firm's outstanding stock to themselves, pumping the value of the stock using boiler room tactics, and then dumping their holdings at the artificially inflated price. To accomplish this end, they set up a series of shell companies through which they engaged in sham transactions to create pre-IPO "debt" for Steve Madden Ltd., which was then "paid off" with SML stock. As a result of this manufactured debt, the company had a negative net worth when it went public—a fact that was disclosed in the prospectus. However, prospective investors had no way of knowing that this debt was simply a means for transferring the proceeds from the IPO stock sale to Madden and Stratton underwriters.

In one of these sham transactions, in June 1992, a shell corporation, the Madden Acquisition Network Group, Inc. (Magnet), was set up in which Belfort and Porush were the principal shareholders. Magnet then made a "loan" of $100,000 to Steve Madden Ltd. in exchange for a debenture that was convertible to 2,040,000 shares in Madden Ltd. common stock. Despite the fact that regulators later could find no evidence that the $100,000 was ever paid to SML, that debt was in fact converted into stock just before the initial public offering. As a result of this transaction alone, over half of the outstanding common stock in SML went to Stratton Oakmont insiders. However, when the National Association of Securities Dealers (NASD)—which had recently investigated Stratton Oakmont for numerous securities violations—got wind of this transaction, they smelled a rat and refused to approve the IPO unless Porush et al. reduced their holdings to less than 4.9 percent of the outstanding common stock. To meet the NASD's requirements while at the same time secretly controlling the stock, the shares that were to have gone to Magnet were transferred to a shell corporation, BOCAP, of which Steve Madden was the sole shareholder. Unbeknownst to the regulators, BOCAP then entered into a secret agreement in which Belfort and Porush retained the power to dispose of the securities as they pleased. In effect, BOCAP was simply a vehicle that was used as a nominee to hold the SML stocks so that on paper they were not directly held by Porush, Belfort, et al., when in fact they were under their control.

On December 10, 1993, shares in Steve Madden Ltd. were made available to the public. The offer ultimately raised $12.5 million in capital. What outside investors in the stock did not realize was that $11 million went to Madden, Belfort, Porush, and their confederates.[46] So what is wrong with that? In theory, companies sell stock in order to raise capital that will be reinvested in the company itself. Investors assume that the money they have transferred to the company in the form of stock purchases represents an investment in the company, not in the individuals involved in the company or in those involved in the sale of the stock.

The impact that these manipulations had on short-term investors was severe. The stock opened at $4 a share in early December 1993 and continued to rise to $7.63 by the middle of the month. However, at the end of March it had dropped to $3 a share and by June 1994 it was trading at $1.75 a share.[47] Thus, those who bought the stock early, got frightened by its decline, and sold in the first six months sustained serious losses. However, unlike the victims of other pump and dump schemes, investors who held on to the stock may have done well. By the end of 1995, the stock was selling at around $8.25 per share. Yet, it could be argued that investors could have done much better had most of the $12.5 million raised when the stock went public gone into the company itself rather than being siphoned off by insiders.

By the beginning of a new decade, the Long Island trio—Belfort, Porush, and Madden—found that their lives and fortunes, which had soared to such heights in the previous decade, had begun to seriously unravel. The charges that led to Belfort's and Porush's arrest in September 1998 were related to a series of IPO schemes the pair had orchestrated in 1994 and 1995 that involved "Regulation S" offerings—securities that need not be registered with the SEC if the stocks are sold to non-U.S. persons or offshore entities. To disguise their ownership of stocks in the IPOs, Belfort and Porush set up several offshore companies and foreign bank accounts in which the shares were parked. As part of the scheme, they employed friends and relatives, including Belfort's wife and her mother, to transport cash out of the United States and into Swiss bank accounts. It was this part of the scheme that ultimately led to their downfall. In August 1994, Porush drove his Bentley to the parking lot of a shopping center in Queens where he handed a bag containing $200,000 in cash to a man who had driven up in a limousine. The transaction was caught on videotape, and a security guard who thought that it must have been a drug deal reported it to the local police. Several years later, federal investigators read the police report of the incident, put it together with other information they had on Porush, and realized it was part of a money-laundering scheme involving securities, not drugs. Belfort was later caught on tape admitting to his accountant that in the money-laundering scheme, he had "totally screwed up."[48] Belfort and Porush entered guilty pleas soon after they were charged.

While awaiting sentencing, Porush was living in Boca Raton, Florida, and running a company that traded in commemorative coins. He was better at hustling stocks than coins; in April 2001 he was arrested and charged with credit card fraud in connection with the business.[49] Belfort also found it difficult to stay out of trouble. In 1999, he chartered a helicopter to transport himself to an Atlantic City casino to gamble and in doing so violated the conditions of his bail. As a result he spent five months in jail.[50] Eventually, both Porush and Belfort were sentenced to four years in prison.

Madden, in the meantime, had his own problems. He was indicted (twice) and charged in connection with his role in the pump and dump schemes at Stratton Oakmont and Monroe Parker. When he entered a guilty plea, for which he received a sentence of forty-one months in prison and was ordered to pay over $5 million in restitution, he told the judge, "I am bloody but unbowed."[51]

One of the reasons for his optimism in the face of adversity may have been the fact that just months before his sentencing Madden had signed a contract with Steve Madden Ltd. that allowed him to stay employed at the firm as the "creative and design chief" at an annual base salary of $700,000 for ten years (a figure that could have eventually gone as high as $35 million when bonuses and other options were included), even while he was in prison![52] News of the arrangement did not sit well with shareholders, who filed a lawsuit against the company for cutting the deal with Madden. The similarities between Madden's situation and that of the Enron executives who were awarded substantial bonuses just before their company went bankrupt did not escape *Slate* magazine, which awarded the former shoe king its "genius of capitalism" award for pulling off the deal.[53]

The similarities between Madden and Enron did not end there, however. In December 1999, Madden was summoned to a meeting with federal prosecutors, who informed him that he was under investigation for violations of securities laws—not an uncommon practice in cases involving white-collar offenders. News of the investigation was not made public, and on May 31, 2000, Madden sold one hundred thousand shares in Steve Madden Ltd. for $16.00 per share. On June 19, the stock closed at $13.13. On June 20, after Madden was arrested and details of his involvement with Stratton Oakmont's securities scams became widely known, the National Association of Securities Dealers suspended trading in the stock. When trading resumed two days later, the stock's price plunged, closing at $6.69. By selling ahead of this information, Madden avoided losses of $784,000 but in the process also engaged in what the SEC would later charge was insider trading.[54] A year or so later, Kenneth

Lay and other Enron executives would employ roughly the same strategy when, sensing that their company's days were numbered, they began quietly selling their stock in the firm before the public got wind of Enron's escalating problems.

Conclusions

In the eighties and nineties, penny stock hustlers refined techniques for ripping off investors. The success of these tactics depended in large part on the willingness of investors to purchase securities issued by companies they had never heard of from brokers they had never seen. In the nineties, this lack of prudence on the part of investors was, in turn, directly related to the prevailing atmosphere of "irrational exuberance," which was built on a number of mythic stock stories, such as Netscape, that made millionaires out of early investors. It also depended on the relatively deregulated environment in which these securities were sold, an environment that allowed crooks to exploit loopholes such as Regulations A, D, and S to deceive both regulators and investors.

By the late nineties, the SEC had moved to close some of these loopholes, modifying Regulations D and S and tightening up the requirements for nonregistration of securities. However, a 1998 report by the General Accounting Office noted that while these changes were helpful in reducing microcap fraud, securities regulators had not implemented a number of policies the congressional research arm had recommended earlier that would have made life more difficult for crooked brokers.[55] In any case, none of these measures would help the thousands of victims of Stratton Oakmont. By December 1998, over three thousand Stratton investors had filed claims with the Securities Investor Protection Corporation—a tax-exempt agency designed to help investors recoup losses from fraudulent brokers—claiming over $130 million in losses. Of those, however, 2,850 had their claims denied by the agency; by 1990, only nine investors had been reimbursed by the agency.[56]

Another source of the problem was that many penny stock crooks were allowed to operate brazenly for years with few serious attempts to stop them because of lax enforcement of regulations by authorities, particularly officials at the National Association of Securities Dealers (NASD), which, in theory, maintained primary oversight over brokers trading in the OTC markets. According to former chairman of the Securities and Exchange Commission Arthur Levitt, "NASD had gradually been taken over by a cabal of dealers who used the NASD's disciplinary process to punish certain players, such as day traders, while failing to prosecute serious infractions by market-makers. . . . The inmates were running the asylum."[57] In his provocative book, *Born to Steal,* about the Mafia's influence at crooked brokerage firm, Gary Weiss provides a good example of this lax enforcement. Weiss describes the plight of a NASD examiner who in the mid-nineties repeatedly documented and reported serious infractions at Hanover Sterling, one of the era's most infamous penny stock firms. When he recommended a full-scale investigation of the firm, his supervisor told him to "mind his own business." Ultimately, the examiner was fired by NASD officials on the grounds that he was "too conscientious."[58]

Even when regulators were willing to pursue penny stock crooks, they were often hampered by a lack of resources. In the nineties, the number of stockbrokers in the United States increased by 50 percent while the staff of regulatory agencies increased by only 18 percent.[59] One of the problems for regulators was retention of high-quality staff members in the face of lucrative job possibilities in the private sector. In 1997, for example, the SEC's regional office in New York lost thirty-two of its eighty-five enforcement attorneys.[60] Many of those lawyers left for considerably higher salaries working for some of the same companies they had been overseeing at the SEC.

In the late nineties, corporate executives who conspired to enrich themselves by artificially inflating the value of their firms' stock were following the outlines of a blueprint sketched out by people like Jordan Belfort and Daniel Porush. This is not to say that they were literally studying boiler room tactics. Rather, the executives were simply following the logic of the marketplace and the rules of a corporate environment that placed a premium on ever-rising stock prices, rewarding those that kept those values rising and punishing those who did not. While football field–sized boiler rooms jammed with cold callers screaming into telephones may seem a long way from glass and steel towers filled with pin-striped MBAs discussing the finer points of the New Economy, in the chapters to come we will show how, despite their outward differences, the business strategies of the companies' insiders turned out to be very similar in both form and consequence.

CHAPTER TWO

The Power Merchants

On January 17, 2001, at one o'clock in the afternoon, residents of the San Francisco Bay Area found out what happens when someone pulls the plug in an electricity-based society. On that day, California officials initiated the first of several "rolling blackouts" in which electrical power was reduced in selected communities in an effort to conserve energy. Two students were stuck in an elevator at their law school in San Francisco for over an hour. Drivers in San Jose had to informally negotiate busy intersections when traffic lights went dark. Teachers at a San Francisco middle school led students out of the building with flashlights. Hundreds of people found themselves without cash as ATM machines across the region shut down.[1]

The next day, President-elect George W. Bush told reporters that the source of California's problems was a dwindling supply of electrical energy caused, in large part, by environmental policies enacted by the state. He also implied that those critics of what he called a "balanced" environmental policy (i.e., one that emphasized opening up protected lands to oil exploration and production) were getting what they deserved: "a lot of the harshest critics of a balanced environmental policy are beginning to have rolling blackouts in their communities."[2]

The Bush administration's position was repeated on many occasions by another former Texas oilman, Vice President Dick Cheney, whom the president, soon after taking office, had appointed to head a task force on energy. While that task force was to have heard from all voices in the energy debate, including conservation groups, early on Vice President Cheney made his position clear. In a speech made in April 2001, Cheney dismissed conservation as a mere "personal virtue," not a "sufficient basis for a sound, comprehensive energy policy." A more realistic solution, he argued, lay in increased energy production, including drilling for oil in previously protected lands, such as the Alaskan Wilderness Area—a pet project for the Bush administration.[3]

This interpretation was quickly challenged by a number of individuals and groups, most prominently the governor of California, who argued publicly that his state's energy problems were not the result of a lack of energy supplies, but rather the tactics of unscrupulous energy companies who were gaming the market in California by artificially driving up energy prices. For Governor Gray Davis and other California officials, the culprits in the situation were the half dozen or so energy companies that had dominated California's electricity market since it was deregulated in 1998. Not only had these companies been instrumental in creating that market, but they had also extracted billions of dollars in illegal profits from the state as Californians saw their electrical energy costs soar. And, for many, the biggest culprit of them all was the Houston-based Enron Corporation, whose CEO, Kenneth C. Lay, personified the corporate greed and insider politics that characterized the energy trading industry. Such was Lay's villainous reputation that just two and a half months after the January blackouts, the normally tight-lipped state attorney general, William Lockyer, told a reporter from the *Wall Street Journal*, "I would love to personally escort Lay to an 8 × 10 cell that he could share with a tattooed dude who says 'Hi, my name is Spike, honey.'"[4]

Despite mounting evidence of market manipulation in the California energy industry, the White House clung to its analysis of the origins of the problem. The report issued by the Cheney task force in May 2001 stated unambiguously that "the California electricity crisis is at heart a supply crisis."[5] Indeed, the words "market manipulation" are nowhere to be found in the report, although there are plenty of references to the California problem.

In sharp contrast, a number of studies—conducted both by government agencies and by independent academic analysts—concluded that market manipulation was a significant factor in California's spiking energy prices.[6] Even the Federal Energy Regulatory Commission, the main energy regulatory agency in the United States, which had early on been accused of dragging its feet in its investigation of misconduct in the California market, was forced, after an exhaustive study, to conclude that "there was clear evidence of market manipulation in western markets."[7] An analysis of electricity prices conducted by the state's Independent System Operator estimated that in a period of a little under three years (April 1998–February 2001) energy companies overcharged Californians $6.2 *billion*—roughly $183 for every man, woman, and child in the state.[8] A big chunk of those overcharges went to a single company: the Enron Corporation. A *New York Times* analysis of Enron's trading activities found that during a three-day period beginning on January 17, the first day of rolling blackouts in California, Enron reaped a whopping $300 million in profits.[9]

By fall 2001, however, the scandal surrounding Enron's involvement in the California energy crisis was eclipsed by the imminent implosion of the company itself. A series of articles published in the *Wall Street Journal* beginning in late October sparked an inquiry that would eventually reveal that the company that claimed to be America's seventh largest corporation, that was widely regarded as the paragon of a New Economy firm, was in fact largely smoke and mirrors. Enron's death certificate was signed on December 2, 2001, when the firm declared bankruptcy and one of the most detailed financial post-mortems of a modern corporation was initiated. The collapse of Enron set off a chain reaction in which (as described in the introduction), in rapid-fire succession, corporation after corporation was charged with illegally cooking their books, misleading investors, and engaging in massive insider enrichment schemes.

In this chapter we begin our examination of boom and bust in the New Economy with a look at the energy trading industry. We will show that despite their differences, energy company executives employed schemes whose essential features resembled the pump and dump schemes developed by the boiler room operators described in the previous chapter. Importantly, we will show that these illegal schemes were not simply the acts of a relatively small group of errant executives, but represented practices that had become common throughout the energy trading industry, practices that were made possible by the nature and structure of the industry itself and the regulatory environment in which it operated—an environment that was, itself, very much intentionally shaped by industry leaders who personally benefited from its many hidden nooks and crannies.

While the Enron Corporation and its illegal practices have received the most public attention, we want to emphasize that Enron was not alone in this misconduct and that many of the other major players in the energy trading industry engaged in many of the same practices. To be sure, Enron's crimes went far beyond wheeling and dealing in energy markets. By the time of its demise, Enron was involved in a dizzying array of markets and industries. Nonetheless, the company's misdeeds were ultimately rooted in the energy business, from which it derived most of its legitimate profits. It is to that industry that our discussion now turns.

The California Electrical Energy Industry: From Natural Monopoly to Free Market

The process by which electricity is produced and consumed is complicated, but can be divided into four major functions: generation, transmission, distribution, and retailing.[10] Electrical power must first be generated through falling water, internal combustion engines, steam turbines, or some other means. Next, the electricity must be distributed to residential and commercial customers along low-voltage lines that run above or below ground. The distribution function also involves a retailing process that includes metering, billing, and other activities related to the sale of electrical energy. In an intermediate stage between generators and consumers, electrical energy must be transmitted from generators to substations and other distribution sites along networks of high-voltage cables. This transmission process involves the coordination of supply and demand in "real time."

One of the distinctive features of the electrical energy industry is that, unlike other sources of energy—coal, oil, natural gas—it cannot be stored. This means that in order to avoid inefficiencies and waste, energy production must constantly be calibrated to meet demand. A related feature is the fact that demand varies widely, determined by time of day, season, weather conditions, and so forth. This results in extreme price volatility. Even under normal conditions, wholesale prices may increase as much as one hundred-fold as producers scramble to meet demand during, for example, a heat wave.

Historically, in order to minimize inefficiencies, these four functions have been vertically integrated by public utilities that have been allowed to operate as "natural monopolies," under the philosophy that in essential industries, competition would be self-destructive. This idea was institutionalized with the passage of the Public Utility Holding Company Act of 1935. Championed by President Franklin Roosevelt, the law was a response to abuses in the 1920s by utility owners who established holding companies which were nothing more than pyramid schemes that allowed them to control the stock of large numbers of utilities in many states. The trend was so widespread that by 1932 eight holding companies controlled almost three-quarters of the investor-owned utility business. The Public Utility Act greatly restricted the ownership of utilities by holding companies and placed electrical utilities under the regulatory authority of the Federal Power Commission. This model of electrical energy being produced and delivered by vertically integrated public utilities that operated under tight state and federal regulations, under which retail and wholesale prices of electrical energy were set by regulatory agencies, would dominate the power industry for the next fifty years. By the mid-seventies, however, a series of events led many policy-makers to question the value of the traditional model of energy production and distribution.

Responding to the energy crisis created by the oil embargo of 1973, the Carter administration proposed a bill that sought to expand the sources of energy. The result was the Public Utilities Regulatory Policy Act of 1978 (PURPA), which "required utilities to buy power from co-generators and small power producers using renewable fuels." While the law did not radically change energy production or distribution, it did lay the groundwork for a much more substantial challenge to the natural monopoly model that emerged in 1992 with the passage of the Energy Policy Act. That law mandated "that owners of regional transmission networks act as common carriers of electrical power, providing interconnection service between independent power producers and wholesale buyers." In other words, it opened up the possibility for independent energy generators to sell energy directly to consumers, or at least wholesale buyers, using the transmission lines operated by public utilities. This was the first step toward deregulation of the electrical energy industry. However, the law left to individual states the critical decision of whether to fully deregulate the industry. Most states moved cautiously to modify their energy production and delivery systems in the wake of the Energy Act, with one large exception: California.

By the early 1990s, Californians were paying 30 percent to 50 percent above the national average for electricity. In 1993, the California Public Utilities Commission, led by its conservative Republican members, issued a report evaluating the electrical utility business and proposing options. One of the options called for a restructuring of the existing system so that the utilities' monopoly on power generation would be broken and consumers would be allowed to choose from a variety of competing energy producers. The next year, that policy was put forth as a recommendation in another CPUC report (known as the "Blue Book," for the color of its cover), which called for "the discipline of markets to replace often burdensome, administrative regulatory approaches." In a word, the electrical energy market in California would be deregulated.

The commission's vision of a new, market-based electrical energy system became a reality in 1998 when California implemented a radically new system for providing electricity to retail consumers. Under the new system, the transmission and distribution of energy remained under the regulatory authority of the state, but generation of power was opened to competition. Much of the electricity consumed by Californians was sold by generators in an auction operated by the newly established California Power Exchange (Cal PX) in which "bids" by electricity buyers were matched to "asks" from electricity sellers. In effect, the auction was a spot market for electricity that attempted to set prices and arrange contracts between buyers and sellers a day ahead or a few hours ahead of the actual purchase and use of power. In theory, the new system was to be more efficient than the old one, constantly adjusting and readjusting prices based on supply and demand.

At the same time, competition was to be enhanced at the retail level by allowing consumers to purchase energy from an array of providers, rather than being forced to buy from a single utility. In addition, consumers were protected from potential increases in prices by a provision in the plan that froze retail prices at or just below their 1996 prices. This was a flaw in the market's design that many would point to later as a major factor in the energy crisis.

The new law also forced the three largest utilities in the state to begin divesting themselves of their power plants, requiring that they sell off half of their fossil fuel–powered generating plants. The idea was to open up the generation process and to create incentives for investors to build

new generation facilities. The utilities went beyond the law's requirements and sold off almost all of that generating capacity to private firms.

The system also created another new body, the California Independent System Operator (ISO), which was generally responsible for ensuring that the energy grid in the state had a constant supply of energy.
This entailed managing the state's electrical power lines and also operating a "real time" market in which energy was purchased an hour before
it was to be used.[11] The primary function of the "real time" market was to
make up for any shortages in energy supplies created when the PX market failed to produce enough power for consumers at any given time.
This might happen when an unanticipated change in the weather drove
up demand in certain areas, and supply was not adequate to cover it.
Under these circumstances, the ISO would first attempt to make up the
difference in the "real time" market. If that failed to produce adequate
energy, it was authorized to purchase electrical power outside the state,
or "out of market." The ISO was also responsible for relieving any congestion that occurred in the system of transmission lines that moved
electricity up and down the state. These lines have a limited capacity for
moving electrical power, and the ISO had to make sure that the energy
contracts entered into on the open markets did not produce loads that
exceeded those capacities. To achieve this result, buyers and sellers of
electrical energy were required to submit schedules to the Independent
System Operator indicating how much electricity they would be sending
across the transmission lines, and in which direction, at any given time.
If after analyzing those schedules the ISO determined that an overload
was possible, the ISO was authorized to, in essence, buy back the energy
from the suppliers, paying them a "congestion management fee" calculated by the agency.

For the first two years, the new system seemed to be working well.
Wholesale prices of electricity remained stable and consumers had
plenty of power as well as the ability to choose their suppliers. Then, in
June 2000, following two months of unusually hot weather in California
that increased demand, the wholesale price of electricity shot up. Prices
on the PX exchange had averaged between $26 and $30 per megawatt
hour in April, but by June they were averaging $116–$125 per megawatt
hour.[12] On June 14, 2000, as temperatures reached a record-popping
103 degrees, authorities declared a Stage 1 emergency as energy reserves dipped and electricity was briefly cut off for customers of Pacific
Gas and Electric in the San Francisco Bay Area.[13] The problem was that

because retail prices were frozen and the wholesale prices had skyrocketed, the utility was losing significant amounts of money on every megawatt of electricity it provided to its customers.

Over the next year, the problem worsened significantly. By December, wholesale purchasers of electricity in northern California were paying an average of $308 per megawatt. The next month, January 2001, the state ordered the first of a series of rolling blackouts, with more occurring in March and May. Despite the fact that in January state regulators had approved a retail price increase for PG&E customers, in April 2001 the utility declared bankruptcy, citing the dramatic increases in wholesale electricity prices. In June, the Federal Energy Regulatory Commission (FERC) acceded to California's request and ordered caps imposed on the wholesale price of electricity. The price caps, combined with relatively cool weather in the summer of 2001, brought electrical energy prices down and started the beginning of the end of the California energy crisis.

The Power Merchants and the New Economy

In the first few months of 2001, as California's electricity crisis worsened, the American public began to learn a lot, not only about that state's energy woes, but also about the theretofore little-known energy trading industry, or "Power Merchants," as they were often referred to. For many Americans, it was the first time they had ever heard of a company called Enron. Before the 1990s, the electrical energy industry was pretty dull. With most energy being sold to consumers by utilities that also generated the power, what trading did occur was mostly between utilities to cover temporary shortages. All of this would be radically altered in the 1990s after several changes in federal laws and regulations opened up the once-staid world of electrical energy to the high-speed culture of Wall Street traders, who, with their dazzling array of tools—derivatives, swaps, futures contracts—would transform the industry into just another financial casino in which they gambled daily, using other people's money.

The move to deregulate the electrical energy markets in the nineties was the natural extension of changes that had taken place in the natural gas industry in the previous decade. In the early eighties, a series of laws and rulings from the Federal Energy Regulatory Commission (FERC) transformed the natural gas industry from a highly regulated monopoly to one in which a number of corporate actors openly competed at a number of levels.[14] These changes made it possible for natural gas to be traded in the same way that other commodities are traded—in a futures market for natural gas contracts. In other words, rather than simply paying whatever price public utilities were allowed to charge for natural gas, consumers were able to negotiate contracts to purchase natural gas in the future at fixed prices, thereby removing the uncertainty of having to respond to wild fluctuations in the day-to-day price. This created the possibility for a market in options to purchase gas at a fixed price, just as there are options markets for many other commodities—wheat, soybeans, etc. Deregulation also created the possibility for companies that owned pipelines and contracted to deliver gas physically to consumers to be more efficient by allowing them to "swap" those contracts, that is, to arrange with another gas distributor to deliver the gas. Options and swaps led to the emergence of whole new markets in which brokers could function as middlemen between natural gas producers and consumers, trading in swaps and contracts.[15] It opened the door, in other words, to the financialization of the natural gas industry.

The newly deregulated natural gas market was used as a model for deregulatory policies formulated for the electrical energy market in the 1990s. When President George H. W. Bush signed the Energy Policy Act in 1992, he told an audience of oil and gas workers that the new law would create jobs, "not by resorting to the failed methods of government control but by *unleashing the genius of the private sector*" (emphasis added).[16] Four years later, the Federal Energy Regulatory Commission completed the work started by the 1992 law by implementing two policy changes that would make California's deregulated system possible.[17]

A number of energy companies were well positioned to take advantage of the changes in the electrical energy markets and quickly moved in and applied the logic and strategies that had served them well in the recently deregulated natural gas industry. The undisputed "first mover" in this market was the Houston-based Enron Corporation. Enron had begun in the rough-and-tumble gas pipeline business, but by the late 1980s, in the midst of a rapidly deregulating environment, it reinvented itself as a commodities trading firm. With a CEO (Kenneth Lay) who came to his position after finishing a Ph.D. in economics rather than by rising up through the ranks of oil field hands and managers, Enron represented something completely new in the power industry: an energy company that was not primarily interested in producing energy, but rather in "making markets." When Lay pronounced that Enron was a "knowledge-based company," he sounded more like Marshall McLuhan than a Texas oilman.

While Enron led the pack and set the standards, by the mid-1990s a large number of companies, including utilities that set up energy trading subsidiaries, had entered the energy trading industry. By 1998 there were four hundred independent trading companies, and seventy-seven utilities were operating in the industry.[18] Despite this apparent high level of competition, by 2000 the industry was dominated by six companies, four of which, Dynegy, El Paso Energy, Reliant Energy, and Enron, were headquartered in Houston's "Energy Alley"—the glass and steel mecca of the energy trading industry. In that year, the six major firms, whose members also included Duke Energy and the Southern Company, had combined revenues of $268 billion.[19] By the late nineties, these companies had transformed (a word that frequently appears in their promotional literature) themselves from energy generators and distributors into "Power Merchants," with broad interests in many markets and products.

Another word that was popular among power merchants was "convergence"—as in "a convergence of technologies." More than simply rhetoric, the idea of converging technologies was put into action in 1999 when Enron opened an online trading platform, Enron Online. With this move, Enron attempted to establish an independent market for transactions, not only in energy, but in a wide variety of other products, including liquid petroleum, pulp and paper, plastics, bandwidth, and even the weather itself. (Enron pioneered the sale of weather derivatives—contracts purchased by companies, like ski resorts, that need hedges against the economic consequences of unusual weather patterns, such as unseasonably high temperatures.) Buyers and sellers could negotiate trades, online, in real time. Enron did not simply match buyers and sellers, but rather served as a counterparty to all trades, which meant that Enron itself was involved in every transaction. Enron's breakthrough was quickly emulated by others; within months, a number of other energy companies had created their own online trading platforms, modeled after Enron's. Importantly, all of these markets operated outside the scope of regulators, such as the Securities and Exchange Commission and the Commodities Futures Trading Commission.

The newly transformed power merchants fully embraced the ideals and the vocabulary of the New Economy. It was the late nineties and the New Economy revolution was in full swing, with the dot-com and telecom industries booming and consulting firms in high gear churning out the rhetoric of the virtual marketplace for their corporate clients. Just as Enron led the energy trading industry in revenues, so did it lead the pack in the production of New Economy babble. In its 1999 annual report, Enron laid out its manifesto for the New Economy:

We are participating in the New Economy, and the rules have changed dramatically. What you own is not as important as what you know. Hard-wired businesses, such as energy and communications, have turned into knowledge-based industries, that place a premium on creativity.

When you define a New Economy company you define Enron. A New Economy enterprise exhibits four traits.

1. *Its strength comes from knowledge, not just physical assets.* . . .
2. *A New Economy Player must operate globally—effortlessly transferring ideas, people and services from region to region.* . . .
3. *New Economy companies understand that constant innovation is their only defense against competition.* . . .
4. *Success in the New Economy requires the adroit use of information to restructure an organization and boost productivity.* (emphasis in the original) [20]

The emphasis on knowledge over hard assets was a key element of New Economy rhetoric, and was reflected in a term used frequently by Enron's chief of operations, Jeffrey Skilling: "asset lite." Not coincidentally, Skilling came to Enron from McKinsey & Company, a consulting firm that was one of the chief architects of the business model that would dominate New Economy firms.

While Enron may have been at the forefront of the movement to create an ideological justification for the emerging energy industry, it certainly was not alone. Across the street from Enron's Houston's headquarters, scribes at Dynegy Energy were hard at work hammering out that firm's corporate identity. In Dynegy's 2000 annual report, the company's chairman described the firm's "transformation to a technology-centric, knowledge-based company, that is highly-connected and leverages the digital community." The concept of convergence appears to have been central to the company's philosophy, as, for example, when the CEO referred to the firm as a "leading convergence player, with an established position in today's hottest commodities markets." The term was also used to explain to shareholders Dynegy's move into the communications industry: "A new kind of *convergence* is on the horizon and Dynegy is building a business to capture the opportunities created by the synergies between energy, communications and technology. In true Dynegy fashion, we are taking an *asset-lite,* wholesale-driven approach to the communications marketplace" (emphasis added).[21]

With its entry into the telecommunications industry, Dynegy was following the lead of several other energy companies, notably Enron and the Williams Companies. Early on Williams had seen the advantage of running fiber-optic cables along its vast network of natural gas pipelines, eventually laying thirty thousand miles of cable that crisscrossed the country. (Prior to this, Williams's executives had briefly considered the idea of transporting milk through its unused pipelines, but dropped the idea after it appeared the milk would turn into butter as it churned through the pipes.) [22]

For several power merchants, once the move had been made from energy to communications, the next step from communications hardware to content did not seem like that big of a leap. One of these companies, Enron, saw the opportunities that lay in the convergence of hardware and software. In the summer of 2000, when the company was at the height of its glory, Enron announced a joint venture with video rental giant Blockbuster to provide videos on demand via its broadband network, boasting that it represented "the ultimate bricks, flicks, and clicks" strategy in the entertainment industry.[23] Despite its auspicious beginnings, the venture never got beyond the stage of a pilot project and eventually fizzled out. It was not, however, a total failure. It was later revealed that (unbeknownst to Blockbuster) the head of Enron's broadband unit had created a structured finance transaction—creatively named Braveheart, after a Mel Gibson movie—around the movie deal. Then, the corporate executives were able to perform a feat of financial alchemy, turning a money-losing venture into a revenue producer by moving $115 million invested by a Canadian bank in another Enron financial vehicle into Project Braveheart, thereby adding $111 million to the broadband unit's quarterly revenue statements. Raising the unit's revenues enabled the executives to exercise stock options, which made these already wealthy men considerably richer. Between February 2000 and June 2001, the unit's CEO, Kenneth Rice, for example, sold over $53 million in Enron stock.[24]

Consistent with New Economy doctrine, energy companies were ardent advocates of deregulation. Here, too, Enron was the clear frontrunner in efforts to spread the deregulation gospel. In a 1996 message to shareholders, Skilling and Lay spoke of the policy in epochal terms: "In North America . . . deregulation is coming, inevitably and day by day. . . . In the developing world, new markets are emerging as governments turn toward privatization. . . . A political scientist would sum up these changes as the retreat of socialism and the advance of free markets. . . . We believe that deregulation is the third major event in the history of electricity. . . . The first took place the day a genius named Edison created an electrical circuit, flicked a switch and the light went on."[25] Other energy companies were equally positive, if less grandiose, in their support for deregulation.

Until the California energy crisis, the power merchants were riding high, and their strength was reflected in their stock prices. In the year 2000, all six of the big power merchants saw their stock prices rise dramatically. The price of Dynegy's stock, for example, more than tripled during the year. As the crisis unfolded and the public began to see news reports of blackouts in California, the tide began to turn against the energy companies. By mid-2002, Dynegy's stock was selling for under $5 a share, having plummeted from a high of over $55 a share in early 2001. Yet, even in the face of mounting evidence that energy companies had manipulated the markets in California, their leaders defiantly defended their behavior. The defensive (and ultimately indefensible) posture of energy executives was best revealed by Enron CEO Jeff Skilling when he responded to a journalist's question about his company's role in the crisis by saying: "We are doing the right thing. We are working to create open, competitive, fair markets, and in open, competitive fair markets, prices are lower and customers get better service. . . . *We are the good guys. We are on the side of angels*" (emphasis added).[26]

Gaming the System

In retrospect, California officials should have seen it coming. They had created a system that was highly deregulated at the wholesale level, allowing energy traders to charge virtually "whatever the market will bear," regardless of how much profiteering was involved, while at the same time retaining the state's ultimate responsibility for supplying consumers with electrical energy at affordable prices. The result was a market that was replete with loopholes and ambiguities that energy traders exploited to the fullest to reap fantastic profits.

It didn't take long for California authorities to realize that the new system created enormous opportunities for legalized theft. Under the new regulations, for example, the ISO was required to pay energy producers for "standby power" to be used when demand was expected to rise higher than normal. There were no limits on what producers could charge for that power. In the summer of 1998, three and a half months after the new rules went into effect, the operators of the ISO encountered a situation where they needed to purchase standby power but found relatively few producers willing to sell it. They eventually paid the Dynegy Corporation $9,999 a megawatt hour for access to electrical energy that normally would have sold for about $10 a megawatt hour.[27] This was only a glimpse of things to come.

In a complaint filed with the Federal Energy Regulatory Commission, California authorities would later claim that during the state's energy crisis, "[energy] sellers engaged in conduct that would be shocking in a fully deregulated market—and that is almost incomprehensible in a market for the sale of a product essential to health and safety." The complaint alleged that energy traders and producers engaged in specific abusive and sometimes illegal practices that included:

- Deliberately withholding energy from the market in order to drive up prices by creating false shortages.
- Submitting false bids in both the PX and ISO real time markets whose only purpose was to drive up prices.
- Scheduling bogus load schedules so as to force trades into the real time market.
- Engaging in "megawatt laundering," by moving energy out of and then back into California in an effort to manipulate Out-of-Market agreements in the real time market.
- Creating false congestion on the electrical lines in order to receive payments for relieving this congestion.[28]

One of the more serious accusations was that a number of energy companies that had recently acquired power generators deliberately withheld electricity in order to create artificial shortages. California authorities alleged that the "Big Five" private electricity generators in the state—AES/Williams, Dynegy, Mirant, Reliant, and Duke—"engaged in deliberate and systematic withholding of energy . . . from the market . . . [which] drove prices significantly above competitive levels."[29] One of those incidents involved the Tulsa, Oklahoma–based Williams Companies, which sold electricity generated from power plants in southern California owned by AES Corp. to the ISO at prices that by the spring of 2000 were running around $63 per megawatt hour. According to FERC investigators, over a two-week period in 2001, Williams/AES shut down two generating plants (ostensibly for repairs) that the ISO considered critical to the southern California power grid. This move forced the ISO to purchase electricity from the other Williams/AES generating plants at prices that were close to the $750 price cap. FERC investigators later determined that the closure of the two plants was unnecessary, and in fact was an intentional ploy to wring more than $10 million in revenues from the ISO.[30] Investigators found smoking gun evidence in the form of taped transcripts of conversations between an AES operator of the plants and a Williams employee, in which the latter explained, "[I]t wouldn't hurt Williams' feelings if the outage ran long."[31] This point, according to FERC's report, was reiterated in a subsequent conversation between an AES employee (Pendergraft) and a Williams employee (Morgan):

> Later that day, Eric Pendergraft, a high-ranking AES employee, followed up this conversation, expressing his understanding that "you guys were saying that it might not be such a bad thing if it took us a little while longer to do our work." Morgan responded by saying, "[W]e're not trying to talk yous [sic] into doin' it but it wouldn't hurt, you know, we wouldn't throw a fit if it took any longer." Mr. Pendergraft responded: "Then you wouldn't hit us for availability?" Ms. Morgan agreed, adding "I don't wanna do something underhanded, but if there's work you can continue to do . . ." Mr. Pendergraft stated, "I understand. You don't have to talk any more." He then stated, "We probably oughta have things we'd like to do in preparation for the summer, so . . . that might work out."[32]

Ultimately, the Williams Companies agreed to refund, without admitting guilt, $8 million to the ISO.

Dude, Where's My Energy?

Even more audacious were the strategies devised by energy companies to bilk the system, and ultimately consumers, out of billions of dollars using a number of trading schemes. After California deregulated its electricity markets, the major power companies set up trading desks at which employees of different companies bartered with each other and the state itself, buying and selling electrical energy. Many of these traders were young and inexperienced, but that didn't stop them from engaging in multimillion-dollar transactions on a daily basis. The public first became aware of these trading schemes on May 6, 2002, when FERC posted a memo from Enron on its website. The memo described the results of an internal investigation that turned up inventive trading strategies with names like "Get Shorty," "Death Star," "Ricochet," and "Fat Boy," all of which came down to "hawking electrons that didn't exist."[33]

Under the "Ricochet" strategy, a trader would buy "energy from the PX in the Day Of market, and schedule it for export. The energy is sent out of California to another party, which charges a small fee per MW, and then Enron buys it back to sell the energy to the ISO real-time market."[34] Investigators discovered a variant on the Ricochet scheme when they investigated trades made from Enron's Portland-based real time trading desk. The scheme took advantage of the fact that (as stated earlier) if the ISO could not obtain sufficient energy from within the state, it could purchase power out of state, and, importantly, the price caps on that electricity were lifted, allowing power marketers to charge essentially whatever they wanted. As an investigator explained in a court document, "The general idea was to buy energy in an earlier market, 'park it' with a power company outside of California, buy it back for a small fee in the hour ahead market, and then sell it to the ISO inside California. When a trader 'parked' energy, he was making a fictional trade. With a parking deal, it was understood that *no electrons would actually move because of the deal*" (emphasis added).[35] In one case Enron traders sold power to an out-of-state utility, New Mexico Power, then a few hours before the power was to be generated bought the same amount of power from New Mexico Power and sold it to the ISO, claiming that the power originated in New Mexico, when, in fact, the electricity never left the state.[36]

The goal of many of the techniques used by traders at Enron and elsewhere was to obtain "congestion fees," that is, fees paid by the ISO to energy companies for not sending electrical energy along lines that would strain their capacity. They did so by fabricating load schedules. Amazingly, several energy trading companies turned over to FERC transcripts of phone conversations of their own traders apparently engaged in just these types of transactions. One of those taped conversations involved traders at Xcel Corp.'s subsidiary Public Service Co. of Colorado (PSCo.) and traders at the Southern Co. Energy Marketing (SCEM), later renamed Mirant, on June 20, 2000.

PSCo: We are starting to get smacked on congestion?
SCEM: Oh see we collected that we scheduled the NP

PSCo: No, I mean, did you go there as your Mead $75 for 13 you got smacked

SCEM: Yeh, but I collected it all back cause if you look at path .26 it was also $75 so it netted zero. Oh yeah, that's right, we actually collected $10 so

PSCo: Yep, that 26 is north to south right now?

SCEM: Yeh, so we are basically scheduling it on PV but scheduling on to load at NP. [Laugh] . . . it has been working pretty well

PSCo: What do you mean you are scheduling to PV

SCEM: That's right

PSCo: You are taking energy out of the north and wheeling it south

SCEM: That's right

PSCo: Oh okay

SCEM: and scheduling it to load at NP . . . [laugh]

PSCo: Yeh, no that makes sense

SCEM: I mean it's just kind of loop-t-looping but it's making money . . . [laugh].[37]

Stripped of the jargon, the conversation shows the Mirant trader telling the Xcel trader that he was intending to tell the grid operators that they were moving electricity from southern California to northern California, when in fact they were moving the power in the opposite direction—"kind of loop-t-looping." Thus, they would earn congestion fees, despite the fact that the congestion was fictional.

Another taped conversation shows an XCEL trader (PSCo) and a Mirant trader (SCEM) discussing a strategy to overschedule a load—in other words, to indicate to ISO that they were planning to send more power through the lines than the lines were capable of carrying, in order to collect congestion fees. The conversation begins with the pair discussing a job opening at Mirant.

SCEM: Yeh

PSCo: What's going on with that . . . are you going to get that?

SCEM: Er no if we do we are going to need lots of bodies—we do something like that we are going to need a lot of people.

PSCo: If you do something like that are you going to hire me?

SCEM: Yep, absolutely we'd be pushing it but we could do it. There are a lot of people in here you know, it's just we need to bring on physical people who can trade physical—you would be 1st on the list.

PSCo: Dude I'm like number 1 man
SCEM: Number 1
PSCo: Number 1 man
SCEM: Hey listen
PSCo: What's up?
SCEM: Here's the deal, er you want um
PSCo: overschedule load at Summit?
SCEM: Yeh . . . I mean like, no no way
PSCo: Smack
SCEM: Hey why not some, we can pick up your 4Cs energy out here
    and send it in to NP if you want to trade congestion
PSCo: At Summit through?
SCEM: No, no no no you send in the 4Cs and we take it up north
PSCo: Yeah dude
SCEM: We collect congestion on about 15 and sell at 26
PSCo: Dude you like rock![38]

The energy traders whose conversations were captured in these tapes often sounded more like stoned surfers than high-paid traders engaged in multimillion-dollar transactions. Because the energy trading businesses was so new, companies were desperate for traders and often hired people right out of college, with little or no experience and, apparently, some with few scruples about bending the rules to profit.

A series of taped conversations among Enron traders and other Enron employees, obtained by a Washington State utility and turned over to FERC, reveal just how pervasive illegal trading tactics were in the energy trading industry. In a phone conversation with an unidentified trader, Timothy Belden, an Enron energy trader who would later be convicted on federal charges, was recorded openly discussing and joking about illegal tactics used by Jeffrey Richter, who headed Enron's energy trading unit in Portland, Oregon, and who would himself eventually be convicted for fraudulent trading practices in the California electricity market.

BELDEN: Is, ah, Richter in short-term California.
PERSON 2: It was 1 point—yeah, OK. [*inaudible*]
BELDEN: Well, he makes—ah, actually he makes between one and
    two a day, um, which never shows up on any curve shift, where he
    just buys it from the day-ahead. He just fucks California. Then,
    another—

PERSON 2: Wait a minute. OK.

BELDEN: He steals money from California to the tune of about a million—

PERSON 2: Will you re-phrase that?

BELDEN: OK, he, um—he arbitrages the California market to the tune of a million bucks or two a day.

PERSON 2: Will that ever stop?

BELDEN: Yeah.

PERSON 2: OK [*chuckling*] Maybe we can put him into an—a special purpose vehicle.[39]

In another conversation, two Enron traders bragged about how much money they stole from California consumers; revealing once again the casual attitude they took toward large-scale theft and its victims.

KEVIN: So the rumor's true? They're fuckin' takin' all the money back from you guys those money you guys stole from those poor grandmothers in California?

BOB: Yeah, Grandma Millie, man. But she's the one who couldn't figure out how to fuckin' vote on the butterfly ballot.

KEVIN: Yeah, now she wants her fuckin' money back for all the power you've charged. . . .[40]

Just in case any energy companies could not figure out how to game the system on their own, Perot Systems, a Texas information technology company headed by former presidential candidate H. Ross Perot, was there to help. Even before the new deregulated system was implemented in 1998, Perot Systems was offering to help energy companies develop strategies for exploiting loopholes in the system.[41] And if anyone knew how to do it, they should have, since they had helped the state create the complicated computer system that was the backbone of the market. In June 1998, representatives of the company gave a PowerPoint presentation at Reliant Energy that noted: "Published protocols governing California markets deviate . . . from theory and physical reality" resulting in "Gaps within a single market" and "Gaps between markets." The presentation went on to assert that these "Gaps in protocols provide opportunities for increased profits."[42] The previous year, an energy consultant who worked with Perot Systems, in a letter to PG&E in which he attempted to market his services to help them understand how to manipulate the new system, wrote: "We have found over a thousand loopholes in the system. For a few years, playing at the edge of the rules will be the name of the game. . . . One would feel very foolish for not taking advantage of the easy money."[43] Appearing before a California Senate panel, Mr. Perot denied the allegations that his firm was marketing strategies for gaming the system but instead was performing a public service by pointing out loopholes in the system that needed to be closed.[44]

The Price Is Not Right

Not only did energy companies manipulate the electrical energy market, but they also artificially drove up prices in the natural gas market, which, because many electrical generators are powered by gas, contributed to increases in the wholesale price of electricity. The techniques used in these schemes were complicated, but distilled to their essence, they involved falsely reporting information on trades to the major indexes that report gas prices. One of the ways that natural gas contracts are valued (i.e., how buyers and sellers establish baseline prices) is by reference to "indexes" published by private firms that record gas transactions on a daily basis. Buyers can refer to these indexes to get a sense of what the current market price is for contracts in a certain region for a certain period of time. Gas traders have an obvious incentive to inflate their transactions in order to raise the prices listed on the index and thus the prices they can negotiate for their contracts. A former employee of one of the firms that publishes a widely used gas index testified before a California legislative committee that "it was common industry knowledge that exaggeration was an accepted industry practice . . . no one acted shocked about the topic."[45] The pervasiveness of the practice was confirmed when some of the largest energy companies in the country—American Electric Power Co., Dynegy, Inc., CMS Energy Corp., El Paso Corp., and Williams Cos.—admitted that their employees had reported false data to the indexes. Investigators at FERC concluded that during the nineties "false reporting became epidemic."[46] While this practice was clearly illegal, as of this writing, few people from the industry have been prosecuted.

Enron and the "Genius of Capitalism"

While a large number of companies were implicated in the California energy crisis, one corporation came to symbolize all that was wrong in that debacle—indeed, it epitomized the process that we refer to as pump and dump. Many volumes have been written about Enron since its spectacular fall, but beyond its specific history, the company, in both its ideology and its practice, represented something greater than itself. The now-disgraced corporation represented a near *ideal type* (to use the sociological concept) of the process known as financialization. Paul Krugman described Enron, just before its collapse, as in the "vanguard of a powerful movement that hopes to 'financialize' (Enron's term) just about everything—that is, trade almost everything as if it were stock options."[47] Enron was a company that started out as very much a part of the Old Economy, laying pipelines and delivering natural gas, and ended up "more akin to Goldman Sachs than to Consolidated Edison."[48]

More than just an ideal-type, during the 1990s Enron was an *ideal* among corporate America and the business press, a model that other corporations were urged to emulate. Therefore, despite all that has been written about Enron—its rise and dramatic fall—the company and its many-tentacled operations still warrant further analysis, particularly as they represent broader trends that were sweeping through the corporate landscape at the end of the twentieth century and which led directly to the corporate crisis that exploded at the beginning of the twenty-first.

There are two versions of the Enron story: one that was told before the company's collapse in the fall of 2001 and one that was told after. The earlier version was almost invariably positive and adulatory in tone, casting the company's executives as visionaries and innovators who were not just creating a very successful company but who were at the forefront of a movement to change the entire economy and thereby usher in a new age of prosperity. The later version of the story (which, interestingly, was often told by the same people who had narrated the earlier version) is, of course, more negative and its main characters are usually cast as sinister charlatans and criminals who duped virtually everyone, including the media. This new tone was captured in the title of a frequently cited article that appeared in *Fortune* magazine (which had previously been one of Enron's most vocal cheerleaders) in December 2001: "Why Enron Went Bust; Start with Arrogance. Add Greed, Deceit, and Financial Chicanery."[49]

As part of the New Economy narrative, Enron symbolized the larger changes that were thought be to taking place in the economy, shifts from hardware to software and an emphasis on "intellectual capital" over financial capital. But more than symbolic value, the Enron story also had instrumental value—instrumental in the sense that it was both carefully constructed by corporate actors at Enron and in the sense that it was strategically used by those actors to legitimate the company's behavior and to suppress critical questions from regulators, the press, and other corporations.

In the emerging New Economy mythology, praise was heaped on individuals and organizations that could "think outside the box." Inspired by legendary Silicon Valley success stories, the heroes of these myths were often rebels and free spirits who were not afraid to break the rules and challenge the existing order. With its particular history and cast of characters, Enron easily fit into this genre. A significant component of the myth-making machine was the business press, which, like Hollywood movie studios, was always on the lookout for a good story that would fit into a proven formula. In April 2000, just eighteen months before it published the highly critical "Start with Arrogance" story, *Fortune* magazine came out with a story on Enron that typified the "New Economy rebels" story line:

> Imagine a country-club dinner dance, with a bunch of old fogies and their wives shuffling around halfheartedly to the not-so-stirring sounds of Guy Lombardo and his All-Tuxedo Orchestra. Suddenly young Elvis comes crashing through the skylight, complete with gold-lame suit, shiny guitar, and gyrating hips. Half the waltzers faint; most of the others get angry or pouty And a very few decide they like what they hear, tap their feet . . . start grabbing new partners, and suddenly are rocking to a very different tune.
>
> In the staid world of regulated utilities and energy companies, Enron Corp. is that gate-crashing Elvis. Once a medium-sized player in the stupefyingly soporific gas-pipeline business, Enron in the past decade has become far and away the most vigorous agent of change in its Industry, fundamentally altering how billions of dollars' worth of power—both gas and electric—is bought, moved, and sold, everywhere in the nation.[50]

Business writers were influential members of a group that we refer to in chapter 5 as "professional pumpsters"—individuals and organizations who (wittingly or unwittingly) helped to "pump" New Economy companies in the late nineties. The Enron pump appeared not only in magazine articles but in the genre of inspirational business books that appeared during the era, books that celebrated the revolutionary aspects of New Economy firms and organizational practices. Typical of these New Economy evangelists was Gary Hamel, whose 2000 book, *Leading the Revolution,* used Enron as a case study of what he termed "gray-haired revolutionaries" in the business world. He observed that "as much as any company in the world, Enron has institutionalized a capacity for perpetual innovation." Just a year before the Enron scandal emerged, Hamel wrote, with no hint of sarcasm: "everyone knows that the champions of business concept innovation get handsomely rewarded. Enron has typically given entrepreneurs phantom equity in the new business they are helping to create."[51] Little did he know that this system of "phantom equity" would soon result in the indictments of people like Enron CFO Andrew Fastow.

By early 2002, the Enron story had changed dramatically, as journalists and government investigators had begun to break through the corporation's facade to lay bare a vast and complex web of fraud and deceit. Still, many prominent public officials dismissed the seriousness of the problem. Appearing on the Bush-friendly Fox News program in January, then–Secretary of the Treasury Paul O'Neill was asked what he thought about the emerging scandal. His reply: "Companies come and go. It's part of the *genius of capitalism*" (emphasis added).[52] To be fair, this "let them eat cake" attitude was not limited to Republicans. Days after O'Neill's statement, journalists uncovered the fact that Democratic National Committee chairman Terry McAuliffe had turned a $100,000 investment in telecom giant Global Crossing into an $18 million profit before the company went belly-up. When asked about his windfall, McAuliffe replied defensively, "If you don't like capitalism, move to Cuba or China."[53]

Making the Rules

The rise and fall of Enron is a story that has been told many times by many people. As of fall 2004, the disgraced corporation had been the subject of over forty congressional hearings, more than a dozen books, countless articles, and one made-for-television movie. Therefore, in our discussion, we will not attempt to recount all the details of this story. Rather, we want to focus on more fundamental aspects of the Enron case that tie it to other instances of corporate misconduct as well as to larger issues concerning the shifting landscape of corporate capitalism in the late twentieth and early twenty-first centuries.

In an incisive article published in the *Columbia Journalism Review,* Scott Sherman raised a fundamental question about the activities of Enron: "Is Enron ultimately a story about people who broke the rules, or about how those rules got shaped?"[54] The answer, we would argue, is: both. What makes the Enron story more than just another tale of corporate crime, greed, and fall from grace is the way in which Enron, along with its many allies, systematically changed the economic rules that govern markets and corporate behavior. To accomplish this feat, the people who ran Enron had to be more than savvy businesspeople. They also had to build an elaborate network of interlocking connections to politicians, regulators, bankers, accountants, public relations experts, and media heads, a network that operated on a system of reciprocal rewards and benefits. And, impressively, the whole system had to operate largely behind the scenes, away from public visibility. We start our discussion of Enron with a focus on how the company was able to successfully manipulate the rules of a game in which it was the perennial league leader.

The Enron story line first began to shift in March 2001 when *Fortune* magazine writer Bethany McLean asked, "How exactly does Enron make its money?" McLean was an astute business reporter, and the question did not reveal ignorance or facetiousness, but rather skepticism about Enron's claims about how it generated revenue. Even Wall Street analysts who were generally bullish on Enron admitted they could not understand the company's business. "Enron is a big black box," said one.[55]

One of the reasons why so many people had trouble understanding how Enron made its money was that the company worked in markets in which accounting standards were ambiguous and in which demands by regulators to explain their operations were minimal. This basic aspect of Enron's business activities was succinctly stated in an internal memo from an accountant at Enron's outside auditor, Arthur Andersen: "Enron often is creating industries and markets and transactions for which there are no specific rules. . . . Enron is aggressive in its transaction structuring."[56] Thus, more than simply choosing those markets, Enron helped to create them. From its very beginning a significant proportion of Enron's activities went into influencing policymakers to create and modify regulations in a way that greatly benefited the company. When Enron executives proclaimed that the company's business was "making markets," they were describing the key to the company's success. But it was not just markets that they were making, but the regulatory environment in which those markets operated as well. While all large corporations lobby politicians and use public relations firms to attempt to influence legislation, Enron's activities took it to a new level.

In response to Kenneth Lay's claim that the California energy crisis was the result of a flawed system, California officials countered that Enron itself was a major architect of that system. "Enron's sophisticated lobbying efforts helped to create the very market it would later exploit," said one California state senator.[57] Enron's representatives had appeared over a dozen times before the California Public Utilities Commission as it deliberated its new deregulated market system. At one of those hearings in 1994, Jeffrey Skilling, Enron's second in command, argued that the state could save as much as $8.9 billion a year by adopting a deregulated system and described what could be done with the savings: "You can triple the number of police officers in Los Angeles, San Francisco, Oakland and San Diego and you could double the state of California construction budget for hospitals. And you could double the number of teachers in Los Angeles, San Francisco, Oakland and San Diego. You could pay all the interest on the California state debt. The stakes are huge, and every minute that we delay bringing competitive markets to California allows the meter to keep ticking."[58] Ironically, $8.9 billion was exactly the amount that Californians were later estimated to have overpaid as the result of market manipulation by energy companies.[59]

But Enron brought more than rhetoric to the debate. It also supplied hard cash to state politicians. The day before the California Public Utilities Commission, whose members were largely appointed by Governor Pete Wilson, issued its Blue Book report on deregulation, Enron gave the governor a $10,000 campaign donation. By 1998, the energy company's donations to California politicians totaled over $100,000.[60]

Even after the energy crisis had peaked and California authorities were seeking radical changes to the system, Enron resisted attempts to alter the system from which it had profited so handsomely. In May 2001, soon after California officials sued energy companies for defrauding the state, Lay organized a meeting in a Beverly Hills hotel, attended by such luminaries as action-movie star Arnold Schwarzenegger and the former junk-bond impresario Michael Milken, to drum up support for a plan that would have further deregulated California's energy market.[61] Lay's plea had little immediate impact. However, two and a half years later, in an amazing turn of events, Arnold Schwarzenegger was elected governor in a stunning victory over sitting governor Gray Davis, who was recalled in large part because the public blamed him, rather than energy companies, for the costs of the energy crisis. Less than a week after he was elected, Governor-elect Schwarzenegger, in one of his first major policy statements, proposed an energy plan that would have once again deregulated portions of California's electricity market.[62]

While Enron's lobbying efforts in California were impressive, it was at the federal level that the company excelled at influence peddling. Over the years, Lay and his colleagues cultivated relationships with powerful figures in Washington and used those connections at critical points when they wanted to influence specific policies. Lay's connections to the Bush family have been well publicized (including then-Governor George W. Bush's letters to his pal "Kenny Boy"), but Enron's Washington campaign was much more extensive and systematic than that single relationship. In 1999 and 2000, Enron contributed more than $2.4 million to federal candidates—72 percent of which went to Republicans—making it the number-one contributor in the energy/natural resources industry.[63] The energy company maintained a government affairs office in Washington (whose 1999–2001 budget was over $100 million) and retained a prominent lobbying firm to do its bidding.[64]

Enron's investments in the political process paid off. In early 2001, Enron used its considerable clout to influence the incoming Bush administration's position on energy policy. This was a critical period for Enron, as the California energy crisis had forced the Federal Energy Regulatory Commission to reexamine its energy policies and, specifically, to consider requests for price caps on wholesale energy prices—a policy that Enron vociferously opposed. One of the company's goals was to influence the selection of FERC's new chairman. On January 8, 2001, Kenneth Lay wrote to Vice President–elect Dick Cheney offering his recommendations on "kinds of individuals we think you should be looking for."[65] Among the names listed was Pat Wood, then the chairman of the Texas Public Utilities Commission and an outspoken advocate of "free market solutions" to energy problems. Eight months later, Wood was indeed appointed as chairman of the Federal Energy Regulatory Commission by President Bush.

The broader goals of the company were to influence FERC to support continued deregulatory policies in California and the country as a whole and to promote the view that California's problems were the result of inadequate supplies of energy and structural flaws, not market manipulation. To help further this goal, Enron representatives met with the White House National Energy Policy Development Group, headed by

Cheney, six times during the period that the group was formulating the administration's energy policy. On April 17, 2001, at a time when environmental groups were having a difficult time gaining access to the vice president, Cheney met personally with Ken Lay—an old friend from Texas. The result of these meetings was a national energy policy that clearly bore the imprint of the Enron Corporation. A report prepared for California congressman Henry Waxman concluded that "numerous policies in the White House energy plan are virtually identical to the positions that Enron advocated . . . [including] (1) policies that promote the deregulation of the electricity market; (2) policies that promote energy derivatives and commodities markets; (3) policies that expand natural gas and oil production; and (4) other policies that benefited Enron."[66] Ironically, Enron's executives never got the opportunity to enjoy the fruits of their labors. Less than nine months after the report was released, Enron declared bankruptcy.

Enron's efforts to influence energy policy under the Bush administration have been well publicized. But over the years, operating in a much more low-key manner, the company reaped incalculable monetary benefits by influencing policy-makers and their actions on specific regulatory issues that greatly impacted Enron's business, but which received very little publicity. The one area that was of the most interest to Enron was the regulation of energy derivatives.

Despite the fact that Enron liked to play up its roots in the rough-and-tumble world of natural gas pipelines, the vast majority of its revenues came from trading, and specifically trading in complicated financial instruments known as derivatives. Even describing them is difficult, but by a simple definition, "derivatives are contracts that promise payments from one investor, or 'counterparty,' to another, depending on future events."[67] Those events—from which the value of the contract is derived—can vary widely, from the value of a stock to weather conditions. Relatively simple derivative contracts include options and futures that are traded on exchanges regulated by the Commodities Futures Trading Commission (CFTC). Other derivatives are traded in the Over the Counter (OTC) market and are not regulated by federal agencies. As discussed earlier, Enron became an innovator in the creation of OTC markets based on futures and options and swaps in energy contracts. Almost all of theses options and swaps fit under the definition of unregulated OTC derivative transactions. Through the nineties, increases in these transactions were a major factor in Enron's spectacular growth. In its 2000 annual report, Enron reported that over 90 percent of its revenues came from "wholesale energy operations and services," a vague category that included most of its trading activities.[68] A post-bankruptcy analysis estimated the notional value of all the derivative contracts on Enron's books at the end of 2001 to have been $758 billion.[69]

Derivatives, then, were at the core of Enron's business, and their unregulated status meant that they were not given the regulatory scrutiny that other financial transactions normally receive. This fact was central to the secretive nature of Enron's activities and to its ability to deceive regulators, investors, banks, and other financial institutions for so long. Thus, a major political objective for Enron, through the years, was to maintain the unregulated status of the OTC derivative transactions that formed a major part of its business. And the best way to do this, Enron executives discovered, was to have the right friends in high places.

In the late 1980s, over-the-counter derivatives were still in their infancy, with only a few financial firms trading in relatively straightforward swaps of various kinds. All of this would change soon, as firms like Bankers Trust would develop sophisticated mechanisms for engaging in complicated derivatives transactions.[70] From the outset, many in the financial community were concerned about the potential for abuse that was inherent in derivatives. Their fears were confirmed in July 1988 when Bankers Trust, then the eighth largest bank in the country, revealed that one of its traders, Andy Krieger, had sustained losses to the bank of $80 million trading in risky currency options.[71] By the early nineties, this incident and other financial scandals involving derivatives led many regulators, and even some prominent individuals in the financial industry, to call for stricter regulation on over-the-counter derivatives. At that point, derivatives that were not traded on major exchanges, such as the New York Mercantile Exchange, were not subject to federal regulation, as they were viewed as private contracts between large, sophisticated investors.

The decision about whether or not to regulate these new financial instruments lay in the hands of the commissioner of the Commodities Futures Trading Commission.[72] In 1992, the commissioner was Wendy Gramm, whose husband was Phil Gramm, a former economics professor and by then a Republican senator from Texas. Throughout the nineties, the Gramms maintained close ties to Enron, particularly Kenneth Lay, and they personally benefited greatly from those ties. In fall 1992, the CFTC was considering extending its regulatory authority over a number of OTC derivatives. Enron was one of nine firms that wrote letters to the regulatory agency arguing that energy derivatives should be exempted from regulation. The issue took on greater urgency in November when Bill Clinton was elected president and Ms. Gramm, a political appointee, realized that she would soon be out of job, and that her successor might take a different view of the policy. On January 14, 1992, Wendy Gramm rushed the issue to a vote before the commission, which normally had five members but at that point had two vacancies (the remaining three members had all been appointed by Bush). The commission voted in favor of the resolution to exempt energy futures and swaps from regulatory oversight. Six days later, Ms. Gramm resigned as the head of the commission. Five weeks after that, she was appointed to the Enron board of directors, all the while denying that there was any connection between her support for the energy derivatives policy and her appointment to Enron's board.[73] In an op-ed piece in the *Wall Street Journal*, Gramm revealed the ideological basis of her support for the energy derivative exemption: "[G]overnment may well pose the greatest risk to this market. . . . Markets can be over-regulated, which imposes costs on users. The danger of over-regulation is that overseas competition is just a phone call away."[74]

Regardless of whether her position was motivated by ideology or pecuniary interest, Ms. Gramm and her husband did well as a result of their Enron affiliations. As an Enron board member, she was paid between $915,000 and $1.8 million (depending on the value of her Enron stock) between 1993 and 2001. Senator Gramm, meanwhile, was the second largest congressional recipient of Enron campaign contributions, taking in $97,000 between 1989 and 2002.[75] When asked about potential conflicts of interest, the couple claimed that they rarely discussed their work with one another. "We talk about my taking out the garbage and Texas A&M football," Senator Gramm told reporters.[76]

During the mid-nineties, several events caused policy-makers to refocus their attention on the catastrophic potential of unregulated derivative transactions. First, there was the bankruptcy of Orange County, California, in 1994, following its loss of nearly $1.7 billion in risky derivatives. Then, in 1998, Long-Term Capital, an international hedge fund that had bet billions on high-risk derivatives and whose principals included two Nobel Prize–winning economists, collapsed, requiring a bailout of $3.6 billion amid fears of calamity in world financial markets.[77] The next year, the President's Working Group on Financial Markets—a policy group whose members included the secretary of the treasury and Federal Reserve chairman Alan Greenspan and SEC chairman Arthur Levitt—issued a report recommending that energy trades not be exempted from federal regulation.[78]

Given this considerable support for repeal of the derivatives exemption from regulation, less politically connected corporate executives might have given up the fight. But not Enron. The company cranked up its in-house lobbying effort. The investment paid off. That year, Congress passed the Commodities Futures Modernization Act of 2000, which, in direct contrast to the recommendations of the President's Working Group, exempted energy derivatives from government regulation.[79] Senator Patrick Fitzgerald, who worked on the legislation, later stated, "[W]e tried to craft a bill that met the recommendations of the President's Working Group; somehow, somewhere in the process somebody slipped in this mysterious exemption for energy and metals trading."[80] That "somebody" was Senator Phil Gramm. In December 2000, as the nation's attention was focused on the Supreme Court's decision that led to the "selection" of George W. Bush as president of the United States, Gramm, as chairman of the powerful Senate Banking Committee, used clever legislative maneuvers to bring a revised version of the bill, with the energy exemptions included, to a vote in Congress as an attachment to a larger appropriations bill.[81]

One might think that after the California energy crisis and Enron's meltdown, policy-makers would have learned their lesson and moved quickly to repeal the energy derivative exemptions. And in fact, just such a bill was proposed in early 2002 by California senator Diane Feinstein, who argued that by exempting from regulatory oversight electronic exchanges, such as Enron Online, the Commodities Futures Modernization Act "created a big loophole. . . . there is no record kept, there is no transparency there, there is no anti-fraud and no anti-manipulation oversight."[82] Senator Gramm, representing the interests of energy companies and the financial services industry, successfully spearheaded opposition to the bill. The bill never made it to a vote.[83] Several months later, in October 2002, Gramm, who had previously stated his intention to retire from politics, announced that he would be joining the investment banking giant UBS Warburg. Perhaps it was only coincidental that the previous February UBS Warburg had purchased Enron's energy trading unit.

The fact that Senator Feinstein's bill was defeated after the demise of Enron makes it clear that the firm was not the only source of support for energy deregulation. However, during its lifetime, Enron led the charge, with powerful allies such as Phil and Wendy Gramm, to shape policies from which it directly benefited. In early 2002, Charles Bowsher, the former head of the General Accounting Office, summed up Enron's influence in Washington: "Money allowed the Enron leadership to come to town. Everyone says they didn't get anything, that the secretary of the treasury turned them down, that the secretary of commerce turned them down. But if you look back over the last five years, what they did get was no oversight."[84]

One of the ironies of Enron was that for a company that vigorously espoused the doctrine of "free markets" and preached against the evils of government intervention in those markets, it spent an enormous amount of time and money in efforts to cultivate political relationships and influence government policies. In late October and early November 2001, for example, as Enron's credit ratings were sinking and its bankers were balking at lending it more money, Enron's newly appointed president, Greg Whalley, did not simply shrug his shoulders and mutter about the "survival of the fittest." Instead, he repeatedly called the Treasury Department's undersecretary for domestic finance in an unsuccessful attempt to persuade the official to contact the ratings agencies (who effectively held Enron's future in their hands) and urge them not to lower Enron's ratings.[85]

Enron's dependency on government support was even more evident in its international operations. From 1992 until its demise in 2001, Enron obtained $7.219 billion in public financing from U.S. government agencies, multilateral development banks (including the World Bank), and foreign governments to fund thirty-eight projects in twenty-nine countries. U.S. agencies, including the Overseas Private Investment Corporation, were particularly helpful, providing $3.68 billion in taxpayer dollars to fund twenty-five Enron projects overseas. In addition, the World Bank made $761 million available to Enron for its foreign projects, as part of the Bank's emphasis on exporting free-market principles to developing countries. In particular, Enron was the primary beneficiary of a World Bank program to bring deregulation to the world's energy markets. According to an analysis by the Institute for Policy Studies, "the World Bank would issue loans for privatization of the energy or the power sector in a developing country or make this a condition for further loans, and Enron would be the first, and often most successful, bidders to enter the country's newly privatized or deregulated energy markets." In 1996, for example, Bolivia received a loan of $10.6 million from the World Bank to "capitalize" its state oil company, which involved breaking it up into separate companies and selling them to private investors. Enron was one of those investors, and as part of its investment gained partial rights to a natural gas pipeline project that would have run from Brazil to Bolivia. The World Bank, in 1997, granted the project a loan of $130 million and later provided it $180 million in loan guarantees. After Enron's collapse the project was put on hold.[86]

Thus, Enron's very vocal public rhetoric about free markets and deregulation was contradicted by its extensive reliance on tax dollars to fund its far-flung enterprises. This contradiction was not limited to Enron, but rather is characteristic of the entire neoliberal project. When advocates of neoliberalism—from Alan Greenspan to Kenneth Lay—argue the virtues of the "free market," they still want a market that operates with rules—more specifically, rules that grant advantages to the largest corporations. And those rules are not to be created by the market itself, but by political bodies. This contradiction has appeared during a number of recent financial crises—from the savings and loan bailout of the late eighties to the bailout of Long-Term Capital Management in the late nineties—when some of the world's largest financial players have successfully pressed a "too big to fail" argument before governments.

Breaking the Rules: The Pump

Enron was, in effect if not by design, a very large-scale pump and dump scheme in which a variety of complex devices were used to inflate the company's assets just long enough so that high-level insiders could profit from their secret and not-so-secret holdings in the firm and its affiliated entities. Then, just as in the schemes discussed in the previous chapter, when the entire enterprise was teetering on the brink of disaster and accounting shell games could no longer hide the enormous losses, the insiders bailed out, leaving investors and employees holding an empty bag. The various post-mortems performed on the once-powerful energy company revealed a variety of intricate schemes, but Enron's crimes (whether or not they were technically illegal) took two basic forms. First, in order to maintain the firm's high stock prices, insiders—with the assistance of cadres of lawyers, accountants, and bankers—concocted a number of ploys that artificially boosted revenues. Second, the company's increasingly large liabilities, which if pub-

licly acknowledged would have dramatically reduced the company's reported profitability, were hidden in off-the-books "special purpose entities" and other deceptive financial vehicles. These schemes served the
purpose of enhancing the picture of Enron's financial health, which
drove up Enron's stock price and enriched the men and women who devised them.

Enron's market capitalization (the value of all outstanding shares)
peaked in 2000 at $70 billion. By late November 2001, that number had
plummeted to less than $1 billion.[87] In just over a year $69 billion in investors' wealth had evaporated.[88]

The primary motivation for Enron executives to pump up the company's financials was the simple fact that their own compensation was
closely tied to the firm's performance. In 1994, Lay, as CEO, was
awarded a compensation package that included 1.2 million options in
Enron stock, most of which could not be sold until the year 2000. An important provision of the contract, however, allowed the executive to exercise a third of the options if the company grew by at least 15 percent a
year.[89] Other executives at the company received similar packages that
were heavily loaded with stock options. These compensation packages,
in which the company's performance could mean differences of millions of dollars in pay, gave Enron executives clear-cut incentives to
artificially inflate the company's numbers—to create the illusion of
rapid growth regardless of the corporation's actual performance. The 15
percent growth rate established as a threshold in Lay's contract was not
an arbitrary number, but was a figure that company spokespersons frequently cited to investors. In Enron's 1996 annual report, Lay and
Skilling told investors: "we expect to achieve compound annual growth
in earnings per share of at least 15 percent from 1996 through the year
2000."[90]

When the Enron debacle was first reported in late October 2001, the
media frequently referred to the company as the seventh largest corporation in the country, based on its reported revenues. Within weeks,
however, even this basic fact about Enron was revealed to be untrue.
Enron accountants had artificially inflated revenues, using a technique
that was simple, common, and legal. Since the early 1990s, the company
had used an accounting method known as "mark-to-market," under
which a firm can record all future revenues and profit from an energy
contract in the quarter in which the contract was signed. Under more
traditional accounting rules, revenues and profits (as well as any losses
on the deal) would be recorded as they came in. Using mark-to-market

rules, however, energy companies could record as revenue on their financial statements the entire amount of an energy contract. So, if the company signed a contract to sell $1 million worth of natural gas, but they also had to buy the same amount of gas for $900,000 in order to re-sell it, they could still record the $1 million as revenue. If a securities brokerage firm had done a similar deal, they would have recorded the difference of $100,000 as net revenue. Using the latter technique, the $101 billion in revenues that Enron reported in 2001 turned into $6.3 billion and the company's ranking in the Fortune 500 dropped from number 7 to number 287.[91]

Enron's financial statements were further enhanced by the fact that mark-to-market accounting requires firms to estimate future profits from long-term contracts. It is very difficult to predict energy prices ten or twenty years into the future, and therefore, it is nearly impossible to estimate profits on energy contracts that span that far. Energy compa-nies were given wide leeway in how they estimated those future profits— a fact that Enron took advantage of to provide rosy estimates of the com-pany's profitability. On its balance sheet these future profits were referred to as "unrealized gains." These figures were often buried deep within Enron's financial statements, but still, they were there for anyone to see. In September 2000, over a year before Enron began to collapse, Jonathan Weil, a reporter for the *Wall Street Journal*, wrote an article in which he questioned Enron's actual performance. Weil pointed out that Enron's financial statement for the second quarter of 2000, for example, showed an overall profit and "unrealized gains" of $747 million. Had those gains not been reported, the company would have had to show a loss for the quarter.[92] Weil's article was published only in the Texas re-gional version of the newspaper and received little attention from the business press and stock analysts, who, not wanting to spoil the party, continued to rate Enron as a strong buy.

These practices were not limited to Enron, however, but were wide-spread throughout the energy trading industry. In his little-noticed ar-ticle, Weil pointed out that 71 percent of Dynegy's reported earnings for the second quarter of 2000 came from "unrealized gains." And at El Paso Energy, about a third of its reported earnings in the same quarter came from estimates of future profits.[93] These details did not dampen the power merchants' enthusiasm for their companies. The cover of Dynegy's 2000 annual report, for example, showed a mountain climber scaling a cliff. The report began with a statement from the company's CEO, who boasted: "[I]n a year when we recorded increases of 230 percent in net income, 91 percent in operating revenues and 218 percent in shareholder returns, and the company was admitted to Standard & Poors 500 Index, a mountain climber on the cover of our annual report seemed appropriate."[94] That mountain climber would soon fall; eighteen months after this statement was made the SEC charged Dynegy with inflating its reported cash flow by $300 million.[95]

For Enron, the beginning of the end was signaled on October 16, 2001, when Ken Lay announced that the firm would reduce shareholder equity by $1.2 billion as a result, in part, of "an early termination of certain structured-finance arrangements with a previously disclosed entity." The next day an article in the *Wall Street Journal* reported that the "previously disclosed entity" was a limited partnership called "LJM2" run by Enron CFO Andrew Fastow, who had earned millions of dollars on the deal.[96] In early November, Enron told the SEC that it was restating its finances going back to 1997, reducing its reported net income by $586 million because of "improper accounting" for transactions involving a number of partnerships.[97] A series of investigations conducted over the coming weeks and months by journalists, attorneys, congressional committees, and forensic accountants all came to the same conclusion: Enron had, for years, been greatly exaggerating the firm's profitability by hiding significant losses in off-the-books "special purpose entities." In one year alone, 2000, Enron (aided by accountants, bankers, and lawyers) used these tactics to erase $10 billion of debt from its balance sheet.[98]

Within a few months of Enron's bankruptcy, several investigations into the company's operations turned up evidence of the extent to which Enron's apparent success was in fact a carefully staged performance in which the major props were "special purpose entities" (SPEs) with exotic names like JEDI and Chewco (apparently Enron executives were enamored of *Star Wars* movies). The operation of these entities was often mind-numbingly complex, involving extremely arcane financial and legal devices. Their ultimate purposes, however, are much easier to understand. They were devised (1) to remove debts from Enron's balance sheets, and (2) to create wealth for the Enron insiders who created them and the invitation-only investors who put money into them. The deals worked like this: Enron insiders would create a partnership as part of a "special purpose entity" and then transfer ("sell") an asset, typically one that was performing poorly and incurring debt, to the partnership, thereby removing the debt from the balance sheets. According to accounting standards, in order for the partnership's finances not to be included on Enron's statements, at least 3 percent of the entity had to be owned by independent outsiders. The remaining 97 percent of the capital used to fund the partnership typically came from banks, usually large Wall Street investment banks such as J. P. Morgan, Citigroup, and Merrill Lynch, in the form of loans or lines of credit. The Enron insiders would include large commissions and fees to be paid to themselves by the partnerships.[99]

To the naïve observer, the big question about this scenario is why sophisticated investment banks would make loans to partnerships whose assets were very unlikely to produce any profits. The answer is twofold: First, Enron would guarantee repayment of the loans with Enron stock, and, if the stock declined in value, with cash. Second, the investment banks were also interested in maintaining their status with the company in order to keep their investment banking business (for example, handling mergers and acquisitions for the energy company), which brought the banks sizeable fees. The first fact is very important, because it meant that in many cases liabilities were being removed from balance sheets and the company's financial health improved at the expense of investors, who ultimately paid for these efforts to temporarily maintain the company's stock value. The role of investment banks in these schemes cannot be overstated. In hearings held in July 2002, the Senate Permanent Subcommittee on Investigations presented exhaustive evidence of the critical role that these firms played in assisting Enron in manipulating their financial statements. In her opening statement to the committee, Senator Susan Collins offered a withering criticism of two of those banks:

> Although many banks ultimately invested in these transactions, JP Morgan Chase and Citigroup were two of the principal banks involved. Their deals enabled Enron to keep some $8 billion of debt off its balance sheet and, as a result, misrepresent its financial status to rating agencies and to the investing public. JP Morgan Chase and Citigroup are two of the Nation's most prestigious financial institutions. That is why I find their involvement so shocking. It appears as though they were willing to risk their reputations to keep an important client—Enron—happy.[100]

The *Wall Street Journal* put it more succinctly when, after reviewing the evidence presented by the committee, it referred to the banks as "Enron's Enablers."[101]

One of the techniques used by Enron and its banking partners to hide debt involved what are called "pre-pay arrangements." As described in Senate hearings, this is "an arrangement in which one party pays in advance for a service or product to be delivered at a later date" (*SC,* 41). These arrangements have legitimate purposes, but in Enron's case, "when all the bells and whistles are stripped away, the basic transaction fails as a prepay, and what remains is a loan to Enron using an investment bank and an obligation on Enron's part to repay the principal plus interest" (*SC,* 14). Over a six-year period, Citigroup and J. P. Morgan Chase, along with a number of other investment banks, structured these pre-pay arrangements in an intentional effort to help Enron obtain over $9 billion in financing while disguising the debt on its books (*SC,* 216). Senate investigators were clear about the banks' knowledge of the purpose of these transactions. When asked by a member of the committee whether the banks knowingly aided and abetted Enron in their deceptions, the chief investigator replied: "Unquestionably. The documents that we have reviewed show that the financial institutions clearly understood what Enron's objective was in engaging in these transactions" (*SC,* 20). One of those documents was an internal memo from a Chase banker which stated: "Enron loves these transactions because it can hide debt from its equity analysts" (*SC,* 161).

In essence, these pre-pay arrangements were vehicles for engaging in circular transactions, which, typically, worked as follows: first, an offshore entity would be set up; the bank would then forward money to the offshore entity to purchase energy contracts at a fixed price from Enron, which the entity would do; then the contracts would be bought back by Enron, or an Enron-related entity, at a price higher than what the offshore entity paid for them. The transaction was booked by Enron as an energy transaction when in fact it was a loan. The transactions were actually more complicated than this, but this is what they came down to. In the early 1990s, J. P. Morgan Chase set up an offshore company in the British Channel Islands known as Mahonia that consisted of a tiny office with many phone lines and no employees. Mahonia became a conduit for doing pre-pays with Enron (see Figure 2.1). A typical transaction occurred on September 28, 2001, when Chase transferred $350 million to Mahonia to purchase natural gas to be delivered the next March (Step 1). The same day, Mahonia paid Enron $350 million for the option to buy natural gas in the future (Step 2). Enron then entered into a contract with Chase to purchase the gas for $355.9 million in March 2002 (Step 3). In effect, Enron got a $350 million loan from Chase, which it booked as positive cash flow, making its bottom line look better, and Chase earned

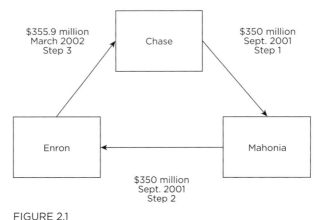

FIGURE 2.1
Mahonia Prepay Transaction
Source: U.S. General Accounting Office.

$5.9 million (*SC*, 249–251). Citigroup engaged in similar circular transactions with Enron using an offshore entity called Delta Energy Corporation in the Cayman Islands. Together, J. P. Morgan Chase and Citigroup engaged in twenty-six pre-pay transactions with Enron in deals that totaled $8.5 billion (*SC*, 214).

Once Chase and Citigroup saw how successful these deals were for Enron, they decided to market them to other companies. Chase developed a standard presentation on pre-pays that referred to them as "[balance] sheet 'friendly'" and eventually sold the idea to seven of its clients (*SC*, 234). Citigroup pitched pre-pays to fourteen clients and persuaded three to go for the idea (*SC*, 241).

Another one of Enron's favorite investment banks, Merrill Lynch, was involved with the energy company in numerous transactions. Likewise, Enron was one of Merrill's favorite clients, having paid Merrill over $43 million in fees from 1997 through 2001, and Merrill was eager to keep its client happy (*SC*, 165). In addition, nearly one hundred Merrill executives had invested more than $16 million of their own money in LMJ2, the SPE created by Andrew Fastow.[102] At the end of 1999, Enron executives proposed a means for Merrill to demonstrate its commitment. Going into the close of 1999, Enron was having trouble meeting its earnings numbers for the fourth quarter—a critical factor in keeping the stock price up. In order to meet those numbers, Enron needed to get rid of some problem assets, at least temporarily. One of these assets consisted of three floating power generators that were to be placed on barges off the coast of Nigeria. Enron executives asked Merrill to purchase the barges from them with the understanding that Enron would buy them back in six months, thereby allowing Enron to book an additional $12.5 million for the quarter. Merrill agreed and put up $7 million in cash to purchase the barges, using a shell company that it hastily created in the Cayman Islands. For its part, Merrill received $250,000 up front and a promise of 15 percent interest when the barges were repurchased. As promised, in June 2000 LMJ2 stepped forward to purchased Merrill's interest in the barges, along with the agreed-upon interest (*SC*, 163–164). The deal served its purpose. In a press release on January 18, 2000, Enron announced, "Enron Continues Strong Earnings Growth," and the stock price stayed up.[103] As the SEC would later charge, the deal was in fact a loan, not an investment by Merrill, whose sole purpose was to prop up Enron's stock price.[104] Eventually, four Merrill executives and two Enron employees were indicted for their involvement in the sham transaction.[105]

In the summer of 2002, a senior vice president at Merrill Lynch appeared before the Senate Subcommittee on Investigations to explain his firm's involvement in the Nigerian barge deal. In his testimony, the banker explained that Merrill had been duped by Enron. "We relied on Enron's accountant's opinions, its board approvals, its lawyers' opinions. . . . At no time did we engage in transactions that we thought improper" (*SC*, 174). Minutes later, after the panel's chairman, Senator Levin, produced internal documents which made clear that Merrill's representatives in the deal were fully aware of the purpose of the deal— to hide Enron debt—and that they regarded the funds Merrill put into the deal as a loan, not an investment that entailed any risk, the Merrill executive, who had earlier used the pronoun "we" when referring to his employer, started to distance himself from the events, stating: "Mr. Chairman, I was not involved in any of these transactions in any detail whatsoever" (*SC*, 180).

Executives from Citigroup and Chase also engaged in some fancy footwork when they appeared before the committee. When confronted with evidence of their companies' involvement in pre-pay arrangements, several investment bankers who gave testimony suddenly became experts on linguistics. A manager at Citigroup's Energy Group, for example, told the Senate panel that, in reference to alleged "secret oral agreements" his firm had with Enron to repay a debt, "there was no binding agreement between Enron and Citibank" (*SC*, 98). When confronted by Senator Levin with a memo the manager had written in which he referred to the fact that Enron had "agreed" to repay the debt, he began parsing words: "'agreement' is probably—is a word that could mean different things" (*SC,* 141–142). Similarly, when Senator Levin asked a banker at Citigroup, "[W]ould you agree that you have a responsibility not to participate in a deception?" the banker responded: "[I]t depends on what the definition of deception is" (*SC,* 138).

The creative techniques—SPEs, mark-to-market accounting, pre-pay arrangements, hidden loans—used by Enron to inflate the company's financials worked. Enron's stock price peaked in September 2000 at $90 a share, thereby ensuring big bonuses and stock option payouts to top executives. But, these strategies could only work for so long, since most were in essence Ponzi schemes that constantly required new injections of capital in order to cover up old debts. In all Ponzi schemes, at some point the new capital requirements outpace the sources of capital and the entire enterprise collapses—which is exactly what happened to Enron. The critical question in all Ponzi schemes is when to get out, knowing when the peak has been reached and the fall is imminent. By the time Enron's stock peaked, it appears that a number of high-level executives knew that the critical point had been reached. While maintaining public postures that everything was great—the company was doing fine and people should keep investing—they knew that in fact the house of cards was on the verge of collapse and so they quietly began to cash out. In other words, even while the pump continued, the dump was starting.

Breaking the Rules: The Dump

Enron was legendary for paying its top executives extremely well and compensating them with perks that included motorcycle races in Baja, expeditions to the Australian outback, and company-paid expense accounts at strip clubs.[106] In the year 2000, as the stock value was peaking, the two hundred highest paid employees at Enron received a total of over $1.4 billion in compensation, averaging $7.1 million apiece.[107] Twenty-six executives were paid over $10 million, and three over $100 million.[108] But what made Enron a really attractive place to work was the generous stock options that were awarded to employees, particularly high-level employees. Between 1998 and 2000, the top two hundred employees received over $1.3 billion in compensation from stock options.[109]

The data displayed in Figure 2.2 show the essentials of the Enron pump and dump scheme. There we see that as Enron's stock price rose, particularly in the first five months of 2000, company insiders sold

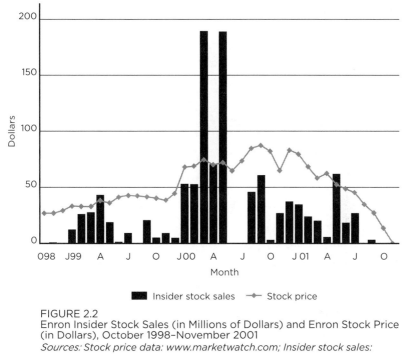

FIGURE 2.2
Enron Insider Stock Sales (in Millions of Dollars) and Enron Stock Price
(in Dollars), October 1998–November 2001
Sources: Stock price data: www.marketwatch.com; Insider stock sales:
Amalgamated Bank v. Lay, et al.

hundreds of millions of dollars in stock. In just three months—March through May 2000—they sold shares worth over $450 million. Soon thereafter, the stock price began to plunge.

In a period of a little over three years—from October 19, 1998, to November 27, 2001—twenty-nine Enron insiders, mostly officers in the company, sold a total of $1.1 billion of their company's stock. CEO Kenneth Lay sold $101 million in Enron shares; Jeffrey Skilling, the company's chief operating officer, sold $66 million; Andrew Fastow, chief financial officer, $30 million. Some of the less well known executives also did quite well. During the same period, Stanley Horton, the former CEO of Enron Transportation Services, sold $45 million in shares; Kenneth Rice, CEO of Enron subsidiary EBS (broadband) sold $73 million; Ken Harrison, CEO of another subsidiary, Portland General Electric, sold over a million shares for profits of over $75 million. But the biggest winner of them all was Lou Pai, CEO of Enron Accelerator, who, during the period, sold stock worth a staggering $353 million![110] When these facts were revealed, along with information about huge bonuses awarded to Enron executives in the company's waning days, public outrage boiled over as many people realized that it wasn't just bad business decisions that sunk the firm but pure greed.

On the other side of these transactions were the individuals and institutions who bought Enron stock under the assumption that the company was playing by the rules and was what it appeared to be: a very prosperous company that would continue to be so in the future. These investors were the victim's of the Enron pump and dump scheme and were generally of three types: (1) the individuals and institutions who purchased Enron stock directly; (2) the individuals who owned Enron stock indirectly through mutual funds and pension plans; and (3) Enron employees who bought Enron stock as part of the company's 401(k) plan and a stock ownership plan.

Among the first group were the thousands of investors who joined class action lawsuits alleging they were misled by Enron. This group included twelve individuals from Brenham, Texas, who bought Enron stock after attending a Chamber of Commerce luncheon where Kenneth Lay gave a speech touting the value of his stock and who later sued Lay, Skilling, and Arthur Andersen (Enron's accountants).[111]

Far more numerous than direct investors were the individuals who owned Enron stock and bonds indirectly through their mutual funds and pension plans. New York City employees lost an estimated $109 million from their pensions when Enron collapsed. Florida's pension plan (whose fund manager *bought* 2.7 million shares of Enron stock just weeks before the company declared bankruptcy) for state workers lost $300 million when Enron's stock plummeted. In Alabama, state employees saw their pension fund decline by $65 million because of the fund's Enron investments. Meanwhile, in Missouri, teachers lost $22.8 million from their retirement fund. These losses from Enron came on top of losses to these funds from their investments in other corruption-ridden companies, such as WorldCom and Global Crossing. As mentioned in the introduction, the New York State Comptroller estimated that in 2002 declines in stock and bond values at corporations hit by accounting scandals cost the New York State Common Retirement Fund (which includes both state and some local employees) around $9.1 billion.[112]

All of the people in these two groups felt the impact of Enron's implosion, but the impact was lessened by the fact that individually they had relatively small proportions of their pensions tied up in Enron stocks and bonds. By contrast, Enron employees who had invested heavily in their employer's stock suffered enormous losses. The firm allowed employees to purchase Enron stock either through its Savings Plan (a pension plan) or its Stock Ownership Plan (which was available primarily to salaried employees). Over twenty-seven thousand Enron employees participated in one or both of the plans. By the beginning of 2001, over half of the assets of the Savings Plan ($1.1 billion) and practically all of the Stock Ownership assets (over $1 billion) were invested in Enron stock.[113] Few employees complained about having so many of their eggs in one basket, since Enron's stock had increased in value dramatically in the late nineties.

The plans were overseen by several committees, whose members included Lay and Skilling, and who, by law, had a fiduciary duty "to prudently oversee the plans' investments and to act solely in the interests of the plans' participants."[114] Instead, the administrators of the plan ignored the interests of the participants and kept them locked into Enron stock, even as the value of that stock plummeted. Moreover, according to a lawsuit filed by the U.S. Department of Labor, CEO Kenneth Lay, in the critical weeks and months leading up to Enron's collapse, intentionally misled employees about the company's health and encouraged them to buy *more* Enron stock, even though he knew the company was on the brink of disaster. On August 14, 2001, when Enron's stock was trading at $40, down from $80 a share at the beginning of the year, Lay told plan participants that "I want to assure you that I have never felt better about the prospects for the company. . . . Our performance has never been stronger; our business model has never been more robust; our growth has never been more certain." The next month, on September 26, 2001, in an online discussion, Lay assured employees that the company was doing great: "The balance sheet is strong. Our financial liquidity has never been stronger."[115] He went on to urge employees to buy more stock: "My personal belief is that Enron stock is an incredible bargain at current prices."[116] Three weeks later the company would reduce shareholder equity—the difference between the company's assets and its liabilities—by $1.2 billion. Apparently, a lot of the employees weren't buying Lay's line. At a meeting with employees on October 23, 2001, the CEO was asked: "Are you on crack? If so, it would explain a lot."[117]

On October 26, 2001, after the revelations about the partnerships, Enron's stock had sunk to around $15 a share, having lost 80 percent of its value since the beginning of year. On that day, Enron officials dealt a death blow to employees when they announced that they were implementing a lockdown period in which participants in both plans could not transfer Enron stock out of their accounts. The lockdown lasted until

November 12, when the stock price closed at $9.24. In this three-week period in which they were prohibited from selling their Enron stock, the plans' participants lost $150 million.[118] On December 3, the day after Enron declared bankruptcy, the shares were selling for around forty cents.

While the image of the typical Enron employee may have been a young, ambitious MBA (and the company did employ many of them), the energy company also employed large numbers of blue-collar workers, many of whom were hit hard when the company's stock nose-dived. One of those was Charles Prestwood, who had retired from Enron at age sixty-two in 2000 after having worked at a gas storage facility in Bammel, Texas, for thirty-three years. When he left Enron his retirement account was worth $1.3 million. In December 2001, after being locked out of his account, it was worth a mere $8,000. Mr. Prestwood described the impact this turn of events was having on his life in testimony before a congressional committee:

> It is a complete turnaround because when I retired from Enron on October 1, 2000, I had plans on doing some traveling, my fiancee [sic] and I, and we had plans of doing a lot of things, see some of this good old beautiful USA. But since everything happened the way it did at Enron, I do good to stay home, and it is awful expensive even to stay home. I didn't have to worry if a refrigerator or water well pump or something like that went. I didn't have to worry about that because I had some money to back it up and I could replace it. Now, it is my prayer every day that everything will hang in there until I can get better financially if I sell a little piece of property that I own or something and kind of tie over my house note and one thing and another.[119]

For many former employees, their experiences with Enron not only impacted their material situation, but also changed their view of the world. As Mr. Prestwood told the committee: "The word 'loyalty'—right now, I do have two definitions of that word. The one that I lived by for 33½ years kind of left me hanging out on a limb when I found out that the real true definition of it wasn't exactly what I was thinking."[120]

Just Deserts?

Two years after the collapse of Enron, the energy trading business was a shell of what it once had been. Most of the firms that had dominated the industry in the late nineties were either bankrupt, teetering on the edge of bankruptcy, or had greatly cut back their energy trading activities. The changed status of the once-powerful energy trading industry was evident when, in the summer of 2002, *Fortune* magazine asked: "Is Energy Trading a Big Scam?"[121] For many people, particularly those who lived in California, the answer was an unequivocal "Yes!" The only question for them was whether the energy companies would be held accountable for their misdeeds. On this, the record is mixed but suggests that, for the most part, the answer is "No."

On the one hand, in the aftermath of the crisis, California and other western states were able to negotiate sizeable settlements with several energy companies, including $425 million from the Williams Companies; over $1 billion (to be paid over twenty years) from El Paso Corp.; and $50 million from Reliant Energy.[122] On the other hand, these and other settlements add up to far less than the $8.9 billion that California authorities claim the state lost due to market manipulation during the energy crisis.

A June 2003 decision by the Federal Energy Regulatory Commission gave Californians some hope that the power merchants would be forced to return some of that $8.9 billion to the state. In that decision, FERC ordered over sixty energy companies to "show cause" that they had not gamed the California energy market and ordered them to appear before an administrative law judge.[123] These hopes, however, were quickly dashed when FERC attorneys moved to dismiss charges against sixteen energy companies and the public utilities that allegedly collaborated with them. In addition, the federal agency approved settlements with a number of energy companies that fell far below the losses attributed to their actions. In spring 2004, California's attorney general asserted that despite the fact that in the two-year period 2000–2001 consumers had paid an additional $40 billion for electricity, FERC had penalized energy companies a paltry $85 million.[124] The outrage felt by Californians toward the federal energy regulator was expressed by another member of the attorney general's office: "It's more of the same of what we've come to expect from FERC and its staff: ladling out the exonerations for price gougers and handing out the justice for Californians with an eyedropper."[125]

The state was dealt an even more expensive blow when, on the same day that FERC implicated sixty firms and utilities in schemes to defraud the state, the federal regulators ruled that $12 billion in long-term energy contracts that California authorities signed with energy companies at the height of the energy crisis, when prices were peaking, had to be honored.[126] The state had argued that it should be able to renegotiate the contracts because they violated a provision in the Federal Power Act of 1935 that required energy prices to be "just and reasonable." In a 2–1 vote (the two Republican members voted to uphold and the lone Democrat voted against), the majority of FERC's commissioners disagreed, ruling that "the contracts were entered into voluntarily in a market-based environment."[127] Even Patrick Wood, the agency's head who was recommended for his post by Enron executives, noted the irony of requiring the state to continue to do business with the very same companies that had ripped them off. "I guess people could go, 'Gosh, these are the same parties that show up in these other [market gaming] cases,'" he noted in an understatement. Then-Governor Gray Davis, who was beginning to feel intense political heat for having approved the contracts in the first place, was considerably less sanguine. "It's like a judge telling a bank robber who's stolen from 10 banks: 'If you promise not to steal anymore, you can keep the money from the first 10 banks.' . . . They're forcing us to keep a bad bargain that was made with a gun to our heads," he told reporters.[128] Four months later, Davis was out of a job, having been recalled by voters who were angry about the way he had handled the energy crisis.

A number of energy companies and their employees were charged in schemes related to false reporting of energy prices to published indexes. In December 2002, a joint venture between Dynegy and another energy company was fined $5 million for submitting false data to the indexes.[129] Four months later, El Paso Corp. was hit with a $20 million penalty for falsely reporting natural gas prices.[130] Reporting false data to the indexes (as described earlier) is a clear violation of criminal statutes, but as of this writing few people from the industry have been prosecuted. The few that have been charged included Todd Geiger, a former vice president at El Paso Energy Corp. in Houston, who reported price data to an index published by FERC on forty-eight trades of natural gas that never occurred. Despite FERC's conclusion that false reporting of trades was "epidemic" in the industry, only one other person, a former trader at Dynegy, was ever prosecuted for reporting phony trades.[131]

Former Dynegy employees, one vice president and two non-officers, were also criminally charged for their role in an Enronesque scheme. By disguising $300 million in loans from banks as revenue from operations, they, by all appearances, boosted the company's income by $79 million.[132]

The company had already agreed to pay $3 million to settle charges filed by the SEC in the case. Part of that $3 million settlement went to resolve charges of "round-trip" transactions by the firm.[133]

In its report on market manipulation in the California energy market, FERC examined the colorfully named strategies (e.g., "fat boy" and "Get Shorty") used by energy traders and concluded: "the trading strategies—while bearing Enron's name—were not limited to Enron but appear to have been widely engaged in by numerous parties. Indeed, it would appear to Staff that the majority of public utility entities, and some nonpublic utilities, engaged in at least some of the trading strategies."[134] Yet, of the relatively few energy traders prosecuted for these offenses, all worked for either Enron or Reliant.

More generally, the weight of criminal prosecution in the energy industry fell overwhelmingly on Enron executives. By early summer 2004, over thirty Enron employees had been indicted, including: Jeffrey Skilling; Michael Kopper, a finance executive; Kenneth Rice, the CEO of the broadband unit; Andrew Fastow, the chief financial officer who pleaded guilty and received a ten-year prison sentence; and the biggest fish of them all, Kenneth Lay, who on July 8, 2004, was led into a Houston courthouse in handcuffs and plead not guilty to an eleven-count indictment. The focus by federal prosecutors on Enron employees is understandable, given that the Justice Department created a special Enron Task Force in January 2002 to "investigate and prosecute all matters relating to the sudden collapse of Enron Corp."[135] Yet, this focus on Enron seems to have displaced a broader focus on the industry as a whole.[136] Indeed, it would seem that in many ways Enron became the "fall guy" for the entire energy industry. Among all power merchants, Enron's misconduct was undoubtedly the most egregious, and the charges filed against Enron executives were fully warranted. Yet, there was considerable evidence that at least some of the tactics employed by Enron executives to mislead investors were also pursued by the heads of other energy companies. A plausible explanation for the apparent failure to punish errant executives at other energy companies is the simple fact that their misconduct did not violate existing criminal statutes. So, for example, while many large energy companies admitted to having engaged in round-trip transactions in an effort to enhance their balance sheets, these transactions were not, in and of themselves, illegal.[137] Thus, the fact that so few energy company employees were ever prosecuted for their misconduct may be less the result of prosecutorial discretion and more the result of the way in which the rules of the energy trading game had been constructed in favor of the energy companies themselves.

Conclusions

In a little over a decade, the energy business was transformed from a highly regulated sector of the economy, dominated by local utility companies, into a wing of the securities industry, but with a big difference: this wing was largely unmonitored by state and federal regulators, allowing the biggest players in the industry to do pretty much what they pleased. This transformation was made possible in large part by deregulatory policies that were intended to work their magic by, in the words of President George H. W. Bush, "unleashing the genius of the private sector." While advocates of neoliberal policies often argue that deregulation is part of a natural and unstoppable process of economic evolution, in this chapter we have seen that deregulation in the energy industry was accomplished through old-fashioned influence peddling aimed at key members of government who had the power to keep specific markets and specific financial instruments free from government oversight. The second factor that facilitated the transformation of the industry was the ideology of the New Economy, which was used to justify extremely risky and sometimes outright illegal ventures while keeping outside observers mystified about the inner workings of these transactions.

The result of these changes was an energy industry that had become criminogenic—whose structure and culture facilitated and encouraged criminal activity. It was an environment that encouraged the heads of legitimate energy companies to use their firms as the vehicles for pump and dump schemes, in which a variety of deceptive tactics were employed to artificially boost the company's stock value, enabling corporate insiders to dump their own shares on the market just before reality caught up with the stocks, causing their values to plummet, leaving naïve investors—both institutions and individuals—holding nearly worthless bags. It was an environment, in effect, that encouraged corporate heads to loot their own companies. While Enron is the best example of this strategy, a number of other energy companies, to a lesser extent, followed the same logic, leading their companies to either bankruptcy or greatly diminished stock values.

In the chapters that follow we will see that the same logic guided the actions of corporate actors in other industries—particularly, the dot-com industry and the telecommunications industry—in the late 1990s. We will see how some of the techniques for inflating revenues that became common in the energy industry were also used by other New Economy firms. What we will see, though, is not just common techniques being employed in these different industries, but the same corporate actors—investment banks, accountants, law firms—collaborating on the application of a common template for corporate misconduct across several business sectors.

CHAPTER THREE

Too Much of a Good Thing
The Rat's Nest in Telecom

Rather than deprive consumers of potential options, the thinking goes, mega-mergers can create companies powerful enough to invade one another's markets and bring competition to the masses. No one is arguing this case louder than Bernard J. Ebbers, the Chairman of WorldCom.

Thirty years ago, few sectors were more criticized for inertia than telecommunications, organized around AT&T's monopoly. Yet, telecom became the vanguard New Economy sector before the term "dot-com" (or for that matter, "New Economy") had caught on. Telcom became hot early on as various interests mobilized to influence and exploit deregulation. Explosive growth in the sector after the 1996 Telecommunications Act helped fuel the long expansion of the 1990s;

between 1992 and 2001, telecom accounted for two-thirds of new jobs produced and one-third of new investment.[1] Backers of the new telecoms proclaimed that growth was boundless—at least in the foreseeable future—based on the "fact" that Internet traffic was doubling every three months. However, the fledgling ensemble, whose future initially seemed so bright, slipped into darkness by the end of the decade, ensnared in a glut of fiber-optic cable and a tangle of deception.

A telling chapter in the reinvention of telecom was the startling rise of an upstart firm that stole the spotlight in the mid-1990s, WorldCom, and the elevation of its CEO—Bernie Ebbers—to the status of charismatic visionary. In the case of Ebbers it was as if Jed Clampet had morphed into Bill Gates. Owner of a chain of budget motels in Mississippi, Ebbers somehow became the head of a small regional telecom and then, in scarcely a decade, ascended a pyramid made up of over sixty acquired firms to become a celebrity, hailed by the business media as the kind of Internet Age entrepreneur who was going to transform America. WorldCom was the epicenter for a circle of reinvention that drew in a host of firms and individuals. First and foremost was Jack Grubman, a former AT&T executive who became a telecom industry analyst for Salomon, which later merged with Smith Barney to become Salomon Smith Barney (SSB). The remaking of Ebbers and his firm went to another level once he hooked up with Grubman (and his bank) in 1996. After several stunning merger deals, WorldCom became the firm to beat (and emulate). For his part, Grubman—identifying himself as a new kind of analyst—used his financial reports, Salomon's clout, and the WorldCom "model" to make himself a power broker, helping dozens of "new telecom" firms raise capital (and expectations).

Myriad individuals who entered WorldCom's orbit had to make over their lives after the firm went bankrupt in 2002, revealing $9 billion in accounting irregularities. Take, for instance, Lorna Barnes, a fifty-two-year-old MCI manager who was laid off from WorldCom in June 2002 and then became a part-time childcare worker and consultant: "I've got a master's degree in computer science and have had a relatively successful thirty-year career. I worked for MCI, then WorldCom took over, and I have to say, when I read about Bernie Ebbers, I was proud to be working for a good Christian man. I was making $84,000 when I was laid off. . . . Now I can't find a job. . . . I think about Bernie, and how he'd spend that getting his shoes shined, and not think twice about it. And I wonder, does he know I'm here?"[2] Many who witnessed the WorldCom saga want to know what Bernie Ebbers and his company were all about.

The early post-mortems portrayed Ebbers as a figurehead who probably was not involved in the inner workings (and frauds) of the firm. One analyst remarked, "Bernie was endearing, but he didn't even have a working knowledge of the business."[3] The *New York Times* proposed that Ebbers might be able to "hold up his poor management skills as evidence of his innocence."[4] This was an amazing about-face, given that the media had earlier saluted Ebbers as a "country-bred genius."[5] Frank Partnoy has rightly stressed the role of Salomon in forging the WorldCom image and Bernie Ebbers persona: "WorldCom was a creation of Wall Street, in the same way Britney Spears was a creation of the entertainment industry. Jack Grubman might as well have propped up a cardboard cutout of a CEO."[6] But new revelations show that Ebbers was a key player in WorldCom's financial machinations who actively worked the relationship with Salomon.

At any rate, the rise and fall of WorldCom was inextricably intertwined with over two decades of policy shifts. The bankruptcy of WorldCom—a firm with $107 billion in assets—was the largest in U.S. history, but only one of two dozen failures (and myriad frauds) among telecoms staking claim to the market terrain freed up by AT&T's breakup. So, how did we get from Ma Bell to the mother of all bankruptcies?

Breaking Up Is Hard to Do

New technology, free markets, and daring risk-taking were all brought together in talk of an Internet-led New Economy during the last half of the 1990s. However, key elements of the narrative predated the Internet hype, having emerged during debates about how to transform the telecom industry. The phone system had been a publicly regulated monopoly since the Telecommunications Act of 1934—the result of a "compact" between the federal government and the industry (i.e., AT&T): in exchange for dependable service, regulators ensured the "stability of incumbents and profitability."[7] Moreover, the rates for local residential service were kept low through charging higher rates for long distance.

In the midst of economic changes in the 1970s, neoliberals began to attack the AT&T monopoly, touting the superiority of markets over regulation, while a new set of telecoms went to court, hoping to hive off AT&T's business customers. A 1983 court order that AT&T divest in its local phone business resulted in the break-up of Ma Bell and the division of the industry into local and long distance segments. After divestiture, the long distance market became segmented between (1) AT&T and other providers that owned their own facilities and (2) a new cohort of "resellers" that purchased long distance capacity from the firms with facilities and resold it (mostly to businesses).

The breakup of AT&T introduced a paradox that is glossed over in free market rhetoric: deregulation does not necessarily create a competitive market, especially when a monopoly formerly existed. AT&T's break-up was actually a matter of re-regulation—it involved government intervention and imposed new restrictions (on the Baby Bells that dominate local markets). The dilemma of how to deregulate while preventing powerful firms from establishing monopolies set the stage for the Telecom Act of 1996.

Debate about the 1996 act pivoted on a claim that computer technology had ended this dilemma. The argument was developed even before the Internet entered the scene. A 1987 study commissioned by the Department of Justice claimed that computers had altered the nature of telecommunications from a hierarchical system to a decentralized network. It concluded that telecom markets now could be competitive even with high levels of business concentration. Patricia Aufderheide notes that with the Internet's arrival, policy debates were dominated by the idea that "new technologies required new approaches."[8] The Internet's rise also fueled talk about a coming "convergence" of different systems and industries, making it possible that a single network could offer video, data, and voice.

For politicians, the main issue was how many restrictions the act should place on various industry interests. The Clinton administration had decided that the development of the "Information Super Highway" would occur through private initiative (but with government encouragement); the privatization of the Internet was completed in 1994 when the National Science Foundation ended its funding. Members of Congress mostly signaled their willingness to go along with the digital flow, waxing about the promise (and inevitability) of convergence. As industry lobbyists exerted great influence and even drafted legislation, Congresswoman Marcy Kaptor called the telecom bill's progress "living proof of what unlimited money can do to buy influence and the Congress."[9]

The efforts of industry lobbyists actually generated powerful political crosswinds as different sectors, and firms competed to promote their own agendas. The main battle lines were drawn between the Baby Bells and their enemies. The Baby Bells, which monopolized local phone service (because of the infrastructure bequeathed them by AT&T) wanted to be free to enter long distance without having to loosen their grip on local markets, while long distance providers wanted the Baby Bells to be forced to provide new competitors with cheap access to their networks. Aufderheide notes that, despite differences, most industry interests argued (successfully) that the ability to get big fast was a *sine qua non* for igniting dynamic competition. The Telecom Act of 1996 "encouraged cross-ownership and concentration of ownership, in an atmosphere in which, industry participants assured legislators at hearings, size mattered. Only large players could attract the investment capital needed to take new risk."[10] Joesph Stiglitz, the former head of the Council of Economic Advisors, recalls that lobbyists touted radical deregulation in the name of competitiveness, but their clients were energized by the prospect of establishing a position to dominate some market: "Those who argued for deregulation said it would produce more competition as different companies vied for market share. But there also was a strong belief in the idea of 'first mover advantage,' the possibility that the first firm in a particular market might dominate. Companies believed they faced a game of winner take all and so spent furiously to make sure they would dominate."[11] The Baby Bells found a powerful ally for their advocacy of a radical deregulation policy giving free play to market forces—Speaker of the House Newt Gingrich. His "Progress and Freedom Foundation" released a position paper by cyberlibertarians (and re-purposed futurists) Alvin Toffler and George Glider. The paper provides a good look at the techno rhetoric of the times. It states, "we are entering new territory, where there are as yet no rules"[12] and advises that as industrial society gives way to a knowledge society, it will generate "new codes of behavior that move . . . inexorably beyond standardization and centralization"; this specifically "spells the death of the . . . bureaucratic organization . . . government being its last great stronghold."[13] The only real concern was that government would not get out of the way fast enough. Their manifesto called for "liberation from . . . rules, regulations, taxes and laws laid in place to serve the smokestack barons and bureaucracies of the past."[14]

Gingrich, in league with a powerful Democrat, John Dingell of Michigan, pushed forward a bill making it easier for the Baby Bells to enter the long distance market while loosening restriction on their local activities. However, a Democratic countermove succeeded in imposing strict conditions on their entry into long distance: each Baby Bell would have to satisfy the Justice Department that it had given new competitors access to their networks—at a "fair" price. However, the law was vague about how a fair price would be arrived at; as a result, the Baby Bells were largely successful in using court challenges to maintain the status quo.

Despite the stalemate regarding the Baby Bells, the 1996 Telecom Act—and the debate around it—had significant effects. It crystallized a new orientation on the part of regulators, who, enamored with the idea of efficiency, became less concerned about monopoly. They opted not to enforce regulations "that interfere with the public interest"—now defined as a "competitive" environment. When a wave of mergers followed, many financial commentators viewed it as conforming to prophecy—that the telecom wars (and convergence) were sure to come: As *Business Week* put it, the largest firms (e.g., AT&T, MCI, Sprint, the seven Baby Bells, and GTE) would leap into the fray, generating a consolidation where "five or so metacarriers" or "one-stop shops" would offer "the whole gamut of phone, data, and entertainment services to consumers and businesses."[15]

However, Aufdeheide argues that the mergers testified to a convergence that was financial rather than technological in nature: large firms expanded to avoid direct competition. Stiglitz adds that a volatile mix of regulatory changes in telecom, finance, and accounting fueled the race to get big fast—and sent telecom on a wayward trajectory: "Deregulation in telecom unleashed a Gold Rush; deregulation in banking allowed the rich to go out of control. Inadequate regulation in accounting allowed the race to go in the wrong direction . . . a race to the bottom; those who won the sweepstakes . . . were those who were willing to be less than scrupulous."[16] Enter a "cowboy capitalist," his banking friend, and his friend's friends.

Get Big Fast (WorldCom's Magical Formula)

An old adage in American sociology says, "[T]hat which men believe to be true, is true in its consequences." Our task then is to examine the "social construction" of WorldCom as the model New Economy telecom and Bernie Ebbers as a New Economy visionary.

Mississippi Messiah (The Milkman Cometh)
Like many New Economy dreams, WorldCom grew out of a coffee shop bull session, though the venue was not Starbucks, but a Days Inn in Hattiesburg, Mississippi. The year was 1983 and four businessmen,

including Bernie Ebbers, talked about opportunities that AT&T's break-up would generate. Ebbers was a native of Edmonton, Alberta, where, among other things, he had been a milkman. He had come to Mississippi on a basketball scholarship in the 1970s and briefly held a job as a basketball coach before he began investing in motels. He owned a chain of thirteen budget hotels when he and three friends started up Long Distance Discount Services (LDDS)—a small firm that resold long-distance phone service it bought from AT&T and other large firms. When his friends asked for more capital in 1984, Ebbers wanted something in return: the CEO's job.

Ebbers, who as a motel mogul had been a deal maker who liked to keep costs down, applied the same strategy to telecoms as he began rolling up other resellers of telecom services. A difference was that after merging with a public company (Advantage Companies) in 1989, LDDS could use its stock as a currency for acquiring firms. By the early 1990s, aggressive acquisitions had made LDDS into one of the largest regional long distance companies in the United States, providing services in twenty-seven states. In late 1995 it changed its name to WorldCom. The next year, WorldCom entered the national spotlight as it used stock to acquire MFS Communications. MFS had local network access facilities in major cities and a subsidiary—UUNet Technologies—that was a leading provider of Internet access.[17] But it was WorldCom's October 1997 bid for MCI that made it and Ebbers the talk of the telecom sector. The $36.5 billion deal was the largest merger in U.S. history at the time.

Ebbers was perceived by many observers to be an extraordinary entrepreneur who embodied larger forces. In the sociological sense of the word, this made him something of a charismatic figure. Though it is easy to dismiss it all as hype, probing his charisma leads us to a critical sociological feature: *the circle of observers, allies, and supporters who bolstered the reputation* of the man (and his company) in the sector. First, a general condition predisposed certain strategic actors to perceive CEOs as extraordinary: since the late 1980s, media and financial commentators treated CEOs as entrepreneurial types who not only personified their firms, but also brought great returns to investors through a special ability to discern the mysterious ways of the market. Ebbers had a magic touch in the most enchanted of markets—the one for stocks. WorldCom averaged an annual return to shareholders of 53 percent in the ten years leading up to 1996; only high-tech powerhouse Oracle did better.[18] If one had invested $100 in WorldCom in 1989, it would have been worth $3,137 by October 2, 1997; the same investment in MCI would have been worth only $132.[19]

Operating from the margins of the New South in the 1980s, Ebbers seemed to have been in the right place at the right time to begin rolling up telecom start-ups; once a firm had a reputation for growth, investors gave it special treatment (and valuations) compared to established firms such as AT&T that would never beat the label of being "value" investments. For one thing, it was the "growth" firms that were likely to be acquired. The head of a research firm noted that WorldCom, despite posting an operating loss of $1.8 billion in 1996, impressed Wall Street—the brokers "treated WorldCom's stock as less like a phone company stock than a hot Internet company, like Netscape."[20]

Moreover, Ebbers was received as the telecom messiah—the embodiment of the free market prophecy that emerged out of the debates surrounding the 1996 Telecom Act. WorldCom's astounding bid for MCI suggested that it was the much-anticipated (and feared) destroyer and creator of worlds. Yet, Ebbers sauntered into the limelight without the usual artifice—or even accessories: he did not carry a cell phone or care to use e-mail. The financial press reveled in reports that he was a "cowboy" who walked through his headquarters in "faded jeans, chomping on a cigar"—a Willie Nelson fan with a real ranch.[21] Coming from rural Mississippi—or the Great White North if you like—he was otherworldly; he did not seem part of the hyped-up world of spinmeisters. Thus, when he justified the MCI bid with a business strategy that resonated with the telecom revolution prophecy, it seemed as if a plainspoken man was passing on a natural fact (with the same folksy manner in which he had once delivered milk). *Business Week* gushed that he was "a visionary . . . a revolutionary" ushering in a "New World Order": "While other phone company executives huddle with consultants, lawyers, and investment bankers to figure out how they can position their companies in the new world of deregulated telecommunications, Bernie Ebbers is at the ramparts."[22] The dominant interpretation by financial analysts and reporters was that Ebbers and his firm embodied revolutionary forces unleashed by deregulation. The day after the MCI offer was made, the *New York Times* remarked that the telecom act "opened the door for the kind of cowboy capitalism in which Mr. Ebbers and WorldCom specialize." A Merrill Lynch analyst proposed, "WorldCom is at the forefront of an unstoppable trend toward very large, vertically integrated companies."[23] Over the next few weeks, most everyone seemed to get on the bandwagon. *Business Week* quoted a TIAA-CREF analyst as saying, "Bernie Ebbers has sent a signal to the rest of the telecommunications industry that this is the way you make an industry-leading firm. You put all the pieces together and organize it quickly"; another telecom analyst declared, "This is the official day the telecom wars began."[24] Another *Business Week* writer advised, WorldCom "is building a new breed of phone company" that could supply customers with "almost all their communications services." Its acquisitions, he added, made WorldCom "the very model of a 21st-century phone company . . . in position to become the first carrier to offer a seamless digital network."[25] Joined with MCI, WorldCom would become "the biggest threat to the Baby Bells."[26]

A key theme was that WorldCom was poised to spur "dynamic" competition because of the "convergence" that the merger would bring. The *New York Times* noted, "[T]he thinking on Wall Street and within the industry these days is that true competition and price reduction will come only through the formation of a handful of national players—companies big and rich enough to build their own networks and compete head on with full lineups of local, long-distance, Internet and other communications services."[27] With the MCI bid, the perspective became linked with the person of Bernie Ebbers. Ebbers defended the merger as "in the best interest of the Telecommunications Act."[28] He played to new regulatory sensibilities stressing competition and efficiency, claiming that the merger would allow the firm to save $3 billion in the first year and $5 billion annually by 2002. This cost-cutting, he added, would free up capital that could be used to expand into other markets. He proclaimed that WorldCom would be the only company to build alternative networks to serve both local residential and business callers.[29]

Much of the commentary was directed toward Washington. Regulators had been agitated by the lack of competition after the Telecom Act and had recently nixed AT&T's hopes to merge with a Baby Bell. Regulators let the MCI deal pass—even though Ebbers let slip that WorldCom's main interest at the local level was the business segment; it would only "look at the residential market as long as it doesn't hurt our stock price."[30]

The Weak End at Bernie's

Through the end of the 1990s, Ebbers and company stunned observers by posting financial reports that indicated extraordinary growth and cost-cutting. *Fortune* noted that "WorldCom seemed to have some kind of secret formula for producing decent margins where rivals couldn't."[31] However, six years after bursting forth on the national stage, the Telecom Cowboy came to the end of the trail, his outfit having turned out to have been a lot like a Hollywood frontier town—a collection of false fronts. Its bankruptcy in June 2002 revealed that an array of ills afflicted every nook and cranny of WorldCom, including systematic fraud. The bankruptcy court examiner, former U.S. attorney general Richard Thornburgh, identified problems with "the culture, internal controls, management, integrity, disclosure and financial statements" (*T,* 6) involving top management, the board of directors (especially its audit and compensation committees), its auditor (Arthur Andersen), and its investment bank (Salomon Smith Barney).

Paradoxically, the core problems in one of the premier "growth" firms were related to growth. WorldCom was an exemplar of organizational dysfunction, with its greatest failures coming in an area that was supposed to be a prime strength: integrating the firms it had acquired so as to increase efficiencies. A *New York Times* story in August 2002 depicted an organizational disaster, due in large part to failures in merging the systems that had been inherited from other firms: "Dozens of conflicting computer systems remained, local network systems were repetitive and failed to work together properly, and billing systems were not coordinated."[32] For example, staff handling "Legacy MCI" accounts could not access "Legacy WorldCom" accounts and vice versa. The firm was plagued by billing errors and ended up taking a charge of $685 million in September 2000, admitting that a big block of its billings were uncollectible. WorldCom shut down three centers that MCI had used to repair and maintain network equipment and then opened twelve centers to replace them, resulting in duplication and unnecessary shipments of equipment. The biggest problem was in local phone networks. WorldCom failed to integrate the expensive exchanges it bought, creating what one employee referred to as a "vast wasteland" with "far too much redundancy."[33]

Second, the great wave of growth expected in Internet traffic—its doubling every three months—never materialized. This faulty "fact" became a self-inflicted wound that led to WorldCom's demise. WorldCom officials revealed in June 2000 that the source of the claim was none other than WorldCom's own Internet unit—UUNet. They also added a rather crucial correction: it was Internet capacity that was doubling every three months, not traffic. And they also acknowledged that UUNet—WorldCom's crown jewel—was actually not profitable.[34]

At the same time, a second sort of growth was giving out—one that was actually more central to what WorldCom was really about. In June 2000, regulators shot down WorldCom's proposed $145 billion acquisition of Sprint, putting an end to the firm's long string of mergers. This deprived WorldCom of the elixir responsible for its stellar financial numbers—accounting tricks it used following mergers to create the impression that its financial picture was continually improving. WorldCom would subtract vast sums from its profits by writing down of some of the assets it had acquired: the basis of the write-down was the cost of expenses it expected to incur in future quarters. This produced a bigger loss in a current quarter but smaller ones in future quarters, making it appear that WorldCom's "profit picture" was always getting better. This technique was widely used by other firms in the 1990s, as was a second that WorldCom practiced—taking charges for assets such as research and development and adding the value to a secret reserve fund that could be drawn on as needed. WorldCom depended so much on mergers to maintain its finances that it came to resemble a pyramid scheme. A former WorldCom executive remarked, "The boost from post-acquisition accounting was like a drug. But it meant bigger deals had to come along to keep the ball rolling."[35] Among other things, this led WorldCom to pay vastly inflated prices for its acquisitions—as was especially evident in the deals for MFS and MCI. WorldCom offered $17 billion more for MCI than British Telecom had. Part of the tradeoff was the payoff in the realm of accounting. WorldCom reduced the book value of MCI's hard assets by $3.4 billion while increasing the "goodwill" (value of intangible assets) gained in the deal by the same amount. Goodwill is amortized over a far longer time than hard assets are depreciated, allowing World-Com to charge smaller amounts against its earnings each year—making it appear that WorldCom was cutting annual expenses for four years. At the same time, WorldCom immediately recognized all of MCI's profits so that its own profits would instantly jump.

As the growth spigot was turned off, the toxic legacies of the race to get big fast began to surface. On the one hand, the costs of its rapid (if not reckless) rate of growth were coming due—the dysfunctional assembly of acquisitions was generating rising costs instead of savings, while the outsized prices WorldCom had paid left it confronting rising debt; on the other hand, revenues in key areas were declining, as was total cash flow. And as the firm's numbers fell, so did its share price. The stock peaked at $96 a share in June 1999; by June 2000 it was down to $46, and by the end of the year the price was $18 (T, 21).

This being the New Economy, the immediate concern on the part of executives was finding a way to make the next quarter's numbers. Under the rallying cry "close the gap," executives scrambled to locate one-time revenue items to boost the revenue total. In the second quarter of 2001 they used such tactics to pump WorldCom's sagging revenue growth from 8 percent to 12 percent; in the third quarter the numbers were inflated from 6 percent to 12 percent.[36]

Thornburgh reported that WorldCom had engaged in bogus accounting of mergers and reserves and improper reporting of revenue since 1999. As WorldCom's situation grew more dire, top officials engaged in accounting frauds that were as crude and more desperate. A criminal complaint charges that in July 2000 Scott Sullivan (chief financial officer) and David Myers (the controller) devised a scheme to hide the firm's growing expenses by moving billions in operating costs around in the books so as to sharply cut annual expenses while pumping profits. Initially, investigators determined that these maneuvers improperly reduced expenses by $3.8 billion—causing quarters to show profits instead of losses.[37] On June 25, 2002, WorldCom announced that it was restating the $3.8 billion as inappropriately reported income. On July 21, 2002, WorldCom filed for Chapter 11 bankruptcy protection. Two weeks later an internal review by the company discovered an additional $3.3 billion of improperly reported earnings for the period 1999 through the first quarter of 2002. Initially, the spotlight was on Scott Sullivan and David Myers; both were arrested on August 1, 2002, and charged with criminal securities fraud and conspiracy. Myers pled guilty to one count each of securities fraud, conspiracy to commit securities fraud, and filing false statements with the SEC. In early October, four members of the financial department pled guilty to criminal counts of conspiracy and securities fraud. Sullivan pled guilty to securities fraud in March 2004.

Investigators eventually found the trail of fraud to extend to Bernie Ebbers. As it turns out, Ebbers was not so hands-off when it came to financial affairs. Ebbers ran WorldCom as his personal fiefdom—keeping his board of directors and top executives corralled. And although he did not dump his stock as the going got tough (as other telecom execs did), he did wrangle over $400 million in loans and guarantees from the company as his personal finances deteriorated with the firm's share price (Ebbers faced immense margin calls on loans as WorldCom stock, which he provided as collateral, fell in value).[38] Ebbers continued to request loans from WorldCom even as it became clear that he would not be able to repay them. This, along with the firm's sinking share price, led the WorldCom board of directors to force Ebbers to resign on April 30, 2002.

Ebbers's use of WorldCom as his own personal piggy bank starkly contradicts the notion that stock ownership automatically aligns the interest of managers with those of shareholders. The age of the "imperial CEO" called to mind Louis XIV, who proclaimed, "I am the state," as more than a few company heads acted as if they "were the company" (and its money was their money).

The public persona of Bernie Ebbers took a mortal hit in June 2003. A pair of reports concluded that he and top managers, "aided by numerous employees, conspired together beginning in the late 1990s to carry out massive and systematic fraud at the company." One piece of evidence was a July 10, 2001, memo from Ebbers to the firm's chief operating officer as executives were mobilizing to "close the gap": "I would ask that you get with John McGuire [senior vice president of finance] and Mike Higgins [vice president of finance] and anyone else who works on these issues and see where we stand on those one-time events that had to happen in order for us to have a chance to make our numbers—we should know those by now." In a later e-mail, Higgins cautioned the group who reviewed the numbers with Ebbers not to pass on "monthly revenue reports" that included the two sets of numbers: "Please do not forward because Bernie is extremely concerned with forwarded or passed on mon rev results."[39] The caution was prudent. On March 3, 2003, Ebbers, handcuffed like a desperado, was brought before a judge, having been indicted on federal fraud charges.

Follow the Leader (and His "Financial Advisor")

The insurgent "spirit" of the new telecoms extended well beyond the boundaries of WorldCom. For instance, after Intermedia lost $57 million in the first half of 1997, its CEO crowed, "We're competing against people [the Baby Bells] who don't know how to compete." Although Nextlink Communications lost $71 million in 1996, its CEO bragged of various advantages it had over the Baby Bells. "They can't compete on price because we don't have unions or golf tournaments"; another advantage, he noted, was that "none of our shareholders even know what net income means." A financial analyst noted, "[T]he root of the enthusiasm is that consolidation is coming to the industry."[40] Indeed, World-

Com's last big acquisition was Intermedia (it spent $5.8 billion in stock and took over $2.4 billion of Intermedia's debt).

Although there were dozens of feisty new telecom start-ups, World-Com served as the model upstart. *Fortune* reported that the entire telecom industry "sought to emulate" WorldCom because of the impressive numbers it posted.[41] A second factor behind WorldCom's leadership was the support of Jack Grubman. The SSB star analyst anchored a network of financial promotion that provided much of the connective tissue (as well as capital) for the new ensemble. An analyst noted, "Jack orchestrated the industry."[42]

In a story entitled "Inside the Telecom Game," *Business Week* proposed that Grubman was able to organize the rise of the new telecoms by covering several bases: he helped raise capital; he gave high ratings to their stock; he aided them in developing strategies; and he helped SSB allocate IPO shares to executives so as to gain banking business. He also attended board meetings to discuss the merits of potential mergers. The minutes of one WorldCom meeting referred to him as a "financial advisor" (*T*, 98).

The fact that his employer was one of the most active investment banks in the sector greatly aided Grubman in positioning himself as a power broker. Since 1996, the year of the Telecom Act, SSB helped eighty-one telecoms raise $190 billion (*T*, 34). The web that Grubman occupied also allowed him to wield cultural and social power. He influenced perceptions of the prospects of the sector and of individual firms. His story line was that "a rapid deployment of broadband connections to consumers and businesses would bring a big jump in Internet traffic, which, in turn, would require the building of new networks with great amounts of capacity."[43] Grubman reassured investors that the markets could easily absorb the new capacity as he endorsed SSB-backed firms such as Global Crossing, Qwest, Teligent, Winstar, Focal, Williams Communications, Rhythms NetConnections, Level 3 Communications, McLeodUSA, and Allegiance Telecom.

WorldCom became an attractive model to hold up to other firms because of the great success it had in using a high-value stock to acquire firms; though WorldCom's share price sometimes dropped immediately following acquisitions, it always rebounded and went up. Thornburgh found that Grubman often touted WorldCom as a leader. In August 1997, for example, Grubman stated, "[N]o telecom company of World-Com's market cap can come close to matching WorldCom's top-line growth . . . [or] strategic position. . . . WorldCom remains our favorite stock" (*T*, 96). Thornburgh reports that from October 1998 to August 1999, Grubman consistently "maintained that WorldCom represented the cheapest S&P [Standard & Poor's] large-cap growth stock at the time, remained the 'must own' large-cap growth stock in anyone's portfolio, represented one of the premier large-cap growth companies in any industry, and represented the single best idea in telecom" (*T*, 91). In August 2002, *Business Week* observed that Grubman used the WorldCom formula as he organized the whole ensemble. A telecom industry analyst commented that "WorldCom delivered such success that Grubman had [other telecom executives] mimic [WorldCom's approach]; he put them up at the pulpit at his conference, where they were the keynotes."[44] For their part, the executives of the upstarts would present story lines that connected with Grubman's master narrative. For example, the founder of Level 3 Communications told investors that "Silicon Economics" would allow start-ups such as his firm to offer more capacity—at lower prices—than old economy firms such as AT&T.

There was little concern about whether the start-ups were making money. *Business Week* noted that "the unspoken assumption was that they would be acquired anyway by the likes of WorldCom, AT&T, or one of the [Baby] Bells."[45] However, investors were wary when a New Economy "growth" firm acquired an established firm; they feared that the rate of growth would drop. Endorsement by financial analysts and the media was critical in these cases. Executives justified such mergers by stressing the need for telecoms to "transform themselves" or "risk certain death"; but their actual motivation may have been to cash in their currencies for hard assets while they could.[46]

It was easy to become an instant player in "the telecom game"— staked to billions of dollars courtesy of Grubman and friends. However, the new telecom players soon found themselves facing the unpleasant task of having to deliver New Economy–quality levels of growth and efficiency—at the same time that prices were being eroded by a flood of fiber-optic capacity. The magical numbers that WorldCom was posting put additional pricing pressure on other carriers.[47] Of course, the WorldCom standard proved to be a perverse one, as its margins were deceptions. Worst of all, after the dot-com sector swooned with the market crash in April 2000, demand for the services of the new telecoms began to tumble. As the network utilization of the new fiber-optic lines became stuck at only 3 percent, the prices starting plunging 50 percent a year.[48]

And so, the journey of the new telecoms into the New Economy took a detour to the dark side.

Ironically, many of the core participants in the telecom insurgency came from AT&T. Jack Grubman had been an executive vice president at AT&T's consumer and small business division; two different CEOs of Global Crossing had been executives at AT&T, as had the man who Grubman helped recruit as CEO of Qwest, Joseph Nacchio. If one did not have experience in telecom, one could still make a go of it as a player if you had a background in the financial sector, as did Global Crossing's founder, Gary Winnick. Winnick had worked with Michael Milken at Drexel Burnham Lambert but had avoided becoming an alumnus of the federal corrections system by leaving the firm in 1985 to found a successful investment company. Although Winnick did not know much about the telecom business, he did know how to raise money. And he had an aptitude for turning Global Crossing into his own personal financial vehicle.

The general idea behind Global Crossing was that the rise of a global economy had created a need for undersea fiber-optic cables that could link continents together. The primary customers would be global carriers, such as AT&T and Deutsche Telecom. *Fortune* magazine reported that Winnick decided to emulate the "growth-by-acquisitions model created by WorldCom" and that he enlisted Grubman to assist him.[49] Partnoy notes that Global Crossing was in a position to use its stock as a currency after a successful IPO in August 1998: it "went on a buying spree, acquiring dozens of telecommunications companies, with Jack Grubman advising on the deals."[50] As a result, Global Crossing ended up with not just an undersea network but one of the largest land-based telecom networks. Highlights included an acquisition of Frontier for $11.2 billion and a bidding war for U.S. West that it lost to Qwest. In all, Global Crossing spent $15 billion on a network that connected twenty-seven countries and over two hundred cities.

Global Crossing never could lease more than a small fraction of its immense global network, and the acquisitions binge left it $7.6 billion in debt. Yet, Winnick gloried in the game of wheeling and dealing with investment banks. The feeling was mutual: Global Crossing spent $420 million in investment banking fees in three years. As one banker put it, "people wanted to do business with Winnick because he was the best game in town."[51] For his part, Winnick talked as if he held the upper hand in the game. A former staffer reported that Winnick walked around the office saying that he "owned" Jack Grubman and J. P. Morgan's Jimmy Lee because of the fees he paid to their banks. Winnick had a special sense of his place in the world—and a special knack for making large amounts of money off Global Crossing even when it was far from making a profit.

The case of Global Crossing offers another look at the aura of royalty that corporate notables gained in the 1990s. At Global Crossing, the CEOs were more like high-paid temps than imperial types—there were five in four years. It was the chairman who was imperial, in terms of his high-level connections and his rather shameless self-dealing. Winnick liked to have people around him who were connected. His co-chairman was a longtime friend of the Bush family, while Winnick himself played golf with Bill Clinton. When Chase Manhattan wanted to woo Winnick, it had one of its executives introduce him to David Rockefeller, who gave him a private tour of the Metropolitan Museum of Art.

Winnick's ability to tap into high society was matched by his ability to tap into the wealth of Global Crossing. Global Crossing contracted with a subsidiary of Winnick's investment company for consulting services— to be performed by Winnick and three other Global Crossing board members. The subsidiary would receive an amazing 2 percent of Global Crossing's gross revenue for advice and marketing help. The contract was cancelled in 1998, but Global Crossing paid a termination fee of $135 million. And although the firm was legally based in Bermuda for tax reasons, Winnick also received rent from Global Crossing for its real headquarters in Beverly Hills—housed in a building that Winnick's real estate company owned. Global Crossing paid $3.8 million for renovations for the luxurious offices, including a room modeled on the White House's Oval Office.[52]

As the telecom market began its nose dive in 2000, the NASDAQ index of telecom stock fell 65 percent. The drop in Global Crossing's share price was even steeper, falling from $61 to $16 a share. Meanwhile, the telecom carriers who were Global Crossing's biggest customers began going bankrupt after their own customer base—the dot-coms—imploded. The same year, Global Crossing began to engage in "swaps" to manipulate its financial numbers. In chapter 2 we saw that energy traders such as Enron became avid swappers to manipulate their financials, and the next chapter will show that many dot-coms did swaps of advertising space for the same reason.

In the telecom version, the swaps typically were of Indefeasible Rights of Use (IRUs), which were long-term rights to make use of bandwidth on a telecom's fiber-optic network. Partnoy notes that the notion of the IRU was created at AT&T and he implies that the practice was carried to other telecoms by executives who were trained at AT&T. IRUs took on a new significance, as far as accounting was concerned, when the SEC published a bulletin in 1999. The SEC hoped to ban the kind of deceptive revenue reporting that appeared in the 1990s (e.g., Al Dunlop's "channel stuffing" at Sunbeam). However, Global Crossing, Qwest, and other telecoms subverted the SEC's intent by "using one portion of the bulletin to justify up-front recognition of revenue while using another portion of the bulletin to justify spreading expenses over time." Thus, the firms came to argue that payments coming in from IRU swaps were revenues that could be booked immediately, while their outgoing payments were a capital expense—and could be spread out over a substantial number of years.

Global Crossing's first experience in swapping was a 1999 trade with Enron's broadband unit. Though it appeared to be legitimate, Partnoy suggests that dealing with Enron taught Global Crossing executives "that financial engineering could be more profitable" than regular business ventures. Lawsuits have claimed that by early 2000 Global Crossing was engaging in bogus swaps with firms such as Lucent and that by the fall of that year it depended on swaps to make its numbers. In March 2001, Global Crossing was doing large IRU swaps, including a $100 million deal with Qwest. When a vice president of finance, Roy Olofson, complained about the practice, an internal study found that less than 20 percent of the deals were defensible. However, Global Crossing did not stop the swaps. Olofson later claimed that $720 million of the $3.2 billion in revenue that the company reported for the first two quarters of 2001 was from bogus swaps. He noted that thirteen of the eighteen swaps occurred during the last two days of quarters, suggesting that their purpose was to help the firm make its numbers.[53] Evidence has surfaced that executives at the highest levels of Global Crossing were already aware of deceptive accounting practices. In a June 5, 2000, memo to several board members, CEO Leo Hindrey Jr. warned, "The stock market can be fooled, but not forever, and it is . . . unforgiving at being misled."[54]

In October 2001, Global Crossing announced that it would not meet the earnings expectations of analysts. As word spread that the firm had engaged in swaps, investors—already spooked by the sudden fall of Enron—began to desert the stock. By December, Global Crossing's stock price was down to $1 a share; Winnick resigned soon after. In late January 2002, the firm filed for bankruptcy. Afterward the firm announced that it would restate its results for 2000 by $230 million because of swaps.

Although Winnick's exit was ungraceful, it was hardly unprofitable. He and other insiders had dumped Global Crossing stock in epic quantities. Winnick cashed in $735 million in stock (one lawsuit claimed it was $860 million), while other insiders sold a combined $4.5 billion. Partnoy reports that many of the shares were sold in February 2000, when the stock was near its peak value—and just a couple of months before the market crashed.[55]

Investors filed some seventy suits charging Winnick and company with fraud. The suits were consolidated and settled in March 2004 for $325 million. Winnick, who agreed to pay $32 million of the sum, had previously contributed $25 million to a fund for workers who had lost money in the firm's retirement plan. Though Winnick's supporters lauded him for his noblesse oblige, his contributions and the settlement itself seem rather puny compared to the billions of dollars that the insiders made. Moreover, Winnick had badly burned the bankers—at least those that showed up late to play. Global Crossing borrowed $2.25 billion from several banks just two months before filing for bankruptcy. However, the "game" may yet turn in favor of the banks. In June 2004, a judge ruled that a $1.7 billion suit could proceed against Winnick and twenty-two former Global Crossing executives. A group of banks, led by J. P. Morgan Chase, claimed that the defendants engaged in fraud to conceal Global Crossing's decline so that it could borrow the $2.25 billion.[56]

When Global Crossing went shopping for its own Baby Bell (U.S. West), it found itself outgunned by one of its peers—Qwest Communications. By picking up the Denver-based Baby Bell, Qwest gained a local phone system that provided service to 25 million customers in fourteen states. With a market valuation of $86 billion at its peak, Qwest had enough "currency" to put together a network that had the capacity to "carry all the voice and data traffic in the US." The buildup in hype by Qwest executives was nearly of the same magnitude. *Fortune* referred to Qwest CEO Joseph Nacchio as "one of the most blustery cheerleaders for the new industry"; for instance, in 1998 Nacchio was quoted in *Wired* magazine as saying, "I feel like an emerging oil baron in 1859." Nacchio also thought big when it came to making forecasts. He stated that by 2005 Qwest's revenues would be increasing at a rate of 15 percent a year and its earning by 20 percent a year—at the time he made the statement, Qwest was losing money and the telecom market was sliding.[57]

Reportedly, Nacchio's promises, and even more so his browbeating, put enormous pressure on subordinates. A former vice president recalled, "The market was collapsing. [There were] unreachable demands: 'We need to sell this many millions of dollars in hosting services in the next 90 days,' when the lead time to sell hosting services was 180 days. You'd ask questions, and it was . . . , 'Don't ask questions. Just go and do it, and if you don't, you're not part of the team.'"[58] Managers learned to boost sales by asking suppliers of equipment to buy Qwest services in return—an exchange that became known as "guns for whiskey." The former vice president remarked, "[T]he premise was, I'm buying a lot of your stuff; We'd like you [to] buy some of our services."[59] It was not long before Qwest was engaged in another sort of reciprocity—swapping. By 2000, a big part of Qwest's business consisted of trading leases that gave access to network capacity, or simply guaranteeing that it would carry the other telecom's traffic. After the first $100 million swap with Global Crossing, Qwest became an aggressive swapper. The swaps included a total of $220 million with Global Crossing, $134.5 million with Tycom (Tyco's network-building subsidiary), and a $242.9 million deal with a British telecom. In the first three quarters of 2000, Quest sold $870 million in capacity while buying $868 million in capacity from the same parties, suggesting that the transactions were round-trips that cancelled each other out.[60]

In 2001, its swap partners included Enron. Especially noteworthy was a deal in which Qwest and Enron swapped fiber-optic network capacity and services at a time when prices had been slashed on account of a glut in supply—and Enron was tumbling toward bankruptcy. Qwest agreed to pay Enron $308 million for a "dark fiber" network running from Salt Lake City to New Orleans. To say it was "dark fiber" meant that further investment in equipment would have to be made to put the line in service. Enron was to pay Qwest $195.5 million for active fiber-optic cable services over a period of twenty-five years. The value the parties put on the deal—$500 million—was called vastly exaggerated by analysts. One telecom industry analyst commented that for Qwest, "[I]t's totally irrational to buy capacity from Enron . . . I can't conceive of any reason they would need more dark fiber in the U.S." Arthur Andersen signed off on the deal, a spokeswoman explaining, "The auditor is not the business advisor and would not advise the company as to the valuation." She neglected to mention that Andersen was actually distributing swap models ("white papers") to its telecom clients. The deal, reached on the last day of the third quarter, helped Qwest boost revenues and profit numbers for the quarter while allowing Enron to avoid recording a huge loss. A former Enron executive remarked, "Qwest said we will overpay for the assets, and you will overpay us on the contract."[61] Qwest and Enron had tried to negotiate an even larger deal in the second quarter of 2001, with the negotiations involving Nacchio and Enron's Jeffrey Skilling.

Qwest used one additional tactic to try to keep itself upright as the telecom market slumped: booking of revenue for services before it delivered them. In the third quarter of 2000, Qwest claimed to have sold $100 million in equipment and $20.5 million in services to Genuity—an Internet service provider. In a civil suit, the SEC claims that Qwest improperly tried to separate the equipment portion of the deal from the services portion, in violation of GAAP.[62] A second alleged fraud, involving a Qwest project to wire Arizona schools, resulted in charges of criminal fraud by the U.S. Department of Justice and of civil securities fraud by the SEC. In January 2001, Qwest had received a $100 million order from the Arizona School Facilities Board to design and install a network linking all Arizona schools to the Internet and local phone service. The government has charged that in the second quarter of 2001 Qwest executives, hoping to meet revenue projections, conspired to make it appear that the board had asked for and received the equipment that had been scheduled to be delivered later in the project. This allowed Qwest to book $34 million in sales for the quarter. In fact, Qwest had not even received the full order from its supplier. Further, the Qwest executives had forged a letter with the letterhead of the Arizona School Facilities Board asking for the early shipment.[63]

Qwest "missed" its numbers in the third quarter of 2001, and the price of its stock began to plummet. After the SEC began inquiries into the company's swaps, the board ousted Nacchio on June 17, 2002. On July 28, 2002, it filed a billion-dollar restatement, admitting that it improperly booked revenue from swaps. Its stock, which had reached a high of $64.50 a share on March 3, 2000, fell to $2.74 by October 18, 2002. Qwest later announced a need for further restatements for 2000 through 2002, bringing the total to $2.2 billion, and warned that more restatements might follow.[64] Developments were all the more aggravating because of the magnitude with which insiders dumped stock. Between 1999 and 2001, Qwest executives made $500 million by selling shares. Nacchio, who has pointed to the fact that he held onto 470,000 shares as evidence of his innocence, sold over 5 million shares for $227 million.[65] And the chairman of the board, Phil Anshutz, rates as the king of the dump, having sold stock for $1.9 billion between 1998 and 2002.

Irate shareholders have joined prosecutors and regulators in trying to hold Qwest executives accountable, but with surprisingly modest results for all. Five shareholder suits were settled for a mere $25 million in June 2004. The plaintiffs' attorney reported: "The review of millions of pages of documents failed to uncover a 'smoking gun' that connected Messrs. Nacchio or Anschutz to the accounting improprieties that were allegedly transacted by Qwest's middle to upper management."[66] With great fanfare, the Department of Justice and the SEC charged several midlevel Qwest executives with fraud, hoping they would, in turn, implicate higher-ups. The actions were announced by Attorney General John Ashcroft and SEC chairman William Donaldson. Donaldson stated, "Accurate financial statements are the bedrock of our capital markets," while the SEC enforcement director trumpeted it as an example "of the extraordinary efforts of the Commission and the Department of Justice to root out corporate fraud and bring enforcement cases against those who would seek to undermine the integrity of the financial reporting process."[67] However, the government actions did little to shore up the financial market or reporting process. Two of the executives were acquitted of criminal charges, while mistrials were declared for two others. These results, along with the mistrials of such notorious figures as CSFB's Frank Quattrone and Tyco's Dennis Kozlowski, underscore the difficulty of establishing criminal intent in white-collar fraud cases.

"Dead Meat Lying on the Sofa"

The question of intent becomes even more problematic in the midst of technological ferment. What did tech executives and promoters believe (and when did they believe it)? Here the case of Enron's ill-fated (and much hyped) broadband venture is instructive, for when the government accused executives at Enron Broadband Services (EBS) of pumping stock through fraudulent exaggerations of the unit's technological capacities, Enron executives and their defenders in the high-tech community argued that such projections were normal in the Silicon Valley tradition of innovation. Jeffrey Skilling declared, "If they're going to send everyone to jail that was optimistic about broadband they would have to incarcerate half of San Jose."[68] Echoes of this defense rang in the remarks of a computer executive familiar with Enron's system who commented, "If they succeed in convicting the Enron developers anyone in Silicon Valley can be sent to jail."[69] Could a firm's involvement with technology provide yet another wormhole for financial manipulators to escape accountability? The question has broad significance, given that so many firms are adopting some sort of digital strategy.

The above attempts to absolve EBS—and by extension, the tech sector—claim that the uncertainty that is inherent in technological innovation make business predictions an imperfect art. A pair of reporters noted that many of the "former customers, suppliers, consultants, employees, partners and competitors" of EBS contended that the unit's problems reflect "the disarray and disappointment that typically accompany product development in the computer industry" where "claims are made for a technology's abilities long before commercially viable products are available."[70] However, one can question whether it ultimately makes sense to distinguish the technological from the commercial capacities of firms that are seeking to develop commercial applications of a technology. A for-profit industry is, in essence, a technological network that is made "commercial" through the addition of paying customers or clients of some sort.[71] Moreover, the ability of a firm to sustain the funding of the ongoing development of its technology typically relies upon its success in connecting with such sources of revenue so as to bankroll its own efforts or to gain/maintain the confidence of investors who provide capital. At any rate, evidence suggesting deception or a lack of faith on the part of executives can make the "disarray" of innovation argument beside the point.

EBS seemed to start out with good intentions, but it faced formidable business and technological challenges that were compounded by unattainable financial targets. The first initiative was to create a premium broadband network that would provide a basis for a broadband trading business. The main idea was that broadband trading "would make it possible for customers to buy only the bandwidth capacity they needed when they needed it" (*ME*, 286). However, real-time switching could only be done if a new kind of operating software was developed; this was the core technological challenge EBS faced. A related task was to build its own broadband network. EBS planned to build a fifteen-thousand-mile network (it would even extend to Europe). The second major initiative was a content delivery business. EBS wanted to develop a viable commercial application—such as video-on-demand—so as to spur demand for broadband. As we will see, this was a daunting endeavor in its own right. Added to these ambitious projects was a financial agenda that was unattainable. From the beginning, Jeffrey Skilling looked to the venture as a financial strategy—an immediate replacement for several failing ventures that could help Enron "fix" its stock valuation. In its efforts to give an immediate boost to the stock, Enron grossly exaggerated the progress of EBS. McLean and Elkin note that an April 1999 press release made it sound as if the new digital network was a reality when it actually "wasn't close to operating on a commercial scale, and much of the promised technology never made it out of the lab," and they call Skilling's briefing of analysts at the January 2000 meeting (featured in the vignette which opened our book) "an act of staggering recklessness"—as misleading as the fake computer hardware on display (*ME*, 285).

Thus, EBS was under immediate pressure to make its numbers. McLean and Elkind report that a November 2000 internal memo outlining a "strategic vision" for Enron broadband stated, "EBS has released key metrics to the analysts on Wall Street and must now deliver on those metrics" (*ME*, 296). Skilling had promised Wall Street that EBS would lose no more than $60 million in 2000; however, the unit had grown to one thousand employees and was burning through $500 million a year as it raced to develop a network. With these kinds of expenditures, it would have to immediately start making a substantial amount of revenue in order to make the numbers that Skilling had promised. McLean and Elkin note that the only way EBS could reach its financial targets was to play accounting games.

Of course, the prospects for creating a broadband trading business soon collapsed, as dot-com stocks crashed and the market was awash in a glut of fiber-optic cable. Enron, which had spent $1 billion on building a broadband network, decided to rely on leasing or trading for capacity to fill the gaps. It warehoused its equipment and let most of its fiber stay dark. This left it relying on its content initiative—video-on-demand.

A video-on-demand service was a problematic venture for big entertainment firms, let alone for a firm with no experience in the area. McLean and Elkin remark that: "Most homes didn't even have the high-speed broadband telephone lines that Enron was planning to use for on-demand video. Those that did were connected to computers: the Enron plan called for video to be streamed into television sets. Providing such digital-TV video required a new kind of set-up box that would cost $500 apiece (while the boxes were under development, one of them burst into flames). And . . . Enron was competing with the cable-television industry . . . which . . . already had wires and boxes in millions of American homes" (*ME*, 287). Solving these problems would take some time—if it was even possible—but EBS was under immediate pressure to make its quarterly numbers. In the first quarter of 2000, EBS entered into swaps of fiber-optic capacity that generated $59 million in revenue. In the second and third quarters it made an acceptable amount of revenue by engaging in complicated transactions with special purpose entities, including Andy Fastow's infamous LJM2. As EBS desperately scrambled to generate revenue for the fourth quarter, it decided to book future earnings from a deal that it had recently made—a twenty-year agreement with Blockbuster to work together on a video-on-demand service.

In an April 2000 pact, Blockbuster had agreed to use its Hollywood connections to line up the content, while EBS promised to develop a system to stream the content into homes—and to absorb all the costs. In return, EBS would receive about $1 for every movie sold. Wall Street analysts were thrilled even though the terms were onerous for the Enron unit.

EBS had some successes in developing elements of the delivery system. Its supporters have stressed several successful tests of the technology: the streaming of video over the Internet from Drew Carey's comedy show, the Wimbledon tennis tournament, and the 1999 Country Music Awards.[72] However, the larger effort was quickly and decisively halted when EBS ran into the "last mile" problem—a rather predictable roadblock. For all the free market rhetoric, the Telecommunications Act of 1996 had left regional phone companies (and cable companies) with a monopoly position when it came to the digital lines that entered a customer's home. EBS attempts to negotiate access from the phone companies were mostly futile. Hoping to keep the Blockbuster deal alive, EBS conducted a trial run of the service, but it provided little credibility for the venture: the scaled-down test included only a few hundred households in three cities and much of the test did not make use of standard DSL equipment. Demand was anemic, with households ordering, on average, 1.8 videos a month. When the head of the effort gushed about the movie proceeds at a meeting, another executive "handed him a $5 bill and said, 'I just doubled your revenue'" (*ME*, 293).

As the prospects for developing a sustainable business faded, Enron resorted to more tested methodology, an especially heroic act of financial engineering that was appropriately named "Project Braveheart." Even though the agreement was on the brink of collapse and had generated zero profits, EBS calculated the value of the twenty-year Blockbuster deal to be $53 million, based on "wildly speculative" projections that "by the year 2010 the company's content business would be operating in eighty-two cities, that 32 percent of the households in those markets would be using DSL lines, that 70 percent of DSL customers using video-on-demand would subscribe to the Enron-Blockbuster service, and that Enron would control 50 percent of the video-on-demand market" (*ME,* 296). To transform the projected earnings into earnings that could be immediately booked, EBS set up an elaborate series of transactions with the kind of "outside" insiders who often figured in Enron machinations. The outside investors were supplied by a joint venture that EBS set up with two partners—aCube, a small video-on-demand equipment firm owned by Oracle CEO Larry Ellison and an investment vehicle owned by an Enron-controlled special purpose entity. The joint partnership then sold almost all profit rights in the Blockbuster deal for $115 million to yet another investment vehicle, which was funded with $115 million from the Canadian Imperial Bank of Commerce (CIBC). In fact, neither aCube nor CIBC really wanted to invest in Braveheart and both have claimed that they had an understanding with Enron that their money was not actually at risk—and would be quickly repaid with a handsome return. In other words, the money was a loan and the accounting statements that outside investors were involved were shams (*ME,* 296).

The figure that EBS arrived at—$53 million—allowed it to meet Wall Street's expectations for the year. Two months after booking the $53 million in profits, EBS beat Blockbuster to the punch, announcing that it was ending the agreement. Yet, EBS proclaimed that this would actually allow it to extend its "entertainment on-demand service"; for the first quarter of 2001, EBS booked another $58 million in profits from Braveheart (*ME,* 297). EBS was not yet finished in pumping the value of Enron stock.

In a December 1999 e-mail, the director of business development complained (a few days before resigning) that the effort to develop a network had reached a dead end: "I don't care what lipstick and rouge you paint that bitch with. She's still just dead meat lying on the sofa, just threatening to stand up and steal the show."[73] The government has charged that little changed over the next year. Shortly before a January 2001 meeting with analysts, Kenneth Rice (the head of EBS) was informed by his staffers that EBS was spending too much, earning too little, and its immediate prospects were poor. An internal report estimated that the unit's losses would hit $149 million for the first quarter of 2001 alone. Yet, during the meeting with analysts, Rice announced that it had been an outstanding year for the content delivery business and that it could depend on a twenty-year relationship with Blockbuster. He stated that EBS's estimated losses for 2001 would total only $65 million and that the unit was now worth $36 billion, with the digital content segment contributing $20 billion of the value—even though an EBS team had just valued the digital content segment at only $8 billion (*ME,* 297).

The final government charge was that Rice used inside information on the unit's dismal prospects to dump stock and options—a total of $53 million from February 2000 to February 2001—while he was head of EBS (*ME,* 299). The government has argued that the fact that Rice unloaded such a quantity of stock at a time when the unit was declaring strong results is evidence that he—and other dumpers—did not believe.

Pie in the Big Sky Country: The Draining of Montana Power

News about scandals and dysfunctions in the telecom sector (as had been the case in energy trading) was dominated by reports of epic misdeeds by corporate giants. But in the shadow of these events one can find smaller cases that help flesh out the contours of the New Economy scandals. We end this chapter with a less publicized debacle that brought together the essential ingredients for disaster in both the energy and the telecom industries. The case involves a Montana utility that was barely known outside the state until the late 1990s, when it made a bold bid to join the ranks of WorldCom, Qwest, and Global Crossing in the heady world of telecommunications, a move that had disastrous consequences for its employees, investors, and many of the state's energy consumers.

The Montana Power Company, created in 1912 by a copper company, became a regulated utility with a monopoly to sell electrical energy to residential and commercial customers. Montana, whose nickname is "Big Sky Country," is large in area but small in population. This fact, combined with the centrality of electrical energy in the mining economy, allowed the firm to wield an inordinate amount of power in state politics.

Montana Power was also a publicly owned utility, with nearly a third of all its shares owned by state residents, several thousand of whom were utility employees who purchased shares through its pension plan. For many years, revenues and stock values were steady and the company paid decent dividends to shareholders. Nobody got rich at Montana Power, but it was a good place to work and retire from. And it was a reliable provider of cheap energy for the energy-intensive mining industry and for consumers who enjoyed electricity prices that were among the lowest in the country.

In the late 1980s, as rumblings of change were being felt in the energy industry, Montana Power's executives began to look for ways to diversify. They purchased a small long-distance telephone service provider in 1990—Touch America—and used its name for a fledgling telecom unit. In 1997, Montana Power's CEO, Robert "Montana Bob" Gannon, and several other executives proclaimed that the company had to either change or die. They argued that the old model of regulated energy utilities would soon become a thing of the past, as the forces of deregulation and the entrance of companies like Enron into the industry were creating a brave new world of electrical energy production.

The first step in the transformation of the firm that would allow it to survive was to change the laws that restricted the utility's range of activities and the rates it charged its customers. Gannon and his colleagues embarked on a campaign to convince state lawmakers to follow the lead of other states and deregulate the electrical energy industry, arguing that deregulation was inevitable and progressive (California is doing it). The Electric Utility Restructuring and Customer Choice Act was introduced at the very end of the Montana legislature's 1997 session and was quickly approved, with little debate.[74] The next month (April 1997) the bill was signed into law, and it went into effect a month later. The legislation allowed utilities to sell off their power-generating facilities and removed price caps on electricity sold to large industrial firms, while at the same time freezing electricity prices for residential customers until 2002.

Montana Power executives had argued that deregulation was necessary for their company to stay in the energy business. Yet, eight months after the legislation was passed they announced their intention to sell off all of their generating facilities—power plants, transmission lines, dams—and effectively leave the energy business. In 1999, they began selling the company's hydroelectric and coal-fired generating plants to PPL Corp., a Pennsylvania utility. The next year they sold its energy distribution unit to a South Dakota company. With these sales the company raised $2.7 billion.

Montana Power used its new capital to embark on a New Economy journey of reinvention, pouring money into a telecommunications network and adopting the name of its subsidiary, Touch America. The goal of the "new" firm was to lay a twenty-six-thousand-mile network of fiber-optic cable throughout the United States, connecting businesses and residences with high-speed broadband from Boston to Seattle. Like other born-again energy companies, Touch America began to pack its annual reports with New Economy rhetoric. In its 2000 report, for example, it let its shareholders in on the big picture: "[W]e are in a world of constant communications where the flow of information . . . defines both the way we live and the way we relate to each other as individuals, enterprises and societies."[75]

Senior executives at Montana Power did not make the decision to move into telecom by themselves. They relied on experts at the Wall Street investment bank Goldman Sachs, who reportedly advised them to get out of the energy business altogether and move into the telecom industry. Representatives from the bank visited the energy company's Butte headquarters *more than one hundred times,* earning substantial fees for Goldman.

Montana Power's makeover was hailed by stock analysts as a bold gambit by Gannon, who had shown himself to be a New Economy maverick. The business press frequently compared the firm to New Economy legends, such as Enron, Global Crossing, and WorldCom. In a 1999 article in *The Motley Fool,* one stock analyst wrote: "Montana Power may not be the sleekest racehorse in the bandwidth stable. Compared to the Global Crossings and Broadcoms of the world, it looks more like an old plow horse. But, in a realm where those companies burning brightest may end up crashing the hardest, Montana Power is quietly building a world-class fiber optic network that rivals them all."[76] "Isn't the free market great?" the analyst gushed. *Barron's* magazine applauded the company, comparing it to Enron.[77] In April 1999, Goldman Sachs (the same company that was advising Montana Power) rated the firm's stock as a "market outperformer."[78]

At first, the enthusiasm seemed justified. The day after the firm announced its rebirth as Touch America in March 2000, the stock hit an all-time high of $65 per share. This was good news for the company's shareholders, including employees, many of whose pension plans were loaded with the stock. But, despite receiving the wisdom of one of Wall Street's most prestigious banks, Montana Power had entered the telecom industry at precisely the wrong moment. By the middle of 2000 it was clear to many that the telecom bubble had burst amid a glut of fiber-optic capacity. To compound matters, Touch America management had made a very unfortunate decision to expand the firm's customer base by purchasing a quarter million long-distance accounts from Qwest. The deal was beset with problems, resulting in a series of suits and countersuits between the two firms. Ultimately, Touch America paid Qwest $60 million to settle.[79] As earnings dropped, Wall Street quickly soured on Touch America. After the March 2000 high of $65, the firm's stock price began to drop—by the end of the year to around $20 a share. Over the next eighteen months, its financial condition worsened, and by August 2002 the stock was worth less than $1 a share before it was finally delisted by the NYSE. The end came in June 2003, when Touch America declared bankruptcy and started e-mailing layoff notices to employees, many of whom had been at the company for most of their work lives.

What makes this sorry tale more than a little sordid are allegations that Gannon and other executives profited from irresponsible wheeling and dealing that left Montana Power investors, employees, and consumers standing out in the cold. In the summer of 2002, as the stock price went below $1, Gannon and three other executives were granted $5.4 million in bonuses under clauses in their contracts that triggered the payouts in the event of a "change of control" in the company— clauses whose usual purpose is to compensate executives who will lose their jobs following a merger. The executives had argued that the sale of Montana Power's energy assets constituted such an event, despite the fact that after the sale they had kept their jobs and salaries. At the time, $5.4 million amounted to 10 percent of the firm's market capitalization.

The executives were not the only ones to benefit from the draining of Montana Power. According to a shareholder lawsuit, Goldman Sachs had contracts with Montana Power that made the investment bank's substantial fees contingent upon the sale of the utility's energy-related hard assets. This, the suit claimed, created an inherent conflict of interest, as Goldman was no longer offering Montana Power advice as a disinterested third party but had a material interest in convincing the firm to get out of the energy business.[80]

While CEO Robert Gannon was living the good life, building a $3 million home on Montana's scenic Flathead Lake, energy consumers in the state were not doing so well. In the newly deregulated electricity market, energy prices for some users rose dramatically. One of the casualties of the changing market was Montana Resources, a mining company that had extracted metal ore from a huge pit in Butte since 1870. The company saw its electrical energy costs rise from $26 a megawatt hour at the beginning of 2000 to $320 a megawatt hour in May 2001. It was more than the company could afford, forcing it to lay off more than 320 workers.[81] This was a heavy blow in a city with only twenty-five thousand adult residents and where the 1999 median household income was $30,516, compared to the national average of $41,994. Other firms reduced production; the AFL-CIO estimated that at least one thousand jobs were lost in the state as a result of rising energy prices.[82] Meanwhile, PPL

Corp., the Pennsylvania utility that purchased many of Montana Power's plants and was now providing electricity to Montana consumers, was doing very well, selling "nearly a third of the plants' power out-of-state at a huge markup, producing record profits."[83] In 2001, PPL's CEO defended deregulation before a congressional panel, stating: "In a deregulated energy marketplace, the mere existence of high prices does not necessarily mean that a market is dysfunctional."[84] One wonders how many Montana residents or laid-off workers shared his view.

Many in Montana wanted to know how a state so blessed in natural resources that had long enjoyed low energy prices could suddenly experience an energy meltdown. For many critics, the blame lay with state politicians and their cozy relationship with energy companies. As former congressman Pat Williams put it, "Montana held the four aces of cheap power, and a corporate-lackey legislature demanded a new deck of cards."[85]

In the world of big energy and politics, it sometimes seems that everyone is connected to everyone else, with very few degrees of separation. The most prominent political sponsor of the 1997 legislation that deregulated Montana's energy market was then-Governor Marc Racicot. When Racicot left office in 2001, he joined a law firm where he became a Washington-based lobbyist for the Enron Corporation. He also lobbied Vice President Cheney on behalf of an energy trade group seeking to repeal EPA regulations.[86] Racicot, who also served in the Bush election campaign, was rewarded for his efforts with the chairmanship of the Republican National Committee, sparking a minor controversy when he refused to give up his lucrative lobbying job while he was in that position.[87] The connections between the former governor and the energy industry draw attention to a political environment that creates revolving doors for government officials who have been admitted to the elite club of corporate chiefs and their minions and who can move effortlessly between public and private life—or, in Racicot's case, somewhere in between as the head of a national political party—all the while consistently advocating the interests of their fellow club members. It is the same setting that allowed Dick Cheney to go from being secretary of defense in the first Bush administration to CEO of energy giant Halliburton (despite having little prior business experience) and back to the vice presidency of the United States.[88]

Once hailed as a hometown hero, "Montana Bob" Gannon became reviled as a profiteer and a puppet of Wall Street financiers. A columnist for the *Bozeman Daily Chronicle* ridiculed the e-mails Gannon sent out to laid-off employees, which read: "Several objectives must be achieved in the course of the bankruptcy proceedings. Touch America's business must be operated until sales of Touch America's assets are closed and we must accomplish an orderly winding down of business. We encourage you to continue with Touch America so it can maintain quality of service for these customers and preserve the value of our network assets." The real message: "In simpler terms: 'You're out of work, too, pal, but if me and my corporate buddies are going to walk away with anything out of this bankruptcy deal, we need you to keep showing up each morning. At least until we can find some sucker to buy the mess we've created. Head up. Nose to the grindstone. Trust me, it'll be better for everybody.'"[89] One reader of an area newspaper column on Gannon proposed a novel solution to the problems faced by Montanans who were ripped off by Montana Power: "I think that we should all move in with Bobby Gannon on his THREE MILLION DOLLAR home on Flathead Lake! The hell with trickle down economics. Let's try some 'move in' economics! That just might show them rich bastards that we're tired of gettin' trickled on!"[90]

One sees in the case of Montana Power familiar elements of New Economy–style pumping and dumping: the reinvention of a firm so that insiders can exploit the stock market; alteration of the rules to abet their activities; and the questionable "assistance" offered by prestigious business intermediaries who had their own agenda. But it is the unique aspects of the case that make it revealing—and perhaps even more alarming.

There were no charges of accounting fraud or criminal wrongdoing; it does not appear that "Montana Bob" Gannon and friends intended to loot their company. Rather, they used legal (if ethically dubious) means to shift financial risk from themselves and onto employees and investors. This transfer of financial risk from corporate elites to employees and small investors was a hallmark of the New Economy. Moreover, the draining of Montana Power reveals how the diversion of capital for speculation distorted the development not only of telecom, but also of other segments of the U.S. economy.

The Great Telecom Dump

The breathtaking extent of corruption in the new telecom sector was matched only by the sheer magnitude of the waste. However, the disaster has not caused as much doubt among the free market faithful as one might expect. Apologists often point to the case of the nineteenth-century railroads—where corruption and overbuilding were similarly epic in scale—as evidence that things will work out (the excess capacity will get used someday). Federal policy-makers have not been able to agree on what caused the meltdown in telecom, leaving the Federal Communications Commission (FCC) free to stay the course set by its conservative chairman, Michael K. Powell. The *New York Times* comments that the FCC "remains committed to reducing regulation and staying largely out of the way of the marketplace."[91] Powell has shown little interest in whether deregulation or abuses of power by business interests may have contributed to the telecom debacle. He stressed stirred-up emotions, ignoring the institutions and organized interests involved: "The Telecommunications Act of 1996 and the commercialization and mass-market adoption of the Internet led to a near-hysterical belief that the opportunities for growth were limitless. Very few did not get swept up."[92] In contrast, Joseph Stiglitz proposes that the telecom fiasco "cannot be explained just by irrational exuberance, by misforecasting; it was the quest for monopoly profits in the new world of deregulation that drove the system so out of balance, at such great costs."[93] Stiglitz, an institutional economist (and Noble Prize winner) who specializes in state regulation and problems of information, agrees that changes in the regulatory system were overdue, given the changes in technology and the economy. However, what was needed was "reformed regulation," not blanket deregulation. He claims that deregulation in the 1990s was too rapid and indiscriminate; in some areas (e.g., accounting) more regulation was appropriate. Stiglitz also points to the damage done in the telecom "gold rush": it distorted the economy and imposed significant costs on society. For the rest of the chapter, we will assess the damage done by the telecom scandals.

The raw economic costs were stark. The new telecom ensemble led the way when the economy went into the tank at the end of the boom. By 2002, half a million were out of work in telecom, the industry had lost an astonishing $2.5 trillion in market capitalization, and twenty-three telecom firms had gone bankrupt.[94] In addition to Global Crossing and WorldCom, the casualties included firms such as 360networks, Winstar, PSINet, Exodus, Iridium, Global TeleSystems, ICO Global, and Arch Wireless.

Importantly, the distribution of benefits and costs was grossly uneven. Insiders exploited ordinary investors on a vast scale through their ability to dump stocks before they crashed. From 2000 to August 2002, eleven executives from telecoms and telecom equipment suppliers gained over $100 million each from stock sales. About one hundred executives from these firms each received $10 million or more; thirteen of them were from Qwest.[95] Indeed, *Fortune* magazine found Qwest executives to be the champion dumpers of all sectors, not just of telecom. Between January 1999 and May 2002, Qwest executives cashed in $2.26 billion in stock.[96] Of course, the beneficiaries of the windfalls (or their hirelings) asserted that they were indeed worthy. The lawyer for former Qwest CEO Joseph Nacchio claimed that his stock sales were "perfectly proper": "Every financial decision was based on the good-faith belief that it was in accordance with all applicable rules and regulations and in the best interest of the company and its shareholders."[97] A spokesman for Gary Winnick, the former chairman of Global Crossing, was more reflective, perhaps because Global Crossing went bankrupt while Qwest merely had most of its stock value wiped out: "Sometimes it takes the markets time to catch up to visionary ideas."[98] Though he was referring to the plan to create a hundred-thousand-mile fiber-optic network spanning the globe, he would have been on firmer ground lauding Winnick's brilliance in the financial sphere, given that he had cleared over $730 million even though his firm went belly-up. The logic of Winnick's successful scheme eluded ordinary folk. For example, Linda Lorch, an elementary schoolteacher who lost $120,000 on her Global Crossing stock, admitted her ignorance on the most elementary of New Economy financial equations: "I don't know how the management of this company did so well while small shareholders did so poorly."[99]

Many employees of telecoms had their pensions devastated or completely wiped out. For example, a local union president reported that workers at Global Crossing lost much of the value of the 401(k) investments they made in the firm's stock because they could not sell it for five years. She remarked, "A lot of workers made their contribution in stock because they had faith in their employer."[100] A more basic injury was the disruption to lives caused by the loss of the job itself, a problem experienced by some half million telecom workers. For many, the loss of a good job meant they were going to have to try to reinvent themselves, an experience that is not nearly as exciting when the impetus is a closing, rather than an opening up, of opportunities. We might recall the case of Lorna Barnes, discussed at the opening of the chapter. Lorna, a middle-aged woman with an master's degree who had made over $80,000 as a WorldCom manager, ended up working part-time in childcare and consulting. Likewise, there is Mike Canaday, age forty-seven, who had been a WorldCom telecommunications engineer. After losing his job, he became a clerk at a pharmacy. Having been displaced from one job after another, he reports he is embarking on a course of "reinvention"—a rather desperate ploy for a middle-aged family man: "I've been through the boom-bust cycle, outsourcing, gone through six jobs as an engineer in a dozen years. I decided to reinvent myself. Now I'm investing six years in studying to be a pharmacist. I'll be working for the rest of my life to pay off loans, but at least I'll have more control."[101]

The sense of things being thrown askew has a parallel at the level of the sector itself. The development of the telecom industry, in various respects, has been as distorted as the flow of financial "information." Financial analysts on the make, in combination with fraudulent financial reports by firms, tainted the entire circuit of financial analysis and commentary. Among other things, executives tried to keep pace with rivals whose performance seemed too good to be true (and was), which in turn led them to engage in their own accounting games and other ploys. The circuit of compromised information also led to the flow of capital out of perfectly viable industries and firms on the one hand, and overinvestment in hot areas on the other. The orgy of investment in the telecom sector was organized in such a manner that the United States has fallen behind countries such as Japan and South Korea with regard to the population's broadband access. Free market advocates criticize such nations for relying on industrial policies because new technologies are supposedly too fast-moving and complex for governments to guide. They hold up "the market" as an alternative mechanism, implying that a multitude of people will be involved in deciding the course of development. Yet, it seems that a privatized industrial policy was generated for American telecoms by a group of elites with narrower interests and much less accountability than government agencies. Recall, for example, the singular influence of Jack Grubman in orchestrating the telecom sector; the *New York Times* reported that he pressured others to accept his view that "the industry should favor corporate customers over consumers."[102] In this light, it is less surprising that U.S. telecoms made so little progress in actually linking consumers to broadband.

Finally, there was the adverse impact of mindsets privileging short-term financial goals over the task of developing viable commercial applications of technology. For instance, the pressure placed on EBS to deliver immediate financial results undermined any hope that it might develop a sustainable business. In the next chapter, we will see that many dot-coms that played the stock promotion game faced a similar situation.

CHAPTER FOUR

The Webs They Weave
Dot-Coms and the IPO Machine

Many pundits assume that New Economy excesses, ranging from speculation to swindle, reflect a breakdown in the market order. Overcome by the "madness of crowds," people lost their individual capacity to make rational decisions—or to control impulses (e.g., greed). Alternatively, we draw on the insights of Charles Tilly, a leading sociologist of historical change. He advises looking for "forms of order hidden in . . . presumed disorder" and focusing on "relationships" rather than "individual mental events."[1] Thus, we will explore the institutional situations and social ties that shaped webs of dot-com fraud.

Previously, we saw that the political debate and business lobbying around the 1996 Telecommunications Act—along with the deregulation that was enacted—greatly contributed to the hype about the revolutionary nature of Internet-related businesses. However, the burgeoning dot-com (or new media) sector of Internet start-ups was the domain that allowed the New Economy—as a body of discourse and practice—to reach critical mass. It was the main arena for refining and applying New Economy doctrines and for marshaling a "rebel" army of web pioneers, entrepreneurs, financiers, executives, and business intermediaries who sought to become New Economy players. Positioned at the nexus of media and financial networks, the dot-com sector played a critical role in feeding the ravenous market for IPOs—supplying the New Economy hit machine with business stories as well as candidate firms.

Though the sector was often cited for its "virtuality," it actually lent a materiality to the New Economy that made it more real—in the form of hundreds of start-up firms, whose funky workplaces and edgy workers testified to the rise of a new kind of firm. Moreover, dot-com clusters provided beachheads for the importation of various norms and practices from Silicon Valley. Finally, the dominance of dot-coms in the ranks of firms "going public" meant that the sector had a preeminent role in minting the "currency" that was a defining feature of the New Economy—stock in new firms. Stock in the New Economy was a preferred medium for acquiring professional services, scarce talent, and other firms.[2] And in the form of IPO allotments, start-up stock also served as a currency for immoral economies. In this chapter we examine the organization of two kinds of dubious activities involving dot-coms: (1) bogus financial reporting and (2) IPOs.

Viva la Revolución!

Revolutionary rhetoric was a standard feature in dot-com promotions, but few images of revolution burned as brightly as those presented by StarMedia Networks, a Latin American online community based in New York. The firm's mission, according to cofounder Fernando Espuelas, was "unifying Latin people around the world" by creating a "central plaza," a "place where people can find each other, can communicate, [and] can share ideas." Espuelas, sounding like a cross between Simon Bolivar and George Gilder, proposed that StarMedia would "break a five-hundred-year pattern of monopolies in Latin America . . . of political . . . social, economic power by giving individuals the ultimate ability to share information and communicate." The liberators in his narrative were the forces of technology and deregulated markets that were unleashing the middle class from state-dominated economies: "[Y]ou can really visual-

ize . . . diversification of this technology. And also democracy that's fueled by open markets and the collapse of the status model, where the
government was making chewing gum and railroads, and everything
else, has created an emerging middle class in Latin America."[3] Founded
in 1996, the firm's strategy was to sell ads and subscriptions for a network
of websites that offered over a dozen "channels," including news, sports,
and personal finance as well as e-mail and chat. It used editors in cities
such as Buenos Aires, Mexico City, São Paulo, Santiago, and Bogotá to
"localize" its content while also providing content that tapped national
and Latin American identities. Espuelas claimed that its competitive edge
was an ability to form a community that would provide Hispanics across
the hemisphere with a special experience—an opportunity to connect
with a larger community.

For all the insurrectionist airs, the background of Espuelas and his
partner, Jack Chen, was solidly corporate. Espuelas worked for various
advertising firms before serving as marketing director for AT&T Carib-
bean and Latin America; Chen graduated with an MBA from Harvard
Business School and then worked as an investment banker at Goldman
Sachs and as a securities analyst at Credit Suisse First Boston. Chief Financial Officer Steven Heller came from the Bay Area software industry,
where, among other things, he had founded a firm that provided finance and accounting consulting services to high-tech firms, while Adri-
ana Kampener, president of one of StarMedia's Mexican units, was a former senior financial analyst at Chase Securities, Inc.[4] StarMedia first
gained attention from its ability to connect with blue chip financiers and
firms. In 1997, it raised $80 million in private funds from sources that
included Intel, Chase Capital Partners, and Henry R. Kravis (the lever-
aged-buy-out specialist).[5]

Indeed, StarMedia proved adept at forming another kind of language
community—a network of financiers who "got it"—the firm's story of
how a Latin American link to the Internet could be highly profitable (as
well as revolutionary). Espuelas recalled:

> What we thought . . . is that this would represent a shift as big as
> the horse to the car, for Latin America specifically. . . . So we thought
> that getting there first and really establishing ourselves as the dom-
> inant player with the big brand would be the key to success . . . it
> was difficult to find the nexus between people who understood
> Latin America and people who understood the Internet . . . it was
> only with Flatiron, who understood the Internet very well, and

Chase Capital Partners who understood the Latin American market very well, that we were able to say to them, look, this is how big the opportunity is.[6]

Flatiron Partners, an affiliate of Chase, echoed the StarMedia story in vouching for it as a promising target for investors. One of Flatiron's principle partners stated, "To believe in StarMedia, you have to believe in Latin America." At any rate, StarMedia already represented an opportunity to catch a financial wave because, the venture capitalist revealed, "I get more calls from people looking to invest in StarMedia than in any other company in our portfolio."[7]

The role of Flatiron Partners was crucial in helping StarMedia hook up with risk capital. Though it was itself a fledgling enterprise, Flatiron quickly became the flagship venture capital firm for "Silicon Alley"— New York's fast-growing ensemble of dot-com firms.[8] Flatiron worked out an arrangement whereby elite institutions and individuals who were members of the New York City Investment Fund could buy into the Internet firms it backed: this was the route through which not only Henry Kravis, but also David Rockefeller ended up buying into StarMedia. And Flatiron ushered StarMedia to a set of powerful investment banks that signed on to underwrite an IPO: Goldman Sachs, J. P. Morgan, Salomon Smith Barney, and BancBoston Robertson Stephens.

The underwriters helped StarMedia write its prospectus. In it, StarMedia touted itself as "the leading online network targeting Latin America" and proposed that its plan was to develop "user affinity to the StarMedia community" by offering Spanish and Portuguese language versions of popular online services such as e-mail, chat rooms, homepages, and instant messaging. It aspired to generate a sustainable revenue stream by continuing to line up advertisements and sponsorships from the likes of Ford, Fox Television, IBM, Nokia, and Sony. Its strategy stressed "aggressively extending our brand recognition."

In terms of the usual standards, the financials in the prospectus were poor: net losses soared from −$3.6 million in 1997 to −$45.9 million in 1998. Yet, New Economy firms argued that they needed to be evaluated with a different set of "metrics." When a firm sought to become a first mover—a strategy that required getting big fast—the numbers that mattered were growth in users and revenues. Thus, StarMedia boasted that the number of web pages its users had accessed per month ("monthly page views") had grown from 7 million in 1997 to 60 million by 1999. And its revenue was exploding—from $460,000 in 1997 to $5.3 million in 1998. However, some 45 percent of its revenue in 1998 came from swaps, where it exchanged ad space with other firms. StarMedia disclosed this fact in its discussion of risks, stating—in all capital letters:

WE HAVE DERIVED A PORTION OF OUR REVENUES FROM RECIPROCAL ADVERTISING AGREEMENTS, WHICH DO NOT GENERATE CASH REVENUE

However, the caution was only one of forty-seven different headings in a discussion of risks that extended for more than ten pages. The barrage of warnings included:

- OUR LIMITED OPERATING HISTORY MAKES EVALUATING OUR BUSINESS DIFFICULT
- WE HAVE NEVER MADE MONEY AND EXPECT OUR LOSSES TO CONTINUE
- WE MAY NOT BE ABLE TO OBTAIN SUFFICIENT FUNDS TO GROW OUR BUSINESS
- IF THE INTERNET IS NOT WIDELY ACCEPTED AS A MEDIUM FOR ADVERTISING AND COMMERCE, OUR BUSINESS WILL SUFFER
- WE MAY NOT BE ABLE TO COMPETE EFFECTIVELY AGAINST OUR RIVALS[9]

Some of the warnings were banal. Moreover, anyone who examined other prospectuses would find similar floods of warnings, giving one the impression that they were looking at some legal template. Finally, the presence of such warnings gave a prospectus a rather schizophrenic flavor, given that most of it was devoted to arguing why the business was well-positioned to take advantage of special opportunities. The question of which message to embrace was not very problematic in practice—not in an era when financial commentators and analysts kept up a steady positive buzz.

The underwriters set a price of $15 a share as the opening price for StarMedia's May 1999 IPO. After the underwriting fee was deducted, this left the firm with $98 million in cash. As was often the case, the IPO released a small portion of the firm's stock—7 million shares—leaving some 53 million shares outstanding. About 46 million of these shares were held by venture capitalists and "strategic investors." Those who went through Flatiron had invested at a price of either fifty cents or $1.50 a share; strategic investors who bought in during April/May 1999 paid $11 a share. The remaining 8,230,000 shares had been allocated to StarMedia executives at an exercise price of $1.92 per share.[10]

After a successful IPO, StarMedia stock value peaked at $67 a share by July 1999; its market capitalization reached $3.7 billion. StarMedia was a bona fide star, as was its front man—Fernando Espuelas. New York's leading new media trade publication saluted StarMedia as "the AOL of Latin America" and noted that the press was calling Espuelas "the Bill Gates of Latin America."[11] *Time* hailed him as one of the "leaders of the millennium." By the end of 1999, Espuelas's shares were valued at $191 million.[12] Like many other dot-com firms that "went public," StarMedia used its IPO cash and its new currency—stock options—to acquire the workers, services, and other firms it needed in its drive to get big fast. It acquired ten firms and by 2000 had offices in Barcelona, San Francisco, Bogotá, Buenos Aires, Caracas, Madrid, Miami, Medellín, Mexico City, Montevideo, Ottawa, Rio de Janeiro, San Juan, Santiago, and São Paulo.[13] The number of employees increased from 270 in 1999 to 779 in 2000; its revenue jumped from $5.8 million to $52.3 million, an increase of $46.5 million (801.7 percent). The "page views" on its network soared from 471 million in 1998 to some 3.6 billion in 1999 (an increase of 675 percent).[14] However, the impressive numbers belied the trouble that the firm was having in turning its users into revenue. Largely because of its huge advertising bills, StarMedia's net losses ballooned from −$46 million in 1999 to −$210.8 million in 2000 (*I,* 184).

So what were Fernando Espuelas and friends really thinking? Founders and new media firms were not usually beset by irrational exuberance, nor were they hucksters. Many were taking an educated guess and had mixed feelings. Though they stressed reasons to believe that their firm could be a hit, they knew the odds were against them. Late in 1999, Espuelas noted, "[W]e always thought that we had two fates: we would either be very successful, or we could crash against a wall and die early . . . a reality for a lot of Internet companies." Yet, at a time when it seemed that StarMedia had made it, he reported that he still had doubts: "What drives me, aside from the upside, is the downside. . . . And the downside here is: there are many, many cases, Apple being the one I think about all the time, of a great company that develops a new category of products, leads in the first couple of years and then goes on to lose it or disappear."[15] In fact, the prospect of dying young reemerged after the stock market crashed in April 2000 and became increasingly likely as the effects rippled through the Internet economy. StarMedia's currency withered with its stock price. By September its stock price had fallen below $10 a share and was feeling the effects of a downturn in Internet advertising. In addition, the firm was experiencing serious competition from an assortment of rivals—some of whom could appeal to a national audience (e.g., Brazil's Universo Online), while others were subsidiaries of large firms with deep pockets (e.g., Terra Networks, a subsidiary of Telefonica). In its bid to be a survivor, StarMedia focused its efforts on keeping the favor of Wall Street analysts. For a time it succeeded, by cutting costs and by reporting "better than expected" financial results in the last half of 2000 and the first half of 2001. Moreover, StarMedia asserted that it would report a profit by the fourth quarter of 2001. However, analysts began to doubt that the firm's cash reserves would hold out long enough for it to make a profit.[16] As of February 2001, the firm's stock had lost 92 percent of its value over the course of a year. Yet, StarMedia still had its believers. In May 2001 it received $36 million in financing from a group of investors (e.g., Bell South) who were attracted to its new forays into the wireless segment.

In the last quarter of 2001, StarMedia issued a statement that stunned Wall Street—not a long-awaited declaration of profitability, but an admission that it would restate its earnings for FY 2000 and the first half of 2001. Accounting errors at two Mexican units had caused StarMedia to overstate its revenues and earnings by over $10 million.[17] The firm's CFO resigned, while Espuelas left his post as CEO (he remained chairman). The NASDAQ halted trading in StarMedia stock, which fell to 38 cents a share, and StarMedia was hit with lawsuits from shareholders claiming that it had misled the market about its financial performance in 2000 and the first half of 2001. By the time the suit was settled for $3.15 million in September 2002, little remained of a firm once considered one of the hottest new media prospects. In July 2002, StarMedia sold its online assets for $8 million, changed its focus to wireless, its name to Cyclelogic, and its headquarters to Miami (*I*, 160).

One last legacy of StarMedia remained. Shareholders filed another suit alleging that the prospectus never mentioned a major catch in the way the IPO was managed—that the underwriting banks set aside allotments of the stock to institutional investors and tech notables in the expectation that they would reciprocate by booking more banking business or by purchasing more stock in follow-up offerings. The suit against StarMedia was later joined to a massive class action involving over three hundred IPOs.

From Silicon Valley to Everywhere

To account fully for the New Economy frauds, we have to understand the technological, financial, and organizational changes that came together in the later half of the 1990s. The dot-com sector provides a unique window for examining how efforts to apply Internet technology spurred the creation and diffusion of new commercial doctrines and identities, new forms of risk financing, and network forms of organization. To some extent, these new forms emerged from particular settings, but many New Economy ideas and practices were imported from Silicon Valley and adapted to new settings.

The dot-com sector originated with experiments with digital technologies (e.g., CD-ROMs, the World Wide Web) by creative types who were interested in new forms of expression. Combining an anticorporate ethos with elements of hacker culture, they hoped the Internet might allow cultural producers to create a "new media" that could bypass the old media. These technobohemians created a subculture (the original "don't you get it" clique) that provided arenas for developing a new identity and status system—and for sharing information on new technologies and techniques. Their initial commercial forays involved webzines and web design services. The anticorporate posture faded as they found that the best means of developing a business was to serve corporate customers. In fact, when major corporations began to discover the Internet in late 1995, their spending on new media services boosted the sector's growth (*I*, 25–37). Though the great majority of new media firms remained modest service providers to corporations, several hundred broke from the ranks in a bid to become national contenders who might dominate some new market—like Microsoft or Cisco Systems had done earlier.

Smart Money (Insider Ties and Exits)

A second major impulse in the formation of the dot-com sector was financial in nature, initially the result of efforts to extend the Silicon Valley institution of venture capital to new settings—a major thrust of the New Economy cultural mobilization. John Motavalli—a veteran of both the old and new media—notes that tech leaders and pundits promoted "the credo that Silicon Valley and its values and innovation would completely change the face of the American Economy."[18] Many new media pioneers became receptive to the message as they tried to establish business credibility. Michael Indergaard's study reports that new media firms in New York grew "interested in hooking up with Silicon Valley–style venture capitalists . . . hoping to gain credibility as well as capital. Establishing the merits of new firms was a daunting problem in an emerging industry where few were making profits. The Silicon Valley model suggested that start-ups could gain credibility by getting the backing of the 'smart money'—venture capitalists whose inside expertise and connections . . . [gave] them an advantage in assessing high-risk ventures."[19] Venture capitalists (both veteran and novice) tried to transplant the Silicon Valley model to new settings. Indergaard observes that venture capitalists disseminated the Silicon Valley model as they created exclusive networks ("circuits") of exchange.[20] "Venture capitalists transformed pools of capital owned by rich individuals and elite institutions into something new—a circuit of exchange with its own set of understandings, obligations, and symbols as well as its own medium of exchange (venture capital itself). . . . They prepared . . . [new media firms] to receive this new currency by creating understandings and ties that bridged the world of new media entrepreneurs and elite financial interests" (I, 60). Venture capitalists educated new media entrepreneurs (and investors) on key Silicon Valley norms, such as "the virtues of risk taking in exchange for equity in a start-up" and "alternative criteria for assessing firms" (I, 60). And they did more than talk. They created new sets of ties between entrepreneurs and a host of entities that possessed assets that start-ups needed. The message was that "who you know" was the magic ingredient that allowed Silicon Valley venture capitalists to turn business models into self-fulfilling prophecies, as is evident from the comments of one dot-com entrepreneur in New York: "Those Claude Perkins guys, and Benchmark [Silicon Valley venture capital firms] . . . have it wired. It is a complete self-fulfilling prophecy. They have capital, they have all the corporate relationships, they have all the head hunting relationships. And the ideas that emanate from them . . . they get the best guys to run them" (I, 62). A basic quality of the venture capital model was discipline. Venture capitalists waited for start-ups to make progress in some product market as well as to grow to the point where they could handle a sizeable investment. For example, in 1996, when Flatiron Partners—StarMedia's financier—began serving New York dot-coms, it told most start-ups that it was too early in their development to be receiving venture capital (I, 63).

Silicon Valley embraced a "risk culture" where failing was "okay"—a sensibility that complemented the venture capital calculus: if some firms in one's portfolio scored big IPOs—or at least received decent buy-outs—it should more than compensate for the failures. Relatedly, finding a lucrative "exit" was a prime goal for venture capitalists.

New Model Army

Apologists for the free market system often blame the New Economy scandals on the character flaws of a few individuals. However, character in the dot-com world was always a work in progress. Reinvention was the typical experience: "[F]irms engaged in endless organizational shifts as they interacted with new partners, explored new markets, or chased new investors. Web design shops reinvented themselves into consultants or e-commerce firms . . . new media people reinvented themselves as they crossed disciplinary, firm, or industry boundaries to join work teams or take new positions" (*1*, 35). Similarly, a study by Wolf Heydebrand and Annalisa Miron showed that organizational boundaries were porous and fluid; the nature of new media work meant that firm reorganization was "potentially unlimited."[21] A host of researchers have documented that these firms relied heavily on networks and project forms of organization.[22]

The above profile has critical implications for trying to understand the nature and significance of dot-com-related frauds. The unfixed nature of firm identities, business models, and boundaries—and the ubiquitous presence of networking—show that neither the *character* of firms nor of individuals is as fixed as conservative moralists intone. In other words, there is strong evidence here for the *institutional and social situatedness* of the New Economy scandals. In addition, the confluence of novel and unstable conditions contributed to the perception of "transformative times"—giving new media participants and investors a reason to believe in what, in hindsight, seems far-fetched; such conditions also may have contributed to the slide of many into fraud and other dubious practices. Finally, many scholars expect these organizational characteristics to endure in cutting-edge firms. Thus, criminogenic aspects of the organizational traits that surfaced in the 1990s may provide challenges for regulators for some time.

Priming the Pump: The IPO Machine

It was a flash flood of capital, roaring down the canyons of Wall Street, that drove the idea of a New Economy into the public consciousness.

References to a "New Economy" in the business press jumped from one thousand in 1998 to twenty thousand in the year 2000, spurred by a historic run of high-tech IPOs—mostly dot-coms.[23] From January 1998 to December 2000, there were 460 tech and Internet-related IPOs.[24] In 1999, IPOs raised $75 billion, the same amount of capital that was raised through all methods during the entire 1980s.[25]

The wild capitalism of Wall Street in the 1980s morphed into a more powerful coast-to-coast phenomenon in the 1990s—cross-pollinating with the technological forces bursting out from Silicon Valley and other West Coast hotspots. Financial developments remained a driving force: mutual funds sent a cascading river of capital into the stock market. In *Dot.con*, John Cassidy shows that the amount invested in stocks accelerated from some $100 billion in 1995 to an average of some $170 billion a year in the period 1996 to 1999. As 2000 came to an end, mutual funds had more than $4 trillion invested in stocks.[26] But while Cassidy suggests that "America" lost its money because it "lost its mind," we will turn the spotlight to the IPO machinery that channeled a sizeable portion of this money toward dot-com start-ups—and their well-positioned backers.

Making New Economy Reputations

Before the boom, the Wall Street investment banks that underwrote IPOs usually waited until a candidate firm had two or three years of profit-making. This changed by 1995 as firms began competing to supply infrastructure to make the Internet accessible to a broader public. Cassidy credits the 1995 IPO for Netscape—the firm that pioneered the graphical browser—for setting a new pattern. Demand for Netscape stock on the opening day so overwhelmed supply that the price rocketed and the value of the stock continued to rise thereafter.[27] From this point, start-ups and their financial backers rushed to launch IPOs— hoping an explosive first day would turn a firm into a hit. But, it was two of StarMedia's dot-com neighbors—EarthWeb and theglobe.com—that helped set off the greatest IPO run of the era in the fall of 1998.

One did not have to be either a gold digger or a scam artist to want to take a firm public. Certainly, some wanted to get rich quick, but there were multiple motives related to bolstering the position of one's firm— for example, getting publicity or gaining capital that could be used to acquire other firms (either to gain capacities or reduce competition). And New Economy doctrine offered several compelling rationales— which a cofounder of EarthWeb evoked in explaining its decision to hold an IPO: "We wanted to be first. Historically, the first-mover advantage is huge. We've seen the big get bigger. We're now at the stage where to win, we have to get as much market share as we can. And the only way to do that is through consolidation and really rapid growth. And you can't do that without some kind of currency, and what people really want is stock."[28]

The EarthWeb IPO provides a look at the distinctive business relationships and practices that launched hundreds of dot-com ventures into the public markets. The November 1998 IPO was a stunning success. Although it was priced at $14 a share, such a tremendous backlog of orders piled up that the stock actually opened at $40 a share. On its first day, it peaked at $89 a share before settling down to $48. Although its IPO was spectacular, EarthWeb was a not-so-spectacular firm. Its core asset was a website that collected technical information of interest to IT professionals, with much of the information being provided by users themselves. Its business rationale was that it would be able to charge premium rates to advertisers who would be eager to reach this strategic demographic. However, EarthWeb's revenue numbers were modest and it faced competition from similar sites. The key factor that allowed EarthWeb to hold an IPO was that there was a chain of "reputational intermediaries" who lined up to endorse the firm.

This system of serial vouching began with having the support of a venture capitalist who was willing to pass a firm on to a set of investment banks. Other reputational intermediaries who vouched for firms holding IPOs were accountants, financial analysts, and the financial media, but the investment banks that were underwriters for IPOs were the linchpin of the system. They provide a firm credibility with prospective buyers. Importantly, the relations between the banks and different sorts of investors were stratified. While the banks reserved blocks of stock (at a relatively low opening price) for institutional investors, less-connected buyers who wanted a little taste of Internet gold would be lined up waiting for someone to resell their shares; as a result, they might pay four or five times as much for a share as an institutional investor. Among other things, this peculiar arrangement set up institutional investors as an enthusiastic vanguard who helped the stock explode out of the gates "with an accelerating price that draws buyers from the general public" (*I*, 69). Under such conditions, the enthusiastic participation of the institutional investors (and underwriters) is neither irrational nor risky. The institutional investors get a chance to resell the stock for a windfall while the banks get 6 percent of the total capital raised, their own publicity, and a bit of reciprocity from the institutional investors (more on that later). The ones left bearing the brunt of the risk are the mass of ordinary investors who join in later on.

The process involved in the EarthWeb IPO is outlined in Table 4.1. The firm hooked up with its investment banks on the basis of the connections of its venture capitalist—Warburg Pincus—and the personal ties of its executives. In a "beauty contest" among banks, EarthWeb selected four banks to act as underwriters, with J. P. Morgan designated to act as the lead underwriter. The underwriters' duties are as follows: "perform 'due diligence'—assess the firm's business record and its prospects in its market segment . . . help the firm prepare a prospectus, which is a detailed analysis of the firm, its history, products, management structure, and financial data . . . [and] any risks . . . set the opening price at which the stock is to be sold and determine the number of shares to be sold" (*I*, 69). The next important stage is the "road show"—a tour where company executives tell the firm's story to groups of institutional investors in hopes of whipping up interest in the IPO. In Earth-Web's case, its management visited thirteen cities, starting on the West Coast and ending on the East Coast. After the road show, the underwriters set the price that the offering is to open at and take orders from institutional investors. Dot-com IPOs commonly underpriced the shares and kept the supply below the level of expected demand in the hope of setting off a feeding frenzy.

EarthWeb raised $24 million in cash from the IPO. An analyst at J. P. Morgan (the lead underwriter) offered a favorable report, repeating the EarthWeb story line: EarthWeb "is able to deliver a very lucrative and attractive market to advertisers that is not easy to reach," meaning that "advertisers are willing to pay much higher rates."[29]

The Sum of All Seers

For market enthusiasts, unfettered competition and capital flows are unqualified blessings. However, hypercompetition and excess capital proved destructive to the infrastructure for reasoned risk-taking associated with venture capital and investment banking. Moreover, these conditions—in combination with certain New Economy norms—helped corrupt a host of business intermediaries who assess the financial status of public firms—and IPO candidates. Most everyone involved in the networks of reputational intermediaries that assess business models and prospects was able "to get it"—how firm after firm fit the New Economy

TABLE 4.1. STEPS IN AN INITIAL PUBLIC OFFERING

Step One: Informal Schmoozing

Make contacts among the investment banking community. When an investment bank underwrites a stock, it is essentially buying the stock from the company and reselling it to portfolio managers, who then sell it on the market on the first day of trading.

Step Two: Bankers' Beauty Contest

Banks make formal presentations explaining how they would underwrite the offering.

Step Three: Due Diligence

The underwriters study the company's business record and prospects in its market segment. Then the company files with the SEC.

Step Four: Quiet Period

After the filing, company employees are prohibited from making public statements about the company until twenty-five days after the stock begins trading. The underwriters set a tentative price for the stock offering based on a comparable group of companies.

Step Five: Road Show

Company management goes on a tour to get institutional investors interested in buying the stock.

Step Six: Taking Orders

The underwriters set the final price for the offering. Institutional investors then place their orders with the underwriting banks.

Step Seven: The Stock Is Traded

In the first day of public trading, institutional investors can reap immediate profits from selling; company management must wait 180 days before selling its stock.

Sources: Adapted from David Ball, "Unearthing an IPO Success," Silicon Alley Reporter 3, no. 2 (1999): 44–49; and Michael Indergaard, Silicon Alley: The Rise and Fall of a New Media District (New York: Routledge, 2004), 70.

template. As their commitment shifted to making sure that they too would "get some," many became blessed with the second sight of a New Economy seer.

The amount of venture capital in the United States increased from some $4.2 billion in 1995 to just over $100 billion in 2000.[30] As new venture capital funds sprang up, even seasoned financiers felt pressured to drop standards and to go with the flow. Among other things, this meant getting involved much earlier in a start-up's life cycle. And venture capital backing—traditionally an indication that a firm has credible prospects in some product market—became a signal that a firm had credible prospects in the IPO market.

The case of Flatiron Partners (StarMedia's financier) suggests that even firms that regretted the deterioration of the venture financing system felt compelled to follow suit. When Flatiron began operations in 1996, it was one of only two or three firms that were funding new media firms in New York. In 1999, New York Internet firms gained as much venture capital as the entire United States had received in 1995. By 2001, over sixty investment funds had offices in New York (*I*, 78). As early as mid-1998, Jerry Colonna (a Flatiron partner) lamented in a *New York Times* opinion piece the "illogical overbidding" for start-ups by venture capitalists. He claimed that "Internet companies are going public that have no business going public"; he suggested that a series of "mind-boggling" acquisitions using stock had contributed, citing Microsoft's $400 million stock swap for Hotmail, a provider of free e-mail services.[31] In early 2000, when the action was more fevered, Fred Wilson (Colonna's partner) cautioned that an oversupply of capital was distorting the start-up process. "People are forming companies for the wrong reason . . . there is so much capital . . . anybody can start a company."[32] Yet, Flatiron kept raising and investing new funds—as did other venture capital firms. And, in fact, Flatiron's partners—and its investors—were making hundreds of millions in profit. Even its star-crossed protégé—StarMedia Networks—was a big success from the perspective of Flatiron's bottom line. Once the six month "lock-in" period after StarMedia's IPO expired in December 1999, Flatiron's investors could sell their shares for as much as $40 a share. This represented a tidy profit, given that Flatiron's investors bought in at 50 cents or $1.50 a share.[33]

The corruption of the IPO process was even more egregious, as it involved a systematic enrichment of insiders at the direct expense of ordinary investors—and a dereliction of professional and legal duties on the part of numerous participants. The IPO system became indifferent (at best) regarding the quality of business ventures, but all too efficient at image making and endorsing New Economy story lines. The investment banks and their supporting cast all seemed to be on the same page. Although webs of fraud permeated the system, the formula seems less the result of a grand conspiracy than of the diffusion process that sociologists associate with institutional processes. Indergaard adds that a set of interests emerged that worked to promote and exploit speculation: "[T]he participants came to possess overlapping interests when it came to revving up the production of IPOs. The IPO process and participant sensibilities changed as the stakes grew, competition heated up, and promotional webs thickened. Between 1998 and 2000, the apparatus became increasingly geared to initiate, sustain, and exploit waves of speculative investment" (I, 71). The peculiar features of the IPO process were taken for granted during the boom: the underpricing of IPOs, the stratification of buyers that favored institutional investors over ordinary folks, and the reliable cooperation of reputational intermediaries who provided endorsements. This taken-for-grantedness would end with the boom.

Keep Hype Alive

The same high-octane imagery that provided a reason to believe in the prospects of many a suspect enterprise that plied the web also abetted cover-ups of accounting fraud. Take the case of Cendant, a firm born of the 1997 merger of HFS International and CUC. HFS contributed hotels (Days Inn, Ramada), real estate (Century 21, Coldwell Bankers), and other franchises; CUC added a consumer services empire that featured auto, shopping, dining, travel clubs—and a set of cooked books that overstated its earnings by one-third.

CUC had manipulated its earnings statements to provide Wall Street with steady earnings, booking revenues far in advance while deferring expenses. As a result, it also amassed earnings at a rate that would have seemed too good to be true, except that it had a hot Internet unit—Netmarket.com. CUC founder Walter Forbes touted Netmarket.com as an "online mall" that "will sell 90% of what you'd want in your home."[34] At a time when Amazon.com was just establishing itself, Netmarket.com boasted 700,000 "members" who had bought $1.2 billion of consumer products—making it a contender for "first mover" in the Web retail niche. However, Netmarket.com turned out to be yet another dot-com whose ability to draw users exceeded its capacity to generate revenue. It said it would generate revenue through having users pay a $69.99 annual fee. However, its impressive user numbers reflected an introductory membership fee of only $1.

Netmarket's online venue was a major attraction of the merger for HFS. For CUC the deal would provide an opportunity to hide its loses in the accounting tricks. And Forbes would own stock options worth $65 million in the new $40 billion firm. However, soon after the merger was completed in late 1997, HFS execs uncovered CUC's suspect finances. When Cendant disclosed its accounting irregularities in April 1998, the stock fell from $40 billion to $10 billion. Seventy investor lawsuits followed; Cendant settled in 2000 for some $3 billion—the largest securities fraud settlement ever. A trial on charges of securities fraud, conspiracy, lying to the SEC, and insider trading against Forbes ended in mistrial in January 2005; his co-defendant, former Cendant vice chairman E. Kirk Shelton, was convicted on twelve counts, including conspiracy, mail fraud, wire fraud, and securities fraud.[35]

The nature of Internet business provided its own opportunities for manipulating the books. Many firms pumped their New Economy credentials by exploiting areas of accounting that became ambiguous in the face of new norms. After the spring 2000 stock crash, firms were sorely tempted to use deceptive accounting to keep their Internet dreams alive.

"Internet Accounting"

A March 2000 *Fortune* story on dot-com accounting tricks opened, "While the Internet hardly invented financial legerdemain, there are disturbing signs that dot-com companies have embraced it with unusual enthusiasm."[36] It reported that the SEC had asked the Financial Accounting Standards Board (the body that oversees GAAP) to examine twenty issues that often occur in Internet companies. Whereas the standards traditionally focused on manipulations of *earnings,* Internet firms—oriented to New Economy metrics—were especially prone to manipulate *revenues.*

One area where revenues were manipulated was in the accounting for coupons or discounts. One of the amusing quirks of dot-coms was their inclination to give things away so as to draw users; however, the SEC was not amused when some firms developed ways to hide the effects of giveaways on sales. *Fortune* offered the following example: "[L]et's say a customer buys a $50 sweater using an electronic coupon that entitles her to 20 percent off. The customer pays only $40, but some companies record the full $50 in revenues and simply tack a $10 charge under 'marketing expenses.'"[37] Some Internet Service Providers offered $400 rebates on computers for users who signed three-year service contracts, then booked the rebates as "deferred subscriber acquisition costs," which they amortized over the life of the contract. AOL did something similar when it tried to hide the enormous costs it occurred when it flooded the land with free diskettes. It argued that its average member subscribed for two years, so the cost of acquiring them was an "investment" that should be recorded over the course of two years.

Another trick concerned accounting for fulfillment costs. One hallowed New Economy myth was that the digital economy was "weightless." In fact, e-commerce firms had to pay the same warehousing, packaging, and shipping expenses that brick-and-mortar merchants incurred. What set online merchants such as Amazon.com, eToys, and 1-800-Flowers apart was that they declared such costs to be "marketing expenses." Among other things, this allowed them to hide operational expenses amid high marketing figures that investors believed were temporary expenses related to establishing the brand. Another maneuver was to report the "entire sales price a customer pays at their site when in fact the company keeps only a small percentage of that amount."[38] An example was Priceline.com—the company that Captain Kirk fronted for in commercials about "naming your own price" for airline tickets and hotel rooms. Priceline took in $152 million in what it called "gross profit" even though it only kept $18 million for itself; naturally, most of the money went to the airlines and hotels that supply tickets and rooms.

The last type of accounting maneuver was one that we saw to be ubiquitous in the energy trading and telecom sectors—barters (swaps). Bartering of advertising is common in the old media, but such transactions rarely exceed 5 percent of their sales. In contrast, it was not unusual for Internet firms to generate half of their revenue from barters. And not all firms were as diligent as StarMedia had been when its prospectus noted a reliance on barters for generating revenues. In fact, *Fortune* noted that StarMedia did not mention swaps in a press release that boasted of increasing revenues by 44 percent in the third quarter of 1999; some 26 percent of the revenue reported in that quarter was based on trading ad space.

The recording of revenue from swaps became increasingly troublesome for observers of the Internet industry. The CEO of an industry newsletter complained, "A lot of things are winked at because of the so-called New Economy. Investors are being duped" with "a practice that is nothing more than fraudulent."[39] This is one case where regulators did plug the gap in accounting standards (belatedly). The Emerging Issues Task Force of the FASB issued a new accounting standard that "prohibits a company from reporting gross revenue from a barter transaction and requires the recognition of expenses."[40] The new standard became operative in January 2000—a few months before the tech stock bubble burst. However, many firms became so desperate that they acted as if the standards had not changed—or tried to hide their violations in more complex deals.

New Economy Barter Circuits

What was it about New Economy sectors (energy trading, telecoms, and dot-coms) that made swapping so attractive? Certainly a prime motivation for start-ups was to conserve their scarce cash reserves. New Economy start-ups were encouraged by investment banks and analysts to use barters of services or stock, rather than cash. For example, in a May 2001 report on Homestore.com, Merrill Lynch analysts observed: "Homestore pays for many of its content, distribution, and marketing expenses using stock instead of cash (which is a legitimate, defendable, and even shrewd decision for a young company with a strong currency, in that it conserves cash)" (*H*, 83). More broadly, such media commentary on the New Economy sought to normalize swapping, as is evident in an article in *Slate*:

> In the mature, old economy, businesses generally paid for goods and services with cash. . . . But as the Internet altered traditional modes of doing business, it also disrupted the traditional relationships between suppliers and business customers. . . . Very few New Economy companies—save the software and hardware firms— were in the business of selling products you could throw in the back of your Jeep. They were selling content, services, placement, and access to networks and customer bases. What's more, the Internet facilitated entirely new means of promotion and marketing: click-throughs, pop-up ads, etc. And so it was natural for companies to strike deals to harmonize their interests.[41]

Swapping also reflected the fact that the energy trading, telecom, and dot-com sectors each relied on a network system. In each system, there were some commodities that just about any member firm could make use of, or exchange (e.g., electrical power, telecom capacity, online advertising). More important, the ambiguous economic values of these commodities abetted swapping economies—as was the case with the stock of New Economy firms (especially, start-ups). The nebulous value provided a great deal of flexibility for firms that wished to manipulate financial statements. In such cases, the real utility of these commodities was that they facilitated collective efforts to engage in financial manipulations. In particular, boosting revenue numbers was an agenda that appealed to large New Economy players as well as start-ups.

In the next section on Homestore (and in the one that follows on AOL), we will examine how firms used special relationships and shared understandings as they collaborated in sophisticated swap deals that pumped up revenues and—after the stock bubble burst—became a survival tool.[42]

Betting the (Home) Store

The classic case of immoral economies organized around elaborate swaps may well be Homestore.com. An Internet start-up that became the largest online provider of real estate listings, Homestore allegedly was the nexus for a series of complex swaps that involved more than a dozen dot-coms as well as major firms such as Cendant and AOL. These swaps eventually included three-legged transactions known as round-trips.

Homestore.com went public in August 1999 and quickly won the praise of stock analysts, which helped the stock briefly jump to a price of over $100 a share. Henry Blodget at Merrill Lynch was particularly impressed with the firm's alliances with other Internet companies, such as America Online, as well as other old economy companies, such as the car-rental giant Budget ("bricks and clicks," as these old/new economy partnerships were called). They were also impressed with the revenues that Homestore was reporting, leading two prominent analysts to compare the firm to eBay (*H,* 60). Then, in a dramatic turn, at the end of 2001, Homestore was forced to restate its financials for the years 2000 and 2001, removing $192 million in revenues and, in a stroke, wiping out millions of dollars of investor's wealth as the firm's stock price plummeted. Investors began to smell a rat, and in a class action suit claimed that Homestore's executives had perpetrated a scam involving various kinds of bogus swaps meant to pump revenue statements. The suits accused the company's top executives, including Vice President Peter Tafeen, of creating "a corporate culture premised on the necessity of Homestore 'beating' the revenue numbers put up by other high-flying technology companies, and never disappointing the analysts. . . . [T]he deals done to meet these goals were known as 'Peter Deals' after Tafeen, and the absolute requirement to meet Homestore's projected revenue targets was known as the 'bogie.' . . . The company became obsessed with hitting the 'bogie' at all costs" (*H*, 5). Homestore executives would create swap deals to "plug" projected shortfalls in meeting a quarterly target. Initially, the swaps were rather conventional in nature. How it was that Homestore ended up engaging in complex bogus swaps is a most instructive tale.

From its inception, Homestore aspired to be something of a network enterprise—a bridge between two giants, Cendant and AOL. The lawsuit asserts that senior managers hoped that Homestore could "monopolize the real estate Internet market by parlaying Cendant's market power over listings, with AOL's Internet market power" (*H*, 104). Cendant controlled some 30 percent of the real estate listings in the United States, while AOL (owner of the prime "real estate" on the Internet) did not have an exclusive real estate channel—a gap that Homestore aimed to fill. Homestore's aspiration to dance with giants—particularly AOL— was a major factor in its slide into complex fraud.

Even before Homestore went public in 1999, it developed a relationship with AOL that involved barter transactions. In 1998, Homestore gave AOL $20 million in cash as well as 1.5 million stock warrants in return for the right to be AOL's exclusive online realtor. Under this arrangement, "an AOL user would simply click on a Homestore link, and be taken to the Homestore web site" (*H*, 105). From this point on, Homestore would make liberal use of its stock as a currency in barter deals. Through participating in these transactions, both Cendant and AOL became major Homestore shareholders.

It was in Homestore's deals with AOL that the barters became ever more complex—and legally suspect—to the point that they used third parties to disguise the nature of the transactions. The point of no return seems to have been a May 2000 agreement by which Homestore gained the right to operate AOL's "House & Home" channel. After a tentative agreement was reached, AOL executives pressured Homestore to accept a revised deal with striking terms. In essence, Homestore had to "bet the store" in order to get the House & Home slot. In order for Homestore to become the exclusive content provider for the House & Home channel (and to get a share of the revenues generated by user traffic), it had to pay AOL $20 million and 3.9 million shares of stock—and *agree to guarantee that the stock would be worth $68.50 a share.* Homestore also had to provide a $90 million line of credit that AOL could draw on for as much as $50 million if the guarantee was not met. Moreover, AOL also gained the right to cancel the marketing deal after three years if the guarantee was not met. The share price contingency resembled a derivative deal. Indeed, it represented a rather amazing bet on the part of Homestore, since its share price as of May 2000 was in the $20 range. This put enormous pressure on Homestore to ratchet up the share price to the guaranteed level of $68.50 a share. The lawsuit claims AOL's demand that the agreement be revised stemmed from its auditor's opinion that in order to recognize revenue from the deal—$287 million over three years—it had to have "the $20 million cash payment, the letter of credit, and the termination provisions" (*H,* 108).

Almost immediately, Homestore found itself hard-pressed to generate the kind of revenue growth it needed to impress investors. Homestore's later restatements of its accounting show that the challenge became ever more daunting as the Internet economy unraveled. For the first quarter of 2000—the last reporting period before the stock market crash—the restatement reduced its reported revenue by $977,000. In the second quarter—the first period after the crash—revenue was reduced by $7,908,000. In the last quarter of 2000, revenues were reduced by over $44 million, and in the second quarter of 2001 they were cut by over $60 million (*H,* 101–102). The lawsuit claims that Homestore began to engage in bogus bartering schemes in FY 2000 involving small firms (mostly dot-coms): "In the first component or 'leg' of each transaction, Homestore paid cash at an inflated price to each company in exchange for advertising and other services. In the second leg, each company recycled the cash received from Homestore back to Homestore as payment for Homestore advertising and/or services, also at inflated prices. The amount of the first leg of each transaction was almost identical to the amount of the second leg of the same transaction. Homestore then improperly recognized the inflated value as revenue on its financial statements" (*H,* 28). Homestore also began using a second sort of scheme, whereby it essentially bought revenue. In late 2000 and early 2001, it developed a third type of scheme—the triangular transactions known as round-tripping. These were the most intriguing, as they were not only more complex, but also involved prominent firms—Cendant and AOL—as well as marginal dot-coms. Moreover, the third leg was "hidden," in large part so as to deceive Homestore's auditor—Price-waterhouseCoopers—which was becoming increasingly concerned about the propriety of the firm's swaps. Once again, Homestore was transforming its own cash into revenues through phony transactions with other firms. The round-trip transactions involving AOL typically were organized as follows: In the first leg Homestore paid companies such as PurchasePro.com, WizShop.com, and Classmates Online cash "purportedly for services, technology, advertising and/or content." This first leg "was a sham transaction because Homestore received nothing of value in return"; the real purpose was "to supply money to these companies so that they could fund the third leg." "[I]n the second leg, AOL paid cash to Homestore for advertising. The third hidden leg was the bridge between these two transactions and was the 'round-trip' which was the quid pro quo for the deal. This is where the third party company used the money received from Homestore to buy advertising from AOL. . . . AOL recycled the money back to Homestore which . . . recognized the same as revenue" (*H*, 30). Such machinations generated large profits for company insiders who sold their stock options at artificially inflated prices before the scheme collapsed. In 2000 and 2001, Homestore's CEO, Stuart Wolff, sold $13.6 million of his stock; Tafeen, the vice president, sold over $12 million; and another vice president, Catherine Giffen, sold over $8 million (*H*, 163–171).

On August 13, 2003, Homestore settled the class action lawsuit by agreeing to pay $13 million in cash and to issue 20 million new shares of stock (valued at $50.6 million) to investors. The SEC has charged eleven individuals for involvement in securities fraud, and seven of these have been criminally charged (four former Homestore executives have plead guilty to criminal charges).[43] Finally, federal prosecutors are trying to line up plea agreements with Homestore executives in order to get information on AOL's possible involvement in fraudulent barter deals.[44]

The Greatest Pump and Dump of All?

The merger of AOL and Time Warner was a fitting grand finale for a decade of over-the-top deal making. It was one of those epochal events that change how we look at things, though not quite in the way that the dealmakers had imagined. Time Warner lunged toward AOL like it was the last passenger catching a rocket ship bound for the stars. As it turned out, it was more like purchasing the last berth on the *Titanic* (indeed, the whole first-class section). And the initiative was really on the part of AOL, which had embarked on the shopping trip of the century, its pockets full of New Economy currency.

The January 2000 announcement that AOL and Time Warner would merge into one company left the business world thunderstruck. Indergaard remarked, it was "the ultimate use of New Economy currency . . . [a]n Internet upstart would use its stock to buy out the world's preeminent old media power" (*I*, 113). Reactions in the business press were mixed. *The Industry Standard* termed the agreement a "bombshell" that signaled "the end of the Internet as an alternative realm outside the bonds of the traditional media."[45] The optimistic interpretation was that the marriage was "a brilliant innovation—the best of both worlds, now working in tandem." AOL had the dominant position on the Internet, while Time Warner controlled a great stock of content and a stable of media properties covering every market. A hybrid firm would bring the convergence of different media systems that New Economy pundits had predicted. However, critics wondered about the new firm's strategic course and the balance of power among two sets of executives. Placating two sets of shareholders was another issue. Indergaard noted, "The merger with an old media firm threatened AOL's New Economy pedigreed and the prospects for 'rocket-like' growth" (*I*, 134). Moreover, the merger would dilute their stock. AOL's market cap was 20 percent higher, but Time Warner shareholders would receive 1.5 shares in the new firm for every Time Warner share, while the ratio for AOL shareholders was 1 to 1. Indergaard concluded, "[T]he New Economy's biggest deal bore a big contradiction: one of its champions was taking over an old media power; yet, its leaders had agreed that its currency was worth 50 percent less than that of the old media conglomerate. Was AOL conquering new domains or cashing in while it still could?" (*I*, 134). In fact, it was Time Warner shareholders who had the most to worry about. Media critic Michael Wolf has reported that when Robert Pittman— AOL's ubersalesman and COO—had approached Viacom's Summer Redstone about a merger deal in late 1999, the seasoned chairman responded, "I really don't trust your currency." In contrast, Time Warner's chairman, Gerald Levin, was smitten with the idea of digital convergence; he reportedly believed that AOL could serve as a "super" division that could bring together Time Warner's unruly fiefdoms. Wolf proposes that Time Warner, like countless Internet start-ups, was seduced by AOL's depiction of itself as the Internet's great mall—a must location where an "anchor tenant" could have "first crack at the legendary mother lode of

AOL eyeballs."[46] AOL's pitch to investors was similar: its past success in enrolling subscribers (i.e., bringing eyeballs to the "mall") would set up its future—collecting revenues from advertisers and firms that engaged in online commerce. AOL had numbers to back up the claim: revenue from online ads and commerce had been doubling.

The Weakest Link

From the time the merger was announced, executives at AOL—and later at AOLTW—had to confront nagging doubts that hung over AOL like a dark cloud. AOL stock immediately dropped in value, from $72.75 on January 10, 2000, to $60.00 on January 12, 2000.[47] The initial concern was getting through the interim period that ran from the announcement of the merger to the time (in January 2001) when it finally closed. AOL's campaign to maintain its credibility soon encountered grave challenges, as the market for Internet advertising eroded after the spring 2000 stock crash. AOL gamely continued to forecast robust gains in revenue from online ads and commerce. At a joint meeting of the AOL and Time Warner boards in July 2000, AOL's COO, Robert Pittman, proclaimed that by 2005 he expected its ads and commerce revenues to reach $7 billion—an audacious call given that the revenues for 2000 would come in at just over $2.3 billion.[48] In October 2000, Pittman responded to concerns about the onset of an Internet advertising depression by stating, "We are benefiting from the current advertising trends of consolidation in the Internet space. It is actually good for us."[49]

In fact, the increase in revenue slowed dramatically in 2001, reaching $2.7 billion (an increase of only 14 percent); in 2002, revenue plunged by 40 percent to $1.6 billion.[50] It was hardly the only sign that the bottom was falling out. In May 2002, AOLTW stated that it would write down $54 billion in "goodwill," meaning that the corporation was admitting that the merger had been vastly overvalued; it soon wrote down another $45 billion for the ensuing quarter—primarily because of the declining value of the AOL division—meaning that the firm was declaring itself to be worth about $100 billion less than had been previously thought. The shocks for investors only kept on coming. In July 2002, the *Washington Post* began a two-article exposé on revelations of accounting improprieties at AOL; Pittman resigned the same day. In August, new CEO Richard Parsons had the embarrassing task of announcing that $49 million of the previous year's earning were suspect—specifically, revenue at AOL. In October, AOLTW reported that the amount of questionable revenue—almost all at AOL—had grown to $190 million and that it would have to restate its earnings for eight quarters in its financial statements for 2000–2002. Both the SEC and the Department of Justice had investigations under way at the firm when, in March 2003, AOL announced that it might have to make another restatement because the SEC was questioning $400 million in ad revenue that AOL had booked from German media giant Bertelsmann.[51] Moreover, the SEC's Homestore investigation had uncovered a connection: former Homestore executives told investigators that AOL executives had spoken of a "pool" of ad spending from Bertelsmann, some of which might be directed to Homestore, which, in turn, could use it to pay for more AOL service.[52]

Far from being the super division in the AOLTW empire, AOL actually turned out to be the weakest link. The financial results for the third quarter of 2002 showed that in the preceding year the cash flow for AOL Time Warner had dropped by 1 percent, but excluding the AOL division from the figures would have shown an 11 percent increase in cash flow.[53] On September 18, 2003, the board of directors voted to drop "AOL" from the AOLTW name; friends of Richard Parsons noted that the move had been considered earlier, but Parsons had been waiting for the right moment to "have the ballast of the AOL name to throw overboard."[54] The ritual sacrifice did little to calm the storm. The new Time Warner faced some forty lawsuits, including state claims by Alaska, California, Ohio, and Pennsylvania—and a federal class action suit led by the Minnesota State Board of Investments. The suits claimed that executives at AOL and AOLTW had engaged in a massive pump and dump, creating sham transactions before and after the merger so as to disguise AOL's deteriorating business and dumping millions of stocks in the same period. The revelations of improper accounting had cost investors dearly; having hit a high of $56.60 in May 2001, AOLTW's stock price had fallen to less than $17 by the time the suits were filed.

Fifty Ways to Weave a Number

The federal securities class action claimed that AOL and AOLTW *improperly pumped the revenue numbers by as much as $1.7 billion before and after the merger.* The charge of massive fraud was hard to reconcile with AOL's popular image. Unlike dot-coms in big cities that touted rebel cultures and edgy workers, AOL was a rather staid business (its home was northern Virginia) that stressed its appeal to middle-class family types. Yet, AOL had a creative streak—not to mention a dark history—when it came to

TABLE 4.2. ALLEGED TYPES OF FRAUDULENT ADVERTISING TRANSACTIONS BY AOL AND AOLTW
Improper barter or round-trip transactions Improper classification of gains as advertising revenue One-time gains in the form of contract terminations or restructuring fees Improper manipulation of advertising contracts to prematurely record revenue Improper classification of legal settlements as advertising revenue Improper recognition of advertising revenue associated with cable channel fees Improper recognition of advertising revenue in broker deal Improper inflation of advertising revenue through cross-platform deals
Source: State of Alaska v. AOL, Inc., et al., *Case No. 1JU–04–503 (Super. Ct. of Alaska, 1st District) ("Complaint").*

the numbers. In 1997, AOL had admitted that it had reported profits for several years when, in fact, it was accumulating $385 million in losses.[55] AOL chairman Steve Case promised to maintain "gold standard accounting,"[56] but a few months later AOL again was forced to restate its quarterly results—turning a profit into a loss. In 1998, the SEC caught AOL taking a large write-off up front on an acquisition—a maneuver that would have allowed it to report bigger profits for years to come.[57] And in 2000, AOL signed a settlement with the SEC pledging to follow accounting rules after several more accounting irregularities surfaced.

Thus, when the time came to set up, and then salvage, the deal of the century, AOL was well practiced in the art of making its numbers—especially revenue. Though the amount involved in the alleged frauds were a small proportion of total revenues, they involved the most strategic area of AOL's business: the online ads and commerce category that AOL held up as its future. The suits argued that AOL was relentless in trying to turn transactions of just about any type into opportunities to book revenue.

The suit by the state of Alaska, for example, outlines eight different types of "fraudulent advertising transactions" that violated GAAP (see Table 4.2). AOL's alleged "improper barter" transactions included a stunning array of deals and partners—ranging from "sixteen sham transactions" with Homestore to deals with uberswappers Qwest and World-Com. In a November 1998 deal with Sun Microsystems, AOL agreed to buy $500 million in computer equipment at full price instead of receiving the kind of discount that a large company would usually get; in return, Sun paid AOL $350 million for advertising services. In an October 1999 deal, AOL placed its Internet service on Gateway computers. Gateway was to receive a fee from AOL each time a Gateway computer purchaser signed up for the AOL service, while Gateway would pay AOL for providing a free year of Internet service. However, since the two payments were for the same amount, the firms "were simply swapping money." As a result, AOL overstated its ad revenue by $340 million in 2000 and $130 million in 2001.[58]

Sometimes the transaction was quite simple: In September 2000, for example, AOL paid Veritas Software $50 million for $30 million in software products in exchange for the software firm's purchase of $20 million in AOL advertising. In other instances, such as the $400 million Bertelsmann transaction, the deal involved a more complex situation. In March 2000, AOL and Bertelsmann worked out an agreement through which AOL could buy out Bertelsmann's 50 percent interest in AOL Europe for some $6.7 billion; the transactions resembled a derivatives deal in that it allowed AOL to choose the timing of the payments and whether to use stock or cash. Bertelsmann initially asked that AOL pay in cash, offering a $400 million discount on the sale price in exchange. AOL suggested, instead, that Bertelsmann apply the value of the discount to a $400 million purchase of advertising from AOL.[59] The Alaska suit also charged that AOL improperly classified various sorts of "gains" as advertising revenue. In a December 2000 deal, AOL paid $9.5 million in cash to PurchasePro in exchange for a repricing of stock warrants (received from PurchasePro in a marketing partnership). The repricing of the warrants from $63 to 1 cent was valued at $30 million; AOL booked the difference, $20.5 million, as "advertising and commerce revenue."[60] Another variation was AOL classification of gains from insolvent dotcoms (termination or restructuring fees) as revenues. AOL usually refrained from suing failing customers for breach of contract because it would draw attention to the fact that the base for its advertising business was withering away. Instead, AOL would restructure contracts—shortening the lengths of advertising deals and requiring the firms to pay a one-time restructuring fee. About 3 percent of AOL's advertising and commerce revenue from July 2000 through March 2001 was derived from termination or restructuring fees from Internet firms such as DrKoop.com.[61] Even in cases when AOL did win lawsuits, it negotiated deals whereby defendants purchased advertising in exchange for satisfaction of a judgment. For example, AOL offered to let Wembley PLC pay off an arbitration award by purchasing $23.8 million worth of ads for its 24dogs.com website by the end of a quarter. As the end of the quarter approached, "AOL began to run ads for Wembley's 24dogs.com site without Wembley's consent everywhere on AOL's website, even multiple ads on a single web page. The ads generated so much customer traffic that Wembley's Internet site crashed. . . . AOL booked $16.2 million of advertising revenue . . . in the quarter."[62] The improper barters continued even after the merger was completed. AOLTW used its leverage "to pressure Time Warner clients to convert cable programming purchases into purchases of online advertising with AOL"; for example, when the Golf Channel agreed to buy $200 million in advertising from Time Warner in order to have its programming run on Time Warner Cable, it was forced to spend $15 million of the advertising on AOL; similarly, AOLTW agreed to have Time Warner Cable carry the Oxygen Channel "if Oxygen would spend $100 million in advertising with AOL."[63]

A second important component in the lawsuits was the charge that top executives used inside information to dump staggering quantities of stock. A California state suit claims that top AOLTW executives earned $936 million in profits from stock sales after the merger closed—and at a time that AOLTW was buying back billions of dollars' worth of its own shares, telling investors that they were undervalued.[64] Case made $100 million selling 2 million shares of AOLTW in the four months following the closing of the merger in January 2001.[65] And Robert Pittman (the relentless promoter of AOL) had almost completely cashed in his stock by the time he resigned.

Who Got Nailed?

In May 2004, the judge in the federal class action rejected a defense motion to dismiss the complaint; legal observers have remarked that the judge's strong opinion hints that the new Time Warner—and a number of its former top executives—will be forced to make a sizeable settlement. The judge dismissed complaints against several individuals, including Steve Case, Gerald Levin, and Richard Parsons. She did stress the strength of the complaints against several former executives. First and foremost was Robert Pittman, who, the judge noted, publicly praised the strength of AOL's advertising even though he allegedly knew that it was plunging. The judge also noted: "During the class period, Pittman sold over 5.3 million shares of AOL and AOLTW stock for proceeds of over $262 million. In the four months following the merger, Pittman sold

1.5 million shares for over $72 million. As of January 31, 2002, Pittman owned just 13,388 shares of AOLTW stock."[66] Other former AOL executives whom the judge singled out included two of its top deal makers—former senior vice president David M. Colburn, who reported directly to Pittman, and former senior vice president Eric Keller. The judge commented that the nature of the transactions they allegedly organized was such as to implicate them without requiring additional evidence of intent. She also said former AOL chief financial officer J. Michael Kelly made public statements in the fall of 2000 about the strength of AOL's business that contradicted information he allegedly had concerning the deteriorating state of its advertising. Finally, the judge concluded that current Time Warner chief financial officer Wayne H. Pace allegedly overstated advertising and commerce revenue by $126 million in a July conference call with Wall Street analysts.[67]

Some anticipate that an unusually large settlement is likely—a gesture meant to send a signal of public indignation. However, the scale of the economic losses incurred in the deal/steal of the century are such that they seem sure to dwarf even a settlement of historic magnitude. On January 10, 2000 (the day the merger deal was announced), AOL's market capitalization was $189.5 billion, while that of Time Warner was $129.0 billion—a total of $318.5 billion. As of January 29, 2003, the value of AOLTW was only $62.4 billion.[68] The damage, in large part, follows the institutional channels for the so-called investor capitalism of our times. Foremost among those injured are some seventy-three thousand Time Warner employees, most of whom have seen their pensions decimated.[69] Then there are the mammoth institutional investors, including state investment plans for their employees and various other groups. The University of California and the Amalgamated Bank claimed to have lost a combined $500 million, and the Minnesota Board of Investments claimed to have lost $249 million.[70] The case of Alaska, which lost over $70 million, offers a sense of the kind of groups harmed: the funds include trusts for public employees, teachers, military personnel, mental health programs, the University of Alaska, public schools, the Exxon Valdez Oil Spill Investment, and Alaskan children.[71]

Old Boys on the Side

The webs of fraud that produced "good" numbers for not-so-good businesses had strong ties to the system for promoting New Economy candidates for IPOs. A strong case has been made that the IPO system itself was riddled with webs of fraud. A massive class action suit has charged that over three hundred firms that filed for IPOs, their top officers, and fifty-five investment banks participated in a scheme to defraud the investing public. Defendants include a half-dozen dot-coms discussed in this chapter: DrKoop.com, EarthWeb (aka Dice, Inc.), eToys, Priceline .com, PurchasePro.com, and StarMedia Networks.

The suit accused the various signers of IPO registration materials of failing to disclose key elements of the process—hidden deals that underwriters organized with what might be called "old boys on the side." The banks granted allotments of initial offerings of hot stocks—typically underpriced—to institutional investors or business notables who were important customers in exchange for their implicit agreement to purchase investment banking business or to participate in follow-up offerings of the stock—a hidden *tie-in* that provided *undisclosed compensation* to the banks and also resulted in the *manipulation of market prices.*[72]

In June 2003, the 309 companies that issued the stock in the IPOs offered to settle the suit with a payment of $1 billion in an agreement that had several contingencies. The firms would end up not actually paying anything if the investors won a settlement of at least $1 billion from the underwriters—a group that includes Goldman Sachs, Morgan Stanley, and Credit Suisse First Boston. The proposed settlement might provide the firms with an incentive to assist in the lawsuit against the underwriters.[73]

The settlement offer came several months after the judge ruled against a motion to dismiss the case, leaving the bulk of the charges intact. That opinion is significant, in part because it refutes an argument that many Silicon Valley interests (and their investment bankers) had made: the "spinning" of IPOs was so common in the 1990s that it became a normal business practice. In contrast, the judge concluded that the "scheme" alleged by the plaintiffs "offends the very purpose of the securities law": "When insiders conspire to frustrate the efficient function of securities markets by exploiting their position of privilege, they have perpetuated a double fraud: they have manipulated the market, and they have covered up that manipulation with lies and omissions."[74] In drawing boundaries for permissible behavior in IPOs, the judge implicitly upheld a line of argument (and enforcement actions) that the SEC had made for some four decades about fraudulent behavior during "hot issues." The foundation the SEC gave for its view was that "a fundamental purpose" of the Securities Exchange Act of 1934 "was to substitute a philosophy of full disclosure for the philosophy of caveat emptor."[75] A special study by the SEC in 1963 noted that severe underpricing and undersupply of shares in IPOs—along with tie-ins—were tactics "encouraging the speculative climate."[76] A 1984 SEC report reviewing earlier episodes of market manipulation during "hot issues" (1959–1962, 1967–1971, and 1979–1983) concluded that "abusive sales and trading practices . . . clearly violate the federal securities laws."[77]

The IPO class action suit interprets earlier "hot issues" as involving attempts to turn hot stocks into "currencies." It also noted the conflicted position of "issuers" that participate in schemes that underprice their own stock. On the one hand, "under pricing itself is not all good for the issuer—in one sense there was 'money left on the table.'"[78] On the other hand, when an underpriced hot issue creates a frenzy, the issuer benefits "from the false impression that the company is so highly valued. The issuer then exploits the impression by using its stock as currency to make acquisitions, or by raising more capital through a higher-priced secondary offering."[79] In the next chapter we will propose that another possible consideration weighed heavily on the thinking of dot-com hopefuls—that "going along" with the IPO gambit circa 1999 was a quid pro quo for a firm to gain access to the IPO circuit.

CHAPTER FIVE

Professional Pumpsters
and Financial Engineers
Looking at the Bright Side (Banking on the Dark Side)

What used to be a conflict is now a synergy. Someone like me,
who is banking-intensive, would have been looked at disdainfully
by the buy side 15 years ago. Now, they know that I'm in the flow
of what's going on.
— Jack Grubman, telecom analyst, Salomon Smith Barney

A merica's love affair with the dot-coms had come crashing to a
halt a few months earlier, but it was still the summer of love for
other New Economy players on the make. Witness the flirta-
tious e-mail exchanges between Frank Quattrone, a Credit Suisse First
Boston (CSFB) banker, and Michael Dell (founder of Dell Computers)
as they discussed the prospects for a "relationship" in July 2000. Two

days before the IPO of Corvis (an optical networking company), Quattrone sent an e-mail to Dell: "My team has gotten word to me that you are personally interested in having Dell Ventures receive a meaningful allotment of the I.P.O. of Corvis. Given the intense interest in this space we anticipate this will be a complete zoo, so I wanted to check if your interest was really there." In fact, what Quattrone was checking out was whether Dell was willing to return the favor if he received an allotment of stock in a hot IPO. He went on to ask Dell if he was available to be the keynote speaker at a CSFB technology conference, an annual gathering for heads of tech companies. Escalating things a bit, he asked if Dell thought that CSFB should hire a certain analyst to cover personal computer makers (Dell is the largest). Dell responded with some relationship talk, but played hard to get, wanting to see how serious his suitor was: "We would like 250 [thousand] shares of Corvis. I know there [have] been efforts on both sides to build the relationship and an offering like this would certainly help." He noted that he would be willing to speak at the tech conference but only if his "investor relations" team "wants him to go" and "they may be waiting to see who your PC analyst is." He added that the proposed analyst was not appealing. A second e-mail to Quattrone—this time by Michael Dell's "personal investments manager"—asked again for an allotment of Corvis stock, and hinted that CSFB will get some action in return. "We are looking forward to making you our 'Go To' banker. We . . . ask for a little help as it is a sincere interest for us."[1] Dell did receive his allotment and was in a position to make a big personal profit. The offering price for the IPO was $36 a share; it opened at $95 and rose to $98. Yet, promises made in the heat of the moment are not always kept. Dell Computers never became a banking client for CSFB. But lest we worry about Frank Quattrone's pain, we should consider that he usually got lucky in his relationships—very lucky. For shepherding 138 IPOs between 1998 and 2000, he made $200 million.[2]

Quattrone's good fortune was due to the fact that the power attached to his formal position in the CSFB hierarchy was greatly amplified by the position he held as an intermediary within a web of relationships that linked start-ups, institutional investors, and the various arms of investment banking. In New Economy deal-making, as in love, "relationships" were a most serious matter, implying understandings, commitments, and obligations. And though, as in many illicit affairs, such things are not necessarily to be taken at face value, they can be of great significance, materially as well as symbolically.

In this chapter we explore why business professionals knowingly went along with organized deceptions. This takes us once again to the question of what happened to the rules and what were the participants in the New Economy scandals thinking? We focus on the development of "normalized corruption" across New Economy networks as well as within individual organizations. We will show nuances in how these rules operated in organizing fraud by focusing on how they were reinforced by material interests and the exercise of power—including not only the kind of power tango that Quattrone and Dell engaged in, but also bald coercion. Finally, we will make the case that in these networks of normalized corruption, power and knowledge were distributed, but not to the point that accountability disappeared, for there were multiple centers where strategically positioned actors took lead roles in orchestrating deceptions.

Our first task is to outline how regulation of business professionals was weakened as politicians joined a bipartisan chorus singing praises for deregulation—and even top regulators became cheerleaders for the high-wire acts of the New Economy.

Friends in High Places

Neoliberal policies, free market ideology, and "soft" corruption of politicians compromised the highest levels of regulation, creating criminogenic conditions for various business professionals with roles in corporate governance. While public regulators were hamstrung by deregulation or by political obstructions, the highest reaches of "self-regulation"—lacking serious government oversight—deteriorated into venues for the promotion of financial interests and for the enrichment of those who brokered the system. When entities such as the Financial Accounting Standards Board (FASB), the independent organization that sets accounting guidelines, did try to make good faith efforts, they were undermined by political allies of industry.

The Best Congress Money Can Buy
The first wave of market-oriented policies that changed the landscape for financial analysts and accountants specifically were actually antitrust actions in the 1970s involving financial analysts at big investment banks and auditing by large accounting firms. Our later discussions of these areas will show that promoting price competition—and a market mentality—among reputational intermediaries ended up producing unan-

ticipated problems in the realm of corporate governance. The key matter of interest here is that Congress blocked the efforts of regulators to respond to emerging problems—and made the situation worse. The issue of accounting for stock options is one of the most grievous examples.

Prior to the 1990s, when the awarding of stock options to corporate executives was a relatively uncommon practice, how this form of compensation was accounted for on a company's books was a technical accounting issue that had little impact on corporate balance sheets. However, in the nineties, as executive salaries grew to astronomical levels, more and more corporations began to reward their high-level employees with significant numbers of shares, to the point where for many companies, particularly start-up New Economy firms, a significant proportion of their outstanding shares were held by their own employees. Now the way companies accounted for options could substantially impact their balance sheets. Existing accounting standards created a "heads-I-win-tails-you-lose" situation for corporations by allowing them not to charge stock options as expenses against earnings, as is the situation for other forms of compensation, while at the same time permitting companies to deduct them from their taxes. The result was a giant loophole that allowed corrupt corporations to deceive investors by artificially inflating their earnings and to transfer wealth from investors to corporate insiders, all the while reducing the companies' tax liabilities. By the end of the decade, these practices had become widespread in corporate America. A study conducted by Merrill Lynch estimated that in the year 2001, if companies in the S&P 500 had treated stock options as expenses, their earnings would have been 21 percent lower than reported. Among firms in the information technology sector the problem was even worse; 2001 earnings would have dropped by 39 percent had options been expensed.[3] The problem is well illustrated by eBay, a dot-com success story, whose total reported net income for 1998–2003 would have gone from $840 million to just $13 million had stock options been recorded as expenses.[4] As one might expect, the Enron Corporation was a master at this game. Between 1996 and 2000, Enron failed to subtract $600 million in stock options from a total of $1.8 billion it reported as earnings on its financial statements, while, at the same time, it deducted those options from its tax liability—a strategy that helped the corporation pay *no* taxes in four out of five of those years.[5]

FASB set off a firestorm in 1995 when it proposed requiring companies to deduct stock options from their earnings on their financial statements. The logic behind their proposal was straightforward and persuasive: stock options were costly to companies and should be treated as an expense just like other forms of compensation. FASB's proposed policy change met with immediate and forceful opposition from several quarters. Large corporations that had gotten into the habit of handing out stock options were, not unexpectedly, critical of the proposal. But the loudest criticisms came from Silicon Valley and the dot-com firms that often used their own stock as a form of currency. Well-established as part of the New Economy mythology were tales of early employees at companies such as Microsoft and Netscape who received stock and later became multimillionaires after the stock's value skyrocketed. The idea also fit into the contrived egalitarianism espoused by dot-coms wherein stock options made even the lowliest employee an "owner" of the company.[6] So engrained were stock options in the Silicon Valley culture that when FASB held hearings in San Francisco on its proposal, rallies were held nearby, attended by hundreds of dot-com employees who chanted slogans such as "Keep our stock options alive."[7] The principal argument was that stock options helped companies attract talent in the start-up phase, when they had little cash with which to pay for it.[8]

In Washington, Congress moved quickly to block FASB's proposed change to the accounting rules on stock options in a campaign led by Senator Joseph Lieberman. In 1995, Lieberman introduced a resolution that condemned the proposal. Speaking on the Senate floor, he advanced the dot-com industry's position: "What's on the line here really is the future of jobs in this country."[9] The resolution passed overwhelmingly with support from several prominent members of Congress. The FASB backed down after these figures threatened to shut the agency down if it continued to pursue its new policy on stock options.[10]

How a reasonable proposal intended to help investors by requiring companies to be clear and honest on their financial statements was stopped in its tracks well illustrates the forces that determined financial policies in the United States in the 1990s. It represents a case study in the exercise of political muscle by corporate America. As one person close to the scene described it, "It was one of the most impressive lobbying efforts on earth. It was protecting CEO's pay packages. . . . They were out in force."[11] And the means they used to get politicians to do their bidding for them was, as usual, campaign contributions.

While the demise of the FASB proposal left investors more vulnerable to deception when they were deciding on which companies to invest in, at roughly the same time, investors' options to take actions after they realized they'd been deceived were greatly limited by the courts and

Congress. In 1994, the Supreme Court issued a ruling that reversed a longtime legal standard, based on an interpretation of the Securities and Exchange Act of 1934, that gave shareholders the right to sue accountants, lawyers, and bankers who "aided and abetted" corporate executives in the commission of securities fraud.[12] While the SEC could still file suits against "aiders and abettors," the ruling effectively shielded accountants and lawyers from shareholder lawsuits in cases where their clients were the principal offenders. Frank Partnoy comments that requiring plaintiffs to show that "advisors" were "primarily liable" was "much more difficult to do"; the 5–4 decision "was a radical decision, and the Supreme Court largely ignored hundreds of judicial and administrative proceedings over sixty years."[13]

Investors were dealt an even more serious blow the next year, when a Republican-controlled Congress passed the Private Securities Litigation Reform Act (PSRLA) of 1995. The act, whose backers claimed it would reduce "frivolous lawsuits that unfairly torture corporations and their accountants," placed significant obstacles in front of shareholders' suits by significantly raising the evidentiary standards for such suits, placing limits on the amounts of damages that could be recovered, and making plaintiffs responsible for defense costs if any of their allegations turned out to be untrue.[14] Opponents of the bill argued that had it been in effect in the late 1980s, many of the investors who purchased junk bonds from S&L crook Charles Keating would not have been able to recover their life savings.[15] When he vetoed the bill (later overridden by Congress), President Clinton stated that the law would have the effect "of closing the courthouse door on investors who have legitimate claims."[16]

In the passage of the Private Securities Litigation Reform Act, one sees the interests of the accounting industry, high-tech companies, and conservative political ideologues converging at a politically opportune moment. Since the 1980s, when accounting firms were hit with hundreds of millions of dollars in lawsuits stemming from the S&L crisis, the industry had been looking for a legislative curb on investor suits.[17] Their efforts were stalled until 1994, when a wave of conservative Republicans were voted into Congress vowing allegiance to Speaker Newt Gingrich and his Contract with America, which proposed, among other things, legislation to limit "strike suits" (lawsuits filed unexpectedly after a company's stock price drops) that "are money-makers for lawyers," but are "frivolous claims" that "destroy jobs and hurt the economy."[18] At the same time, high-tech companies, particularly those located in Silicon Valley, were beginning to flex their political muscles and complaining about the effects of strike suits on their profits. These arguments were voiced by industry representatives who complained of "professional plaintiffs" and "predatory attorneys" who were "stalking" the high-tech industry.[19] The complaints were repeated by one of PSRLA's congressional sponsors, Representative Chris Cox of California, who referred to the trial bar as a "national scandal of corruption" and lawsuits on behalf of shareholders as "legalized extortion."[20]

The accounting industry was particularly vocal in its support of the Private Securities Litigation Reform Act, claiming that there was an "epidemic" of class action suits aimed at accounting firms. Industry representatives portrayed the situation in cataclysmic terms, casting lawsuits and the lawyers who filed them as the forces of evil that threatened to bring the entire economy to a standstill. The CEO for one of the big six accounting firms told Congress: "Just as the doctors stopped delivering babies, they couldn't take the risk any longer, we are rapidly approaching our equivalent situation: the unwillingness to bring to market the engines of commerce, the job creators, the emerging growth companies. To me it is almost un-American to deny services and therefore access to the capital markets to these companies that are so vital to the economy. . . . Yet, it is the inevitable consequence of a system that seeks to hold us liable as deep-pocket guarantors of their financial success."[21] However, the number of class action securities lawsuits filed had not increased during the early nineties. As Representative Edward Markey pointed out in hearings he chaired in 1994, "There has been no explosion in securities fraud litigation in the past 20 years. . . . The figures for the early 1990s are remarkably similar to the numbers for the early 1970s."[22] A number of observers have argued that the changes brought about by the Private Securities Litigation Reform Act had the effect of encouraging executives to commit fraud by removing the threat of sanctions that would have otherwise deterred their behavior.[23]

The effect of this changed regulatory environment was to "define deviancy down" in the corporate world, to loosen standards so that conduct once considered to be harmful and that once violated widely accepted norms of conduct in the business community were now deemed as acceptable and routine business practices. The concept of defining deviancy down was first proposed by senator and sociologist Patrick Moynihan, who applied concepts borrowed from nineteenth-century French sociologist Emile Durkheim to argue that "we have been re-defining deviancy so as to exempt much conduct previously stigmatized, and also quietly raising the 'normal' level in categories where behavior is abnormal by an earlier standard."[24] Moynihan applied his idea primarily to violent street crime. More recently, New York Attorney General Eliot Spitzer has suggested that a similar process was at work in the corporate community in the nineties where one sees a "pattern of tolerance for impropriety over time that ultimately debased the standards we lived by."[25] In other words, the relaxation of formal standards and the reduction in the legal liability of business professionals contributed to a change in the cultural norms that govern behavior on Wall Street, in the offices of accounting firms, and in corporate boardrooms. As Lynn Turner, the former chief accountant at the SEC, told an interviewer: "It's a symptom of something larger. It's beyond Enron; it's beyond Andersen. It's embedded in the system at this time. . . . There has been a change in culture that arose out of the go-go times of the 1990s. Some people call it greed. But I think it is an issue where we got a lot of financial conflicts built into the system, and people forgot, quite frankly, about the investors."[26]

Defenders of the Faith

The first Clinton administration witnessed the growing influence of financial sector regulators who were advocates of free markets and industry self-regulation. The most notable case was a holdover from a previous administration, Federal Reserve chairman Allan Greenspan. Greenspan's power and status steadily climbed. He even gained something of a charismatic aura because of a growing perception that he had a special ability to understand and influence the mysterious forces of the market. His power increased as he took the role of a behind-the-scenes crisis manager, and Democrats joined conservatives in giving him free rein to set monetary policy.[27] But more generally, the shift in regulatory tone was due to the influence of financial industry political contributions and lobbying.

To start, Clinton, who had received strong financial backing from Wall Street, appointed two Wall Street veterans to top regulatory posts: Robert Rubin, the former co-chairman of Goldman Sachs, became secretary of the treasury, and Arthur Levitt Jr., a former stockbroker and president of the American Stock Exchange, was made director of the SEC. Although by the end of the 1990s Levitt became known as the lonely voice warning of growing reliance of firms on financial deception, Partnoy shows that early on Levitt tended to advocate self-regulation when abuses arose. This is apparent in the responses made by Congress and regulators to a serious crisis in 1994 involving financial derivatives (the crisis in which Orange County went bankrupt and many firms, mutual funds, and other institutional investors had huge losses on derivatives because of an unexpected rise in the interest rate). Although there was momentum for regulating derivatives, the industry lobby mounted a fierce campaign to turn back the effort; moreover, in the strategic 1994–1995 period, Congress, the Supreme Court, and regulators made a counterintuitive response, as they greatly weakened the liability of the business professionals who advise corporations. When the General Accounting Office recommended that derivatives be regulated, the industry lobby, Levitt, and other top financial regulators opposed it, endorsing industry self-regulation instead.

Providing a hint of a stance that was to dominate the rest of the decade, the derivatives industry association aggressively challenged whether skeptics understood the new practices. It tried to intimidate congressmen and the media by questioning their credibility and competence in the area. It went so far as to bully newspapers such as the *Wall Street Journal* from even using the word "derivative" in its reports about financial problems.[28] While some suggested this was a case of market failure that required regulatory redress, Greenspan reiterated in his 1995 testimony to Congress that his faith lay in market fundamentals rather than in regulation: "It would be a serious mistake to respond to these developments by singling out derivative instruments for special regulatory treatment. Such a response would create artificial incentives to structure transactions on the basis of regulatory rules rather than of the economic characteristics of the transactions themselves."[29] The derivatives industry lobby also received support from Wendy Gramm, the former head of the Commodities Futures Trading Commission (CFTC) who had helped deregulate swaps in the energy industry before leaving her position to become a member of the Enron board. In an opinion piece in the *Wall Street Journal,* she reiterated the industry line about those who don't get it: "[W]e must all resist the urge to . . . over-regulate what we just do not understand."[30] Levitt joined in, giving a speech to fifteen hundred mutual funds executives in May 1994 in which he stated that the SEC did not have enough resources to regulate mutual funds and instead blamed the funds for their losses with derivatives: "in the final analysis, compliance is the principle responsibility, not of the . . . [SEC], but of each investment company."[31] However, when an industry body did try to take a principled stand—namely, the FASB accounting reform proposals—Levitt caved in to the pressure of lobbyists from the big accounting firms and Silicon Valley tech firms.

The more general pattern evident in this period is the attempt of industry interests and their allies in Congress and among regulators to try to police policy discourse so that it became difficult to articulate anything but a deregulatory position. Partnoy provides a graphic illustration involving Wendy Gramm's successor at the CFTC. When she suggested that "government should at least study whether some regulation might make sense, a stampede of lobbyists, members of Congress, and other regulators—including Alan Greenspan and Robert Rubin—ran her over, admonishing her to keep quiet."[32] Of course, by the end of the decade Arthur Levitt became, it seemed, the lone voice in the wilderness, warning of excesses in the stock market and counseling that inadequacies in the regulation of areas such as accounting had turned much of the corporate economy into a "numbers game." But by then it was difficult for his warnings to take hold. They did not fit into the dominant framework through which people interpreted economic developments—a framework that placed unquestioning faith in markets and gloried in the wonders of a "New Economy."

The President of Capitalism (Grasso Rules)

When the New York Stock Exchange reopened at 9:30 A.M. on the Monday after the 9/11 attacks on the World Trade Center, a national television audience saw a moving scene as the exchange observed two minutes of silence in tribute to the victims and then joined in to sing "God Bless America." Though the familiar balcony (where the opening and closing bell is rung) was filled with political notables, including New York senators Charles Schumer and Hillary Clinton, the television coverage opened with a shot of a little bald man with his head bowed, and then joining the floor in singing. The man was Richard Grasso, the chairman and CEO of the NYSE, and his prominence in what seemed a national ritual was not so surprising when one considered that he was the one who made the rules at the NYSE—and it was he who had orchestrated the reopening ceremony. In fact, the NYSE was the only exchange that refused to cooperate with the SEC's effort to coordinate the reopening of all the exchanges, because Grasso wanted to have two minutes of silence followed by "God Bless America."[33] It could be argued that Grasso outranked everybody else on the balcony. He was, after all, known as the

"President of Capitalism."[34] As it turned out, he was paid more like a king; his 2003 contract specified that he would immediately receive $139.5 million and be paid another $48 million over the next four years, for a total of over $187 million.

Even before news of Grasso's high pay broke in August 2003, institutional investors had been unhappy with the NYSE governance system and its trading practices. As the details of Grasso's pay package gradually trickled out, the NYSE board, dominated by CEOs of Wall Street firms, became the center of a firestorm of controversy, as the NYSE was a non-profit body that was supposed to be a regulatory mainstay for the financial industry. For many observers, the pay fiasco highlighted the contradiction of depending on self-regulation by the financial industry and, more generally, the shortcomings of corporate boards as governance mechanisms. Grasso resigned his post on September 17, 2003.

The NYSE's role as a regulator was conflicted with its market "interest" as a competitor with other exchanges, especially the NASDAQ. When Grasso became CEO in 1995, his bonus was tied to the "market" share of stocks listed, which was of economic importance for the exchange and its trading specialists. Grasso was quite successful in this area; the NYSE's share of the nation's stock trading increased from 70 percent in 1995 to 90 percent in 2003. More than half of the companies that are listed there were added during his tenure.[35] In fact, Grasso was more of a high-octane marketer than a regulator. He was able to get celebrities to join him in ringing the opening bell each morning, and during the late 1990s this ceremony was often a routine part of network newscasts (the backdrop when the day's Wall Street "numbers" were reviewed). The *New York Times* commented that the NYSE became the symbol of the New Economy and "an American icon . . . a symbol of the kind of capitalism that can produce wealth for everyone, not just the high-born."[36] Former SEC chairman Arthur Levitt Jr. noted that Grasso worked hard to fuse the imagery of capitalism and nationalism: "[Grasso] has waved the flag often enough to persuade investors and the world and public opinion that the NYSE is an American icon."[37] Moreover, Grasso had a flair for getting "out in front of a company," helping it gain credibility; as a result, the NYSE became a showcase for IPOs.[38] And the NYSE spent a great deal in a marketing campaign in which it stated that firms which were listed on it had met governance standards that "are amongst the highest in the world." A NYSE official noted the pitch is an "important part of the [NYSE] brand."[39]

However, critics claim that Grasso did little to enforce good governance. For example, he invited Citigroup's CEO, Sandy Weill, to join the board as a representative of the public just after Citigroup had agreed to pay $325 million to settle an investigation into conflicts of interest involving its research analysts (after an explosion of criticism, Weill withdrew).[40] The *New York Times* stated that Grasso operated the NYSE through "intimidation and an old-fashioned favors system" in a manner that "resembled the dealings of a 19th-century ward boss."[41] When he did wield the exchange's regulatory power, it often seemed to benefit a close associate. A floor trader reported, "[D]ifferent rules at different times seemed to be the order of the day. Grasso rules."[42]

John Reed, the interim head of the NYSE, and New York State Attorney General Eliot Spitzer have both launched investigations of how it was that the NYSE board came to award Grasso such a lucrative pay package. Reed has demanded that Grasso return to the exchange $120 million. Spitzer has filed suit, claiming that the level of Grasso's pay violated a state law on compensation for officers in nonprofits and that Grasso violated his fiduciary duties in accepting it. Among other things, the state complaint also charges that Grasso was able to exert improper influence on the process through which his compensation was decided. In part, the complaint places the blame on "conflicts of interest" that were created by "the NYSE's governance structure and Grasso's regulatory authority over the NYSE's Directors."[43] The complaint noted past instances when Grasso had exerted pressure on members of the board's compensation committee or, conversely, came to the assistance of board members when their firms had problems with NYSE units or regulators. For example, in 2002 Grasso called the head of the National Association of Securities Dealers on behalf of Kenneth Langone (a member of the compensation committee and close friend) when the NASD investigated IPO allocations by Lanone's investment bank. The state also charged that conflicts of interest caused Grasso to "take no regulatory action when confronted with evidence of fraud relating to the equity research analysis being offered by many of the largest NYSE member firms."[44] The complaint proposed that Grasso knew of the fraud because he attended a series of meetings on the issue from November 2001 through early 2002 called by Harvey Pitt (then SEC chairman) that were attended by representatives of Citigroup, Merrill Lynch, CFSB, Goldman Sachs, and Morgan Stanley. It suggests that Grasso's inaction was due to the fact that two of the bank representatives were on the NYSE compensation committee while a third was on the board that would vote on compensation packages. During the span when the meetings with Pitt were being held, the NYSE compensation committee awarded Grasso $30.6 million in compensation for 2001.[45]

This amount, and the pay packet agreed to in 2003, far exceeded the amount that he would have received if the regular formula for setting his pay had been used.[46] Still, a number of prominent friends have spoken strongly in Grasso's defense. First and foremost is Kenneth Langone, the founder of Home Depot, who is reportedly worth $1 billion— and the member of the NYSE compensation committee who is thought to have been instrumental in setting up the pay agreement. His first line of defense is that Grasso cannot be faulted for an agreement that the compensation committee and the board voted to accept. Furthermore, he argues that Grasso was worth the money. While the CEO of Merrill Lynch, for example, received $28 million a year for running a firm, Grasso "ran the fountainhead of capitalism in America."[47] Furthermore, he and some prominent friends hint that Grasso was a national hero for helping the NYSE reopen after 9/11. Rudy Giuliani commented, "Grasso got the NYSE up and operating without a glitch. When billions are made, you get rewarded." Ross Perot proposed that Grasso's pay level was commensurate with his celebrity standing: "What about Elvis, Michael Jackson, and A-Rod?"[48]

Deal Teams and the Celebration Circuit

Swarms of veteran executives, newly minted MBAs, and professionals of various stripes swarmed toward the sweet spots of the New Economy in the second half of the 1990s. Though the hodgepodge character of the recruits assembling might bring to mind some sort of disorderly mob, a great many embarked on the crusade precisely because their "calling" was to help bring order in the midst of flux and upheaval. Hundreds of young consultants left McKinsey & Company to follow in the footsteps of Jeffrey Skilling, though the path to glory for most led to dot-coms and venture capital firms.[49] The army that joined the dot-com cause included a sizeable financial brigade, some of whom had held a high rank in the old economy. For example, Robert Lessin, the vice chairman of Salomon Smith Barney, began acting as an investor and consultant to dot-coms in 1997 and then resigned his banking position in 1998 to work full-time on Internet business. The trickle from Wall Street became a flood as dot-coms began a sensational run in the market for IPOs in 1998. By late 1999, Wall Street investment banks were hit by an exodus of bankers who left to join Internet firms (often as chief financial officers).[50] Tagging along with the investment bankers and their financial analysts were yet more professional "carriers" of new business sensibilities and models—accountants and lawyers, who were inclined to also act as consultants.

Another participant that contributed mightily to the efforts to make sense of it all was a new financial media. At the larger level, there seemed to be a new structural relationship between the media and the financial industries. In his book on the new media, *Silicon Alley,* Indergaard comments that "as the cultural and financial industries have become interwoven in a 'symbolic' economy, the content of cultural industries increasingly concerns financial news and commentary while the financial sector has taken on the structure of certain cultural industries."[51] More concretely, firms that wanted to become "hits" in the stock market— either through IPOs or by finding other means to gain a reputation as a "growth" firm—had to make a successful entree into "a new circuit of media coverage and commentary."[52] *Business Week* referred to this circuit as the "Wall Street Hype Machine" and noted that Wall Street's unprecedented interest in advertising dovetailed with the rise of the new financial media; coverage of finance was being transformed by the proliferation of cable television outlets and personal finance sites on the Internet.[53] Some of these journalists attained celebrity status, as did a number of the Wall Street financial analysts who made regular appearances on their programs. For example, Merrill Lynch analyst Henry Blodget appeared on television seventy-six times in 1999 and forty-six times in 2000, often on CNBC and CNN.[54]

Importantly, almost all reputational intermediaries had material interests in participating in New Economy circuits of financial commentary and analysis. For the media, New Economy firms were a lucrative source of advertising, while insiders (i.e., financial analysts, executives) were also an important source of content for stories. Financial analysts had an interest in supporting the business of their investment banks, as their success in this area influenced their compensation, standing at work, and public reputation. The investment banks themselves had an interest in boosting the reputation (and finances) of client firms so as to maximize the fees they received. Accounting firms hoped to win more lucrative consulting business at the firms they audited.

For our purposes, two kinds of settings were important as sites for assorted executives and professionals to come together to pursue these material interests: teams of "professional pumpsters" who sought to directly boost the values of stocks and teams of financial engineers who sought to affect stock prices indirectly through manipulating financial results. The latter includes, for example, "cross-disciplinary teams of lawyers, accountants, and investment bankers" that aided Enron in creating "Rube-Goldberg–like transactions"—the structured-finance deals it used to manipulate its balance sheets.[55] Sites of stock promotion and financial engineering were strategic points for incorporating diverse actors into normalized corruption.

Friends of Frank

Perhaps no figure better exemplifies the conflicts of interest inherent in a system that relied on inside connections between the tech and financial sectors than Frank Quattrone, the New Economy's preeminent power banker who possessed a unique ability to broker relations between Silicon Valley and Wall Street. According to *Business Week,* Quattrone was "an architect of Silicon Valley's financial culture."[56] His stature reportedly grew to the point that "his web of interwoven dealings . . . underpinned the Internet economy."[57]

Quattrone joined Morgan Stanley and set up an office in San Francisco in 1981—the first representative of a major investment bank to do so. He was reportedly a "world-class schmoozer" who took the geeks on ski trips to Utah and showed up at their watering holes to sing karaoke. The insights and relationships he developed helped him to become involved in some of the biggest IPOs—including Silicon Graphics and Cisco Systems—as network computing took off. In 1995, he managed the Netscape IPO—the event that thrust the Internet, and a heating up market for tech stocks, into the public consciousness.

It appears that out of that happy accident, Quattrone rediscovered one of the favorite games of investment banking—manipulating "hot issues." In doing so, he had a singular role in developing the signature investment banking practices of the New Economy. He pushed Morgan Stanley to give him control over its research arm—the unit that housed financial analysts. Up to this time, research had been kept separate from investment banking so as to avoid conflicts of interest. When Morgan Stanley turned him down, he departed, taking along eight coworkers to set up a new tech banking unit at Deutsche Bank Securities (which granted his request). Within two years he moved to CSFB.

At CSFB, Quattrone received an astonishing compensation package—he and his team would get 33 percent of the revenue they brought in over their quota ($150 million). In 1999, his unit produced $600 million in revenues, meaning that he had almost $150 million to distribute among his close associates. In addition, they also were collecting profits on the personal investments that they were able to make in venture capital firms or start-ups. The position of power that Quattrone was given at CSFB was equally amazing (and had a lot to do with the amount of revenue he was able to generate). The heads of three key units all reported to him—investment banking, research, and private-client services. When Quattrone or some of his associates wanted to woo a CEO for the right to manage his IPO, they could take a dream team with them: "investment bankers to talk about how much money they could bring in, analysts to show off their knowledge of the competitive landscape, and client-services people to offer up a menu of personal investment services. In other cases, commercial bankers were brought along to discuss raising debt."[58] The clincher was the same enticement offered in the courtship of Michael Dell—allotments of stock in upcoming IPOs. CSFB created more than three hundred accounts for "Friends of Frank" who were eligible for IPO allotments in the hope that they might reciprocate by giving CSFB some banking business.[59]

The system of IPO allotments set off a number of investigations by federal and state authorities. As we saw at the end of the last chapter, one of the allegations—made in the class action suit—is that the special arrangements for allocating shares in IPOs and the compensation that underwriting banks received was not disclosed. Another allegation, which has been the subject of both SEC and criminal investigations, is whether the allocations represent a form of kickback. One damning type of evidence are claims that smaller institutional investors and wealthy individuals who would not normally generate enough investment banking fees to receive IPO allocations did receive allocations in return for paying commissions equal to a certain percentage of the profits they had made on the IPO. CSFB salespeople would remind people if the amount of banking fees they had paid was too paltry relative to the IPO gains they had realized. For example, a trader at a hedge fund reported that a CSFB salesman told him, "'You've made $2 million in IPO profits, but you've paid us $500,000 in commissions.' They were saying, 'Listen, can you step it up?'"[60]

As the federal government and New York attorney general launched investigations of Quattrone's role in IPO allocations, *Business Week* reported that a host of his Silicon Valley "friends" have risen to his defense, claiming that he "is taking the fall for an ambiguous regulatory system that failed to restrain behavior that became commonplace as markets and investors stampeded out of control."[61] Perhaps the more important point is that other banks adopted the tactics that Quattrone pioneered to the point that they became seen as normal business practices. In fact, there was reportedly a sense that Silicon Valley itself was on trial, since many of the practices that have come under critical scrutiny as a result of the New Economy scandals actually originated in Silicon Valley. A business professor at St. Clara University commented that the legal attention challenges "the Silicon Valley culture of friendships, networking and partnerships," with the heart of the concern being the fact that "an extra portion of the wealth created is directed to insiders."[62] *Business Week* stressed that the same relationships which contribute to the innovative prowess of Silicon Valley are highly susceptible to conflicts of interest. The system "locks together the interests of venture capitalists, bankers, lawyers, and entrepreneurs. . . . This sharing of information and advice often improves the performance of companies and hastens innovations to market. Yet the system creates conflicts of interest. Even now, lawyers continue to talk equity and sit on the boards of client companies. Banks still invest in startups they take public. And tech executives still get rich off the money they sink into their venture backer's funds."[63] In the wake of the New Economy scandals, one chairman of a software firm commented, "We can no longer think we're this cute little outlaw place were we make our own rules."[64] However, one suspects he is in the minority, given the vehemence with which Silicon Valley interests have continued to lobby to protect certain accounting rules that facilitated countless abuses in the 1990s.[65] In connection with a federal investigation of IPO allocations, Quattrone was criminally charged with obstruction of justice.[66] He allegedly sent an e-mail to his CSFB employees on December 5, 2000, urging them to purge their files because he wanted to prevent federal investigators from seeing this evidence. A first trial ended in a mistrial, even though Quattrone seemed to undermine his own credibility by maintaining that he did not make allocations of IPO stock.

However, Frank Quattrone's luck may have finally run out. In a second trial, he was found guilty of obstructing justice.

There's Something About Mary

Given the buzz set off by the Telecom Act, 1996 was a propitious time for a nice young woman with a vision to do big things—for example, to set off a crusade to commercialize the Internet and, in the process, vanquish the old economic order. So it was that Mary Meeker, a Morgan Stanley financial analyst, became the "Queen of the Net" (as *Barrons* dubbed her). What Meeker could see that others could not was a path by which Internet start-ups could become not only commercially viable, but also transformative forces in the economy more generally. A 1996 report that she wrote with a research assistant—*The Internet Report*—proved to be a major theoretical tract, packed with ideas that would become core tenets in New Economy doctrine. In his book *Dot.con,* John Cassidy observes that Meeker drew much of her inspiration from having participated in the Netscape IPO. That IPO had prototyped a new way of financing firms. As Cassidy puts it, "[T]he days were gone when start-up firms had to spend years building up a track record of profitability before going public. In the post-Netscape world, stock market investors were willing to play the role of venture capitalists, funding companies much earlier in their development in the hope of making high returns."[67] Meeker proposed that the Internet pioneers would have a similar experience to that of Bill Gates: the Internet, like the personal computer, would end up in every home, and the Internet firms who moved first could potentially reap the same kind of financial reward. It followed, Meeker argued, that a different set of criteria was appropriate for determining the value of an Internet stock—not the standard one of current earnings, but some measure of its potential. What mattered, then, was some indication of the firm's success in grabbing market share—for example, the number of subscribers that AOL enrolled. Cassidy notes that Wall Street gleefully picked up the argument to use in justifying the stunning prices that were being paid for Internet stocks—which is how analysts ended up measuring things like "eyeballs" (i.e., website traffic).[68]

Some one hundred thousand copies of *The Internet Report* circulated around the United States, and it ended up being published as a book. This helped establish Meeker as a national figure, as did the connections that she developed with Silicon Valley based on her status as a protégé of Frank Quattrone while he was at Morgan Stanley. In fact, Morgan Stanley was inspired by Meeker to develop another characteristic tenet of the New Economy—that an investment bank should use a high-profile analyst to attract banking business. Meeker gained a reputation that allowed Morgan Stanley to draw not only Internet IPOs, but also major firms such as AOL and Time Warner. The practice became institutionalized across the major investment banks, which corporate clients came to rely on for a package deal: when they did investment banking with a bank, they would get not only coverage from its star analyst, but inevitably, positive ratings as well.[69]

When the head of Morgan Stanley's investment banking unit tried to explain Meeker's emergence as a celebrity, he commented, "Mary is one of a kind, and that has to do with her personality, her dedication," but he also noted the role of the "space" she was in as an Internet analyst. "Mary is the right person in the right place at the right time."[70] Meeker was not one of a kind as far as celebrity analysts are concerned—Henry Blodget of Merrill Lynch and Jack Grubman of SSB ended up with reputations of the same magnitude and a level of compensation that equaled (or surpassed) that of Meeker, who reportedly was paid $15 million in 1999 (Grubman received $25 million the same year). In 2000, the average pay for a top financial analyst averaged $2 million.[71] However, the Morgan Stanley banker was certainly right in citing the importance of larger circumstances.

For one thing, the position of the financial analyst had been changing for over two decades—beginning with the deregulation of securities analysis in 1975, which forced the large investment banks to compete on the prices they charged for analysis. As a result, financial analysis could no longer pay for itself. The banks gravitated to treating their research departments as appendages that would have to earn their keep by supporting the investment banking units—even though the securities industry's rules required that research and investment banking be kept separate (by the infamous "Chinese wall"). A second major kind of change came in the early 1990s as the shareholder value model spread in importance. Journalists pushed financial analysts to offer up "target prices" for stocks to reach so as to go beyond qualitative ratings. This task became a lot easier after the onset of a bull market gave analysts confidence that stock prices were generally going to rise, especially for tech firms. The exercise took a new twist when some analysts became famous after seemingly outlandish predictions for rises in a stock's value proved accurate—and the very fact that they made the forecast was seen as contributing to the explosive rise of a stock. The classic case of the self-fulfilling prophecy was Henry Blodget's call (while he was with CIBC Oppenheimer) that the share price of Amazon.com would rise from $230 to $400 (which it did within two weeks).[72] Thus, having a signature big call that came true became seen as the way for an analyst to become a national celebrity. As *Red Herring*, a flagship New Economy business publication, put it, the "risk" for an analyst was that he or she would set the target "too low" and "won't get noticed": "Send a jolt into a stock by doubling your price target and day traders and market makers will be singing your praises, the financial press will fawn on your astute timing, and the man on the street will come to know your name."[73]

However, as Meeker and the other star analysts found out, while it was nice to ride high on the rocketing New Economy bandwagon, it was difficult to dismount. In Cassidy's account, Meeker was particularly troubled by the indiscriminate success of IPOs for even mediocre Internet prospects, which made it nearly impossible to hold to her original standards. When she did hold to those original standards, and a firm that she ignored or criticized had a celebrated success, it threatened to bring down her reputation. In sum, a responsible analyst like Meeker wanted to make assessments based on the long term, but the basis of a reputation in the New Economy circuits of financial commentary was rooted in the short term. Meeker predicted market corrections several times that failed to transpire and then began to go with the flow. After trading on his new celebrity to move on to Merrill Lynch, Blodget also offered critical assessments that forecast downturns in Intenet stocks. Where both Blodget and Grubman got themselves in trouble with regulators was in their going along with investment bankers who pressured them to maintain high ratings for firms they actually had negative views about.

New York's attorney general, Eliot Spitzer, began his offensive against the abuses of the New Economy with an aggressive assault against the major investment banks for offering "conflicted" financial analysis. His first target was Blodget's Internet research team at Merrill Lynch. He found evidence that the analysts were directly involved in supporting the firm's investment banking business and that this was an important consideration in their compensation. For example, when a company became an investment banking customer, Blodget's group would begin covering it with research reports. Most serious was Spitzer's determination that the analysts offered positive stock ratings that were at odds with their true opinions, as evidenced in their private notes and e-mails. The group never published even one reduce or sell rating for any of the Internet stocks it covered between the spring of 1999 and the fall of 2001—even though their in-house comments on some of the firms referred to them as "such a piece of crap," "fundamentals horrible," or "a powder keg."[74] In 2002, Merrill Lynch agreed to pay the state a fine of $100 million.

Spitzer's finding in his investigation of Jack Grubman and Citigroup (Grubman's last employer) offers a look at the economics that biased financial research as well as Grubman's unsuccessful struggle to maintain integrity while under pressure from SSB investment bankers. The report concluded that Grubman's analysis was conflicted in several respects: he helped the investment banking unit of SSB obtain clients, maintain good relations with clients, and generate revenue. It found that in the period 1999 through 2001, SSB earned more than $790 million in investment banking business from telecoms that Grubman covered—and that between 1999 and August 2002 (when he left) Grubman earned $67.5 million, including a severance package. The most serious findings were that Grubman issued two reports on telecoms that were "fraudulent," in that they were contrary to his true views, and that he issued reports on six firms that were "misleading," in that they concerned telecoms that he expressed a need to downgrade, but did not because of pressure from investment bankers.

The impact of the investment bankers on Grubman's reports is vividly illustrated in his frustrated exchanges with coworkers and associates. In a May 2001 e-mail to one of the analysts on his team, Grubman complained that the bankers had no reason to criticize him. "If anything the record shows we support our banking clients too well and for too long." The analyst agreed, responding that he told an investment banker "to look at all the bad deals we sold for them in the past. He agreed." In a June 2001 e-mail to a research associate, Grubman said, "Screw [the investment bankers]. We should have put a Sell on everything a year ago." The next day he e-mailed the head of a stock research unit, "[M]ost of our banking clients are going to zero and you know I wanted to downgrade them months ago but got huge pushback from banking." An angry Grubman e-mail to two investment bankers on February 21, 2001, concerned Focal, one of the firms he later was accused of supporting with a fraudulent report. Focal management had complained to the investment bankers about reservations Grubman expressed about the firm in a research note, even though he still gave it the highest rating ("buy"). Grubman bitterly complained to the bankers, "I hear [the] company complained about our note. I did too. I screamed at [the analyst] for saying 'reiterate buy.' If I so much as hear one more fucking peep out of them we will put the proper rating ["underperform," the second lowest rating] on this stock which every single smart buysider feels is going to zero. We lose credibility [on better firms] when we support pigs like Focal."[75]

Of course, after the New Economy went belly-up, Grubman and all the star analysts lost credibility (and their jobs). However, their post-celebrity lives have varied. Henry Blodget wrote a book. Jack Grubman was banned from working in the securities industry again, but as part of his severance agreement with Citigroup had a $19 million loan forgiven and received some $12 million in Citigroup stock. Mary Meeker, the Queen of the Net, took a decidedly unglamourous turn as a cover girl on May 14, 2001, for a *Fortune* magazine story entitled "Can We Ever Trust Wall Street Again?"[76]

A One-Stop (Favor) Bank

In 1997, Congress struck down the Glass-Steagall Act, the Depression-era law that kept the retail loan end of banking separate from more speculative investment banking. The firm that has taken advantage of deregulation more than any other is undoubtedly Citigroup, formed by the 1998 merger of Travelers' Insurance and Citicorp. In fact, many observers think that as CEO of Traveler's, Sanford Weill actually pushed the hand of Congress on Glass-Steagall by announcing the merger before the law was repealed. Touted as a financial services supermarket, Citigroup has produced stellar earnings since the merger—housing a brokerage unit and insurance company as well as major investment and consumer commercial banks. However, its disastrous and seedy relationships with WorldCom and Enron have raised questions about the one-stop bank model. In particular, critics ask if gaps in monitoring and conflicts of interest aren't inevitable in a situation where there are strong temptations for different types of banking units to work together.[77]

The Biography of Account X

When companies merge, the entity that results finds itself dealing with assorted "legacies" of the original business entities—for example, a legacy computer system. When Citigroup was formed from Salomon Smith Barney (a unit of Travelers' Insurance), the new superbank inherited a legacy that dated back to the days of Salomon: a relationship with World-Com that was personal as well as organizational. The relationship between WorldCom and its investment bank—in its various incarnations—always pivoted on the ties between WorldCom CEO Bernie Ebbers and Jack Grubman, the financial analyst. To trace how this personal-organization relationship formed and evolved over time provides an interesting look at the dynamics involved in normalized corruption.

At first glance it might seem that there is not all that much to this story. It is tempting to write off Ebbers and his dysfunctional operation as just another set of props in the games that investment banks play. The elevation of Ebbers to the status of Telecom Sun King seems akin to Chance—the simple gardener in the Peter Sellers's movie *Being There*—becoming CEO of a global food conglomerate. Certainly Jack Grubman, backed up by the power of his bank, played a central role in the make-over of Ebbers and his company. It was only after Ebbers hooked up with Grubman that he and his firm became stars. As the *New York Times* put it, "Suddenly, the company known as WorldCom had an investment story to offer about the value of combining long distance, local service and data communications."[78] All the evidence points to Grubman, not Ebbers, as the head coach here.

However, there is much more to this story than the notion that the "banker made me do it," for Ebbers possessed the leverage to play his own brand of hardball in pitting investment banks (and their financial analysts) against their respective rivals. Moreover, when the Wall Street types hooked up with Ebbers and company, they too were changed by the new relationship. This is most true of Jack Grubman himself, who was transformed from a rather standard-issue analyst to a multimillionaire celebrity who could imagine himself a peer of the super elite—or at least aspire for his kids to become the peers of their children.

Interestingly, Ebbers and Grubman shared an inclination to position themselves strategically so as to maximize their influence over deal-making. Ebbers liked to personally handle financial-related matters that corporate heads would usually delegate to others. Based on its investigation of ties between Ebbers and Citibank, the *New York Times* noted that, because Ebbers "ran WorldCom as a personal fief," he was in a position to provide two important things to an investment bank: "immense fees for its help in conducting various investment bank and trading operations, and a product—stocks and bonds—for the bank to sell to its clients."[79]

Thornburgh, the WorldCom bankruptcy examiner, claims that Salomon regularly tried to use allocations of IPOs to corporate executives to influence them to give their investment banking business to the bank—a practice known as "spinning." He asserts that Salomon's awareness of Ebbers's role in investment banking decisions led it to make overtures to him, including offers of IPO shares.[80] Grubman was instrumental in this effort. He tried to set himself up as a go-between who—by mediating ties between Ebbers and Salomon's investment bankers—could provide a service package wherein financial analysis and investment banking

TABLE 5.1. ALLOCATIONS OF MCLEOD IPO SHARES TO SALOMON RETAIL CUSTOMERS

Private Wealth Management Client	Shares Allocated
Bernard Ebbers	200,000
Customer 1	47,500
Customer 2	25,000
Customer 3	25,000
Customer 4 (5 family members)	10,000
Customer 5	7,500
Customer 6	7,500
Customer 7	6,000
8 other PWM clients	5,000 each

Source: In re: WorldCom, Inc., et al., *Case No. 02-15533 (Bankr. S.D. N.Y. 2002)* *("First Interim Report of Dick Thornburgh, Bankruptcy Court Examiner").*

were intimately linked. However, Ebbers influenced the terms of the relationship, putting Grubman and company off for two years until the pot was sweetened—for himself personally as well as for his firm.

The evidence provided in Thornburgh's report strongly suggests that Ebbers and Grubman worked out a mutual understanding about collaboration (and reciprocity) during a sequence of events wherein Salomon influenced WorldCom to acquire MFS. One can go further to say that talks about MFS appear to be the forum in which Grubman and other Salomon representatives helped WorldCom develop the new business strategy that was to draw national attention to the firm and Ebbers.

Thornburgh cited the size and timing of the IPO allocations to Ebbers as highly suspicious. The size of the allotments was extraordinary, as can be seen in the case of the McLeod IPO. The amount allotted to Ebbers— 200,000 shares—dwarfed that of Salomon's other "retail" customers— also referred to as "Private Wealth Management" (PWM) customers (see Table 5.1). While Ebbers led the list with 200,000 shares, the next highest total was 47,500, and only five parties received as much as 10,000. Ebbers's allotment was even high compared to that received by institutional investors, whose allotments were much greater than those received by retail customers (see Table 5.2). Only two institutional investors received a larger allocation than Ebbers's 200,000 shares—Fidelity at 250,000 shares and Firstar Investment Management at 215,000 shares. And only Fidelity—one of the largest mutual funds in the United

TABLE 5.2. LARGEST IPO ALLOCATIONS TO INSTITUTIONAL INVESTORS
AND BERNARD EBBERS WITH NUMBER OF SHARES REQUESTED

Name	Number of Shares Allocated	Number of Shares Requested	Percent of Request Allocated
Fidelity	250,000	1,200,000	20.8%
Bernard Ebbers	200,000	1,000,000	20.0
Capital Guardian Trust	200,000	1,000,000	20.0
Alliance	200,000	1,200,000	16.7
Dreyfus Corporation	200,000	1,200,000	16.7
Putnam Management Co.	200,000	1,200,000	16.7
State Street Research & Mgt.	200,000	1,200,000	16.7
Firstar Investment Mgt.	215,000	1,500,000	14.3
Capital Research & Mgt.	200,000	1,500,000	13.3
Massachusetts Financial Svs.	200,000	1,500,000	13.3

Source: In re: WorldCom, Inc., et al., Case No. 02-15533 (Bankr. S.D. N.Y. 2002)
("First Interim Report of Dick Thornburgh, Bankruptcy Court Examiner").

States—received a higher percentage of its request (20.8 percent) than Ebbers, who received 20 percent.

Thornburgh found SSB's explanations for the huge allotment of IPO shares to Ebbers to be without any credibility whatsoever. In response to a congressional investigation in 2002, SSB suggested that Ebbers received a large allotment because he was one of the bank's "best" retail customers for the Private Wealth Management (PWM) unit, which did personal brokerage services for wealthy individuals and corporate executives. However, Thornburgh found that Ebbers was not even a retail customer of the bank when he received the initial allocation for the McLeod IPO. A second explanation was given in the course of Thornburgh's own investigation: Salomon's former managing director claimed that Ebbers received the allotment as a reward for helping spark interest in the McLeod IPO, which was said to have drawn little interest from institutional investors initially. Ebbers supposedly agreed to invest a sizeable amount in the IPO and to let the underwriters cite his support in marketing the issue. Ebbers was an influential figure, since he was a "pioneer" in finding ways to exploit the deregulated market and was a "thought leader" in the sector. He was "smart money" that would give the IPO credibility. However, Thornburgh found "no credible evidence" to back up this argument (*T,* 155–157). For one thing, in the chart that was used to show the underwriters the amount of shares that each institutional investor had requested and the amount they were actually allotted, Ebbers's allotment was not listed under his name but under the moniker "Account X." So, instead of being revealed to the underwriters as a high-profile investor they could cite in marketing the issue, Ebbers's involvement was actually hidden. Furthermore, all the evidence pointed to there being a very high degree of interest in the McLeod IPO from the outset.

The suspicious timing of the allotments to Ebbers takes us to the heart of the matter—the fact that he received a massive personal benefit and then finally agreed to give Salomon some investment banking business. Moreover, this is the series of events—involving WorldCom's acquisition of MFS—through which the relationship crystallized between Ebbers and Grubman (see Table 5.3).

Jack Grubman joined Salomon in March 1994 and initially was a rather conventional financial analyst. From early on, however, he trained his sights on Ebbers. In August 1994, he introduced Ebbers to Salomon investment bankers in New York, and in March of the next year he traveled to Mississippi to introduce two Salomon investment bankers to Ebbers and his CFO. Independent of this, WorldCom and MFS began to meet informally in 1995 to discuss possible business relationships. In its research reports and in its communications with WorldCom, Salomon began to link it with MFS. On May 30, 1996, Salomon solicited business from WorldCom, sending Sullivan information on its lead role in a large equity offering for MFS; the same material also mentioned Salomon's lead role in an upcoming McLeod IPO. A week later (June 6, 1996) Salomon investment bankers met with Sullivan and WorldCom comptroller David Myers to discuss a document prepared by Salomon—"Project New Wave." Project New Wave contained an analysis of MFS and its acquisition of UUNet—the most important Internet network. The document also discussed the prospects for a hypothetical merger of WorldCom and MFS. June 6 was also an eventful day for the relationship between the bank and WorldCom for another reason; on this day Bernie Ebbers opened his first account with Salomon's retail banking unit. The timing leads Thornburgh to propose, "Mr. Ebbers apparently opened this account for the sole purpose of having an account in which Salomon could place the McLeod IPO shares that would soon be allotted to him" (*T,* 135). It was four days later, on July 10, that Salomon allocated the 200,000 shares in the McLeod IPO to Ebbers.

**TABLE 5.3. CHRONOLOGY OF EVENTS LEADING
TO WORLDCOM-SALOMON RELATIONSHIP**

Date	Event
March 1994	Jack Grubman joins Salomon as telecom financial analyst.
August 1994	Grubman introduces WorldCom CEO Bernie Ebbers to Salomon investment bankers in New York.
March 23, 1995	Grubman visits Mississippi, taking two Salomon investment bankers to meet Ebbers and WorldCom CFO Scott Sullivan.
August 1995	WorldCom and MFS Communications executives discuss business relationships and mutual provision of network services.
May 30, 1996	A Salomon investment banker sends Sullivan materials that highlight Salomon's role in MFS $1 billion secondary offering and mentions its role in the upcoming McLeod IPO.
June 6, 1996	Salomon investment bankers meet Sullivan and WorldCom comptroller David Myers and discuss Salomon document entitled "Project New Wave." It analyzes MFS, its acquisition of UUNet, and a hypothetical WorldCom/MFS merger.
June 6, 1996	Ebbers opens his first brokerage account with Salomon.
June 10, 1996	Salomon allocates 200,000 shares to Ebbers in McLeod IPO.
July 11, 1996	Ebbers and Sullivan meet with MFS executives to discuss commercial and strategic issues.
August 7–9, 1996	Ebbers telephones Grubman, informing him that WorldCom might, within the week, hire Salomon as financial advisor for a MFS merger. Grubman calls investment banking head.
August 13, 1996	Ebbers asks Grubman to arrange a meeting with Salomon investment bankers later that day on a MFS merger.
August 15, 1996	WorldCom engages Salomon as its financial advisor for the MFS transaction for fees totaling $7.5 million.
August 23, 1996	The WorldCom board approves the merger. Grubman and a Salomon banker help prepare public announcement.

Now Salomon was on track to get investment banking business from WorldCom. Thornburgh reports that sometime between August 7 and 9, 1996, Ebbers telephoned Jack Grubman to inform him that in the next week WorldCom might seek Salomon's services as a financial advisor for a possible merger with MFS. Grubman relayed the information to Eduardo Mestre, a co-chairman of investment banking at Salomon. The next week (August 13), Ebbers called Grubman and asked him to arrange a meeting with Salomon investment bankers later that day regarding a merger with MFS. Two days later, WorldCom finally hired Salomon as its financial advisor for the MFS deal, which brought the bank a total of $7.5 million in fees. About a week later (August 23) the World-Com board met at Salomon's New York office; Grubman and Salomon investment bankers attended in order to discuss the proposed transaction. On August 25, the WorldCom board approved the merger terms; Grubman and several Salomon investment bankers assisted WorldCom representatives in preparing a public announcement of the merger.

Everything now came together. WorldCom, Ebbers, and Grubman would become some of the biggest names on the New Economy circuit while the material basis for their relationship remained much less visible. For the next year and a half—the period of WorldCom's intense efforts to use acquisitions to make itself the leader of the new telecoms—Salomon kept a steady stream of extraordinary allotments flowing to Ebbers, who made the decisions that kept a steady stream of fees flowing to the investment bank. Between June 1996 and November 1997, Ebbers received a total of nearly 750,000 IPO shares (and 90,000 secondary offering shares), which returned him a total profit of $11 million; Salomon received a total of $65 million in fees from WorldCom (*T*, 140).

The most controversial assistance to Ebbers during the Citigroup era came in response to an escalating crisis in his personal finances—an area that he managed as ineptly as he did WorldCom. Here again Grubman played a key role as an intermediary between Ebbers and the bank. As was discussed in chapter 3, Ebbers turned to WorldCom for financial assistance when the declining value of WorldCom stocks began to destabilize his personal finances. He used loans from WorldCom to meet margin calls from banks on loans that were backed by his World-Com stock. However, in September 2000 the compensation committee of WorldCom's board denied a second loan request. Ebbers was forced to sell 3 million shares of WorldCom stock. When his sale was publicly disclosed in October 2000, the stock price dropped more than $2 a share. Ebbers then turned to SSB, requesting that it provide financial assistance so he could avoid selling more stock to meet margin calls. Grubman backed Ebbers, and the highest levels of SSB approved the request, including its CEO and the head of investment banking. Thornburgh reported that SSB staff he interviewed said that the action was unprecedented. SSB entered into a complex arrangement with its affiliate, Citibank.[81] In November 2000, when WorldCom's stock fell in value again, SSB helped out Ebbers by refraining from selling the stock securing the $55 million loan. In June 2001, SSB agreed to ease the terms that would allow it to sell the stock. In early 2002, SSB agreed to release a lien on Ebbers's Colorado townhouse so that he could receive the sale proceeds (over $1 million) (*T*, 125).

Part of what made the bank's assistance illegitimate in the eyes of the bankruptcy examiner was the implied quid pro quo, that this personal assistance to Ebbers was being made so that in his capacity as a WorldCom executive he would continue to make decisions that favored SSB. Thornburgh claims that in January 2001 Ebbers made the reciprocal nature of this relationship explicit. In a meeting with representatives of SSB and Citibank, Ebbers allegedly told them that he was considering replacing Bank of America with Citibank as WorldCom's lead commercial bank because he was angry at Bank of America "for its personal treatment of him on its loan to him" (*T*, 126). Afterward, the Citibank executives handling Ebbers's loan wrote the following memo: "Our efforts to 'weather the storm' with Ebbers during WCOM's price volatility have apparently paid off, as he is looking to expand our relationship."[82] The same day Grubman wrote a glowing report calling WorldCom's shares his top pick. Ebbers never followed through on replacing Bank of America with Citibank. However, there was a most significant piece of investment banking business that Ebbers did send to his benefactors.

In May 2001, WorldCom was preparing to make a $12 billion bond offering—the third largest in history. A SSB investment banker asked Grubman to put in a word with Ebbers about giving SSB part of the action. As a result, SSB served as the co-lead manager for the offering, earning over $20 million in fees. However, WorldCom imposed a major condition, which vividly illustrates our claim about the leverage that Ebbers and his firm exercised. The co-lead role was available "provided that Citigroup committed at least $800 million to a revolving credit line WorldCom was trying to refinance."[83] Citibank did commit $710 million, not knowing that the finances of Bernie Ebbers's firm were as shaky as his personal finances. This illustrates another point of leverage that WorldCom had vis-à-vis its collaborators: as was the case with Arthur

Andersen, Citibank did not have accurate information on the true state of the firm's financial health. Its special relationship with Ebbers and company was to cost the bank dearly, although the individual notables at the bank would do surprisingly well. When WorldCom declared bankruptcy, Citibank found itself in the creditors' queue because of the $710 million credit line. Much worse, WorldCom shareholders filed a class action suit against the bank for its role in abetting the fraud of WorldCom executives. In May 2004, Citibank agreed to a stunning settlement, agreeing to pay WorldCom investors $2.65 billion—an amount that was second only to the Cendant settlement.[84]

A Good Preschool Is Hard to Find

A final example of Citigroup's utilization of New Economy relationships of the dubious kind was cited in the allegations made by the New York attorney general concerning biased financial analysis and conflicts of interest. It seems unlikely that there is a better example of how rancid relationships linked the corporate and the personal than the tangled tale of how Jack Grubman's effort to gain his children seats in an exclusive preschool became linked to Sandy Weill's campaign to help oust a rival from the Citigroup board.

The affair began in July 1998 when AT&T management complained about Grubman's ratings to Sandy Weill, then co-CEO and chairman of Citigroup—and a member of the AT&T board of directors. The CEO of AT&T, a member of the Citigroup board (and before that a member of the Travelers' board) told Weill that Grubman's comments made it difficult to do business with Citigroup's investment banking unit, SSB. From 1993 through November 1999, Grubman gave a "neutral" rating on AT&T; he also occasionally made disparaging remarks about the firm in his reports. In October 1998, AT&T again complained to Weill about Grubman, and Weill passed the complaint on to top SSB officers. As a result, Grubman wrote a letter of apology to Weill and the SSB heads, which they reviewed and approved—and then forwarded to AT&T (with Grubman's encouragement). Grubman's letter contained the following statement: "I view AT&T as one of the most significant companies in this industry, a company that I hope we can build a long and valued relationship with and one where I truly am open-minded about changes in investment views." A few months later, Weill requested that Grubman "take a fresh look" at AT&T, hoping that Grubman might alter his views of the company. After several exchanges between Grubman and AT&T,

Grubman and Weill traveled on August 5, 1999, to AT&T's headquarters for a meeting with its CEO. Two weeks later, Grubman wrote to AT&T's CEO asking for more information: "When my analysis is complete and if the results are in line with what you and I are both anticipating, once I'm on board there will be no better supporter than I. . . . As I indicated to you at our meeting, I would welcome the role of being a 'kitchen cabinet' member to you." On October 29, 1999, Grubman and Weill talked on the telephone about the progress Grubman had made in his "fresh look" at AT&T. At that time, or shortly thereafter, they also discussed Grubman's hopes of sending his children to an exclusive preschool in New York City at the 92nd Street Y. On November 5, 1999, Grubman forwarded a memo to Weill with the title "AT&T and 92nd Street Y." The memo outlined the steps Grubman would take in reevaluating AT&T. In addition, Grubman asked for Weill to help in getting his children admitted to the 92nd Street preschool: "[T]here are no bounds for what you do for your children . . . it comes down to 'who you know.'. . . Anyway, anything you could do Sandy would be greatly appreciated. As I mentioned, I will keep you posted on the progress with AT&T which I think is going well." In late November 1999, Grubman upgraded AT&T from a "neutral" (3) to a "buy" (1) rating and issued a thirty-six-page report providing a rationale. Afterward, Grubman told an analyst and an institutional investor, in separate discussions, that he upgraded AT&T so that his children could get in the 92nd Y preschool. A year later, Grubman stated in an e-mail to a friend that he was able to exploit a power struggle on the Citigroup board involving Weill: "I used Sandy to get my kid in 92nd Y pre-school (which is harder than Harvard) and Sandy needed [the AT&T's CEO's] vote on our board to nuke [John] Reed in showdown. Once coast was clear for both of us (i.e. Sandy clear victor and my kids confirmed) I went back to my normal negative self on . . . [AT&T]. [AT&T's CEO] never knew that we both (Sandy and I) played him like a fiddle." After Grubman upgraded AT&T, Weill helped his children get admitted to the preschool. In mid-December 1999, Weill called a member of the 92nd St. Y board and said he would be "very appreciative" if she could help Grubman. The term "very appreciative" strongly suggested a quid pro quo would be forthcoming. In March 2000, Grubman's children were admitted to the preschool. The board member then called Weill, suggesting that he make a donation to the Y. Weill indicated to the president of the Citigroup Foundation that it should make a $1 million donation to the Y.[85]

A Friend in Need . . .

Enron's dealing with investment banks provides a final example of the rancid nature of the "relationships" and "understandings" that animated networks of corruption and a vivid illustration of the distributed nature of power and knowledge in those networks. In a *Fortune* magazine story, Bethany McLean and Peter Elkind presented strong evidence that Enron and myriad investment banks were "partners in crime." They found numerous internal documents from the banks that showed that they were "helping Enron mask debt as cash flow from operations and to create phony profits at the end of a quarter"; moreover, when Enron CFO Andy Fastow solicited the banks to invest in his infamous special partnerships (e.g., Raptors), "almost all of them put money" in "because of—not in spite of—their potential for abuse."[86]

In the later half of 1999, Fastow approached the dozens of financial institutions that Enron worked with in an attempt to enlist them in special purpose entities that he had set up (the special purpose entities allowed Enron to appear as if it was dealing with an outside actor in various complex financial transactions—and allowed Fastow and his inner circle to loot the firm). McLean and Elkin report that Fastow's briefings of banks left them astounded by the conflict of interests entailed in having Enron's CFO participate financially in entities that would be negotiating transactions with Enron. Fastow sidestepped their concerns by stating that his inside position would allow the special entities to deliver returns of over 30 percent on the banks' investments. Importantly, he also linked participation to his criteria for an institution to have "tier one status" as an Enron financial partner, telling one banker, "All of our significant relationships are coming."[87] Indeed, Fastow who had hoped to draw a total of $200 million from the banks, ended up receiving $400 million. The "buzz" about the deal was so strong at Merrill Lynch that ninety-seven individual employees put up a total of $16.6 million in personal contributions.[88]

As we have seen in other cases, the illicit nature of the deals had a certain appeal to the banks, as they felt they had an understanding with Enron that some reciprocity would be forthcoming when they helped it in such situations. This can be seen in an exchange within Chase Manhattan after Fastow asked it to contribute $20 million toward his new LJM2 fund in August 1999. Rick Walker, the bank's "relationship manager" for the Enron account, began the sequence by sending a memo to his superiors in support of the request. He proposed that they see it as a "relationship-driven exercise" that would mean "continued deal flow from Enron Corp." He also tried to frame the "invitation" as a sort of favor to the bank—"a carrot from Andy to Chase." In a follow-up note, he said a $20 million commitment would generate "deal flow out of the fund" and "a closer relationship with Enron leading to more M&A [merger and acquisitions] and corporate financing opportunities." After the bank contributed $10 million, one of Walker's bosses sent him a memo: "Rick—Now that you got your $10 million, we need an M&A mandate—something big & high profile. When do we go ask Fastow for this order?"[89]

There is a glaring paradox here. The banks knew that Enron was breaking rules and that Fastow was deceiving Enron to some degree, yet, they perceived that their relationships with Fastow were trustworthy. This is quite evident in the case where Canadian Imperial Bank of Commerce (CIBC) provided equity that was really a disguised loan in late 2000 for Enron's Project Braveheart (discussed with regard to EBS in chapter 3). CIBC expected that it would receive some sort of favor in return for going out on a limb in a deal that was not only legally dubious but also required them to take Fastow's verbal guarantee that the money would be repaid with interest. One CIBC banker noted in an internal memo, "Unfortunately there can be no documented means of guaranteeing the equity . . . we have a general understanding with Enron that any equity loss is a very bad thing. . . . We have done many 'trust me' equity transactions with Enron over the last three years and have sustained no losses to date."

Thus, as Enron became ever more desperate for capital to stave off bankruptcy, major banks vied to take advantage, sensing that they could now gain an extra measure of leverage over Enron (and Fastow). On October 23, 2001, Fastow sent an extraordinary e-mail to Rick Walker (now J. P. Morgan Chase's "relationship manager" for the Enron account): "The key thing right now is to get JP Morgan Chase fully comfortable with Enron. I think you know the credit and the business as well as (and better) than anyone in the world, so I'm counting on you to lead the way. While JP Morgan is already one of the few most important financial institutions for Enron, a strong, timely action . . . would be a 'transforming' event in our relationship." Though the SEC had opened an investigation into Enron's special partnerships the day before, Walker saw no danger in Enron's dire state, but a huge new opportunity for the bank.

In an e-mail to a colleague, he bragged that Fastow was "reaching out and offering gigantic new opportunities for us" and added, "obviously these guys are going to need some equity."[90]

In their eagerness to exploit the "dark side," banking friends of Enron, like those of WorldCom, set themselves up to be duped in turn. In scarcely two weeks (November 8), Enron would disclose that it had overstated profits for the previous five years by $586 million. And less than a month later (December 2) it would file for bankruptcy protection.

CHAPTER SIX

Counting on the Upside
Accountants and Lawyers Who "Got It"

[I'm] trying to kinda cross lines and . . . become more of just a
business person here at Enron. . . . Being here full time . . . day to
day gives us a chance to chase the deals with them and participate in the deal making process.
— Two Arthur Andersen auditors in a promotional video

In 1999, Veba (a German utility) backed away after having engaged
Enron in talks about a possible merger. Its consultants from PricewaterhouseCoopers had advised that Enron's "aggressive accounting
practices" made it look stronger than it really was. One of the participants representing Veba remarked, "[W]e were wondering why this
wasn't common knowledge, or why it wasn't discovered by those people
whose business it was to discover these things."[1] Of course, it was com-

mon knowledge to many of Enron's partners. Enron's own auditor—Arthur Andersen—had at least as much information about Enron's financial high jinks as the investment banks discussed in the last chapter. And one suspects that both Andersen and the banks knew a lot more than PricewaterhouseCoopers uncovered for Veba. The real issue then is not information per se, but the framework used to interpret it. Most firms with inside information about Enron were "partners" who saw its financial gamesmanship to be a source of opportunities—not a potentially lethal condition.

A second incident, in early 2001 (when Enron's hidden financial crisis was in a much more advanced stage), is perhaps even more revealing. When Bethany McLean, a *Fortune* reporter who was struck by the lack of crucial information in Enron's financial reports, issued the first critical challenge to the firm in a national publication, in a story that asked, "How exactly does Enron make its money?" Enron rushed to have the story suppressed. Its CEO, Ken Lay, called *Fortune*'s managing editor, three executives were sent from Houston to *Fortune*'s New York offices, and Jeffrey Skilling, the chief operating officer, tried to discredit the young reporter, implying that she did not understand Enron—and was "unethical" for not doing more research. *Fortune* held firm and published the story.[2]

Most interesting was that McLean herself was not that skeptical about Enron's financial viability. She later commented that she had known that Andy Fastow, Enron's CFO, was a principle in two Enron partnerships, but left it out of the article: "I knew it was weird, but the accountants had signed off on it."[3] Such was the power of accounting on one's sense of economic reality.

Lies My Accountant Bought and Sold

U.S. officials who touted the superiority of neoliberal policies to other nations in the 1990s stressed our reliance on Generally Accepted Accounting Principles (GAAP). While many other nations focus on accounting *principles,* the United States stresses adherence to accounting *rules.* Ironically, as the decade progressed, the SEC became increasingly concerned about accounting abuses involving conflicts of interest and the gaming of the rules. In the fall of 1998, SEC chairman Arthur Levitt Jr. launched an offensive, declaring, "Accounting is being perverted. Auditors and analysts are participants in a game of nods and winks."[4]

Accounting industry representatives responded with their usual line: accounting firms could be counted on to police themselves because of their concern for their reputation. As the president of the American Institute of Certified Public Accountants (AICPA)—the industry association—had put it in 1997, "The reputational capital of a firm is one of its prime assets. You have a built-in check and balance system."[5] But, in fact, the basis for an accounting firm's reputation has changed dramatically over the last twenty or so years—from guardian of professional and legal rules to a creative collaborator of corporations. This shift was reflected in a second kind of defense the industry presented in the 1990s: the practice of accountants was validated by impressive stock prices, which were taken to reflect public trust in the corporate clients they certify.[6]

Since federal securities regulation began in the 1930s, the accounting profession has been given great autonomy while serving as the front line for ensuring corporate compliance. In his book *The Number,* Alex Berenson warns us not to exaggerate the pristine state of accounting in earlier times; over the last thirty years, the accountants that audit corporations have often proved pliable in eras when their clients became inclined to engage in financial deceptions. Yet, the 1990s was undeniably a watershed in the transformation of corporate accounting (and in its complicity in fraud). Several developments contributed. First, the threat of antitrust actions in 1977 against the Big Eight accounting firms for price fixing caused the AICPA to abandon rules that limited competition for public audits on the basis of fees. Audit fees fell as competition heated up.[7] This reinforced the impact of a second factor—the growing role of consulting in generating fees for accounting firms. In 1981, 13 percent of the revenue for large accounting firms (now the Big Five) was derived from consulting; by 1999 the figure was 50 percent.[8] A third factor was the reduction of liability resulting from the 1994 Supreme Court ruling and related legislation in 1995. Accounting firms became more willing to take risks and to give clients the benefit of the doubt.[9]

Consequently, the distinctive American focus on complying with the rules became a perverse game. Rules were followed in a technical sense, but oftentimes their intent was thoroughly subverted. In particular, economist Joseph Stiglitz notes that "techniques that had been invented to deceive the IRS were now employed with a little modification to deceive shareholders"—especially the devices that were used to move items off a firm's balance sheet.[10] The profession's ethics declined in importance throughout the whole system of governance. Whereas most CFOs in 1990 were CPAs, by 2001 only 20 percent of the CFOs at *Fortune* 500 firms were CPAs while 35 percent had MBAs—a degree that stressed creativity rather than respect for numbers. The *Economist* magazine remarked that, in the 1990s, "CFOs became strategic planners, playing a big part in mergers; taking charge of information technology; devising complex financial instruments; and above all, managing relations with investors."[11] Model CFOs were no longer pencil pushers, but financial engineers like Enron's Andrew Fastow (MBA) or WorldCom's Scott Sullivan (Business Administration)—both of whom were awarded "excellence" awards by *CFO* magazine. The new cultural emphasis in corporate accounting was complementary. Barbara Ley Toffler, whose book on Arthur Andersen (*Final Accounting*)[12] was based on her experiences as a partner there, commented in an interview that Andersen became dominated by the "aggressive-win-at-any-cost, make-big-bucks culture" of consulting; she also observed that the culture of conformity that big accounting firms had traditionally promoted was shifting from stressing adherence to accounting rules to conforming to the new priority of maximizing revenue and pleasing clients.[13] The most striking aspect of the consulting ethos that overtook accounting in the New Economy era was the value placed on *breaking the rules.* A November 2001 article in the *Journal of Accountancy* stressed the role of New Economy consultants in creating new models and the virtue of breaking rules: "An innovative environment can be consciously created if a company is willing to abandon old rules, shed old habits, and upend cherished conventions. The key is recognizing that past achievement mitigates against future adaptability, by creating well-worn ways of doing things that cause a company to undervalue or ignore rule-breaking insights."[14] Of course, the rise of a rule-breaking ethos bodes ill for an accounting system based on following the rules.

Sociologists caution that culture is more messy, fluid, and filled with contradictions than is ordinarily thought. Such was the cultural situation in accounting during the 1990s. In 1995, the chief executive of Andersen's audit and tax practice wrote an essay in a newsletter on a recent conversation he'd had with a Japanese executive concerning the cultural differences between the firm's audit and consulting practices. He recalled that the Japanese executive had observed, "Andersen Consulting partners tend to be 'Merchants,' while Andersen . . . [audit] partners tend to be more like 'Samurai' . . . the Samurai Spirit . . . involved . . . absolute loyalty, a strong sense of personal honor . . . , devotion to duty, and courage. . . . A Samurai highly values a sense of shame. . . . The Samurai does not always pursue profits, which are necessary in one's life but are only secondary in the life of a Samurai." The Andersen executive added an aside: "By the way, this sounds much like Arthur Andersen's words of October 27, 1936. 'We want to . . . measure our contribution more by the quality of service rendered than by whether we are making a good living out of it.'" Though it might sound like the head auditor was using the story to stress how his unit's cultural ethos resonated with that of its nearly mythic founder, he went on to discuss how the firm's culture was changing (and had to change): "As in all matters, there are few absolutes and universal truths. Those who are concerned with the possibility that we may be losing some ground on the professional side, and becoming merchants, may well have some basis for this concern. At the same time, the market is changing rapidly and what worked 20 years ago doesn't necessarily work today. I believe that we must find a way to be both Merchant and Samurai."[15] However, the "Samurai" were actually an endangered breed at Andersen and in the big accounting firms in general. As time passed, the "Merchants" increased in numbers as well as in economic importance. More and more, the ranks of the old-school accountants were culled through forced retirements and lay-offs.

Don't Ask (Don't Tell)

When the SEC raised concerns that audits were being compromised when accounting firms also did consulting with an audit client, accounting executives asserted that consulting would actually result in better audits. They claimed the better you knew a client, the more accurate the audit would be. And they noted that the new relationships were only informal, not "contractual."[16] In fact, development of consulting relationships put accountants in an ambiguous and oftentimes conflicted position. And as we will see throughout the rest of the chapter, informal relationships place few limits on the demands that others can place on you, while in contracts demands are usually specific and well defined.

Accounting firms found themselves auditing work that their own people had done or that of their business "partners." For example, Ernst & Young drew the scrutiny of the SEC for its relationship with PeopleSoft, a software firm. The SEC found that it had violated rules on auditor independence by jointly marketing with PeopleSoft—its auditing client—consulting and tax services. Ernst & Young's revenue from the non-audit work with PeopleSoft dwarfed the revenue it received from auditing it—creating a powerful incentive for its auditors to avoid disrupting the relationship. In 1998, Ernst & Young had earned $150 million from implementing PeopleSoft software and only $372,000 for auditing the firm. A

judge fined Enrst and Young over $2.4 million in 2004, and the SEC
proposed to ban the firm from taking on any new audit clients for six
months.[17]

In general, auditing tended to be subordinated to other lines of business, a "loss-leader" that got the firm in the door with a chance to sell
more lucrative services, such as consulting or tax shelters. Lou Lowenstein, a professor of finance and law at Columbia University, observed,
"Auditing is a marvelous marketing tool. You are already doing the
audit. You say their internal controls are no good. Well, who are they
going to call to fix it?"[18] And in the case of auditors and their clients, it
appears that familiarity breeds fraud. *Fortune* magazine observed that
"the marquee accounting scandals" in the 1990s all happened in cases
where the same auditor had been used ten years or more: Waste Management, Enron, WorldCom, Tyco, Adelphia, HealthSouth, and Xerox.
Some firms (e.g., HealthSouth, WorldCom) reportedly used their knowledge of their auditor's methodology to hide problems. More basically,
"the same firm can continue to do a company's audit ad infinitum, so
the pressure remains for any single audit partner not to rock the boat with
a client that generates millions in fees for the firm."[19] In some cases, auditors who approved of problematic accounting treatments later became nervous and advised executives that they should cease or alter the
practice. We saw, for example, that Homestore.com (chapter 4) added a
third leg to its swaps to hide them from PricewaterhouseCoopers after
the auditor became concerned about the use of swaps. Investigations at
WorldCom found that its executives repeatedly deceived their auditor,
Arthur Andersen. They altered key documents and denied auditors access to the database where the most sensitive numbers were stored. For
example, the WorldCom executive who was the head of regulatory reporting altered documents submitted to Andersen in the third quarter
of 2001 when WorldCom pumped its revenue growth up from 6 percent
to 12 percent. In another instance, the head of WorldCom's United
Kingdom unit sent an e-mail reporting that she withheld information
from Andersen in a 2001 meeting: "Pretended ignorance! . . . we ran
them through selected pages of our monthly [report]." The head of regulatory compliance replied, "Thanks Lucy. Great Job."[20] However, Andersen's categorical claim that it did not know about WorldCom's suspect accounting because they were lied to does not hold up: evidence
has surfaced showing that at least one WorldCom executive who was
alarmed by its financial practices notified Andersen in mid-2000.[21]

The cat-and-mouse game that clients played with them was one the auditors did not necessarily want to win. It often seemed they preferred not to know about (or ignored) the dubious deeds of clients. And in more than a few cases, accountants were intimately involved in constructing financial frauds.

A Rosetta Stone for Fraud

Accountants and other business professionals (bankers, lawyers) took multiple institutional roles in financial deceptions. Besides exercising their roles as professional monitors in approving transactions, they also actively participated in constructing deals—either through supplying expert advice or how-to models. Moreover, the transfer of expertise often occurred when accountants crossed over to work in the client firms they had previously audited. For example, the three Homestore.com executives who pleaded guilty to charges that they engaged in fraudulent swaps all came over from PricewaterhouseCoopers.

Instructive is the case of a white paper that Andersen developed on swaps. An executive at another accounting firm referred to it as "the Rosetta Stone" for telecom fraud. According to *Fortune* magazine, Andersen argued that "when a telecom sold 20-year leases of telecom capacity, it could immediately book all the revenue. Even better, when it leased capacity from a company like Global Crossing—the magic of the swap— it could stretch the costs over 20 years. When two telecom companies traded leases for each other's networks, both could show big short-term revenues and profits . . . even when . . . no cash changed hands."[22] The history of this "Rosetta Stone" illuminates the subtle (and not-so-subtle) dynamics of how accountants participated in not only developing suspect practices, but also in carrying them across entire sectors. The starting point was Andersen's work with Global Crossing. The Andersen executive in charge of the Global Crossing audit, Joseph Perrone, wrote a two-page memo (dated February 10, 1999) that advised how best to account for swaps of fiber-optic capacity. One suggestion was to keep the contracts sixty days apart, "apparently," the *New York Times* surmised, "to avoid suspicion that the deals were reached merely to help each party meet its quarterly financial objectives."[23] A second suggestion was that each partner in the swap submit separate cash payments. Soon after, Global Crossing hired Perrone as senior vice president for finance; after his arrival, Perrone's robust promotion of swaps helped undermine the opposition offered by another financial vice president, Roy Olofson (discussed in chapter 3).

In late 2000, Global Crossing began using a new accounting treatment for swaps that allowed it to book what it sold as revenue and to treat what it bought as a capital expense (which does not appear in operating results). The *Wall Street Journal* reported that this idea came from Andersen's Professional Standards Group, which had developed it after having received numerous questions from its telecom clients. Thereafter, Andersen included its treatment of swaps in its white paper for telecoms, which reportedly became "a must-read in the telecom world." Andersen began making PowerPoint presentations on it in an effort to attract new clients. An attorney recalled, "It almost was a cookbook recipe."[24]

A Penny for Your Thoughts ($20 Billion for Your "Foresight")

Another major venue for fraud during the 1990s was the burgeoning system of tax avoidance that *Business Week* referred to as "the Wall Street Tax Machine."[25] Corporations pumped earnings (and thus stock prices) while wealthy individuals minimized taxes through use of tax avoidance schemes, which essentially dumped their share of taxes on the rest of us. Accountants, along with investment banks and lawyers, served multiple roles in the development, spread, and utilization of these schemes. Some tax avoidance scams were crafted for specific clients, while others took the form of recipes.

An unusual scheme that KPMG developed for WorldCom is a striking example of a custom tax avoidance scheme. In early 1997, WorldCom engaged accounting giant KPMG to provide advice on the restructuring necessitated by WorldCom's rapid growth through acquisitions. One component in the package KPMG developed was a strategy to reduce WorldCom's state taxes. The strategy focused on "transfer pricing transactions" between WorldCom and its affiliates: the rationale was that WorldCom was licensing certain "intangible" assets to these units, which, in turn, would be charged royalties. The subsidiaries could count the royalty charges as a business expense that was deductible for state tax purposes. Part of the appeal of the accounting treatment was that many of the states in which WorldCom operated imposed little if any taxes on the royalties that WorldCom itself would earn. Intangible assets usually involve such things as trademarks or brands. KPMG added an innovative wrinkle. Richard Thornburgh reports that "KPMG advised WorldCom that it possessed an unusual type of intangible asset—the 'foresight of top Management'"—which "appears to have been nothing more than former Management's vision to create a horizontally and vertically integrated corporate structure to provide a full range of telecom services to its customers."[26] Although the reasoning behind the strategy seems intellectually modest, the value that KPMG gave to the so-called royalty payments was anything but modest—over $20 billion from 1998 to 2001, which allowed WorldCom to avoid hundreds of millions of dollars in state taxes over the period. Thornburgh found the argument that "management foresight" was an "intangible asset" to be wholly unsupportable. KPMG itself originally seemed to have had its doubts as well. The initial drafts of its applications to the state of Mississippi and the District of Columbia did not disclose that "management foresight" would be the cornerstone of the program; instead, they indicated that "the royalty income would be the result of the licensing of traditional intellectual property, such as trademarks, trade names, and service names and other unspecified intangible assets."[27] At least thirty-seven states have filed documents challenging the tax deductions—no doubt thinking that the management "foresight" that led to the largest bankruptcy in history was not much of an asset of any sort.

That WorldCom was headquartered in Mississippi, one of the poorest of states in terms of income and state services, makes its tax evasion especially egregious. In fact, nearly every tax jurisdiction in the United States got cheated during the New Economy frenzy to pump earnings (and individual fortunes). In 1965, U.S. corporate taxes amounted to 4 percent of the gross domestic product; by 2000 the figure had dropped to 2.4 percent, as compared to 3.6 percent for OECD (Organization for Economic Cooperation and Development) nations taken as a whole. As firms used aggressive tax avoidance strategies to help boost their earnings totals, U.S. corporate taxes plunged to only 1.5 percent of GDP by 2002. The New Economy decade punctuated a long-term dumping of tax burdens from corporations to individuals. In 1940, companies and individuals each paid 50 percent of U.S. taxes; in 2003, companies paid only 13.7 percent while individuals paid 86.3 percent.[28]

Enron's bankruptcy brought attention to the new face of tax avoidance, especially the use of a new generation of tax shelters that used derivatives. Congressional investigators were stunned to find that Enron did not pay taxes in four of its last five years. In fact, Enron considered its tax department another business unit and even provided it with revenue targets. The unit more than met its dual charge; its twelve tax avoidance transactions between 1995 and 2001 created over $2 billion in tax savings, which it somehow turned into $2 billion in current income.[29] The transactions used technical tricks to allow Enron "to deduct some dollars from its tax liabilities more than once, treat some of the company's capital as an expense and generate tax losses while creating the appearance of profit."[30] Enron's tax shelters, like those of some other large corporations, were so complex that the IRS reportedly "has been unable to understand them."[31] Enron inundated the IRS with paperwork, filing 2,486 tax returns in 2000 alone.[32] It created 881 offshore subsidiaries, 692 of them in the notorious tax haven of the Cayman Islands. However, Senator Max Baucus (a Montana Democrat and member of the Senate Finance Committee) remarked that Enron was not the only example: "[T]his is not just Enron alone. It involves lots of other companies and how they inundated the I.R.S., out-complexed the I.R.S. The I.R.S. just cannot handle the complexity of some of these transactions."[33] Large corporations have been much more able than small firms to engage in this financial engineering: the large firms can pay premium fees to accountants, lawyers, and investment banks that design the tax shelters. As a result, the top tier of U.S. companies—the 10,380 firms with assets of $250 million or more—paid a real tax rate of 20.3 percent in 1999 compared to a rate of 38.7 percent for the 13,632 firms with assets of $25 to $50 million. A study of corporate tax shelters by a Harvard economist suggests that they may cost the U.S. government as much as $54 billion a year in taxes.[34] *Business Week* reported that those supporting Enron and others with tax shelters are "many of the brightest, most highly credentialed investment bankers, lawyers, accountants in the country," including Ernst & Young, Deloitte & Touch, Merrill Lynch, and J. P. Morgan Chase.[35] They often charge contingency fees of up to one-third of what they save in tax payments.

During the heyday of the New Economy, accountants also found it extremely lucrative to develop tax avoidance shelters to help individuals protect their windfalls from taxes. For example, KPMG worked with the top two executives at Sprint in an attempt to help them avoid paying taxes on almost $200 million in stock options.[36] It received more for this work ($5.8 million) than it did for its audit ($2.5 million) and related services ($2.6 million) combined.[37] The General Accounting Office estimates that these schemes to shelter individuals' wealth from the IRS cost the government $11–15 billion annually between 1993 and 1999.[38]

An accountant can collect tax accounting fees of as much as $2 million a year—four times what the average partner makes. Tax consulting is the biggest single portion of non-audit revenue that large accounting firm generate—ranging from 30 to 40 percent. The SEC has settled suits with PricewaterhouseCoopers and Ernst & Young for abusive tax shelters; but it is KPMG's tax operations that have drawn the most notice from regulators and a Senate panel. In 1997, KPMG set up a Tax Innovation Center in Washington, D.C., staffed by a dozen employees whose job was to develop tax shelters that could be marketed to multiple clients. In conjunction, it opened up a telemarketing center in Fort Wayne, Indiana, to cold-call prospective clients. Jeffrey Stein, KPMG's deputy chairman, challenged KPMG partners to develop "a new tax strategy every week." Most striking was the sleaziness of the calculations that KPMG partners made about the relative merits of breaking a rule that required certain tax-reduction strategies to be registered with the IRS. In 1998, a tax partner wrote a memo to Stein arguing that KPMG should not register the strategy known as OPIS (so that the IRS would not see it). The OPIS shelter used complex financial transactions to create losses that would offset capital gains. His memo said, "The rewards of a successful marketing of the OPIS product far exceed the financial exposure to penalties that may arise."[39] He proposed that KPMG would generate fees averaging $360,000 per OPIS shelter, while the penalty was only $31,000 per sale. KPMG sold the OPIS shelter to 111 individuals in 1998 and 1999, producing revenues of $28 million; in 2001, the IRS identified the OPIS strategy as potentially abusive.

A senior partner made a similar argument in a 1999 e-mail about another dubious strategy, know as BLIPS. It sheds light on the misuse of opinion letters as well as the logic that the firm should get extra compensation for bending the law: "I do believe the time has come to shit [or] get off the pot. Have we drafted the opinion with the appropriate limiting bells and whistles? Are we being paid enough to offset the risks of potential litigation resulting from the transaction? My own recommendation is . . . we should be paid a lot."[40] Stein replied, "I vote for shit" (i.e., sell the shelter). KPMG sold BLIPS to over 185 wealthy individuals in 1991 and 2000; in 2000, the IRS deemed BLIPS to be a potentially abusive strategy and began auditing some KPMG clients.[41]

KPMG's appearance before a Senate panel in 2003 did nothing to redeem its image. It claimed that is had discontinued sales of aggressive tax shelters, but during a three-hour grilling Senator Carl Levin, a Democrat from Michigan, found the testimony of its representatives to be so evasive that he wondered aloud if he would "ever get an honest answer" from the firm. Levin asked the supervising partner of KPMG's tax shelter unit why it was selling investment strategies whose sole aim was to avoid taxes, which invalidated them. Although the KPMG partner refused to admit this was the case, Levin showed him e-mail messages he had written that discussed only tax avoidance issues, making no mention of investment attributes. When the exchange continued in much the same manner, the KPMG partner remarked, "I don't know how to change my answer." Levin retorted, "[T]ry an honest answer." Later, Levin challenged the assertion of KPMG's vice chairman for tax services, Richard Smith, that the "investment" strategies it sold were not "tax products." Levin rephrased the question six times and finally got Smith to admit that they were tax shelters—after he showed Smith a stack of papers which listed five hundred tax products that KPMG still was selling.[42] Two months after the Senate appearance, KPMG announced that Richard Smith was resigning and that Jeffrey Stein would retire within a month. Senator Levin welcomed the changes, citing "a culture of deception inside KPMG's tax practice."[43] Forty-nine former shelter users have filed a $1 billion lawsuit against KPMG, and the government has pressured KPMG, as well as PricewaterhouseCoopers and Ernst & Young, to reveal the names of the clients to whom they sold the shelters.

The Last Samurai

The fatal plunge of Arthur Andersen provides a special glimpse of the changes that caused the frontline guardians of investor interests to become accessories to fraud. The case also illuminates the kind of close relationships with corporate clients that compromised the roles of accountants and other business intermediaries in the New Economy era.

After Arthur Levitt Jr. issued his call for new restrictions on the ability of accounting firms to consult with the same firms that they audited, W. Robert Grafton—then CEO of Arthur Andersen—was said to have declared, "This is war."[44] That the head of Andersen was calling accountants to the barricades to defend their commercial interests says a lot about the changes in the industry. Andersen had once been the lead defender of professional ethics; the principled stand of its founder (and namesake) against a shady railway operator in 1913—at the cost of losing his business—had been the company's founding myth.

In later years, the guardianship of the professional ethos (or the "Samurai" orientation, if you wish) at Andersen had been embodied in its Professional Standards Group (PSG). The steady slide of that ethos relative to the commercial ethos was evident in the changing position of the PSG relative to the office of the managing partner. Once, there had been frequent contact between the two, which were located only fifty feet from one another. By the 1990s, the PSG was seven layers of management removed from the managing partner—and located in Chicago, while the managing partner had begun to operate out of New York.[45]

Andersen had been at the forefront in developing a consulting practice. A bitter conflict between the consultants and the auditing practice led to a split-up in 2000, when an arbitrator ruled that the consultants could leave to form their own company (they named it Accenture) if they paid Andersen $1 billion. The auditors were stunned, as they had expected to receive as much as $15 billion. As it built a new consulting unit, Andersen, which had gone from being the largest of the Big Five to the smallest, put even more emphasis on increasing its revenue.

Andersen's lethal experience with Enron graphically illustrates the fallacy of the claim that close ties with clients would result in better audits. Boundaries between the two firms became quite faint. Some ninety Enron employees had previously worked at Andersen; one hundred Andersen accountants who worked on the account were housed in Enron's offices. Andersen accountants not only conducted external audits but also helped Enron perform its internal audits. In 2000, Enron paid Andersen more for consulting—$27 million—than it did for audit work—$25 million.[46] McLean and Elkin report that Andersen accountants worked so closely with Enron that "they came to see the world in the same way as Enron Executives" (*ME,* 142). And Enron, according to one of its former accountants, had "an absolute conviction that clever accounting could alter the business reality" (*ME,* 142). Enron's own accountants worked alongside Fastow's team to structure financial deals. They considered themselves "advisors . . . who guided the deal makers by telling them what the accounting ramifications would be," and they viewed their efforts as "creative rather than misleading" (*ME,* 142). Though he didn't know accounting, Fastow's expertise meshed well with the ethos of New Economy accounting—working to rule. Fastow was "rule-driven," as he searched for ways in which he might realize his financial goals "while following the precise letter of the rules, even if it meant violating their intent" (*ME,* 136).

Indeed, McLean and Elkin note that many of Enron's financial ruses were "arguably" legal; however, they propose that Enron clearly went over the line when Fastow devised special purpose entities (SPEs) through which the company began complex and deceptive dealings with itself. Hundreds of firms used SPEs for legitimate purposes, commonly to lower their borrowing costs for some part of their business that was a reliable performer with less risk than other segments—the assets that are reliable generators of income (e.g., rents, movie receipts) can be transferred into a SPE and thus borrow capital at a lower interest rate.[47] In contrast, Enron often transferred underperforming assets to SPEs, where they could be used in transactions to generate cash and income without the other side of a transaction showing up as debt on the balance sheet.[48]

Andersen rated Enron to be a "maximum risk" client. Its memos noted that Enron depended on "form over substance transactions." Yet, McLean and Elkin note, "the Andersen team always had a rationale as to why they [Enron] weren't breaking the rules" (*ME*, 147). When the auditors did object, Enron pressured them to go along. An ex-Enron employee said of Andersen, "they were pretty easy to push around and bully into doing whatever we wanted them to do" (*ME*, 148).

In late 1999, Carl Bass was appointed to Arthur Andersen's Professional Standards Group. As one of the firm's top technical experts, Bass spent much of his time reviewing issues at Enron. Whereas the regular Andersen team at Enron pretty much fit the "Merchant" archetype, Bass was an old-school accountant—more of the "Samurai" mold. According to McLean and Elkin, Bass became "the leading in-house critic of Enron's financial maneuvers" (*ME*, 295). He disapproved of Enron's Project Braveheart (discussed in chapter 3), which sought to book future profits from Enron's joint venture with Blockbuster Video. He also complained when Enron failed to book a loss when the Blockbuster deal fell apart and criticized the special purpose entities that Enron used to hide loans and losses—the Raptors and LJM. Bass found that most of his objections were ignored or rejected by David Duncan, the lead Andersen partner who headed the Enron team. Duncan often seemed to act more like he was an employee of Enron than of its auditor. Bass complained to the head of the Professional Standards Group that Duncan's unit had allowed Enron to know "all that goes on within our walls" (*ME*, 318). In fact, without his knowledge, Duncan wrote memos reporting that Bass had signed off on the accounting issues involved in the Raptors and LJM (*ME*, 363).

On February 5, 2001, Duncan and thirteen other senior Andersen partners held a meeting to discuss whether they should keep Enron as a client. They discussed LJM and conflicts of interests entailed in having Fastow—Enron's CFO—head what was supposed to be independent entity—and they worried about Enron's reliance on "intelligent gambling" and "transaction execution" to meet its financial targets. They also noted that the fees they collected from Enron might reach $100 million a year. In the end, they concluded that they should keep the account: they felt they could maintain their independence (and manage the risks). Finally, they decided to request that Enron's board create a special committee to monitor LJM transactions. Duncan never made the request; a week later he told Enron's board that Andersen would give an "unqualified" approval of its "internal controls" (*ME*, 317).

At the end of February, Andersen CEO Joseph Berardino paid a courtesy call to Enron's Houston headquarters, where he met with Duncan and Enron's chief accounting officer, Richard Causey. Causey, who had once worked for Andersen on the Enron account, was "angry that Bass had refused to sign off on Project Braveheart and the Raptors." Duncan's notes from the meeting commented that Carl was "too technical" and there was "some push by client to get Carl out of engagement team" (*ME*, 317). A week later, Bass, arguably Andersen's last "Samurai" at Enron, was pulled from the account.

What followed is the best-known incident in the New Economy scandals: after Enron went bankrupt and the SEC had started to investigate, Duncan ordered the destruction of Andersen records on its Enron work. Subsequently, Andersen was convicted of "obstruction of justice" and went out of business, leaving its eighty-five thousand employees out of work (by law an auditing firm convicted of a felony cannot audit a public firm). Though it is often seen as a tragic result of one foolish act, it was really a matter of the firm's recent history and new ethos catching up with it.

The immediate bit of history that, more than anything, doomed Andersen was the $1.4 billion Waste Management accounting scandal. The SEC, finding evidence in Andersen's files that it knew of the errors, fined it $7 million in a June 2001 settlement—and got Andersen to pledge that it would refrain from wrongdoing in the future. But the real lesson that Andersen learned was not to keep old notes from its audits. It created a policy whereby it would preserve audit work but destroy notes, e-mails, and drafts as soon as possible.

Andersen's Enron team in Houston neglected to purge such materials (due to staff cuts). When senior auditors at Andersen's headquarters in Chicago perused a cache of old Enron notes in September 2001, they were alarmed to find memoranda that suggested that Chicago had approved suspect accounting for some of Enron's SPEs. The entities were becoming a big issue, as $1.2 billion in accounting errors had just been discovered at Enron in August. As the Chicago auditors debated how to change the memoranda, an in-house lawyer—Nancy Temple—reminded them of the policy on destroying unnecessary records. The partner in charge of global risk management made the same observation. Chicago began to destroy Enron material, and by October 10 the director of Andersen's Houston practice was passing on the word that notes and such should be destroyed. On October 12, Temple sent an e-mail to the Enron team in Houston suggesting that they change a draft memorandum about problems with Enron's Raptor entities. Before Duncan could destroy old notes, the SEC had sent a letter to Enron requesting financial documents. On October 22, Duncan heard that a letter from the SEC was imminent that would request Enron's accounting files. Duncan began the intensive document shredding sessions the next day and asked the Enron team to get their files in compliance with Andersen's document retention policy. In three days, twenty-six trunks and twenty-four boxes of Enron records were destroyed. On November 9, Duncan ordered a halt to the shredding after hearing that Andersen had received a SEC subpoena.

On January 10, 2002, Andersen disclosed the document destruction, setting off a firestorm of public criticism and ridicule. In March federal prosecutors revealed that they were considering indicting Andersen for obstruction of justice—a felony that would effectively be a death penalty for an accounting firm. Andersen made public pleas for a chance to reform itself, but prosecutors reportedly were incensed that the firm had engaged in a coverup only a few months after its Waste Management pledge. One member of the prosecutor's team commented, "[T]he question finally comes down to, 'How many times do investors have to lose millions of dollars because they relied on Andersen before somebody finally charges them with a crime?'"[49] On June 15, a jury convicted Andersen of obstruction of justice. Despite the attention placed on document shredding, members of the jury reported that they found the firm guilty because of deletions that Nancy Temple (the Andersen lawyer) ordered for a draft copy of a memo that discussed Enron accounting. A House panel asked the Department of Justice to purse a criminal investigation of Temple for making false statements to Congress: although she had stated that she had not been concerned about Enron-related litigation when she sent e-mails about document retention, the panel unearthed notes she made which said that a SEC investigation was "highly probable."[50]

Lawyers in the Deal Flow

In contemporary U.S. business, no complex financial transaction, or fraud, is complete without one or more lawyers on the team. Like accountants, lawyers have a government-mandated role in certain transactions and a special status that unethical practitioners can exploit to support frauds. In fact, many of these frauds are possible only because lawyers are willing to sign off on a transaction.

The role of lawyers in the New Economy era owes much to the Silicon Valley model of vested business professionals. In Silicon Valley, lawyers commonly accept equity in exchange for their services, provide advice on a broad range of business issues, and act as "carriers" who diffuse the venture capital model to new sites. A lawyer noted that the intimate role of lawyers in helping organize Silicon Valley had changed how they practiced law: "[Y]oung lawyers in particular took a very fresh look at what it means to assist a client. And they gave these clients not only legal advice, but business advice, about how to run themselves and to maneuver . . . and how to get funded. . . . If you had very traditional, conservative, risk-adverse legal activity, I'm not sure it would have happened. . . . Whatever it was the lawyers did by partnering with their client . . . they've helped create a . . . New Age kind of thinking and business modeling."[51] Though this "new age" lawyer was most evident in the case of the dotcom sector—where they often exchanged services for equity—it also was reflected in a more general inclination of lawyers to place themselves in "the deal flow."

Lawyers seeking a position in the New Economy deal flow had a special resource to offer—the status of a trusted defender of the law who has sworn to abide by an elaborate code of ethics, including a prohibition against helping "a client in conduct that the lawyer knows is criminal or fraudulent." More practically, this special status meant they had the ability to issue an expert opinion on the legality of a transaction—a letter that can serve as a "get-out-of-jail-free-card" because it usually absolves executives of responsibility even if the transaction is later ruled to be illegal (the letter provides cover on "intent"). And a professor of ethics at the University of Virginia Law School commented, "All the financial incentives are for clients to seek out lawyers who give them the advice they want to hear. And all of the financial incentives are for lawyers to give it."[52]

The involvement of lawyers in tax avoidance schemes and mutual fund schemes has begun to draw the attention of regulators. A partner at a law firm that is litigating over ten suits against tax shelter promoters exclaimed, "Law firms were definitely part of the Axis of Evil in the tax shelter industry."[53] The IRS is concerned because lawyers issue opinion letters on tax schemes that lead clients to believe that they will not have to pay a penalty if the IRS disallows the tax strategy. The opinion letters are often scores of pages long and sell for as much as $1 million each. They usually assert that a tax strategy is "more likely than not" to pass an IRS audit, but they are often based on unrealistic assumptions and are not tailored to match the specifics of the taxpayer who purchases the letter.[54] Some law firms wrote such letters for a type of tax shelter known as "Son of Boss," which the IRS declared to be illegal in 1998. Between 1997 and 2001, some five thousand wealthy individuals used Son of Boss shelters to evade more than $6 billion in federal taxes. The government has begun to take actions against these law firms. For example, it forced Jenkens & Gilchrist to reveal the names of one thousand shelter clients; the law firm has also settled a lawsuit with one hundred clients for $75 million.[55]

Regulators have just begun to scrutinize the role of lawyers in the mutual funds scandals. In 2003, a SEC commissioner commenting on the mutual fund scandals declared that Sabines-Oxley placed explicit duties on lawyers: "An attorney who is aware of credible evidence of a material violation of the securities laws, or a material breach of fiduciary duty, must report this evidence up the chain of command." A Boston University law professor remarked that the SEC's message to lawyers is, "[Y]ou are the law's gatekeeper. You are public servants. You're not selling justice and you're not selling income-producing property. That means you have to tell the client sometimes 'I know you want to do it, but you know something? You can't.'"[56] That regulators and ethics experts felt compelled to make such declarations in the wake of the New Economy scandals speaks volumes about the inability of the legal profession to police itself.

It is the role of lawyers in the big corporate accounting scandals that has drawn the most attention. Although it is rare that attorneys face criminal charges for abetting fraud, two top counsels at Tyco and Rite-Aid have been indicted. Another legal scandal emerged at Global Crossing in 2001 when a law firm was asked to investigate charges by a vice president that the telecom was deceiving investors. The lawyers concluded that nothing was wrong, even though they never talked to the executive who made the allegations.[57]

The most important case is undoubtedly that of lawyers who assisted Enron's financial engineers not only by writing opinion letters vouching for the legality of financial machinations, but also by helping to draft the documents for the transactions. A number of Enron's in-house lawyers were assigned to assist CFO Andrew Fastow, who seemed to think that they were his own personal counsel. The orientation of the legal department was reflected in a commemorative knickknack it handed out in 1998, which outlined its mission: "To provide prompt and first-rate legal service to Enron on a proactive and cost-effective basis. Translation: We do big, complex and risky deals without blowing up Enron."[58] Enron's outside lawyers mainly came from two Houston law firms—Vinson & Elkins and Andrews & Kurth. The two firms handled almost all of Enron's SPEs, including 98 percent of the twenty-odd transactions that accounted for over $2 billion in hidden debt that Enron disclosed in November 2001.[59]

Enron's use of SPEs often made both its lawyers and its accountants uneasy. Yet, the fees for handling structural-finance deals were enticing—especially for lawyers. Their fee typically reached as much as $175,000, which was more than three times what the accountants received. The role of the lawyers was to first construct the SPE (which could be an independent firm, partnership, or trust that has its own managers and complex rules). Then the attorneys usually created "layers of corporate shells" and executed a number of complex transactions among the different entities they created. Because they could be a source for liability, the opinion letters the lawyers wrote for the SPEs could be worrisome—both for their own interest and for that of the accountants involved. Before they issued a letter attesting that the SPE conformed with the law, they performed due diligence, and it usually had to be approved by a general partner committee. On the kind of SPEs that Enron commonly used (which involved stocks or some other financial asset), a lawyer had to write two kinds of letters that guaranteed to SPE investors (e.g., investment banks) that the assets they had a right to would not be secured by other creditors in the event that Enron went bankrupt.[60]

A collaborative process often came into play when there was concern on the part of the lawyers or the accountants on the contents of a letter—especially when the SPE in question looked like a disguised loan. An in-house Enron lawyer noted that they would negotiate the deal's form: "The law firm might say to the deal team, 'Listen, under these circumstances, we cannot deliver a[n] . . . opinion. In order for us to deliver one, we need X, Y, and Z to happen.' The accountants then look at what results from the legal changes and say, 'Under those circumstances, we can't reach the accounting result we would like to reach.'"[61] The parties would go back and forth until they negotiated a deal that achieved the financial team's goal—for example, taking some asset off the balance sheet.

Although the lawyers, like the accountants, claimed after Enron's fall that they did not have access to enough information to be able to discern the larger picture, critics stress that they knew the intricacies of the deals they worked on and surely found out a lot about Enron after engaging in repeat transactions. Moreover, the bogus nature of some SPEs had to have been evident from the reactions of other participants. For example, when investment banks invested in SPEs, they were the ones who should have been most acutely concerned about the opinion letters. In fact, a court-appointed examiner found that Enron and Andersen were much more worried about the letters than the banks they were supposed to protect. The banks were not concerned because their supposed investments were really disguised loans that Enron had secretly committed to repaying with interest. A legal ethics expert at Boston University observed that Vinson & Elkins and Andrews & Kurth "had to have a bag over their head not to see that there was something fishy going on here"; the disinterest of the banks in the letters "is a blatant sign of possible fraud."[62]

Don't You Get It (Want In)?

Having examined three sectors and numerous professions, we are in a good position to revisit our key question: Why did so many professionals and executives go along with organized deceptions? (And what were they thinking?) Those who study complex white-collar fraud often note that "the devil is in the details." This section will look for "the devil" in the details of complex social relations and shared understandings. We will focus on the use of power to enact and enforce New Economy rules, especially those of "normalized corruption."[63]

We wish to make a decisive break with outdated theories of the irrational crowd and to go beyond recent accounts that revolve around some generalized culture infused by irrationality—for example, Partnoy's *culture of greed,* or the *culture of fear* found in Maggie Mahar's book, *Bull!*[64] Mahar portrays a climate where financial analysts and reporters went along with the positive flow of commentary that marked the New Economy out of a fear for their careers; they avoided taking stances that were contrary to the general view. More usefully, she observes that intimidation also came in the form of rebukes by powerful actors—for example, editors who dissuaded reporters from focusing on bad news.

We propose that the conformity seen in New Economy scandals has more to do with the active use of power pressuring people to go along than a general cultural orientation. Our task is to examine the intersections of power relations, material interests, and culture—treating culture as the "making of meaning" rather than as an all-encompassing blanket.[65] The business world is a political realm where actors use social ties and cultural constructions in their individual and collective efforts to muster power—whether in the cause of shaping "the rules" for hidden realms of corruption or for legitimate arenas.[66] More generally, the exercise of power by business actors typically involves offering ways of looking at the world that they see as complementary to their interests.

When actors have the power to define the situation (e.g., which actions, actors, or topics are valued in a firm), they have "symbolic power."[67] This capacity usually is derived from some other base of power they enjoy—for example, the authority of top corporate executives vis-à-vis employees, or the leverage of brokers over those who want access in a network. Executives can wield several "levers" in (re)producing normalized corruption: (1) promotion of an organizational culture that is conducive to fraud (e.g., conformity); (2) hiring and screening processes; (3) evaluations, ranging from formal personnel reviews to less formal exposés; and (4) the routinization of corrupt activities so that participants will take them for granted as regular work tasks.

The reliance of New Economy scandals on interfirm networks involved a second kind of power—brokering access. The use of the broker's leverage—by prominent reputational intermediaries as well as executives—was instrumental in leading many business professionals to go along with frauds. As we have seen, assorted business professionals had a significant material interest in participating in New Economy circuits of financial analysis and commentary. These material interests gave them motives to go along with dominant New Economy story lines and interpretations. For one thing, their ability to participate depended on their ability, in terms of words and actions, to make sense to others in the circuit. To be a capable participant, one had to know and speak the language in all its nuances and tacit assumptions. In turn, their material interest in the circuit gave great leverage to those who were in a position to broker access—including strategically positioned intermediaries (e.g., Jack Grubman, Frank Quattrone) as well as corporate executives (e.g., Andy Fastow). This could involve more routine situations where business professionals were competing with others for some block of business, or it could involve access to the insider circles where the most lucrative (and most dubious) deal-making was carried out. And, like corporate employees, these professionals could be subjected to coercion—not only by executives who could freeze them out of their firm, but also by better-positioned peers who had the status to question their credibility as experts.

You Must Imagine This

How two or more parties interpret a problematic situation they share depends a great deal on the nature of their relationship—especially the balance of power between them. When the parties involved are equals, it is likely that they will use a process of negotiation to develop a shared interpretation of a situation. For example, in August 2001 a Global Crossing sales executive sent the following e-mail to her counterpart at Qwest as they tried to put a swap together. "I understand quirky, we do quirky all the time. We'll be happy to help as long as we don't go to jail or something." The Qwest executive assured her that the deal was not that risky, making a joke about prison uniforms: "Believe me, I would never ask you to do something that would end with that result—[I] don't like orange, and although I like Black and white, I don't prefer those stripes."[68]

In many other cases, the political tone was more one of domination, particularly when the relations involved corporate superiors and subordinates. To start with, top executives can shape a firm's culture to intensify their control. Though they seemed havens for nonconformity on the surface, the cultures of New Economy firms were often highly conformist. WorldCom's bankruptcy examiner criticized its "culture," where, among other things, "critical questioning was discouraged."[69] We saw in our telecom chapter that much the same could be said of Qwest. A former employee of HealthSouth, site of yet another massive accounting scandal, recalled that it "was like being in a cult."[70] Many dot-coms were exercises in studied excess—symbolized by their over-the-top company parties; their strong cultures gave at least some of them a cult-like atmosphere.[71] Jeffrey Skilling compared Enron to a start-up and said he wanted to nurture an environment that the "weird" people who generated new ideas would feel comfortable in. Besides embracing a number of dot-com sensibilities—including the inclination to discredit those who saw things differently—Skilling also stressed that deal-making and risk-taking were to be valued over everything else.[72]

A more direct use of executive power was the routinization of corruption. Fraudulent activities were organized in such a way as to focus people on the task at hand while blocking off questions of whether what was being done was appropriate. A central activity in accounting frauds—the quarterly effort to manipulate the financial results—was encoded in a way that encouraged one to treat it as a regular task that did not need to be thought out. Participants geared up to "plug the bogie" (Homestore.com), "make the numbers" (Qwest), "close the gap" (World-Com), or "make the overview" (Enron). The importance of routine for normalized corruption was evident in the irritation (or rage) that was directed toward those who broke with it. A vivid example can be seen at WorldCom, where CFO Scott Sullivan sent the following e-mail to a staffer (and the employee's supervisor) when the employee prepared a budget using actual (as opposed to manufactured) cost estimates: "This is complete, complete garbage. . . . What am I supposed to do with this? *What have we been doing for the last six months* [our emphasis]. This is a real work of trash."[73] Routinization limited what could be discussed (and with whom). A WorldCom executive who was alarmed by the accounting that the CFO ordered for his unit found that top financial executives "were reluctant to discuss it and simply continued to refer back to the fact that the entry had been made at Scott Sullivan's direct instruction." When he suggested that Arthur Andersen check the accounting, an angry controller forbade him to discuss the issue with Andersen.[74] If one wrote a critical memo at Enron, one was likely to receive an intimidating literary critique. After an Enron lawyer sent a memo warning that a deal ran a high risk of being seen as a manipulation, his superior responded that he "had used unnecessary inflammatory language and editorialized too much."[75]

When the exercise of power was across firm boundaries, actors who were strategically positioned in networks aggressively promoted their own story lines. A former CEO noted that Jack Grubman shaped the sense of reality in telecom, concerning which strategies and actors had credibility—and who had "obligations" to him: "Jack had great power. If he didn't endorse a deal or a strategic direction, it wasn't going to work. But he held you hostage. In order to endorse the deal, he and Salomon had to get a major chunk of the banking business. He was very blatant. He would tell you what his expectations were in terms of investment banking for the firm."[76] Thornburgh compiled a series of supportive statements that Grubman made over time in WorldCom's behalf. The subtext to analysts and investors was clear: for your actions to make sense—for you to have credibility—you must do/think this. For instance, on August 20, 1999, Grubman "declared that any investor who did not take advantage of current prices to buy every share of World-

Com should seriously think about another vocation." On February 15, 2000, he "attributed WorldCom's declining stock price . . . to the market's ignorance in assessing the realities of the Company's compelling story and to the fact that the market instead was acting on sentiment." In June 2000, Grubman proclaimed that analysts who worried about World-Com "would be surely disappointed that they downgraded the stock." On February 15, 2001, he "advised investors to take advantage of misguided analysts by aggressively buying WorldCom stock."[77]

Interestingly, Grubman would meet with WorldCom executives to help them manage how other analysts perceived them. He would consult with them about "the opinions and actions of other Wall Street analysts and Mr. Grubman's reactions to negative press reports regarding WorldCom."[78] As confidence in WorldCom began to fray—and its stock started to plummet in February 2002—Grubman took extraordinary steps to try to restore confidence in the firm, coordinating his reports with the public comments of Bernie Ebbers; in an e-mail, he coached Ebbers on the script he should follow in an upcoming conference call with analysts. He especially stressed the need for Ebbers to confront questions about the firm's liquidity, debt, and accounting, and about his loans. Grubman then published a research note on WorldCom that reiterated his strong buy rating, stating that its stock had been "unduly punished" by investors worrying about accounting issues. He also set the stage for Ebbers's upcoming call with analysts: "We feel confident that investors will see on Thursday . . . morning that Mr. Ebbers is very engaged in the business and that he feels 1,000 percent that WCO is executing better than in any time over the past 10 years. Also, despite any issues he may be personally facing, we believe he is quite on top of the tactical, financial and strategic challenges facing the company." The *New York Times* reported that Ebbers followed Grubman's script "almost to the letter," with the result being that the stock rose over 12 percent that day. Along the way, Ebbers challenged the credibility of analysts who doubted WorldCom: "I would like to clear the air on the rumor mill, most of which should be classified as unfounded nonsense. . . . Let me be clear we stand by our accounting. . . . Bankruptcy or a credit default is not a concern. To question WorldCom's viability is utter nonsense. . . . I hope you know me well enough to know that I take WorldCom's finances very seriously and I take my debt to the company very seriously. . . . It has been 10 years since WorldCom has been so well positioned from an operating perspective." The next day, Grubman published a report on the comments Ebbers and other WorldCom executives made, and repeated

his recommendation of the stock: "Perhaps the most significant out-
come of WCOM's earnings release was its very clear denial of the unfounded rumors surrounding its liquidity position, balance sheet and
accounting."[79] Some five months later, WorldCom filed for bankruptcy
protection.

Bully (in the) Pulpit

A large body of evidence has surfaced about the pervasive role of coercion in the New Economy frauds. Ironically, those in the corporate and
professional ranks who yearned to be free from state controls found that
when it retreated they were left more vulnerable to coercion by superiors, major clients, and others who brokered access. The threat of state
sanctions had actually protected those who wanted to resist demands
that they engage in illegal or unethical acts.

As it turns out, there were many more instances of people questioning or resisting dubious practices than was previously thought. The reason why most drew little notice is because they lacked "champions" or alternative story lines to link up with—and the fact that they were usually
repressed or otherwise bullied, threatened with marginalization, ostra-
cism, or expulsion.

Instructive is the fate of Roy Olofson—the vice president of finance
at Global Crossing who raised concerns about the appropriateness of
swaps. On August 6, 2001, Olofson sent a letter to Global Crossing's
general counsel (who was also the chief ethics officer) warning of accounting abuses. The Global Crossing general counsel consulted with
an external attorney, and after a few days responded that the company
already knew about the accounting practices. A few days later, the general counsel retired (at age thirty-nine), citing "personal reasons." Olofson was fired in November 2001.[80] Enron's treasurer, after raising issues
with Jeffrey Skilling about conflicts of interest entailed in Andy Fastow's
role in SPEs, had to face an irate Fastow (Skilling told him of the complaint) and was then advised by Skilling that he should accept a transfer
to another position (*ME*, 210–211).

Importantly, intimidation was used not just to punish those who refused to go along, but also *to establish the fact that one was dependent* on certain figures—those who exercised control over whether you retained
your job or whether you would have access to the deal flow. There was
a synergy between the doling out of rewards/punishments that were
used to amplify control through heightening greed/fear. Many central

figures in the New Economy scandals sculpted their immediate surrounding to their liking, dangling a carrot from one hand while waving a stick (or club) in the other. Enron's CFO, Andy Fastow, was just such a figure—an infamous bully who often unleashed tirades to get his way. He also made use of rewards and punishments to gain the cooperation of subordinates and even Enron's in-house lawyers. One general counsel was allowed to invest $5,800 in the LJM partnership and enjoyed a return of over $1 million in a few months. Conversely, *Business Week* reported that "lawyers Fastow disliked were clubbed with big sticks." He reportedly fired one general counsel and tried to sack a staff lawyer because they both "resisted his direction." A high-ranking executive who worked on many of the deals recalled that "Andy clearly surrounded himself with people he though would be loyal to him and whom he could influence or pressure."[81]

This Little Light of Mine . . .

One powerful instrument top executives could use on a regular basis was the ability to subject subordinates to evaluations, which might be formal reviews or ad hoc ambushes that had the flavor of exposés. An example of the former was Enron's dreaded "rank and yank"—a performance review process introduced by Skilling wherein employees were evaluated by management at regular intervals and the lowest-ranked were fired. The process was infamous as an opportunity for managers to engage in power plays to further the interests of their cliques. A technology officer who was purged complained that it was a mechanism for enforcing conformity. "If you disagreed with anything, if you spoke what you thought was the truth, you didn't fare too well."[82] HealthSouth's CEO, Richard Scrushy, used a regular evaluation ritual of sorts to intimidate subordinates. Every Monday morning senior employees had to gather in a meeting where Scrushy would "grill" them about "the numbers." The employees called the sessions "Monday-morning beatings," as Scrushy typically would identify some shortcoming and then go on to publicly humiliate the manager he deemed culpable. In an interview in 2002, he commented on the method to his madness: "Shine a light on someone—it's funny how numbers improve."[83] It is tempting to think that such tactics had something to do with the fact that HealthSouth ended up ensnared in a massive accounting fraud—at last count, $1.4 billion in misstated revenue from 1999 through 2002. From its investigation, the *New York Times* concluded that Scrushy "surrounded himself with people who believed they owed him nearly everything. He played on their insecurities, their fears."[84] Qwest CEO Joesph Nacchio reportedly used ambushes to create fear: "Managers were terrified they wouldn't match Nacchio's expectations. In meetings he would pretend not to listen when he was unhappy, then suddenly zero in on what he thought was the weakest point of an executive's presentation." *Fortune* magazine claimed that Nacchio "used every technique at his disposal to goad his executives and salespeople to deliver" on impossible revenue targets; he "had a preternatural ability to push the buttons of fear and greed that would make his salespeople 'make the numbers.'" An example of the tactics he used to intensify his control was on display at a Las Vegas conference: "Nacchio threw out tennis balls, each one cut open and stuffed with bills, to a cheering crowd and watched as salespeople with mid-six-figure incomes pushed and dived for the few bucks." A former senior vice president noted that the threat always hung over one's head that they would be told they were "not part of the team."[85]

When CEOs bullied top executives, it often set off a dynamic of trickle-down intimidation, wherein the executives would, in turn, run roughshod over their subordinates. *Fortune* reported, "Down through the hierarchy, Qwest managers believed they had to make their numbers in any way possible."[86] WorldCom provides a rich illustration of the same condition. *Business Week* stated that CEO Bernie Ebbers usually "publicly belittled" directors and top executives "who dared question him." For example, two former board members recalled an instance in 2000 when WorldCom CFO Scott Sullivan questioned Ebbers's cutback in a project; Ebbers responded by gathering information "that undermined" Sullivan and then revealed it in the next meeting of the board. As one former director put it, "Ebbers treated you like a prince—as long as you never forgot who was king." The core of his support was a block of longtime cronies—a group of four directors known as "Bernie's Boys"—who he bestowed favors upon (e.g., use of the corporate jet, financial support for pet projects). In some cases, multi-billion-dollar acquisitions were approved after thirty minutes (or less) of discussion, without the board having been given even a single piece of paper with information on the deal. As the telecom industry collapsed in 2001, the board accepted Ebbers's assurances that it was a passing squall. As a result, they did not dump their stock, and their holdings went down with the ship.[87] The bankruptcy examiner noted that Ebbers also played hardball with staff on the matter of his loans. When WorldCom's general counsel took steps to try to obtain collateral from Ebbers's personal assets, Ebbers "fiercely resisted," going "so far as to criticize . . . [the counsel] in harsh terms, placing the in-house counsel in an untenable position."[88] Ebbers's behavior was so blatant that in February 2002 WorldCom's compensation committee retained an outside lawyer to work on the matter so as to shield the in-house lawyer from further abuse. Another WorldCom report revealed striking cases of high-level executives pressuring subordinates who resisted going along with (or questioned) dubious financial manipulations. When the acting CFO of WorldCom's UUNet unit twice refused to free up $50 million in reserves, David Myers, WorldCom's comptroller, flamed him an e-mail: "I guess the only way I am going to get this booked is to fly to DC and book it myself. Book it right now, I can't wait another minute." And after an employee asked Buddy Yates, director of general accounting, for an explanation of a large accounting discrepancy, an anonymous employee who witnessed the exchange quoted Yates as replying, "Show those numbers to the damn auditors and I'll throw you out the fucking window."[89]

Circuit Jerk

The other realm where power plays were used to enforce normalized corruption was that of reputational networks. Business professionals who worked in networks that extended across firms were kept in line by major clients and by peers who held power as brokers—positioning that allowed them to control access (e.g., to their firm's business or to financing networks) or to impact one's reputation.[90] For example, one dot-com executive reported that his start-up was under pressure from its investment bankers to count advertising swaps as revenue—otherwise they would not support an IPO.[91] *Business Week* cited the case of a Silicon Valley firm as evidence of why it was important to be a "Friend of Frank." When Brocade Communications Systems did not pick CSFB to handle a debt offering, the day that the offering was announced a CFSB analyst wrote a negative research note (causing the stock to drop in value). Later that day, Brocade's CEO received an e-mail from one of Quattrone's bankers suggesting that he might want to consider using CSFB in the future.[92]

An investment banker noted that "[W]hen Grubman said something it was go along or be left behind."[93] Grubman battered rival analysts who departed from his line. For example, in January 2001, when a Kaufman Brothers analyst questioned the prospects of Winstar (a firm Grubman backed), Grubman blasted him in a research note: "We believe this is highly irresponsible of the analyst since they do not have coverage of [Winstar], nor did they speak with senior management."[94] He also criticized the analyst in Winstar's quarterly conference held a few weeks later (Winstar filed for bankruptcy two months after the conference). Ebbers used Grubman's faithful support to leverage other analysts. A banker remarked, "Mr. Ebbers routinely chastised analysts who were not as favorably disposed as Mr. Grubman toward WorldCom and told their firms that they would not receive any of his business until their analysts adopted a rosier viewpoint." There were numerous other cases in which executives tried to punish or intimidate financial analysts. When a Morgan Stanley analyst publicly questioned why Qwest was becoming increasingly reliant on capacity swaps, Qwest's CFO wrote a note, "Quietly close Morgan Stanley out of company" and listed banking and stock options as areas where they should not give Morgan Stanley any work.[95] Enron was less subtle when it came to maintaining an upbeat buzz about its financial prospects. In the summer of 1998, Merrill Lynch replaced a research analyst, John Olson, who angered Enron by giving the firm a "neutral" rating. The purge came after two Merrill investment bankers, eager to land more of Enron's banking business, sent a memo passing on Enron's criticisms of Olson. They stated that the bank had lost a big underwriting deal because Enron executives had a "visceral" dislike of the analyst. They added, "our research relationship with Enron has been strained for a long period of time" and that Olson "has not been a real supporter of the company, even though it is the largest, most successful company in the industry."[96] A broker at UBS Paine Webber suffered a similar fate when in August 2001 he advised a group of Enron employees to sell their shares, warning that the firm's "financial situation is deteriorating" and that they should "take some money off the table." Of course, he was only too accurate. But the Enron executive in charge of the company's stock option program blazed an angry e-mail to Paine Webber executives: "Please handle this situation. This is extremely disturbing to me"; Paine Webber fired the broker three hours later and sent his clients a retraction stating that Enron's share price was "likely heading higher than lower from here on out."[97] And as we saw at the beginning of this chapter, Enron was just as aggressive in trying to intimidate reporters and publishers who strayed from the firm's official story.

Accountability (Does Anybody Get It?)

After Arthur Andersen went out of business, its former CEO, Joseph Berardino, made the standard "I was responsible but . . . " comment. In an interview with *Business Week* he stated, "Do I bear responsibility? No question." But he blamed investors for not studying financial filings and the WorldCom board of directors for not asking enough questions. He also recalled that when he first heard reports that WorldCom would be restating $3.8 billion in revenue, he had "watched in outrage"—not because yet another Andersen audit client had been sunk by an accounting scandal, but because he felt the media was "talking down the stock." His successor as CEO, Aldo Cardoso, criticized Berardino—not for failing to ensure ethics, but for failing to fight dirty against the Department of Justice: "He probably should have been a street fighter and told them they were a bunch of liars who weren't interested in the public good. The Justice Department is responsible for the collapse of the financial markets because they caused our collapse."[98] More typical was the excuse made by David Duncan, the head of Andersen's Enron team who ordered the destruction of documents. His lawyer claimed that Duncan was innocent of obstructing justice because "he followed the instructions of an Andersen in-house lawyer."[99] The lawyer for Jeffrey Skilling, former chief operating officer and CEO at Enron, stressed that he had acted with the knowledge and approval of dozens of accountants, lawyers, and board members: "If the C.O.O. can be indicted for transactions that were reviewed and recommended by dozens of experts, then no C.O.O. should go to work tomorrow morning, because if something goes wrong with the company, they are in danger of being indicted."[100] And Enron's former chairman and CEO, Ken Lay, has made the obligatory (but heavily qualified) confession: "I take full responsibility for what happened at Enron. But saying that, I know in my mind that I did nothing criminal." He claimed that criminal charges loomed because of his political connections: "If anything, being friends with the Bush family, including the president, has made my situation more difficult because it's probably a tougher decision not to indict me than to indict me."[101]

Lay blamed the fall of Enron on the fact that his former CFO, Andrew Fastow, and Fastow's inner circle committed crimes to enrich themselves—and on the media coverage that followed revelations of those crimes. In fact, Lay denied that Enron was failing. He said there were sound business reasons to let his CFO manage the special purpose entities that were supposed to be independent of Enron. And Lay pointed to the fact that when he received Sherron Watkins's memo warning of grave dangers with SPEs, he retained an outside law firm—Vinson & Elkins—to investigate the entities. Vinson & Elkins concluded that Enron was in the clear because Arthur Andersen had signed off on the entities. And in an appearance before the House Energy and Commerce Committee in March 2002, the managing partner of Vinson & Elkins remarked, "There's nothing that I'm aware of that we would change. We never saw anything at Enron that we considered illegal"; another partner claimed, "[I]f you are working on a deal, you don't always see the rest of the elephant"; likewise a partner at Kirkland & Ellis—a law firm that often represented the SPEs that Enron created—declared, "We were not responsible for any of Enron's accounting judgments or any of its disclosure judgments."[102]

If we take these defenses at face value, it seems that we are back to Frank Partnoy's "daisy chain," where no one party can be held accountable—each stayed within the formal rules and lacked knowledge of how their actions interacted with those of others in the chain.[103] However, when one scrutinizes the cases more closely, the alibis become suspect. For example, it was dubious that Lay choose Vinson & Elkins to lead an in-house investigation of Sherron Watkins's concerns about Fastow's SPEs—and equally dubious that the law firm accepted the job—given that Vinson & Elkins was so intimately involved with the SPEs.[104]

The daisy chain metaphor does capture the network character of the organized deceptions and the fact that the power and knowledge of participants was distributed. However, we have shown that while the frauds did not usually involve a single power center, they did involve multiple centers from which strategically positioned participants exerted power over others in the course of organizing frauds and other deceptions. Some, such as Jack Grubman, exercised a more informal sort of power within networks extending across firms, while others, such as Bernie Ebbers and Andrew Fastow, used both formal hierarchical power as well as informal network power. Among other things, these characters were the prime shapers of "rancid rules" through their ability to define which practices (and actors) within a firm or a network were to be valued. Such actors took many direct and indirect roles in organizing others to engage in deceptions. But to know that sociological relationships exist is a different matter from proving intent to commit fraud. Eliot Spitzer notes that with regard to proving intent, white-collar fraud is analogous to Mob cases: "You have the trigger guy down the street who committed the crime. But how do you prove that the soldier reported in to the capo who reported in to the crime boss."[105] It seemed for a time that Partnoy might be correct about the alegality of many New Economy scandals— especially as figures such as Ebbers, Skilling, and Lay avoided indictment. However, when Skilling and Lay were indicted in mid-2004, all three had been charged with criminal offenses for having taken lead roles in orchestrating fraud. The last indictment—of Lay on July 8, 2004—added him to a case pending against Skilling and Richard Causey, Enron's ex-chief accounting officer. This indictment calls Lay one of the "leaders and organizers of criminal activity," stating that Skilling "spearheaded" the scheme until he left in August 2001, and that Lay then "took over leadership of the conspiracy." Lay is charged with misleading analysts, investors, and Enron employees by claiming that all was well when he knew it was not. The government lists the following "objectives of the conspiracy":

- reporting recurring earnings that falsely appeared to grow smoothly by approximately 15 to 20 percent annually and thus created the illusion that Enron met or exceeded the published expectations of securities analysts . . . ;
- touting falsely the success of Enron's business units;
- concealing large losses, "write-downs," and other negative information concerning its business units;
- masking the true magnitude of debt and other obligations . . . ;
- deceiving credit ratings agencies in order to maintain an investment-grade credit rating; and
- artificially inflating the share price of Enron's stock.

And when it comes to identifying violations of rules, the indictment is a *tour de force,* belying Partnoy's fears that regulators and prosecutors might not be able to hold anybody accountable for deceptions. It accuses Lay, Skilling, and Causey of using (or causing others to use) "secret oral side-deals, back-dated documents, disguised debt, material omissions, and outright false statements to further the scheme." It cites the following specific devices as being used to further fraud:

- structuring financial transactions in a misleading manner in order to achieve earnings and cash flow objectives, avoid booking large losses in asset values, and conceal debt, including through the fraudulent use of purported third-party entities . . . ;
- manufacturing earnings and artificially improving Enron's balance sheet through fraudulent overvaluation of assets;
- fraudulently circumventing accounting standards . . . in order to conceal the amount of Enron's debt and to create the false appearance of greater earnings and cash flow;

- concealing large losses and failures in Enron's two highly-touted new businesses, Enron Broadband Services ("EBS") and EES;
- manipulating earnings through fraudulent use of reserve accounts to mask volatility in Enron's wholesale energy trading earnings . . . ;
- fraudulently circumventing accounting standards applicable to the disclosure and recognition of impairments to goodwill; and
- making false and misleading statements and omissions of facts . . . about Enron's financial condition.[106]

It seems, then, that professional pumpsters and financial engineers are not the only ones with the ability to construct reality. So too can state agents when they commit to enforcing laws and regulations that protect ordinary investors. The question we turn to now concerns just how deep this commitment is at the highest reaches of the government.

CHAPTER SEVEN

Forgive and Forget

Responses to Corporate Corruption

U.S. policy-makers have offered their main responses to the New Economy scandals, making it a good time to ask what, if anything, they seem to have learned from the free market experiments of the 1990s. We propose that the wave of corporate fraud provides an opportunity to test two key assumptions underlying neoliberal policies. One is that pushing risk-taking and responsibility down to the level of ordinary individuals is in their interest (and society's), as it unleashes creativity and initiative. The second is that markets are self-correcting—in terms of *prices* because the actions of self-interested actors (in the aggregate) will cause prices to move toward their "true" value, and in terms of *behavior* because business actors will refrain from fraud out of a concern for their reputation (if you become known as a cheat, others will not do business with you).

Our examination of the New Economy scandals casts serious doubts on these assumptions. Ordinary investors who were left to their own devices were systematically deceived by groups of insiders. To say that they will come to recognize frauds—or the real worth of commodities such as stocks—is beside the point; frauds such as Ponzi schemes (and speculative markets) are usually organized so that enlightenment comes after the damage is done and the predators have moved on. By definition, New Economy insiders who pumped and dumped got out before deceptions surfaced. Our study also has made clear the social and institutional nature of these misdeeds; the motives and acts cannot be reduced to the level of individuals. The scandals were the work of clusters of actors within organizations—or within networks that bridged organizations. While the perpetrators were indeed concerned with their "reputations," these concerns turned out to be motives for engaging in misdeeds. There was a broad concern with establishing one's credibility as a New Economy actor, including not just displaying the requisite norms and sensibilities, but also measuring up to financial criteria, such as share prices and quarterly statements. And the reputational concerns of those seeking entry to the heart of the action—the more exclusive circuits of insider exchange—led them to go along with deceptions that preyed on outsiders. Professional ethics had little pull in comparison, especially where state oversight was weakened. In sum, business actors inhabit social worlds that possess multiple sets of rules and status systems. As it turns out, state institutions matter quite a lot in determining the relative influence of different sorts of guidelines.

Unfortunately, government responses have not indicated much in the way of learning about the perils of promiscuous deregulation or utopian ideology. This is not surprising, as neither free market ideals nor policies were adopted with the intention of putting them to a test, for the embrace of market fundamentalism was, and still is, a "faith-based initiative"—intertwined with the naked self-interest of the powerful.

Government Response

Cracking Down on Corporate Corruption . . . Sort of

From the very beginning of the corporate scandals, the Bush administration was on the defensive. Not only were they very pro-business, but Bush and his colleagues had direct and extensive ties to top Enron executives. Moreover, the public soon came to learn that George W. Bush and

Vice President Dick Cheney had, in their previous careers, been involved in business deals that were strikingly similar to the shady transactions at Enron. In the late 1980s, while his father was vice president and president of the United States, George W. Bush was on the board of an oil company, Harken Energy, from which he received loans to buy stock in the company. These loans were unusual in that they did not require any of the principal to be repaid for eight years. In June 1990, Bush sold 212,000 shares of the stock for nearly $850,000. Two months later, Harken surprised analysts when it announced a $23 million loss for the second quarter. The next day Harken's stock price fell by 20 percent, and within six months it had lost nearly two-thirds of its value. The SEC investigated the Bush stock sale for possible evidence of insider trading, ultimately concluding that he had not, technically, violated the law. Bush's critics, however, point out that the head of the SEC at the time had been appointed by and was a close friend of his father, President George H. W. Bush. When President George W. Bush was asked, in 2002, about the transactions, his reply might as well have been written by Kenneth Lay: "[I]n the corporate world, sometimes things aren't exactly black and white when it comes to accounting procedures."[1]

Meanwhile, Bush's vice president had his own explaining to do. Prior to his nomination for the vice presidency in 2000, Dick Cheney was the CEO of Halliburton Corp., a large Texas energy and construction company. In 1998, while he was the chief executive, the company changed its accounting practices (with the approval of its outside accountants, the ubiquitous Arthur Andersen) so as to book as revenue more than $100 million in disputed cost overruns. Had the more traditional accounting method been applied, more than half of one quarter's profits would have been wiped out.[2] When he left for the White House, Cheney was given a "retirement package" worth $20 million.

These facts, combined with the cavalier attitude toward the emerging corporate scandals displayed by other members of his administration (the Treasury secretary's "genius of capitalism" comment, for example), increased the pressure on the administration to take forceful action against corporate corruption. Bush himself did not help matters with tepid statements in the early days of the Enron investigation, telling reporters, for example, that his own mother-in-law had recently purchased stock in the company that had become worthless.[3] From the start, the administration's efforts to go after Enron were hobbled by close ties not only between the White House and Lay, but also between federal law enforcement agents and Enron's thousands of employees. The entire investigation had to be taken over by the Justice Department after the U.S. attorney in Houston decided to recuse himself and virtually every lawyer on his staff from the case because of personal connections with Enron employees.[4] Even at the Justice Department, Attorney General John Ashcroft was forced to recuse himself from the Enron investigation after critics pointed to the fact that he received $57,000 in campaign contributions from Enron when he was a U.S. senator.[5] Finding a prosecutor anywhere in Texas who did not have some ties to the energy company proved to be difficult. Even the state's attorney general withdrew from the investigation because he had received $193,000 in contributions from the company.[6] In Washington, the "get tough" rhetoric escalated in July 2002 when the president announced that he was creating a Corporate Fraud Task Force that would function as a "financial crimes SWAT team."[7] But from the outset this new squad was beset with questions about conflicts. Named to head the task force was Assistant Deputy Attorney General Larry Thompson, who, prior to joining the Justice Department, had served on the board of directors of a credit card firm that was forced to pay $400 million to settle charges that the company had defrauded consumers.[8]

At the same time that the White House was feeling pressure to act, members of Congress were feeling the heat from constituents who were unhappy to learn that their representatives, both Republicans and Democrats, had accepted campaign contributions from some of the largest corporate malefactors. Senator Joseph Lieberman, for example, who headed a Senate committee investigating the Enron debacle, acknowledged that he had taken funds from both Enron and Arthur Andersen.[9] A number of congressional bills were proposed to close the loopholes in corporate governance. The one that gained the most support and ultimately became the cornerstone of the government's efforts to reform corporate accountability was the Sarbanes-Oxley Act. The law's sponsors and namesakes were a political odd couple. Paul Sarbanes was a Democratic senator from Maryland, and Michael Oxley a Republican congressman from Ohio with deep connections to the financial services industry. Oxley (who the *Wall Street Journal* characterized as having "carried oceans of water for the [accounting] industry") had, in spring 2002, crafted a reform bill in the House that met with the approval of the accounting industry.[10] The law would have created an oversight board to regulate the accounting industry, but it would not have been independent. Rather, it would have been under the jurisdiction of the SEC, which at the time was headed by the industry-friendly Harvey Pitt.[11] Meanwhile, in the Senate, Sarbanes was working on a similar bill that called for more regulation of the securities and accounting industries, a bill whose opposition was led by none other than Phil Gramm. For a while it looked like the powerful Gramm and his allies would win, but then the tides turned in June, when WorldCom announced the discovery of a multibillion dollar accounting fraud scheme within its ranks. With this event, many members of Congress realized that the public would not stand for any measure that appeared to be watered down and quickly signed on to a bill that combined elements of both the House and Senate versions.[12]

When President Bush signed the bill in late July 2002, in a ceremony held in the East Room of the White House under a banner that read "Corporate Responsibility," he said that the measure signaled that "the era of low standards and false profits is over."[13] The signing was attended by a number of prominent lawmakers and regulators, but not Vice President Cheney, who was conveniently in Iowa at a fund-raising breakfast, where his presence was protested by the state's Democratic party with a costumed character named "Hallibacon" the "corporate crime-fighting pig."[14]

The law's provisions (1) created an independent Public Company Accounting Oversight Board to police the accounting industry; (2) required that CEO's certify the accuracy of their companies' financial statements and included stiff criminal penalties for violations; (3) created new criminal penalties of up to twenty-five years in prison for document shredding and defrauding shareholders; and (4) directed the U.S. Sentencing Commission to revise sentences for a number of white-collar crimes.[15] The law was intended to symbolize a new "get tough" response to corporate corruption. On signing the bill, President Bush said, "No more easy money for corporate criminals, just hard time."[16]

Despite the fanfare with which Sarbanes-Oxley was enacted, critics argued that it did not go nearly far enough, complaining of key omissions.[17] In particular, two critical gaps in investor protection that were opened in the 1990s were left unfilled. First, the law did not require corporations to list stock options as an expense on financial statements. This was a key issue in the debate over corporate governance. Many firms had deceived investors by failing to list executive stock options as charges against earnings, the way that other forms of compensation are listed; had they done so, their financial pictures would have changed significantly. Second, the new law failed to reverse court rulings and legislation that curtailed the right of shareholders to sue executives and their pro-

fessional accomplices for securities fraud. Why it was that post-Enron reformers would leave such serious gaps takes us back to the political roots
of the scandals themselves.

No Shame in My Game
(The Congressional Take . . . on Reform)

The reform impulse was a nondenominational affair involving the "people's" branch of government—Congress—as well as the executive, and
Republicans along with Democrats. In that respect, it was not all that different than the bipartisan romance with "the market" (and corporate
contributions) that helped set the scene for fraud in the first place. Indeed, many who led the charge to make the rules "mean something
again" were the same figures who had helped gut or subvert effective
regulation seven or eight years before.

This paradox speaks volumes about the gaps in the major reform
efforts. It also provided Enron's chief operating officer, Jeffrey Skilling,
with a rare bit of fun during a 2002 Senate appearance. Between 1996
and 2000, Enron had failed to subtract $600 million in stock options
from the $1.8 billion it reported as earnings on financial reports, while
at the same time it deducted those options from its tax liability—a strategy that helped the firm pay no taxes in four out of five of those years.[18]
Skilling told a Senate committee that the practice was indeed "egregious." But, after a tart exchange with Senator Barbara Boxer of California, he gleefully reminded the senators that "FASB tried to change that,
and you introduced legislation in 1994 to keep that exemption."[19]

The event that Skilling referred to was the attempt by the Financial
Accounting Standards Board (FASB) to require firms to deduct stock
options from their earnings on their financial statements. The rationale
was that stock options were costly to companies and should be treated as
an expense just like other forms of compensation. Skilling was all too accurate in hinting that today's lead reformers had been the biggest enablers of yesteryear, for the leader in the successful 1995 campaign to
block the FASB proposal—Senator Joseph Lieberman—would become
the head of a Senate committee that seven years later was investigating
the failure of the financial gatekeepers (federal agencies, auditors, stock
analysts) to protect the public in the Enron fiasco. From this new pulpit,
Lieberman piously warned of the threat to middle-class investors who
"without sound information—or even worse, with misleading informa-

tion . . . may as well go gambling."[20] But he did not acknowledge his own role in opening the door for corporate accountants to provide "misleading information" in the form of deceptive earnings statements.

This sort of post-Enron hypocrisy was displayed by a number of prominent political figures, including those who had sponsored the Private Securities Litigation Reform Act (PSRLA)—the 1995 law that greatly reduced the accountability of accountants, lawyers, and bankers who aided corporate executives in the commission of securities fraud. Several backers of the act—described in one 1995 op-ed as a "gift to the boiler room crowd"—also later went on to become prominent figures in efforts to rein in corporate corruption after the collapse of Enron.[21] One of the bill's sponsors was Representative Michael Oxley, who would later co-author the Sarbanes-Oxley Act. Another was Representative Billy Tauzin of Louisiana, who would later head a House Commerce Committee investigating Enron and, specifically, the shredding of Enron documents by Arthur Andersen.[22]

So what were the people's representatives thinking back in 1994 and 1995? There is reason to believe that more lay behind the bipartisan drive to liberate big business from regulation than free market ideology. Arthur Levitt, the head of the Securities and Exchange Commission during the period in question, later reflected on the role of campaign contributions in the 1995 campaign to stop FASB reforms: "There was no question in my mind that campaign contributions played the determinative role in that Senate activity. Corporate America waged the most aggressive lobbying campaign I think that they had ever put together on behalf of this issue. And the Congress was responsive to that."[23] Much the same dynamic (and the same corporate donors) factored in the political mobilization for the 1995 Private Securities Litigation Reform Act. One sponsor—Congressman Tauzin—held the dubious distinction of having received more campaign contributions from Arthur Andersen ($57,000 from 1989 to 2001) and from the accounting industry as a whole ($289,000) than anyone else in the House of Representatives. He wasn't the only well-placed beneficiary of the accounting industry's largess. After President Clinton vetoed the 1995 act, the campaign to override the veto in the Senate was led by Christopher Dodd, a Democrat who, like Senator Lieberman, represented the state of Connecticut, home to a number of large accounting firms. Dodd was far and away the leading Senate recipient of contributions from the accounting industry, taking in $482,453 between 1989 and 2001.[24] In the 1995/1996 election cycle, as the PSRLA was being debated in Congress, Dodd received nearly a quarter of a million dollars from the accounting industry even though he was not up for reelection. As one observer put it, "Dodd might as well have been on the accounting industry's payroll. He couldn't have helped them any more than he did as a U.S. Senator."[25]

The lesson, it would seem, is that a second form of corruption—a "soft" corruption resulting from the commodification of politics—has not only contributed to the onslaught of corporate corruption in the 1990s, but also hamstrung current efforts at reform.

The Law in Action

The legislative response to corporate corruption, then, was seriously flawed. But it was not just the "law in the books" that was deficient, but also the "law in action"—the specific actions that were taken to implement the law—that was woefully inadequate. The tough talk in Washington was followed with half-hearted campaigns to clamp down on corporate misconduct, watered-down reforms, and foxes-in-charge-of-the-henhouse appointments to enforcement positions. This foot-dragging response was not only the result of the many personal and financial connections between the White House, Capitol Hill, and corporate America, but also the result of the particular view of the world (and, specifically, the role of corporations and their agents in it) shared by the members of these groups. In this view, the vast majority of corporate actors are honest individuals whose contributions to society far outweigh the misconduct of a minuscule number of businesspeople who have crossed the fine, technical line between legal and illegal behavior. This view found expression in the idea, oft-repeated by members of Congress and the Bush administration, that the corporate scandals of the late nineties were the result of a "few bad apples" rather than evidence of systemic problems in the marketplace. To punish the many with fundamental changes in the system for the bad acts of a few would, from this perspective, not only be unjust but would seriously impede the ability of corporations to make their essential contributions to the progress of society.

As the evidence of stock manipulation at Enron, Global Crossing, and other firms mounted in early 2002, it was the SEC that was primarily responsible for taking action. The agency's new head, Harvey Pitt, came to the SEC after a long career as a lawyer on and around Wall Street, where he represented the accounting industry (and in the 1980s notorious insider-trader Ivan Boesky). He vowed to change the agency, telling business leaders that they would see a "kinder, gentler SEC," by which he meant an entity that was less interested in enforcing rules than in co-operating with business.[26] From the start, Pitt attempted to minimize the scope of the corporate scandals, comparing the situation to Lincoln Steffens's 1931 essay "I Create a Crime Wave," in which the former reporter described how he had created the perception of a crime wave by writing more sensationalist crime stories, when in fact no surge in crime had occurred.[27] He also disparaged the notion that the Private Securities Litigation Reform Act or the way that stock options were accounted for played any part in the accounting scandals of the late nineties.[28] In line with the industry's position, he favored private sector regulation of the accounting industry rather than regulation by an independent government agency. After only fifteen months on the job, Pitt was forced to resign as commissioner of the SEC after even his staunchest supporters began to see him as a liability.

The straw that finally broke Pitt's back was the appointment of William Webster, the former FBI director, to head the Public Company Accounting Board, an independent agency created by the Sarbanes-Oxley Act to oversee the accounting industry. Early on, John Biggs, the head of the TIAA-CREF pension plan, was the frontrunner for the post, in large part because he did not have extensive connections to the accounting industry or Wall Street. However, the accounting industry opposed Biggs because, in the words of the *Wall Street Journal,* he was "not in the tank for the remaining Big Four" accounting firms.[29] Specifically, he favored expensing stock options and placing restrictions on accounting firms' doing consulting work for the companies they audit (as Arthur Andersen did with Enron).[30] The SEC chairman bowed to the accounting industry's demands and replaced Biggs with Webster as the lead candidate. Only after the SEC commissioners voted to appoint Webster was it revealed that the individual selected to head an agency that was meant to instill confidence in investors had until recently been the chairman of the audit committee at a company whose financial reporting was under investigation by the SEC.[31] A week after these facts were made public in early November 2002, Chairman Pitt resigned. A few days later Webster followed suit. These events were indicative of the administration's unwillingness to enact real reform and willingness to conform to the financial services industry's version of reform.

This industry-friendly attitude was confirmed by a rare insider account of high-level discussions in the executive branch by former Secretary of the Treasury Paul O'Neill. In his controversial memoir, O'Neill described internal discussions between himself, Harvey Pitt, White House aides, and cabinet members that led up to a March 7 speech by President Bush in which he outlined a "Ten-Point Plan to Improve Corporate Responsibility." O'Neill had proposed changing the legal standards by which executives could be held liable for misstatements in their company's financial reports from the current standard that required the government to prove "recklessness" on the part of executives, which requires proof of intent, to one that required only proof of "negligence," a lesser standard that would prevent them from claiming they were out of the loop and unaware of misstatements (as Ken Lay and other CEOs had). At a meeting held on February 22, 2002, Pitt reacted negatively to O'Neill's proposal, arguing: "It's not the government's job to protect shareholders from the risk of bad management." Pitt preferred language that referred to "conscious avoidance"—a standard that O'Neill saw as "a hair's breadth from recklessness—you'd have to prove intent." Also in attendance at the meeting was Lawrence Lindsey, the administration's top economic advisor, who opposed any change in the standard: "Better incentives for better behavior by CEOs can, I think, be achieved in the existing framework."[32] Lindsey, perhaps coincidentally, had earned $50,000 two years earlier as a consultant to Enron.[33] O'Neill refused to back down and days later publicized his proposal at a luncheon for financial services executives. Their reaction was immediate: "[T]he phones in the West Wing rang. CEO contributors to the Bush campaign were weighing in. The calls were mostly of a single message: 'I know O'Neill's supposed to be one of us . . . but rein him in!'"[34] And reined in he was. The president's Ten-Point Plan made no mention of a "negligence" standard for executives, and eight months later O'Neill resigned as secretary of the treasury.

Too Big to Jail

Consistent with policy-makers' failure to enact real, structural reforms of corporate governance, White House officials and their congressional allies frequently characterized corporate corruption as the result of individuals and their personal flaws, rather than as evidence of a breakdown of the checks and balances that ensure integrity in the system. In a speech delivered at the New York Stock Exchange in July 2002, George W. Bush, the first MBA president, declared: "In the long run, there is no capitalism without conscience; there is no wealth without character. And so again today I'm calling for a new ethic of personal responsibility in the business community, an ethic that will increase investor confidence, will make employees proud of their companies, and again regain the trust of the American people."[35] Shifting the locus of responsibility for the corporate crisis onto individuals and their ethics naturally suggested a policy that would focus on imposing tough criminal sanctions on those members of the business community who had lost their sense of "personal responsibility."

As evidence of its successful pursuit of this goal, in July 2003, the White House announced that the President's Corporate Fraud Task Force had charged 354 defendants with some type of corporate fraud and had won over 250 convictions, 25 involving former CEOs.[36]

Impressive as these numbers may sound, their significance is difficult to assess. The great majority of these prosecutions were undertaken by U.S. attorney's offices across the country. White-collar and corporate crime cases were a normal part of these offices' caseloads before the Corporate Fraud Task Force was created, as well as after. In the absence of baseline data on corporate crimes and their prosecution, one has no way of determining whether the cases reported by the task force represent a significant increase in the number of corporate crime prosecutions undertaken by federal prosecutors. The best one can do is to examine trend data on white-collar crime cases (a category that includes corporate crimes) prosecuted by U.S. attorneys in federal court.[37]

The data in Figure 7.1 show that despite the rhetoric of the Bush administration, there was no significant increase in white-collar prosecutions in the post-Enron years of 2002 and 2003. The data show that white-collar prosecutions peaked in 1995 and remained relatively stable from 1998 through 2003. In these data, white-collar crime is a broad category that includes a number of different offenses, and it is difficult to determine where corporate crimes of the sort described in this book might fit in this scheme.[38] However, had there been a significant increase in corporate crime prosecutions, one would expect that it would show up in these data.

These trends are generally consistent with data from the FBI on the number of that agency's white-collar crime investigations that resulted in convictions (including pre-trial diversions). Those data, as reported in the attorney general's annual report for 2003, show that white-collar convictions *decreased* by 28 percent between 1998 and 2003, with much of that decline occurring in 2003, when white-collar convictions dropped by 17 percent from the previous year.[39] The FBI data are admittedly imprecise—lumping complex corporate crimes in with all other white-

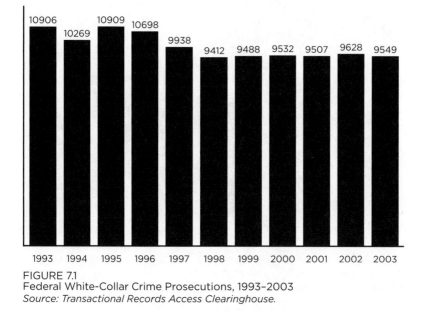

FIGURE 7.1
Federal White-Collar Crime Prosecutions, 1993–2003
Source: Transactional Records Access Clearinghouse.

collar offenses—but nonetheless, they clearly show that, in the midst of a corporate crime wave, the principal federal law enforcement agency did not step up its efforts to pursue white-collar criminals.[40] A report from the Department of Justice's inspector general concluded that the FBI's declining interest in white-collar crime was directly related to the post-9/11 decision to transfer over three hundred agents out of white-collar crime units and into units devoted to investigating terrorism.[41]

By contrast, data from the Securities and Exchange Commission on their enforcement activities show significant increases. The data in Figure 7.2 show that total enforcement actions increased by 42 percent, from 477 in 1998 to 679 in 2003. More specifically, enforcement actions involving what the SEC refers to as "issuer financial statements and reporting cases"—instances in which false claims are made on financial statements—rose by 152 percent, from 79 in 1998 to 199 in 2003. The increased workload at the SEC was also reflected in the fact that the number of investigations opened each year by the agency more than doubled between 1997 and 2003.[42]

These data, limited as they may be, suggest that corporate crimes in the late nineties and early years of the next decade were dealt with primarily through civil and administrative rather than criminal means. This is not to deny that many corporate criminals were, in fact, charged with criminal wrongdoing, particularly in high-profile cases such as Enron.

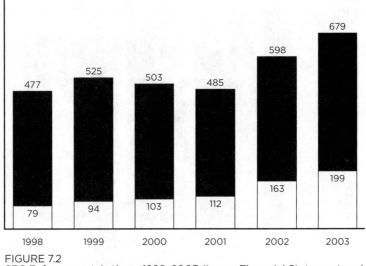

FIGURE 7.2
SEC Enforcement Actions, 1998–2003 (Issuer Financial Statement and
Reporting Actions in Unshaded Areas)
Sources: SEC Annual Reports, 1998–2003.

Yet, compared to the scope of the phenomenon as indicated by the very
large numbers of financial restatements and class action securities fraud
lawsuits filed, the statistics on indictments and convictions leave one
with the impression that many corporate miscreants and their professional confederates in the legal, banking, and accounting industries
never faced the prospect of doing any time in jail. The corporate crimes
described in this book were nothing if not complex, typically involving
scores of individuals acting in a variety of capacities, and with varying degrees of legal culpability determined by their role in the scheme, their
knowledge, and their intent. In the criminal case against Enron's Jeffrey
Skilling, for example, prosecutors listed 114 unindicted co-conspirators,
including "individuals from some of the big financial institutions, law
firms and other businesses with which Enron fostered close ties."[43] This
suggests that, in general, the number of those individuals and organizations potentially subject to criminal sanctions in the New Economy scandals was far greater than the number actually charged.

Why, then, weren't more of these individuals or their companies
charged with crimes? Two explanations seem plausible. The first is that
while many of these acts of deception may have met the definition of
civil fraud, they may not have violated any criminal laws. For example,
the practice of round-tripping—two companies engaging in identical

trades with each other in order to boost revenue—has been illegal in the securities industry for some time, but in the energy industry these trades in and of themselves do not violate the law, in that they are seen as transactions between private individuals. This distinction is not just a quirk of the law, but an exemption that energy companies fought hard to retain.

Other examples of this criminal-but-not-illegal conduct include the issuing of biased research reports by stock analysts at investment banks. New York Attorney General Eliot Spitzer argued that existing laws made prosecution of most of these acts difficult if not impossible: "The rules were corrupt. The analyst on the street by and large were playing by a set of corrupt rules but rules that had been accepted by the regulators. And so we had to change the rules. And you couldn't look at an analyst and say to 'em, well, you violated the new rules but you were playing by the old rules but we're gonna send you to jail for violating the new rules."[44] One of the major difficulties in these cases, Spitzer argued, was that to obtain criminal convictions prosecutors would have been required to prove that stock analysts had an intent to defraud rather than had simply given bad advice to clients.[45] The General Accounting Office reached a similar conclusion in its analysis of the role that investment banks played in the structured-finance deals that involved offshore entities such as Mahonia. Securities regulators would have had a difficult time bringing and winning civil fraud suits in these cases because of legal standards that require proof that the bank's agents had "actual knowledge" of Enron's intentions in the deals.[46]

A second and complementary explanation for the relatively low rates of criminal prosecution begins with an observation of the pervasiveness of some corrupt business practices, indeed their embeddedness, in certain industries. The reporting of false data to natural gas indexes, for example, was referred to by the Federal Energy Regulatory Commission as "epidemic," and an industry insider testified that "exaggeration was an accepted industry practice" (see chapter 2). On Wall Street, the conflicts of interest between stock analysts and investment bankers that led to biased research were not just found among high-profile analysts, such as Jack Grubman and Henry Blodget, but afflicted the entire industry. Spitzer described how he and his colleagues reached this conclusion: "At a certain point, we looked at each other and said, 'This is fundamentally corrupt. This isn't merely one aberrant act. This is pervasive.' There was a tipping point, where we went from viewing this as a problem that was isolated and could be carved out, probably one analyst or two analysts and no more, to the recognition that we had suddenly arrived at—that the entire structure was fraud."[47] Under these conditions, where fraud was endemic to an industry, it would have strained the resources of investigators and prosecutors to pursue all or even most of the individuals who had engaged in these practices. The pervasiveness of corrupt practices was even argued by attorneys representing white-collar defendants, who claimed that their clients were being singled out for prosecution for practices that were commonplace in their industries.[48]

Rather than pursuing individuals, an alternative strategy would have been to charge individual companies under corporate crime statutes. By and large, however, this strategy was not applied to the energy trading industry, the dot-com industry, the telecommunications industry, or to Wall Street investment banks. The decision not to pursue criminal charges against either individuals or corporations came in for considerable public criticism in the "global settlement" worked out by the New York attorney general's office, the SEC, and ten large Wall Street firms.[49] In response to these criticisms, Elliot Spitzer argued that had charges been filed against these large investment banks, the consequences could have been devastating, not only to the companies themselves but to the financial services industry and the economy as a whole. His explanation for his decision to work out a settlement with Merrill Lynch, in which Merrill agreed to pay a $100 million penalty and make changes in the way it did business, rather than indict the bank illustrates the general principle: "What we are seeking here is to reform the system and restore integrity and driving Merrill Lynch out of business wouldn't have made sense. [If criminal charges had been brought against the firm,] [t]hey would have a brokerage house that is under indictment, that if convicted criminally of the sort of behavior that I think we probably could have convicted them of, would go out of business."[50] Spitzer's explanation is more than a rationalization; a criminal conviction or even an indictment can often mean a death sentence for companies in the financial services industry. Arthur Andersen is a case in point. A little over two months after being convicted on obstruction of justice charges, the company closed its doors after its clients fled en masse out of fear of being associated with the tainted firm.

The attorney general's explanation is consistent with a broader policy position that has surfaced in a number of recent financial scandals and crises: the "too big to fail" argument. Following the savings and loan crisis of the 1980s, federal regulators made the decision to guarantee all thrift deposits, not just those under $100,000 as the law required, under a philosophy that was meant to ensure stability in the banking industry. Similarly, in 1998, Long-Term Capital, a secretive hedge fund that controlled $125 billion in assets, was on the verge of collapse after a series of highly risky investments did not pan out. Alan Greenspan, the chairman of the Federal Reserve, arguing that the firm's collapse would threaten the entire economy, organized a private sector bailout.[51]

In the post-Enron context, the question this position raises for corporate criminals was put succinctly by business reporter Ari Weinberg: "[A]re bankers and analysts these days too big for jail?"[52] If the answer is "yes," then the regulatory/law enforcement system creates perverse incentives for corporate actors in essential financial industries to engage in criminal activities because the deterrent effect of criminal sanctions has been effectively lifted in exchange for economic stability. A similar conclusion was reached by Kitty Calavita and her colleagues in their study of the savings and loan crisis. "The government's response to the savings and loan debacle can be seen, then, as an effort directed less at penalizing thrift wrongdoers for their misdeeds than at limiting damage to the industry, preventing comparable damage in other financial sectors, and containing the hemorrhage of government-insured capital."[53] In short, the government was more interested in "damage control" than "crime control." Much the same policy, we would argue, was followed by the government in its response to the large financial firms on Wall Street and elsewhere that aided and abetted corporate pump-and-dumpers in their crimes.[54]

This situation points out a contradiction in the neoliberal position on markets and regulation. Neoliberals, particularly those from the Chicago school of economics, are fond of asserting that fraud and abuse are best dealt with by market discipline; individuals and firms that engage in corrupt practices will suffer reputational losses, lose customers and clients, and eventually go out of business. Under "too big to fail" policies, however, one sees exactly the opposite: individuals employed by very large corporations, deemed to be essential, are given immunity for their violations and their firms are kept afloat through government intervention in the markets. Two of the principals at Long-Term Capital, for example, were well-known neoliberal economists who frequently touted the Chicago-school line about free markets and deregulation. Yet, they were more than willing to accept the Federal Reserve's efforts to organize the fund's bailout. As one commentator put it: "You wonder what definition of capitalism they use to bail out the arbitragers and the speculators, but insist that the people who make automobiles and steel and textiles must live and die by the market."[55]

Spitzerkrieg (The Little Regulator Who Could)
In contrast to top federal regulators (who often seem to be members of the "club" they are charged with monitoring), state regulators have been more willing to shake up the status quo. Commenting upon his office's pioneering forays against abuses by mutual funds, New York Attorney General Eliot Spitzer offered a thinly veiled indictment of federal regulators: "Before we began our investigation nobody had ever viewed [market] timing as being a civil violation, much less a criminal case. We could not simply wake up one day and say we're criminalizing practices *that had been known to regulators and where they'd done nothing*" (our emphasis). Or as a *Fortune* reporter put it, Spitzer has "exposed some of the worst practices on Wall Street—issues federal regulators wouldn't touch." The more activist stance of this state-level unit—and the robust results achieved—suggests that political commitments matter much more in regulatory responses than the level of resources. New York's Attorney General Spitzer has fifteen lawyers at his disposal, compared to over one thousand at the lethargic SEC. The posture of Spitzer's office stands out in yet another way—Spitzer acts less like a prosecutor and more like a policy-maker, which is reflected in his "method": "uncover an endemic problem, apply pressure by bringing high-profile cases and generating withering public attention, then use all that leverage to produce change—almost always through negotiated settlements."[56] Spitzer amplifies his modest legal leverage by using exposés to challenge the credibility of entire industries with investors or other clients. His activism also has challenged the legitimacy of the SEC, which has reacted indignantly—as if some unspoken rule or gentleman's agreement had been broached.

Spitzer's initiative vis-à-vis financial analysts in particular seems an intriguing success story. The settlement requires that ten major Wall Street firms pay $1 billion in fines and agree to spend $438 million for independent research that will appear alongside their own research reports over the course of five years. And the firms have to adopt rules to ensure that analysts no longer link their efforts to investment banking: "Analysts now have to get approval from a 'research recommendation committee' before they can initiate coverage of a new stock or even change a rating on a stock. Their public appearances are monitored closely—if they're even allowed. Though analysts are still supposed to vet banking deals, they can no longer attend the meetings where the investment bankers pitch underwriting business. . . . Analysts have to add new disclosures when they put out research reports, including a certification that 'all the views in the research report accurately reflect our personal views.'" Insiders propose that investment banking clients generally still expect analysts to support them and that the analysts can signal their cooperative attitude with "winks and nods." However, the new rules for how financial analysts are to behave may not be as important as rules about how they are paid and organized structurally. The settlement mandates that "analysts can no longer be paid for helping to generate banking deals, and research can no longer view itself as an adjunct to the banking department."[57]

The intervention appears to have spurred not just a crisis for the financial analysis industry, but also its restructuring. Pay for analysts has been slashed, highly paid stars have been replaced by junior analysts, and large research departments have cut their staff by a third or more. More profoundly, dozens of insurgents (research boutiques) that claim to offer research that is specialized and independent are challenging the incumbent firms and business models that had dominated—the large firms that linked financial analysis to investment banking. For example, *Fortune* cited the case of a mid-sized research firm that sent out a letter to its clients (large institutional investors) stating that it would discontinue "unfortunate practices" that had tarnished the field: it would no longer issue "buy, hold, sell" ratings, nor would it release quarterly earnings notes; instead, it would stress "good investment ideas" and "proprietary information" that represented the sort of research not easily duplicated by its competitors. The founder of a research boutique declared, "The old research model is dead"[58] by the fact that the institutional investors who buy Wall Street research have joined the rebellion; Spitzer's exposés have led them to complain about the quality of research and to demand that the banks unbundle the fee for research services from the rest of the commission they receive.

One's satisfaction at seeing "small" states enjoy some successes vis-à-vis "big" capital is tempered by indignation that they seem to be the main site for serious policy reform. The sense of a dereliction of duty at the federal level is only intensified by the fact that legislation has been introduced in Congress to put an end to the kind of activist regulation that Spitzer and some other state attorneys general have engaged in.[59]

Though the immediate political climate makes passage unlikely, one anticipates that sponsors of similar bills will—like thieves in the night—return when no one is watching.

The Unrepentant: Responses from the Business Community and Beyond

The sudden plunge in the stock markets that began in 2001 followed by the revelations of widespread corruption in corporate America had the potential to provoke a crisis of faith among the true believers in the New Economy and the cheerleaders of the nineties economic boom. It was increasingly difficult to ignore accumulating evidence that the era was greatly overblown through the use of smoke and mirrors—a generalized illusion of endless prosperity that abetted carefully constructed ruses whose purpose was to fleece investors. Faced with these facts, one might expect that chastened executives, along with media pundits and other "professional pumpsters," would, if not publicly recant their beliefs, at least express some doubt or remorse about business practices that inflicted so much damage on the average worker and investor during the late nineties.

In fact, with a few exceptions, what one saw in the wake of the corporate scandals was a tendency by business leaders to defiantly deny responsibility for these events. Specifically, in the emerging revisionist interpretation of events of the late nineties one sees a number of distinct themes: (1) an attempt to depict financial crimes as a matter of moral failure rather than the consequences of institutional imbalances; (2) a tendency to defend, or at least minimize the harm in, corporate misconduct by arguing, in essence, that fraud and abuse were the necessary correlates of economic innovation and prosperity; (3) a related effort by a number of corporate leaders to resist the imposition of tighter regulations on the grounds it would reduce incentives for "risk-taking," which, they argue, is normal and necessary under capitalism; and (4) a tendency to blame investors or regulators for the problems. The business community, or more specifically the community of big businesses, does not speak with one voice. But one does find a certain consistency expressed in the views of CEOs, conservative politicians, professional pundits, business consultants, and academic theoreticians, particularly in schools of business. In the post-Enron period these views formed not so much a coherent ideology as a set of defensive postures that could be used to thwart any serious discussion of the broader sources of corporate corruption.

Corporate Crime as Moral Failure

The corporate-crime-as-moral-failure theme was at the center of President Bush's speech at the New York Stock Exchange, where he declared that "there is no capitalism without conscience." In that same speech Bush asserted that business schools were the key to the rehabilitation of business leaders: "Our schools of business must be principled teachers of right and wrong and not surrender to moral confusion and relativism."[60] The reference to "relativism" was a subtle nod to the Religious Right's critique of public education as amoral. The linkages between capitalism and Christian virtue, implicit in Bush's speech, were made explicit in an essay by Rick Santorum, a Republican senator from Pennsylvania, entitled "Accounting for Corporate Misconduct": "No viable economic order can survive without the moral underpinnings of personal responsibility, honesty in business dealings, and Judeo-Christian values . . . democratic capitalism taps into individual creativity and initiative and relies on self-interest—not to satisfy individual greed but to benefit others, the principal other being the family. Such a system not only produces wealth but also virtuous people whose worldly enterprise compliments the work of the Creator."[61]

Other conservative commentators were more specific about the sources of the "moral confusion" that had resulted in corporate malfeasance, pointing the finger directly at the Clinton administration. This accusation was made in the early days following the collapse of Enron by the editors of the *Wall Street Journal,* who wrote: "We'd say it's also impossible to understand Enron outside of the moral climate in which it flourished. Those were the roaring '90s, when all of America reveled in the economic boom. They were also the Clinton years, when we learned that 'everybody does it.'"[62] The blame-Clinton theme was picked up by congressional Republicans who, faced with a number of embarrassing relationships between Enron and their party officials, fought back with the more abstract connection between a perceived decline in moral standards under the Democratic administration and acts of corporate malfeasance. The House Republican campaign chairman, Tom Davis, for example, argued that the origins of the scandalous behavior lay in the "culture of dishonesty and situational ethics that flowed directly from the White House. A lack of accountability, dishonesty, evasion and dissemblance are the true legacies of the Clinton era."[63] Claims that individuals and their personal ethics were at the root of the problem served to divert attention away from the need to change institutions and the rules that guide them in order to avert future crises.

Corporate Criminals as Innovators

Many members of the business community and their allies in the media and academia were uncomfortable with the vagueness of the "moral decline" argument. For them, a much bolder revisionist interpretation of the corporate scandals was needed, one that acknowledged some wrongdoing but kept intact the basic tenets of neoliberalism. The solution was to view the situation from a wider angle, to see corporate actors who broke the rules not as powerful individuals motivated by greed, but as agents of positive social change. Note, for instance, a Michael Lewis essay in the *New York Times Magazine*:

> It is deplorable that some executives fiddled their books and stole from their companies. But their behavior was, in the grand scheme of things, trivial. Less than trivial: expected. A boom without crooks is like a dog without fleas. It doesn't happen. . . . Is it possible that scandal is somehow an essential ingredient in capitalism? That a healthy free-market economy must tempt a certain number of people to behave corruptly, and that a certain number of these will do so? That the crooks are not a sign that something is rotten but that something is working more or less as it was meant to work? After all, a market economy is premised on a system of incentives designed to encourage an ignoble human trait: self-interest. Is it all that shocking that, when this system undergoes an exciting positive transformation, self-interest spins out of control?[64]

A similar view was expressed by influential academics, such as Nobel Prize–winning economist Gary Becker, who defended Enron in a magazine column: "Enron's actions, while self-serving, were generally good for the economy as a whole. The company promoted greater competition in electric power." According to Becker, the disgraced company's negative behavior was far outweighed by the good it did: "Enron's total expenditures on political influence were tiny compared with the potential benefits to consumers from competition in energy markets."[65] Becker's comments were significant not only because he was a Nobel laureate but also because he was one of the chief theoreticians for the neoliberal project and his views thus influenced other conservative economists. Among them were two prominent business school professors who wrote: "[W]e must be careful not to indict everything the firm did . . . the firm moved entrepreneurially into new areas and put itself to the ultimate test of the market. Without that spirit of innovation, the process of capitalism would grind to a screeching halt."[66]

To say that Enron put itself to the test of the market is absurd, given its tireless efforts to hide its performance. In truth, this revisionist interpretation recycled the "New Economy rebel" narrative: despite their faults, the radicals at Enron and elsewhere had struggled to cast aside government's oppressive yoke, thereby liberating consumers from costly, inefficient markets. This provided a convenient ideological escape route for New Economy evangelists whose prophecies about the coming of a new era of prosperity suffered seriously in the aftermath of the dot-com crash. One of these was telecom guru George Gilder. In a provocative article in *Forbes* magazine, Gilder claimed that he trusted disgraced executives such as Gary Winnick, former head of Global Crossing, because, like scientists, they "tested" their ideas in the laboratory of the marketplace. Going further, he argued that, contrary to conventional wisdom and securities law, insider trading is an essential element of capitalism: "If people are not allowed to put their money in companies they understand, capitalism loses its advantage over socialism, since what makes capitalism succeed is the assignment of capital to the insiders who earned it—and thus learned how to invest it profitably."[67] Gilder's essay was just one example of the logical contortions that New Economy apologists had to go through to in order to reconcile the illegal and destructive behavior of corrupt executives with visions of a bold, new society based on new economic rules.

The corporate-criminal-as-innovator argument has a history dating back to at least the late 1980s, when junk-bond impresario Michael Milken was charged with orchestrating a massive insider-trading scheme.[68] His many supporters argued, at the time, that while he may have crossed a legal line in some of his transactions, he also revolutionized markets and invented new financial strategies that made those markets more efficient.[69] The Milken defense was revived in the post-Enron era by at least one observer, writing in the conservative *Weekly Standard*: "Whether in the course of his assault on the status quo Milken bent or broke some of the rules governing financial transactions is still being debated . . . [but] . . . there can be no denying that the Milken-financed revolution turned many companies over to a breed of entrepreneurs. . . . Lean and hungry predators replaced fat cats, to the benefit of consumers and investors."[70]

Statements like these become part of what legal theorist Thurmon Arnold referred to as the "folklore of capitalism." Writing in 1937, Arnold looked back at the previous decade of boom then bust and saw the importance of a mythology, or "folklore," surrounding business enterprise, created in large part by lawyers and economists. This folklore "consisted of a series of very simple mental pictures" that personified corporations, replacing their abstract nature with images of the nineteenth-century individual businessman. One of the consequences of this personification of the corporation was that it "protected any expenditures, however fantastic, from investigation or criticism, provided they were made by great industrial organizations . . . [since] such spending was considered that of a free individual spending his own money."[71] At the same time, this folklore served to justify policies that limited the government's role in the economy. What one saw in the 1990s was a folklore of the New Economy, one that incorporated many of the same elements of the 1920s version.

Reform as Persecution of Risk-Takers (The Great Terror)

One prominent theme in the folklore of contemporary capitalism is the role of risk and risk-taking in business. This theme produces many metaphors that transform the images of business executives from the reality of pin-striped symbolic analysts who spend most of their time behind richly veneered desks in comfortably furnished offices into explorers in the wilderness, adventurers on safari, or ship captains on rough seas—all the images that one encounters in self-promotional materials generated by corporations. It was this theme of risk-taking that business leaders fell back upon when, as public outrage over corporate scandals began to build, they were confronted with efforts to impose real reform measures on business practices.

Almost one year after his firm agreed to pay $100 million to settle charges involving tainted stock research, Stanley O'Neal, Merrill Lynch's CEO, was neither repentant nor chagrined, but instead was boldly defiant, defending himself, his company, and Wall Streeters in general. In an opinion piece that appeared in the *Wall Street Journal,* he sparked a controversy when he wrote:

> In the atmosphere of cynicism and potential retribution that dominates the business landscape today, CEOs seem to want

nothing more than a low profile. They are reluctant to undertake new and untested business initiatives, want no visible risk and are loath to speak out on corporate governance matters. It's all very troubling: Risk-taking is essential to capitalism. Without it, the system can't function. . . . Of course, in any system predicated on risk-taking, there are failures, sometimes spectacular failures. But for every failure to be viewed as fraudulent or even criminal bodes ill for our economic system. The message to CEOs, to entrepreneurs and to venture capitalists right now is that you cannot afford to be wrong.[72]

O'Neal's remarks met with swift rebukes from regulators and members of Congress. But, not long after, similar public statements were made by a number of influential figures in the business world, including the new head of the SEC, the president of the U.S. Chamber of Commerce, and numerous CEOs.[73] This attitude soon became dominant among corporate leaders. A survey conducted in the fall of 2003 asked fourteen hundred CEOs in forty countries to rank the most serious threats to their businesses' growth prospects. Leading the list was "overregulation"—with 59 percent of those surveyed indicating that it was either a "significant threat" or "one of the biggest threats." By contrast, only, 40 percent listed global terrorism in either of the two categories.[74]

A more radical theme in the rhetoric against reform held that in the post-Enron era corporative executives were being persecuted and normal business activities criminalized. Scott McNealy, CEO of Sun Microsystems, complained that the atmosphere surrounding corporate America was similar to a "mob lynching."[75] Complaints began appearing in the business press about the difficulties of finding people willing to sit on corporate boards for fear of the liability that might go with those positions. Former senator John Danforth, in a *New York Times* op-ed, railed against oppressive law enforcement actions taken against corporations and their officers, including forcing executives like Adelphia founder John Rigas to endure a "perp walk" in which he was paraded before cameras in handcuffs.[76] This new defiant attitude was expressed in the title of a *Business Week* article on SEC reforms, "Big Biz Says Enough Already."[77] A chief complaint in these reports was that post-Enron, corporate behavior was under a microscope and normal business practices were being redefined as criminal violations. After the passage of Sarbanes-Oxley, a columnist in the conservative *Washington Times* angrily denounced the legislation: "Acting on the premise that 'business is theft,' the U.S. government has tarred all corporate executives with the misbehavior of a few and is rushing to enact a blanket crackdown on 'business fraud.'"[78] Articles in *Forbes* magazine and the *New American* took this argument further, declaring that with laws like Sarbanes-Oxley, the government was "criminalizing capitalism."[79] The author of the *New American* article claimed that by "blaming corrupt corporate officers for the recent stock market slide, both the White House and Congress are imposing socialist 'reforms' that will exacerbate the downturn."[80]

It might be difficult for many ordinary Americans, particularly those who lost significant amounts of money in the post-boom stock market, to think of multi-millionaire corporate executives as persecuted victims, but this is a classic theme in neoliberal economic thought. In 1961, Ayn Rand, the avatar of libertarian and neoliberal economics (and Alan Greenspan's mentor), gave a speech entitled "America's Persecuted Minority: Big Business" in which she boldly declared:

> If a small group of men were always regarded as guilty, in any clash with any other group, regardless of the issues or circumstances involved, would you call it persecution? If this group were always made to pay for the sins, errors, or failures of any other group, would you call *that* persecution? If this group had to live under a silent reign of terror, under special laws, from which all other people were immune, laws which the accused could not grasp or define in advance and which the accuser could interpret any way he pleased—would you call *that* persecution? If your answer is "yes"— then ask yourself what sort of monstrous injustice you are condoning, supporting, or perpetrating. That group is the American businessmen.[81] (emphasis in the original)

This idea was more fully developed by one of the deans of contemporary neoliberalism, Austrian-born economist Friedrich Hayek, who complained about "the condemnation of profit and contempt for trade" among intellectuals that stems, in large part, from an ignorance of the "mysteries of trade and money."[82]

Blaming Investors and Regulators

Another element of the revisionist interpretation of the corporate scandals was an attempt to shift blame from corporate decision-makers to investors and regulators. In this accounting, greedy investors created the bubble by throwing money into risky ventures and regulators interfered with the natural forces of the marketplace, creating perverse incentives for deception. Support for this view came from various quarters. From the media, journalist Michael Lewis argued that the real "culprits" of the 1990s were the "reckless speculators" who were later "recast as the victims."[83] From the political realm, billionaire mayor Michael Bloomberg (whose media outlets were a major source of market hype in the nineties) stated publicly: "People who were buying stocks in the stock market at multiples that never made any sense should look at themselves in the mirror. They're as responsible, I think, as those who actually committed the crimes of misstating earnings and fudging the numbers."[84] Yet, the strongest statement of this view came from the bench. In July 2002, a ninety-six-year-old federal judge dismissed a suit against Merrill Lynch that claimed investors were misled by Merrill stock analysts. In a decision that conjured up the spirit of the nineties (the 1890s), the judge blasted the investors:

> The record clearly reveals that plaintiffs were among the high-risk speculators who, knowing full well or being properly chargeable with appreciation of the unjustifiable risks they were undertaking in the extremely volatile and highly untested stocks at issue, now hope to twist the federal securities laws into a scheme of cost-free speculators' insurance. Seeking to lay the blame for the enormous Internet Bubble solely at the feet of a single actor, Merrill Lynch, plaintiffs would have this Court conclude that the federal securities laws were meant to underwrite, subsidize, and encourage their rash speculation in joining a freewheeling casino that lured thousands obsessed with the fantasy of Olympian riches.[85]

The judge's decision touched on a theme expressed by other revisionists: for the courts (or legislature) to act on behalf of investors would be to contravene the market's natural mechanism for punishing those who invest unwisely. The visible fist of the government should be replaced by the invisible hand of the market.

Related to this response was an effort by free-market apologists to lay blame at the feet of government regulators and the regulations they enforced. While many policy-makers were arguing that the crisis in corporate responsibility was evidence of the need for stricter oversight of big business, a number of politicians, pundits, and particularly economists argued the contrarian view that the situation demanded less, not more regulation. This view was frequently applied to the California energy crisis, where true believers in neoliberal economics saw the problem not as the failure of deregulation, but the failure to fully and properly deregulate. Despite the public outrage over the tactics of energy companies in California, a number of prominent observers defended these tactics, arguing that the power merchants had simply taken advantage of a dysfunctional market. In March 2001, as the dimensions of the crisis were becoming clear, Kenneth Lay, CEO of Enron, argued in an op-ed piece, "What has happened in California over the past four years is not deregulation. It is misguided regulation."[86] The root of the problem, this argument held, was that a market had been created that at the wholesale level had been deregulated, but at the retail level remained tightly regulated (consumer prices were fixed). Economist Gary Becker similarly wrote: "Had states fully deregulated their electricity markets, the Enron political scandal would have been largely avoided."[87] Becker's views were also reflected in the statements of other economists. For example, Benjamin Zycher (a Rand Corporation economist) argued that while "many Californians, with ample support from both Sacramento and the media, believe the crisis was the result of greedy power companies, particularly Enron, manipulating a deregulated marketplace . . . California's electricity crisis was entirely due to poorly designed public policies." As to allegations that energy producers deliberately withheld electricity at certain times in order to drive up prices, Zycher responds: "This is not 'manipulation.' Rather, it is the allocation of generating capacity to time periods when it is valued more highly by consumers."[88] In short, from a neoliberal point of view, what appears to be market manipulation turns out, on finer analysis, to be rational responses of energy companies to an imperfect market system—imperfect, because political forces attempted to meddle in the "natural" relationship between consumers and producers of energy.

Ironically, the "regulators-made-me-do-it" argument had been used to explain a major economic crisis in California a little more than a decade earlier. In the eighties, California had moved beyond federal efforts to deregulate the savings and loan industry, with disastrous consequences: scores of the state's thrifts failed, leaving taxpayers to cover billions of dollars in federally insured deposits. In the aftermath, conservative politicians and neoliberal economists argued that the problem was not deregulation but the fact that deregulatory policies had not gone far enough. By leaving in place federal deposit insurance, policy-makers had created a situation of "moral hazard"; knowing that their money was insured, depositors lost their incentives for holding thrift owners accountable for what they did with their money.[89] Even some corrupt S&L owners blamed regulators for their problems. Don Dixon, the owner of an infamous Texas S&L whose failure cost taxpayers $1.3 billion and who was later sentenced to five years in prison for looting his institution, told reporters at one of his court appearances: "So far the government has been successful in hiding behind the so-called crooks. We are the easy target. All the stories you've heard about the millions of dollars the savings and loan crooks took—it's totally dead wrong. The true villains are the politicians, the regulators. The whole system of deregulation was improperly handled."[90] While few condoned Mr. Dixon's crimes, a number of influential observers agreed with his assessment that the government was more to blame for what happened at Dixon's failed S&L, including the author of an op-ed piece in the *Wall Street Journal* who noted that "yes, he broke laws, but his guilt cannot explain the collapse of the thrift . . . the blame goes to federal deposit insurance, which encourages high-risk lending."[91] Dixon's defense was roughly analogous to gangster Al Capone's arguing in the 1920s that he was only minimally culpable for the crimes associated with his bootlegging empire and that the government, because it had enacted Prohibition laws, was the bigger culprit.

America Held Hostage

The corporate scandals of the late 1990s were of such a magnitude that they demanded responses: responses by the government to reevaluate and possibly change the rules that govern the marketplace and responses in the way of sanctions against those who had violated those rules (laws). The government's response to corporate crime was characterized by bold rhetoric and symbolic statements about the need to "get tough" on white-collar criminals in the immediate aftermath of the collapse of Enron, WorldCom, and other corporate giants, at a time when investors' confidence in the markets was plummeting, followed by generally tepid efforts to impose criminal sanctions on offenders. While popular critics often focus on the personal ties between officials in Washington and executives at suspect companies, our discussion has suggested two less visible—but likely more important—factors for the failure to criminalize corporate misconduct. First was the fact that many of the abuses may not have technically violated any criminal statutes. This situation is consistent with the historical tendency for the legal system to treat white-collar offenses as regulatory or civil violations rather than criminal wrongs. A number of leading academics have noted the limits of the law in defining corporate misconduct.[92] Second, the reluctance of authorities to vigorously pursue criminal charges against offending corporations may reflect what Calavita et al. refer to as a policy that emphasized "damage control" over "crime control." That is, the priority for policy-makers has been stabilizing economic institutions whose legitimacy has been threatened by revelations of massive insider corruption, rather than punishing those responsible in actions that may have further exposed the rot within those institutions and caused investor confidence to erode even more.

The crisis provoked by the corporate scandals also begged for a cultural response. For nearly a decade Americans had enjoyed unprecedented prosperity as stocks steadily increased in value and unemployment hit all-time lows. The good times had been explained, in part, by references to a "New Economy" that had purportedly ushered in an era of nearly limitless growth. But by the end of 2002, there was increasing evidence that much of that growth was illusory and many of the business visionaries of the era were little more than snake oil salesmen. Political leaders, business leaders, and their allies in the media and academia who had earlier linked their economic and political philosophies to the boom were now hard pressed to explain the sudden reversal of fortunes. We might have expected an unraveling of the dominant ideological framework or, at the least, that policymakers would learn something about the limits of indiscriminate deregulation and utopian aspirations—or that they would realize that the tech economy had its own "issues" (the legacy of Silicon Valley's insider capitalism and a reliance on nebulous forms of organization). What actually emerged in the aftermath of the scandals was a fragmentary revisionist account of the late nineties—an ideological patchwork whose various strands served to normalize corporate corruption by minimizing the harms caused and diverting attention away from its systemic sources. The broader goal of the revisionists was to prevent substantial changes in the fundamental rules that govern corporate behavior.

Though this campaign was not wholly successful (and one remains hopeful that a day of reckoning may still come), we are left with the sensation of a nation held hostage—to the "too big to fail" syndrome, to the utopian vision of market fundamentalists, and to the power that big business holds over our government. Corporations get special breaks because legal sanctions are often organizational "death penalties" that would harm large numbers of innocent stakeholders. Yet, corporate executives are not held accountable to this larger interest. The market fundamentalists intone—as impractical ideologues must—that the revolution has not gone far enough. And our political system is engulfed in a flood of corruption that threatens to pull us away from our democratic moorings.

Conclusions

An article published in *Business Week* magazine in August 2002 declared that a new day had dawned on corporate America: "In the post-Enron, post-bubble world, there's a yearning for corporate values that reach higher than the size of the chief executive's paycheck or even the latest stock price. Trust, integrity and fairness do matter, and they are crucial to the bottom line. The corporate leaders who somehow forgot that are now paying the price in a downward market roiled by a loss of investor confidence."[1] The last sentence suggests that this shift was taking place because the market was righting itself, punishing those who had strayed too far from traditional values and rewarding those who had stuck to the straight and narrow. The idea that the market had inflicted its own punishment on corporate wrongdoers by handing death sentences to companies such as Enron and Global Crossing was popular among neoliberal economists who interpreted the economy's response to the corporate scandals of the late 1990s as evidence *not* of the failings of unregulated markets, but as evidence of the strength of that system—and proof that government regulations are largely un-necessary.[2] In this view, which was not confined to economists but shared by business leaders and influential policy-makers, the late nineties were an aberrant period in the history of American business—a period in which, in the words of Alan Greenspan, the business community was gripped by "infectious greed" resulting in a "once-in-a generation frenzy of speculation that is now over."[3]

In this concluding chapter we look at the New Economy scandals in a broader context and consider some of the larger questions they raise. We start with the fundamental question raised above, one that we touched upon in the introduction: Were these scandals an aberration, a depar-ture from contemporary business practices, or were they, in large part, products of the neoliberal framework instituted in the 1990s? If these scandals are a consequence of our economic institutions, then we can expect to see more of the same if those institutions are left intact. A full answer lies beyond the scope of this book, but we can at least consider some of the evidence that would point us in the direction of an answer.

New Chapters in an Old Book

By 2004, many of the elements that fueled the incendiary financial envi-ronment of the late nineties were gone: the high-tech stock boom was over; after California's experience, few states were considering deregulat-ing their energy markets; the number of IPOs had declined dramatically; stock analysts operated under tighter restrictions imposed by Sarbanes-Oxley; and the New Economy evangelists had toned down their rhetoric considerably. Maybe, then, the corporate scandals of the late nineties will join the S&L crisis and the insider-trading scandals of the 1980s in the history books, rather than remaining in the headlines.

Yet, as we write this, there is troubling evidence that additional finan-cial shell games are out there waiting to be discovered. First, in 2004 the number of companies filing financial restatements increased to 414—28 percent more than the previous year and a 77 percent increase since 2000.[4] Similarly, 2004 class action securities fraud lawsuits increased 17 percent from 2003 and involved potential market capitalization losses that averaged $3.7 billion.[5]

Furthermore, one wonders what effect the U.S. campaign in the 1990s to promote its financial practices has had in the rest of the world. There is some evidence that creative accounting schemes have spread beyond U.S. borders. In late 2003, the Italian dairy and food conglomerate Parmalat—whose name is familiar to many Americans from the cartons of milk they regularly consume—publicly acknowledged that a Cayman Islands account shown on their books to hold $4.85 billion (40 percent of the company's assets) did not exist. Within days, Parmalat's stock, which had been selling for around $4 a share, became practically worthless. Investigators would uncover a massive scheme that had been going on for years in which Parmalat executives had been hiding significant losses in certain of its companies by surreptitiously transferring funds to those companies from the more profitable businesses it ran and covering the transfers with phony bank accounts, special purpose entities, and a series of sham transactions. As with Enron, the purpose of the scheme was to give the appearance of a strong economic performance, thereby maintaining investor confidence, while insiders looted millions of dollars from the company. The firm ultimately declared bankruptcy, leaving $17 billion in debt and many of the company's top officers, including its founder, under indictment.[6]

Another non-U.S. corporate scandal emerged in January 2004, when the British-based Royal Dutch/Shell Group (Shell Oil)—the third largest oil producer in the world—was forced to cut by 20 percent its estimate of its "proven" oil and gas reserves—a figure that is important because it is taken by analysts as a measure of an oil company's future productivity and therefore profitability. Evidence later emerged that suggested that Shell officials may have intentionally overstated reserve estimates not only to keep investors satisfied but also to please government officials in Nigeria, where many of Shell's reserves are located.[7] As yet, no one has suggested any criminal wrongdoing in the Shell case, but a number of observers have indicated that the problem could be widespread, as gas and oil companies, faced with declining production, have in recent years maintained the value of their stock by artificially boosting their reserve estimates.[8]

Beyond accounting-based scandals involving individual companies, there is emerging evidence that corrupt practices may infect whole sectors of the financial services industry. Indeed, it appears that one need not look very hard to find abuses in any number of financial institutions, as Eliot Spitzer's office has shown. In September 2003, Spitzer set in motion an inquiry that would quickly roil the $7 trillion mutual fund industry when he accused Canary Capital, a hedge fund, of engaging in numerous illegal trading practices, including what is known as "late trading." As the name implies, late trading involves buying mutual funds after the 4:00 P.M. deadline at the price established for the fund that day. It gives an obvious advantage to investors who might have information that would affect the next day's price. It is, in effect, like betting on yesterday's horse race. Spitzer's complaint implicated four major mutual funds in the scandal.[9] It would soon become clear, though, that this was just the tip of the iceberg and that illegal practices were common throughout the industry. A study conducted by the SEC found that among mutual fund broker-dealers, 25 percent admitted to having allowed customers to place orders after 4:00 P.M.[10] By March 2005, over thirty mutual funds (including some of the largest in the country), hedge funds, and brokerage firms had been implicated in the growing scandal.[11] One analyst estimated that just two of the illegal practices identified as common at many mutual funds cost the typical middle-income American family $3,750.[12] Coming on top of the scandals examined in this book, the mutual funds scandals raise yet another question mark about the substance of the so-called shareholder capitalism of our time.

Spitzer's office continued to expose rot in the financial services industry when, in spring 2004, it publicly disclosed that it was investigating illegal payments from insurance companies to brokers who steer their clients to the companies. The payments, which insurance insiders claim has been common practice in the industry for decades, present a clear conflict of interest, since insurance brokers are theoretically supposed to be acting in the best interests of their clients, recommending to them insurers that offer them the best deal, not those that offer the broker the best deal. The investigation seems to be a logical extension of Spitzer's earlier investigations. As one noted law professor and corporate crime expert put it: "This is a book about conflict of interest on Wall Street, and the commercial insurance brokerages appear to be the next chapter. It is the same story, but just the names of the characters have changed. Chapter One was the conflicts of security analysts. Chapter 2 was the mutual funds. Chapter 3 was the securities brokers marketing products from the mutual funds. And now Chapter 4 appears to be unfolding as conflicts of interests in the insurance industry."[13] By fall 2004 it was clear that Spitzer's office had uncovered another huge patch of normalized corruption in the financial services industry. In October his office filed a civil suit against the largest insurance brokerage firm in the country,

Marsh & McLennan (the suit also implicated several of Marsh's largest competitors), charging that the firm engaged in contract-steering and bid-rigging and stating that these practices were widespread in the industry.[14] Given that Spitzer accomplished all this with an extremely small staff, one wonders how much more corruption might come to light, and how many billions of dollars consumers might save if federal and state regulators, who collectively have thousands of employees, would give the same kind of critical scrutiny to these industries that the New York attorney general's office has.

One post-Enron financial scandal that Spitzer's office did not expose emerged from the ongoing inquiries of the Senate's Permanent Subcommittee on Investigations, which in November 2003 held hearings on abusive tax shelters. Our brief account revealed the emergence of a large tax shelter industry comprised of accounting firms, banks, law firms, and investment advisors. And, as was the case with corporate stock promotion efforts in the 1990s that resembled two-bit pump and dump schemes, the high-status providers of tax shelters had begun, in the words of the Senate subcommittee, "employing the same tactics employed by disreputable, tax shelter hucksters: churning out a continuing supply of new and abusive tax products, marketing them with hard sell techniques and cold calls; and taking deliberate measures to hide their activities from the IRS."[15] Here again, it seems that major enterprises were cashing in on the position of institutionalized trust they occupy.[16] Moreover, these undeserved tax breaks were an important—and especially egregious—mechanism through which U.S. society was made more unequal during the New Economy. A PBS *Frontline* documentary, for example, showed how First Wachovia, one of America's largest banks, used a complex tax shelter that involved leasing underground sewer pipes in a German city to pay no taxes in 2002, despite the fact that it reported $4 billion in profits.[17] The General Accounting Office estimates that abusive tax shelters cost American taxpayers nearly $85 billion over the last decade.[18] The shelters are yet another means of shifting the tax burden from corporations to individual taxpayers.

These reports of widespread, continuing corporate corruption are difficult to square with rosy predictions of a new era of honesty and integrity in the business world. Indeed, one is justified in asking whether corruption—the routine use of subterfuges to evade the rules that govern the marketplace—has become institutionalized, a normal feature of neoliberal capitalism, as practiced in the United States.

Return of the Public?

As we finished this book in March 2005, a flurry of actions suggested that more serious efforts to enforce the law were beginning to bear fruit: The Federal Reserve issued an order barring Citigroup from making acquisitions until it fixed regulatory problems;[19] Time Warner, Inc., agreed to pay $300 million to settle a SEC complaint about AOL overstatements of revenue (in addition to its previous agreement with the Department of Justice to pay $210 million in fines);[20] the IRS reported that it had recovered $3.2 billion from 1,165 individuals who had participated in an abusive tax shelter known as Son of Boss;[21] and thirteen more banks agreed to settle with New York's Common Retirement Fund for their role in helping WorldCom sell bonds, bringing the total payout in the WorldCom investors' class action to over $6 billion (a record in a securities class action).[22] Most dramatic of all was the conclusion of the trial of former WorldCom CEO Bernie Ebbers. Once lauded for his genius as a telecom visionary, Ebbers testified that his "marks weren't too good" in college and declared, "I don't know about technology and I don't know about finance and accounting." Rejecting defense claims that Ebbers was merely the "coach" at WorldCom, a jury convicted him of securities fraud, conspiracy, and seven counts of filing false reports with regulators. Ebbers could be sentenced to as much as eighty-five years in prison, but is more likely to receive a sentence of five to ten years. Observers commented that the conviction sent a message that top executives could be held accountable after all.[23]

When former Enron CEO Ken Lay was indicted in July 2004, it provided a sense of closure for some of the firm's many victims. For example, the director of a group representing eleven hundred former Enron employees commented, "We know seeing Ken Lay in handcuffs won't return what we lost. At least it's a milestone in terms of putting this chapter of our live behind us."[24] However, after an earlier Enron indictment— that of ex-CFO Andrew Fastow—maverick economist Paul Krugman remarked that the key problem which had yet to be addressed was a political system that allowed corporations to "get away with just about anything," ranging from accounting scams to bogus tax shelters. Krugman advised, "The wave of scandals was made possible, if not caused, by a political climate in which corporate insiders got pretty much whatever they wanted. Since the politicians who did their bidding haven't paid any price, that climate hasn't changed."[25] This view complements our contention that it was a political mobilization—not markets or new technologies—that changed "the rules" in a manner that opened the door for a wave of fraud. Despite the rhetoric concerning a shareholder revolution, changes in the institutional environment in the 1990s weakened protections for ordinary shareholders, leaving them to be deceived and cheated at nearly every turn. There is considerable evidence that the post-Enron reforms have done little to change this situation. Institutional investors such as CALPERS have rejoined the battle over control of the firm, demanding that corporate governance be reformed to protect the interests of investors. Among other things, they have requested that investors be given more influence over corporate boards. However, they have been hard pressed to overcome the opposition of business powers (e.g., the Corporate Roundtable). And efforts to rein in risks that are beyond the control of individuals—such as are posed by hedge funds and derivatives—have been stymied by industry lobbies and their political allies. For example, when SEC chairman William Donaldson proposed to require that hedge funds register with the SEC, he faced strong opposition from several senators that recalled the anti-regulatory tactics of the 1990s. Senator Wayne Allard of Colorado raised the question of whether the regulators really understood hedge funds: "People who deal with hedge funds are highly sophisticated, highly educated, and they are trading with each other. I wonder if regulators even understand how this market works."[26] And Senator Robert Bennett of Utah offered a thinly veiled threat to SEC staff: "We are involved in funding you."[27]

Senators fronting for elite financial interests brings to mind another basic finding from our review of the New Economy scandals—the fact that neoliberal policy often involves the active support of specific corporate interests. This was especially evident when top regulators acted as cheerleaders for New Economy ensembles and endorsed the general story line. In sum, the neoliberal state did not withdraw from the economy but exerted great power in constructing the sense of reality for economic actors.

We have seen evidence that it could be otherwise—that regulators, too, can make applications of rules that serve the larger public interest by defining the situation in ways that impose limits and consequences on powerful firms and elites. For example, state attorneys general—especially New York's Eliot Spitzer—have been creative in using the state's power to publicly sanction wrongdoers and to institute settlements that include requirements that the firms involved adopt model practices. Court rulings on the culpability of bank executives who abetted Enron's frauds—which cited the rise of a new industry of corporate advisors for structured finance—show that law enforcement and regulators can respond to the development of novel business practices. And the case of Richard Grasso shows that the SEC and Congress can apply effective leverage on a self-regulating industry body such as the NYSE. The day that began with the SEC director issuing a stiff challenge to the NYSE regarding Grasso's pay package—and Congress discussing the matter—ended with Grasso's resignation.

More basically, we need to rethink the standing of the general population in the matter of the New Economy scandals. Most of us were not "active" investors any more than we were "players." Thus, while there is a need to protect ordinary shareholders, the rubric of "shareholder interest" is not by itself adequate for defining the interest of the majority of the population. What needs to be revisited, if we have any ambition of remaining a democracy, is the conception of the public interest in the national economy.

However, our leaders have uttered few critical reflections about policies that undermine the public sector while encouraging people to entrust their futures to the stock market. On the contrary, President Bush has touted the notion of an "ownership society" as he promotes "personal accounts" as a viable alternative to Social Security. Though the public has responded skeptically, the Bush administration has shown a remarkable ability in the past to use the media to shape how reality is perceived. Indeed, Frank Rich (a reporter who covers art and culture for the *New York Times*) has noted that the administration's use of staged events and "fake" news to produce favorable media coverage calls to mind the tactics of none other than Enron.[28]

At a point in U.S. history where there is a sense of widespread institutional failure, the area that needs the most urgent attention is turning around the corrupted politics that supports the short-term interests of elite economic elites over the long-term interests of the many. However, if we as a citizenry are to respond to the New Economy scandals in the name of a broader public interest, we need to better comprehend what exactly it was that we as a complex society—not a crowd or a herd—experienced during the New Economy.

We Just Want to Celebrate (Don't We?)

As students of culture remind us, images and labels that are placed on buildings, stamps, flags, and other manmade objects are important symbolic statements about the people and ideas that are valued in a culture. But, for all the fanfare, the cultural imprint of the New Economy has proved to be rather ephemeral—leaving us uncertain about what kind of people we were at that time and what kind of people we are becoming now.

During the late nineties the iconography of the New Economy began to appear in a wide array of institutional arenas—sports, education, the arts—suggesting that the New Economy was becoming The Economy and that the culture of Silicon Valley was becoming the dominant business culture. Yet, as quickly as the NASDAQ index plummeted, it became apparent that the legends of the New Economy culture were quickly forgotten, and its icons easily erased from the cultural landscape. This has nowhere been more evident than in the world of professional sports. During the tech-boom of the late nineties, a number of New Economy companies—flush with cash from the sale of their stocks—paid top-dollar to sponsor professional sports stadiums and obtain the considerable prestige and publicity that came with them. Many of those firms quickly suffered serious reversals of fortune. In 1999, the Houston Astros baseball team began playing in Enron Field after the energy company bought the naming rights to the stadium for $100 million. Two seasons later, after the company collapsed, the team was playing in the newly renamed Minute Maid Park. Across town, the Houston Texans football team began the 2002 season playing in Reliant Stadium, named for Enron's former rival. In April 2004, Reliant was named in a criminal indictment for allegedly manipulating the California energy market. And in Tennessee, workers at Adelphia Coliseum (home of the Titans, Tennessee's professional football team) had to remove their sponsor's signs from the stadium after the company crashed amid allegations of massive frauds by the firm's chief executives.[29]

A similar debacle befell a number of universities. In the good times, college officials were eager to plaster the names of corporate moguls, who had pledged substantial donations to their institutions, on campus buildings. When their benefactors were implicated in shady business deals, those officials found themselves in a quandary: return the money and face the financial consequences or keep the money and live in the shadow of a tainted name. Seton Hall, a Catholic university in New Jersey, was particularly hard hit. Students at the university can attend poetry readings in Kozlowski Hall, named for Dennis Kozlowski, who made a reported $5 million donation to the school before he was charged with looting over $600 million from his firm, Tyco; they can find books in the

Walsh Library, named for another Tyco executive, Frank Walsh, who was implicated in some of Kozlowski's schemes; or they could (until the name was changed in late 2002) have worked out in the school's gym, named after Robert Brennan, the former head of a penny stock securities firm who was convicted in 2001 on charges of bankruptcy fraud and money laundering.[30] At the University of Missouri, students may find themselves taking classes from the school's occupant of an endowed chair in economics named for Kenneth C. Lay, who donated $1.1 million to the university in stock options.[31] And, at the State University of New York at Stony Brook, students and faculty may attend conferences at the Charles B. Wang Center for Asian-American Studies, named after the founder of Computer Associates, a Long Island software company that has been under investigation for inflating its sales during the late nineties.[32]

The media, a crucial watchdog institution in our democracy, was just as easily co-opted by the lure of New Economy bucks and buzz. A year before Enron collapsed, the *Columbia Journalism Review* warned that the media was not critically reporting on the New Economy and that journalists had generally been "blinded by the boom": "Coverage of the current prosperity can be read like a sports page when the home team is on a roll: cheerleading can drown out the occasional story pointing out weaknesses in the squad or the challenges coming up in the schedule. Journalistic scorn is reserved for the players—or in this case stocks— that don't make their numbers."[33] It was not as if the facts were buried too deep for reporters to uncover; on the contrary, they were hidden in plain sight. In 1998, Arthur Levitt, who was then the head of the Securities and Exchange Commission, gave a speech at New York University's school of business entitled "The Numbers Game" in which he warned of an "earnings game" being played by companies desperate to meet Wall Street's expectations, a game whose tactics revolved around various forms of "accounting hocus pocus"—in other words, the very tactics that several years later would be revealed to be at the heart of the scandals that engulfed many corporations.[34] Levitt's admonitions were met with polite silence by the mainstream and the business press, which, on the whole, dutifully noted his remarks in their back pages and quickly returned to the larger task of celebrating the New Age of endless prosperity. Only after its champions were engulfed in crisis and scandal was the hold of the New Economy story line shattered. Even now, few members of the press have admitted their failure to heed the warning signs that something was seriously wrong with the picture they were presenting. In December 2001, just two weeks after Enron declared bankruptcy, the editors of *Business Week* excoriated the press and themselves for having "blithely accepted Enron as the epitome of a new, post-deregulation corporate model when it should have been more aggressive in probing the company's opaque partnerships, off balance sheet maneuvers, and soaring leverage."[35] This form of self-criticism, however, was rare, as most members of the business press preferred to take the position that they, too, were duped by the sophisticated corporate miscreants of the era, rather than admitting that they were complicit—and that coverage of New Economy firms by media corporations was tainted by conflicts of interest.

Though the icons, imagery, and "insights" of the New Economy have proved fleeting, their acceptance by a host of institutional gatekeepers, such as the ubiquitous tagging of the landscape by marketers, points to a deeper cultural condition—the dominant influence of corporations in our culture (as well as our politics). In our age, few American institutions can match the symbolic power of big business—an ability to define the situation that is so pronounced that it is generally assumed that corporate interests are equivalent to those of the public. The epitome of this condition is the flag waving on Wall Street—and flag hanging— namely, the draping of a massive American flag on the front of the New York Stock Exchange like so much star-spangled packaging.

The institutional underpinnings of this symbolic power were evident in the politics of deregulation and in the New Economy celebration circuit. The new structural nexus of media and finance in this circuit was conjoined with politics, as politicians became dependent on corporate contributions to help fund their campaigns—capital-intensive media affairs that drew on the art of marketing. This financial-entertainment-political apparatus increasingly transformed us from a body of citizens into individual consumers—altering our ethical obligation from deciding how to best promote our collective interests as members of a public, to calculating how to get the best possible deal for ourselves.

For most of us, the cultural connection to the New Economy was superficial—something that infused the marketing, news coverage, and entertainment that was directed our way. Their standing in this circuit allowed the central figures in New Economy frauds to cloak their exploits as legitimate (or "normal")—and to avoid serious questioning of their motives and means until the damage was done. In this they were like the grand swindlers of earlier eras who exploited their inside connections as they charmed and bribed their way into high society while plotting to steal millions.

The Way We (or Some of Us) Live Now

Periods of stock speculation and swindle have been commonplace in the country's history, from the railroad stock scandals of the nineteenth century to the various stock swindles associated with the oil boom of the 1920s. But it is not just the United States where one finds these periods, which are commonly attributed to investor mania. Victorian England witnessed a number of financial scandals, many of which involved joint-stock companies. The spirit of the era was best captured in the novels of Anthony Trollope, particularly his classic *The Way We Live Now*, first published in 1875.[36] At the center of the novel is Augustus Melmotte, a financier with a checkered resume who arrives in London from Paris around 1871 and immediately establishes his family in London's high society and himself within the city's business elite. He secures his connections to these circles by creating a speculative scheme to build a railroad in America that would join Salt Lake City and Veracruz, Mexico (though no one seems to know why connecting the two cities would be economically beneficial), and persuading many of London's most prominent citizens to invest in the venture. Despite their doubts about the scheme and Melmotte, the investors eagerly hand over their money to him, in part because, like today's New Economy speculators, they were impressed with his connections with reputable figures—as well as to new technologies that defined the era: the railroad and the telegraph.[37] And like many contemporary speculators, Melmotte's investors were more interested in the value of the stock than in the commercial viability of the railroad project. They understood that their "fortune was to be made, not by the construction of the railway, but by the floating of the railway shares."[38]

In the post-Enron era, a number of writers have pointed out the similarities between the fictional Melmotte of Victorian England and real-life contemporary characters such as Sam Waksal, the CEO of ImClone and close friend of Martha Stewart who was eventually convicted of insider trading after he advised relatives and friends to sell their shares in his company following a decision by the FDA not to approve ImClone's cancer treatment drug for sale in the United States. Like Melmotte, Waksal cut a broad swath in high society, hosting salons at his Manhattan loft that were attended by the many celebrities, intellectuals, and financial wizards he counted as friends. One of those drawn to Waksal and the charisma he exuded was David Denby, a film critic for *The New Yorker* and a novice, but extremely enthusiastic investor in the stock market during the late 1990s. After his tech-heavy investments went sour, causing him to lose $900,000, Denby wrote an insightful and often eloquent memoir in which he describes how he got caught up in the exhilarating atmosphere of the late nineties stock market: "At that moment, in early 2000, you were sure that if you could just grab hold of the flying coattails of the New Economy investments, you could get rich very quickly. The newspapers and CNBC were filled with stories of twenty-four-year-old millionaires, start-up companies going through the roof, initial public offerings outlandishly doubling and tripling their price on the first day of trading." Denby befriended several of the central characters in the drama of the late nineties financial boom, including stock analyst Henry Blodget, about whom Denby wrote: "I wanted to believe in him . . . I needed to believe in him." By late 2002, as his losses mounted and the full dimensions of the corporate scandals became public, Denby's admiration for these characters turned to contempt as he realized that he had simply been a mark in a large-scale confidence game in which his former heroes were shills: "We had been blinded by our own desire and by the dazzling lies. Chumps! Suckers! Some of the insiders stole from us— from ordinary shareholders, and in some cases from employees, too. They stole from *me*" (emphasis in the original).[39] In his bitter reappraisal of the nineties boom, Denby expresses the feelings of many other Americans who also came to see themselves as suckers in a carefully orchestrated swindle whose perpetrators included not only entrepreneurs and stock analysts like Waksal and Blodget, but also investment bankers, accountants, energy traders, politicians, and pundits, most of whom walked away from the scheme with bags of cash, chuckling *caveat emptor*.

Yet, despite the anger that many Americans currently feel toward corporate leaders, it is not at all clear how long that anger will last or on what it will eventually focus. Given the interests of the celebration circuit, it may not be long before we find ourselves once again suckered into believing that the next big thing is just around the corner and that we should get in on the ground floor. Even David Denby acknowledges at the end of his memoir that, despite all of his financial misfortunes, he was once again considering investing in a new technology, wi-fi (wireless fidelity)—the devices that allow computers to connect to the Internet without physical connections—telling himself, "the market will always come back . . . eventually."[40]

The fact that elements of culture promoted speculation in the United States in the late nineties—and in Britain in the nineteenth century—

does not give credence to accounts of the era that refer to "herd thinking" or "maddened crowds." Denby, for example, stresses the influence of powerful executives and media commentators—not his peers—and we saw in Perrow's account of the railroad era the leading role of organized elites who changed the institutional environment for business. Still, given the disorienting shift in perceptions at the end of the New Economy—when its champs suddenly morphed into chumps—it might seem that irrational sentiments of some sort must have overtaken many people and perhaps the culture itself. However, this book has shown that the cultural climate that encouraged gambling in the stock market was created by a circuit of professional pumpsters—the business press, stock analysts, etc.—and that suspect perceptions and expectations of many people were the result of deceptive information provided by networks of high-status executives and business professionals who occupied positions of trust.

Perhaps even more important is the fact that most of the people who lost money in the corporate scandals were not speculators. They were simply people whose money and futures were tied up in the stock market through pension plans or mutual funds, over which they had limited control. These were not people caught up in a speculative mania, day-trading their financial futures away. Rather, they were ordinary Americans who entrusted their earnings to professionals and institutions that had legal and ethical obligations to look out for their interests, but which ultimately betrayed that trust.

Our findings also clash with efforts to depict corporate corruption in the late nineties as the outgrowth of general cultural shifts. The author of one popular book on the "cheating culture" in our society has argued that corporate corruption was not simply "due just to lax regulators or huge financial temptations" but was more fundamentally "explained by the moral climate of corporate America, a place where the troubling value shifts in our society have played out with notable intensity."[41] This argument—versions of which have been repeated by other commentators—is belied by the facts. The corporate crime wave of the late nineties occurred during the very years that levels of street crime were showing unprecedented declines. This is a point worth emphasizing. The crimes described in this book were not committed by the lower-class individuals who dominate crime statistics reported by the police, but by corporate elites and their agents who had not only the opportunities to carry out these acts but also the power to shape the rules that created those opportunities. The implication is that we do not need a general moral rejuvenation plan for society. We also do not need more vague bromides about "personal responsibility" or "wealth without character."

In sum, this book has shown that the rationality involved in the New Economy scandals cannot be reduced to a stylized portrait of a generic individual actor who can be extrapolated to account for the rationality and behavior of entire groups or social segments. Rationality is framed by larger institutions (e.g., laws, ideologies, policies) in a society as well as by the particular networks that people belong to—and their respective positions within those networks. The population is also differentiated by sets of material interests and power relations that reside in particular networks.

The fallacy of stylized portraits of actors and rationality is most obvious when it comes to the divide between elite insiders and the rest of the population—inhabitants of distinctive social worlds that vary tremendously in terms of material interests, access to economic information, and their general perceptions. We saw ample evidence that the world of elite insiders is further segmented by the formation of the small world of normalized corruption where participants in fraud come to develop distinctive sets of understandings—for example, about "relationships" and "reciprocity."

Rather than blaming individual investors and enjoining them to be more diligent in taking care of their affairs, we need to change how corporations conduct business and how they are governed. We can start by rejecting neoliberal canards about "self-regulating markets" and the evils of government "interference" in the marketplace. Recent deregulatory policies—from the savings and loan industry of the 1980s to the electrical energy markets of the 1990s—have led to widespread fraud and corruption and have had disastrous consequences for consumers and taxpayers. These events contain several lessons for American democracy. One is that a democracy depends upon the power of its state to ensure that those entrusted with protecting the public interest live up to their obligations (rather than cashing in on the market value of their institutional status). The second is that democracy and capitalism are not the same thing: the destructive tendencies of modern capitalism threaten to undermine our democracy and the stability and security of our society. If we fail to heed these lessons, we can expect further re-engineering of institutions that will, in effect, redistribute the resources of our society and of ordinary citizens to generate deal flow for networks of elite insiders. And market fundamentalists may enjoy increasing success in instituting their project: a future in which individuals—left to their own devices—place their trust not in public institutions or their fellow citizens, but in their own ability to come out on top in a Darwinian competition. To the degree to which these partisan interests are successful in undermining the economic role of the "public" interest, one can anticipate a hollowing out of our democracy itself.

NOTES

Introduction

1. Bethany McLean and Peter Elkind, *The Smartest Guys in the Room: The Amazing Rise and Scandalous Fall of Enron* (New York: Portfolio, 2003), 243.
2. Senate Committee on the Judiciary, Subcommittee on Crime and Drugs, "Penalties for White-Collar Crime," 107th Cong., 2nd sess., 19 June 2002, 9–11.
3. Gary Fields and Dennis Berman, "FBI Begins Preliminary Inquiry into Global Crossing's Practices," *Wall Street Journal*, 8 February 2002, sec. A, p. 4.
4. Securities and Exchange Commission, "SEC Charges CSFB with Abusive IPO Allocation Practices," press release, Washington, D.C., 2002.
5. *United States v. Arthur Andersen LLP*, Case No. Cr-H–02–121 (S.D. Tex. 2002) ("Indictment").
6. *Securities and Exchange Commission vs. Dean L. Buntrock, et al.*, Case No. Cv–02–C2180 (N.D. Ill. 2002).
7. Office of New York State Attorney General Eliot Spitzer, "Merrill Lynch Stock Rating System Found Biased by Undisclosed Conflicts of Interest," press release, Albany, N.Y., 8 April 2002.

8. *Securities and Exchange Commission v. Xerox Corporation,* Case No. Cv–02–272789 (S.D. N.Y. 2002).

9. Mitchell Benson, Chip Cummins, and Jonathan Sapsford, "Trade Disclosures Shake Faith in Troubled Energy Markets," *Wall Street Journal,* 13 May 2002, sec. A, p. 1.

10. Simon Romero, "WorldCom Facing Charges of Fraud; Bush Vows Inquiry," *New York Times,* 27 June 2002, sec. A, p. 1.

11. Deborah Solomon and Susan Pullman, "Qwest Faces Criminal Probe Over Accounting Practices," *Wall Street Journal,* 5 July 2002, sec. A, p. 3.

12. Senate Committee on Governmental Affairs, Permanent Subcommittee on Investigations, "The Role of Financial Institutions in Enron's Collapse—Volume I," 107th Cong., 2nd sess., 23 and 30 July 2002.

13. David Kirkpatrick, "AOL Accounts Under Scrutiny from the S.E.C," *New York Times,* 25 July 2002, sec. A, p. 1.

14. Marcia Vickers and Mike France, "How Corrupt Is Wall Street?" *Business Week,* 13 May 2002, 36.

15. Robert Merton, "Three Fragments from a Sociologist's Notebook," *Annual Review of Sociology* 13 (1987): 1–28.

16. General Accounting Office, *Financial Statement Restatements,* GAO: 03–138, 2002, 2.

17. Ibid., 15.

18. Ibid., 25.

19. These data are derived from the website (http://securities.stanford.edu) maintained by Securities Class Action Clearinghouse, Stanford University Law School.

20. Carol Graham, Robert Litan, and Sandip Sukhtankar, "The Bigger They Are, The Harder They Fall: An Estimate of the Costs of the Crisis in Corporate Governance" (Washington, D.C.: Brookings Institution, 2002).

21. New York State Office of the State Comptroller, "Impact of the Corporate Scandals on New York State" (Albany, N.Y.: Office of the State Comptroller, 2003).

22. Frank Partnoy, *Infectious Greed: How Deceit and Risk Corrupted the Financial Markets* (New York: Times Books, 2003), 299.

23. Donald Cressey, "Why Managers Commit Fraud," *Australian and New Zealand Journal of Criminology* 19 (1986): 196.

24. John L. Campbell, "Institutional Analysis and the Role of Ideas in Political Economy," in *The Rise of Neoliberalism and Institutional Analysis,* edited by John L. Campbell and Ove K. Pedersen (Princeton, N.J.: Princeton Univ. Press, 2001), 159–189.

25. Keith Faulks, *Political Sociology: A Critical Introduction* (New York: New York Univ. Press, 2000), 74.

26. See, for example, Jamie Peck and Adam Tickell, "Neoliberalizing Space," in *Spaces of Neoliberalism: Urban Restructuring in North America and Western Europe,* edited by Neil Brenner and Nik Theodore (Malden, Mass.: Blackwell, 2002), 33–57.

27. Joseph E. Stiglitz, *The Roaring Nineties: A New History of the World's Most Prosperous Decade* (New York: Norton, 2003), 100.

28. Partnoy, *Infectious Greed,* 264.

29. Paul DiMaggio, "Introduction: Making Sense of the Contemporary Firm and Prefiguring the Future," in *The Twenty-First-Century Firm: Changing Economic Organization in International Perspective,* edited by Paul DiMaggio (Princeton, N.J.: Princeton Univ. Press, 2001), 20.

30. Partnoy, *Infectious Greed.*

31. Neil Fligstein, *The Architecture of Markets: An Economic Sociology of Twenty-First-Century Capitalist Societies* (Princeton, N.J.: Princeton Univ. Press, 2001), 227.

32. Craig Johnston, "Advising the New Economy: The Role of Lawyers," in *The Silicon Valley Edge,* edited by C. Lee, W. Miller, M. G. Hancock, and J. Rowen (Stanford, Calif.: Stanford Univ. Press, 2000), 325–341; Mark Suchman, "Dealmakers and Counselors: Law Firms as Intermediaries in the Development of Silicon Valley," in *Understanding Silicon Valley,* edited by Martin Kenney (Stanford, Calif.: Stanford Univ. Press, 2000), 71–97.

33. Michael Indergaard, *Silicon Alley: The Rise and Fall of a New Media District* (New York: Routledge, 2004).

34. Asaf Darr, "Gifting Practices and Interorganizational Relations: Constructing Obligation Networks in the Electronics Sector," *Sociological Forum* 18, no. 1 (2003): 31–51.

35. Randall Smith and Susan Pullman, "U.S. Probes Inflated Commissions for Hot IPOs," *Wall Street Journal,* 7 December 2000, sec. C, p. 1.

36. Gretchen Morgenson, "The Fall of a Wall Street Ward Boss," *New York Times,* 19 October 2003, sec. 2, pp. 1, 10–11.

37. McLean and Elkind, *The Smartest Guys in the Room,* 151.

38. Bethany McLean and Peter Elkind, "Partners in Crime," *Fortune,* 27 October 2003, 78–100.

39. Michael Piore, "Society as a Precondition for Individuality: Critical Comments," *Socio-Economic Review* 1, no. 1 (2003): 121.

40. Mark Suchman, "Managing Legitimacy: Strategic and Institutional Approaches," *Academy of Management Review* 20 (1995): 574.

41. William D. Schneper and Mauro F. Guillen, "Institutions, Power, and Corporate Governance: A Cross-National Study of Hostile Takeovers," The Wharton School and Department of Sociology, University of Pennsylvania, March 2002.

42. James Burk, *Values in the Marketplace: The American Stock Market Under Federal Securities Law* (Berlin and New York: Walter de Gruyter, 1988); Mitchell Y. Abolafia, *Making Markets: Opportunism and Restraint on Wall Street* (Cambridge, Mass.: Harvard Univ. Press, 1996).

43. Lauren B. Edelman, "Legal Ambiguity and Symbolic Structures: Organizational Mediation of Civil Rights Law," *American Journal of Sociology* 97, no. 6 (1992): 1568.

44. Partnoy, *Infectious Greed.*

45. Peter Gourevitch, "Collective Action Problems in Monitoring Managers: The Enron Case as a Systemic Problem," *Economic Sociology European Electronic Newsletter* 3, no. 3 (2002): 3–16, http://econsoc.mpifg.de/archive/esjune02.pdf (accessed 15 June 2002).

46. Blake E. Ashforth and Vikas Anand, "The Normalization of Corruption in Organizations," *Research in Organizational Behavior* 25 (2003): 3.

47. Charles Perrow, *Organizing America: Wealth, Power, and the Origins of Corporate Capitalism* (Princeton, N.J.: Princeton Univ. Press, 2002).

48. Fligstein, *Architecture of Markets.*

49. H. Rowen, "Serendipity or Strategy: How Technology and Markets Came to Favor Silicon Valley," in C. Lee et al., eds., *The Silicon Valley Edge,* 189.

50. Fligstein, *Architecture of Markets.*

51. Michael Useem, *Investor Capitalism: How Money Managers Are Changing the Face of America* (New York: Basic Books, 1996); Fligstein, *Architecture of Markets.*

52. Partnoy, *Infectious Greed.*

53. Indergaard, *Silicon Alley*.
54. Kevin Phillips, *Wealth and Democracy* (New York: Broadway Books, 2002).
55. Karl Polanyi, *The Great Transformation* (1944; reprint, Boston: Beacon Press, 1957).
56. Perrow, *Organizing America*.

Chapter 1. The Classic Pump and Dump

1. David Lefer, "Stock Scams Are Eyed in Dual Slay," *New York Daily News,* 7 November 1999, p. 27.
2. Gary Weiss, "A Message from the Mob?" *Business Week,* 20 December 1999, 142.
3. Lefer, "Stock Scams."
4. *SEC v. Cavanaugh, et al.,*1 F. Supp. 2d 337; 1998 U.S. Dist. LEXIS 5450; Fed. Sec. L. Rep. (CCH) P90,204.
5. Deborah Lohse, Jason Anders, and Aaron Elstein, "Death Puts Focus on Web, Penny Stocks," *Wall Street Journal,* 29 October 1999, sec. C, p. 1.
6. David Barboza, Leslie Eaton, and Diana Henriques, "Penny Stock Fraud Is Billion-Dollar Game," *New York Times,* 19 November 1999, sec. A, p. 1.
7. Ibid.
8. New York State Attorney General, *Report on Micro-Cap Stock Fraud,* Albany, N.Y.: 1997, http://www.oag.state.ny.us/investors/microcap97/report97a.html (accessed 7 August 2003).
9. Senate Committee on Banking, Housing, and Urban Affairs, Subcommittee on Securities, "Fraud and Abuse in the 'Hot Issues' and 'Penny Stock' Markets," 98th Cong., 1st sess., 15 December 1983, 13.
10. Ibid., 2.
11. Ibid., 20–36.
12. General Accounting Office, *Penny Stocks: Regulatory Actions to Reduce Potential for Fraud and Abuse,* GAO/GGD–93–59, Washington, D.C., 1993.
13. Michael Schroeder, "Despite Reforms, Penny-Stock Fraud Is Roaring Back," *Wall Street Journal,* 4 September 1997, sec. A, p. 12.
14. New York Stock Exchange, *Share Ownership 2000* (New York: NYSE, 2001), 7.
15. New York State Attorney General, *Report on Micro-Cap Stock Fraud.*
16. Ibid.
17. Securities and Exchange Commission, "Microcap Stock Fraud: A Guide to Investors," January 2003, www.sec.gov/investor/pubs/microcapstock.htm (accessed 22 April 2003).
18. Ibid.
19. New York State Attorney General, *Report on Micro-Cap Stock Fraud.*
20. Ibid.
21. Leslie Eaton, "States Lead a Crackdown on Telemarketing Brokers," *New York Times,* 30 May 1997, sec. D, p. 2.
22. Selwyn Raab, "Officials Say Mob Is Shifting Crime to New Industries," *New York Times,* 10 February 1997, sec. A, p. 1.
23. *United States v. David Houge,* Case No. MD–98–0637M (E.D. N.Y. 1998).
24. Sharon Walsh, "Mob Ties Seen on Wall St.," *Washington Post,* 17 June 1999, sec. E, p. 1.
25. Gary Weiss, "The Mob on Wall Street," *Business Week,* 16 December 1996, 92.
26. Ibid.

27. House Committee on Commerce, Subcommittee on Finance and Hazardous Materials, "Organized Crime on Wall Street," 106th Cong., 2nd sess., 13 September 2000, 134.

28. Susan Harrigan, "Boom to Bust," *Newsday* (New York), 26 March 2001, sec. C, p. 14.

29. Susan Harrigan, "Castles Made of Sand," *Newsday* (New York), 25 March 2001, sec. A, p. 3.

30. R. Khalaf, "Steaks, Stocks—What's the Difference," *Forbes,* 14 October 1991, 82.

31. Securities and Exchange Commission, "In the Matter of Richard J. Puccio," Admin. Proc. File No. 3–8438, 22 October 1996, 2, www.sec.gov/litigation/opinions/3437849.txt.

32. David Halbfinger, "Money Machine," *Newsday* (New York), 16 July 1995, p. 1.

33. *United States v. Jordan Ross Belfort,* Case No. Cr–98–859 (E.D. N.Y. 1998) ("Superseding Information").

34. Halbfinger, "Money Machine"; Susan Antilla, "Look Who's Selling Solomon-Page," *New York Times,* 13 November 1994, sec. 3, p. 15.

35. Congressional Record—*Senate,* Tuesday, April 26, 1994 (legislative day of Monday, April 11, 1994), 103rd Cong., 2nd sess., 140 Cong Rec S 4794.

36. Glenn Simpson, "D'Amato Flips Stock for $15,000 in a Day Firm That Sold IPO Later Sanctioned by SEC," *Roll Call,* 16 June 1994. In 1996, D'Amato was cleared by a Senate ethics panel of wrongdoing in his transactions with Stratton Oakmont (Irvin Molotsky, "Ethics Panel Clears Senator in Stock Deal," *New York Times,* 21 September 1996, sec. 1, p. 21). As part of their investigation, the panel interviewed Jordan Belfort. In 2000, at the trial of Stratton's former accountant, Belfort testified that he had lied to the Senate ethics panel about his involvement with D'Amato, at the request of D'Amato's best friend. In his court testimony, Belfort recounted a conversation he had with D'Amato prior to making the controversial transaction. In it, D'Amato asked him: "Can you make me some money?" Belfort responded by saying that it was not a good idea since Stratton Oakmont was under investigation by the SEC at the time, to which D'Amato reportedly replied: "Who cares about that? Is it illegal for you to make me money?" (Michele McPhee, "D'Amato Broker: I Lied for a Senator," *New York Daily News,* 25 October 2000, p. 17).

37. Paul Vitello, "Crime Richly Rewarded," *Newsday* (New York), 26 September 2004, sec. A, p. 8.

38. Harrigan, "Castles Made of Sand."

39. Ibid.

40. *United States v. Steven Madden,* Case No. Cr–00–601 (E.D. N.Y. 2001).

41. Harrigan, "Castles Made of Sand."

42. John Sullivan and Leslie Kaufman, "Shoe Designer Is Charged with Fraud," *New York Times,* 21 June 2000, sec. C, p. 1.

43. Much of the information about Madden's illegal activities is drawn from court documents filed in the following cases: *United States v. Steve Madden,* Case. No. 00–Cr–601 (E.D. N.Y. 2000); *Securities and Exchange Commission v. Steve Madden.* Case No. 00–Cv–3632 (E.D. N.Y. 2000); *United States v. Steven Madden,* Case No. 00–Cr–00557 (S.D. N.Y. 2000).

44. Johanna Berkman, "Steve Madden: Crisis of the Sole," *New York Magazine,* 26 February 2001, 40.

45. Ylonda Gault, "Week in Review," *Crain's New York Business,* 11 December 1995, p. 51.

46. Senate Committee on Government Affairs, Permanent Subcommittee on Investigations, "Fraud in the Micro-Capital Markets Including Penny-Stock Fraud," 105th Cong., 1st sess., 22 September 1997, 167.
47. Gault, "Week in Review."
48. Harrigan, "Boom to Bust."
49. Sonja Isger, "Prince of Securities Fraud Coins a New Scam," *Palm Beach Post*, 20 April 2001, sec. B, p. 1.
50. Harrigan, "Boom to Bust."
51. *U.S. v. Steve Madden*, Case No. 00–Cr–601 (E.D. N.Y. 2000) ("Transcript of Proceedings," 23 May 2001, 12).
52. Elizabeth McDonald, "High-Priced Heel," *Forbes*, 1 April 2002, 42.
53. Rob Walker, "Genius of Capitalism: Steve Madden," *Slate*, 10 April 2002, http://slate.msn.com (accessed 7 February 2003).
54. *Securities and Exchange Commission v. Steve Madden*, Case No. 00–Cv–3632 (E.D. N.Y. 2000) ("Complaint").
55. General Accounting Office, "SEC Enforcement: Responses to GAO and SEC Recommendations Related to Microcap Stock Fraud," GAO/GDD–98–204, Washington, D.C., 1998, 16–17.
56. Susan Harrigan, "Many Unhappy Returns: Ex-Stratton Customers Still Fighting to Recoup $130 Million," *Newsday* (New York), 20 December 1998, sec. F, p. 6.
57. Arthur Levitt, *Take on the Street* (New York: Pantheon, 2002), 184, 186.
58. Gary Weiss, *Born to Steal: When the Mafia Hit Wall Street* (New York: Warner Books, 2003), 73–76.
59. Senate Committee on Governmental Affairs, Permanent Subcommittee on Investigations, "Fraud in the Micro-capital Markets Including Penny Stock Fraud," 105th Cong., 1st. sess., 22 September 1997, 6.
60. Paul Beckett, "Departure of Many Lawyers at SEC Stretches Its Resources, Delays Cases," *Wall Street Journal*, 19 November 1997, sec. B, p. 13.

Chapter 2. The Power Merchants

1. Chuck Squatriglia, Justino Aguila, Patrick Hoge, Matthew Stannard, "Rolling Blackouts Hit," *San Francisco Chronicle*, 18 January 2001, sec. A, p. 1.
2. Tom Raum and Ron Fournier, "Bush Rules out Federal Intervention in California Energy Crisis," Associated Press, 18 January 2001.
3. Dick Cheney, "The Energy Crisis Is Serious, Not Perplexing," *Vital Speeches of the Day*, 15 May 2001, vol. 67, no. 15 (2001): 474.
4. John Emshwiller, "California Blame Game Yields No Score—Probes Reveal Little Evidence Suppliers Acted Illegally," *Wall Street Journal*, 22 May 2001, sec. A, p. 2.
5. White House Energy Task Force, *National Energy Policy: Report of the National Energy Policy Development Group* (Washington, D.C., 2001), I-3.
6. For a review of these studies, see: General Accounting Office, "Restructured Electricity Markets: California Market Design Enabled Exercise of Market Power," GAO–02–828, Washington, D.C., 2002.
7. Federal Energy Regulatory Commission, "Commission Readies Tough Action Based on Staff Report Citing Market Manipulation, Other Violations," press release, Washington, D.C., 26 March 2003.

8. Eric Hildebrandt, "Further Analyses of the Exercise and Cost Impacts of Market Power in California's Wholesale Energy Market" (Folson, Calif.: California Independent System Operator Corporation, 2001).

9. "California's Pain, Enron's Gain," *New York Times*, 12 December 2002, sec. A, p. 1.

10. Sources for the discussion of the electrical energy industry include: Paul Joskow, "Restructuring, Competition and Regulatory Reform in the U.S. Electricity Sector," *Journal of Economic Perspectives* 11, no. 3 (1997): 121; Richard Hirsh, *Power Loss* (Cambridge, Mass.: MIT Press, 1999), 17; Richard Hirsh, "Powering America," Smithsonian Institution, http://americanhistory.si.edu/csr/powering/ (accessed 17 July 2003); Matthew White, "Power Struggles: Explaining Deregulatory Reform in Electricity Markets," in *Brookings Papers on Economic Activity, Microeconomics: 1996*, edited by Martin Neil Baily, Peter C. Reiss, and Clifford Winston (Washington, D.C.: Brookings Institution Press, 1997), 207.

11. Congressional Budget Office, "Causes and Lessons of the California Electricity Crisis," Washington, D.C., 2001, 22.

12. California Energy Commission, "Record of Day-Ahead Prices in the PX Monthly Average, Per Megawatt-Hour (MWh)," www.energy.ca.gov/electricity/wepr/monthly_day_ahead_prices.html (accessed 23 August 2003).

13. Henry Norr, "Searing Heat Tests PG&E's Limits," *San Francisco Chronicle*, 15 June 2000, sec. A, p. 19.

14. John McArthur, "Anti-Trust in the New Deregulated Natural Gas Industry," *Energy Law Journal* 18 (1997): 1–112.

15. Peter Fusaro and Ross Miller, *What Went Wrong at Enron* (Hoboken, N.J.: John Wiley & Sons, 2002), 30–33.

16. President George H. W. Bush, "Remarks on Signing the Energy Policy Act of 1992," 2 November 1992, *Weekly Compilation of Presidential Documents* 28, no. 44 (1992): 2093.

17. Federal Energy Regulatory Commission, Order No. 888, 24 April 1996; Federal Energy Regulatory Commission, Order No. 889, 24 April 1996.

18. Mark Golden, "Young and Wild: Electricity Trading Is Fast Becoming One of the Biggest Commodity Markets in the Country," *Wall Street Journal*, 14 September 1998, sec. R, p. 13.

19. The figure for the combined revenues was derived from the companies' annual reports for 2000.

20. Enron Corporation, *Enron Annual Report, 1999* (Houston, Tex.: Enron Corporation, 2000), 2.

21. Dynegy, Inc., *Dynegy 2000 Annual Report* (Houston, Tex.: Dynegy, Inc., 2001), 5, 12.

22. Chip Cummins and Elliot Spagat, "Boom and Bust: At Willlams Cos. Two Trendy Bets Yield Snake Eyes for Williams," *Wall Street Journal*, 5 September 2002, p. 1.

23. Rebecca Smith and John Emshwiller, *24 Days* (New York: Harper-Business, 2003), 161.

24. *U.S. v. Kenneth Rice, et al.*, Case No. Cr–H–03–93–01 (S.D. Tex. 2003) ("Superseding Indictment").

25. Enron Corporation, *Enron Annual Report, 1996* (Houston, Tex.: Enron Corporation, 1997).

26. Interview with Jeffrey Skilling from PBS video *Blackout*, transcribed at www.pbs.org/wgbh/pages/frontline/shows/blackout/interviews/skilling.html (accessed 30 June 2003).

27. Scott Thurm, Robert Gavin, and Mitchel Benson, "As Blackouts Hit California,

Traders Manipulated Market," *Wall Street Journal,* 16 September 2002, sec. A, p. 1.

28. *San Diego Gas & Electric Company v. Sellers of Energy,* Case before the Federal Energy Regulatory Commission, Docket No. El–00–95–000 ("Investigation of Practices of the California Independent System Operator and the California Power Exchange, California Parties' Supplemental Evidence of Market Manipulation by Sellers, Proposed Findings of Fact, and Request for Refunds and Other Relief," 3 March 2003), 3–8.

29. Ibid., 4–20.

30. Federal Energy Regulatory Commission, "AES Southland, Inc., Williams Energy Marketing & Trading Company. Show Cause Order," Docket No. IN01–3–000, 3 March 2001.

31. Federal Energy Regulatory Commission, "Non-Public Appendix to Order Directing Williams Energy & Trading Company and AES Southland, Inc., to Show Cause," Docket No. IN01–3–000, 3 March 2001, 3.

32. Ibid.

33. Chris Taylor, "California Scheming," *Time,* 20 May 2002, 42.

34. Memorandum from Christian Yoder and Stephen Hall to Richard Sanders, "Re: Traders' Strategies in the California Wholesale Power Markets/ISO Sanctions," 6 December 2000, reprinted in Federal Energy Regulatory Commission, "Fact-Finding Investigation of Potential Manipulation of Electric and Natural Gas Prices," Docket No. PA02–2–000, 7 May 2002, 19.

35. *U.S. v. John Forney,* Case No. Cr–c–03–302–0 (N.D. Cal. 2003) ("Affidavit of Steven Coffin"), 10.

36. Ibid.

37. Federal Energy Regulatory Commission, "Refiling of Letter and Data from Xcel Energy, Inc. in Response to Letter Issued on May 8, 2002 under PA02–2," Docket No. PA02–2–000, 23 May 2002.

38. Ibid., 35–36.

39. Federal Energy Regulatory Commission, "Motion of Public Utility District No. 1 of Snohomish County, Washington for Leave to File Limited Supplemental Testimony and Exhibits Related to Audio Recordings of Enron Phone Conversations, Ex. SNO–222," Docket No. EL03–180–000, 17 May 2004, 3.

40. Federal Energy Regulatory Commission, "Motion of Public Utility District No. 1 of Snohomish County, Washington for Leave to File Limited Supplemental Testimony and Exhibits Related to Audio Recordings of Enron Phone Conversations, Ex. SNO–224," Docket No. EL03–180–000, 17 May 2004, 1.

41. Miguel Bustillo and Tim Reiterman, "Energy Scheme Details Emerge," *Los Angeles Times,* 8 June 2002, sec. B, p. 1.

42. "Perot Systems Presentation," document submitted to the California Senate, Select Committee to Investigate Price Manipulation of the Wholesale Energy Market, July 2002, http://republican.sen.ca.gov/web/38/News/select.asp (accessed 14 January 2004).

43. California Senate, Select Committee to Investigate Price Manipulation of the Wholesale Energy Market, "Hearings Re: Review of Perot Systems' Role in California's Energy Crisis," Sacramento, Calif., 11 July 2002.

44. Ibid., 8.

45. Chip Cummins, "Misreporting of Energy Prices to Indexes Was Commonplace," *Wall Street Journal,* 19 November 2002, sec. A, p. 1.

46. Federal Energy Regulatory Commission, "Final Report on Price Manipulation in Western Markets," Docket No. PA–02–2–00, ES–6.

47. Paul Krugman, "Enron Goes Overboard," *New York Times,* 18 August 2001, sec. A, p. 19.

48. Wendy Zellner, "Power Play: Enron, the Nation's Largest Energy Merchant, Won't Let California Stand in Its Way," *Business Week,* 12 February 2001, 70.

49. Bethany McLean, "Why Enron Went Bust; Start with Arrogance. Add Greed, Deceit, and Financial Chicanery," *Fortune,* 24 December 2001, 58.

50. Brian O'Reilly, "The Power Merchant," *Fortune,* 17 April 2000, 148.

51. Gary Hamel, *Leading the Revolution* (Boston: Harvard Business School Press, 2002), 216–217.

52. Bob Herbert, "Silencing the Alarm," *New York Times,* 14 January 2002, sec. A, p. 15.

53. Frank Rich, "State of Enron," *New York Times,* 2 February 2002, sec. A, p. 19.

54. Scott Sherman, "Enron: Uncovering the Untold Story," *Columbia Journalism Review* 40, no. 6 (March/April 2002): 22.

55. Bethany McLean, "Is Enron Overpriced?" *Fortune,* 5 March 2001, 122.

56. Memo from Michael Jones, partner in Andersen's Houston office, to Enron lead audit partner David Duncan, 6 February 2001, reproduced at *AccountancyAge .com,* 18 January 2002, www.accountancyage.com/News/1127349 (accessed 28 September 2003).

57. Joseph Dunn (California State Senator), "Testimony on Electricity Price Manipulation in California before the Senate Committee on Commerce, Science and Transportation" (11 May 2002), text from *Federal News Service,* available from *LexisNexis Congressional* (online service) (Bethesda, Md.: Congressional Information Service, 2002).

58. Nancy Vogel, "Enron Vision Proved Costly to Firm, State Energy," *Los Angeles Times,* 28 January 2002, sec. B, p. 1.

59. Paul Krugman, "Another Friday Outrage," *New York Times,* 2 September 2003, sec. A, p. 23.

60. Vogel, "Enron Vision."

61. Christian Berthelsen and Scott Winokur, "Enron's Secret Bid to Save Deregulation," *San Francisco Chronicle.* 26 May 2001, sec. B, p. 1.

62. Zachary Coile, "New Push to Deregulate Energy," *San Francisco Chronicle,* 11 October 2003, sec. A, p. 1.

63. Public Citizen, *Blind Faith: How Deregulation and Enron's Influence Over Government Looted Billions from Americans* (Washington, D.C.: Public Citizen, 2001), 14.

64. Senate Committee on Governmental Affairs, Staff Memorandum, "Committee Staff Investigation of the Federal Energy Regulatory Commission's Oversight of Enron Corp.," Washington, D.C., 12 November 2002, 8.

65. Ibid., 43.

66. House Committee on Government Reform, "How the White House Energy Plan Benefited Enron," Washington, D.C., 16 January 2001, 1.

67. Daniel Atlman, "Contracts So Complex They Imperil the System," *New York Times,* 24 February 2002, sec. 3, p. 1.

68. Enron Corporation, *Enron Annual Report, 2000* (Houston, Tex.: Enron Corporation, 2001), 21.

69. Randall Dodd, "The Bigger They Come, the Harder They Fail, Enron's Lessons for Deregulation," in Senate Committee on Agriculture, Nutrition and Forestry, "CTFC Regulation and Oversight of Derivatives," 107th Cong., 2nd sess., 10 July 2002, 95. The term "notional" refers to the value of the underlying assets that the derivative contracts are based on. It does not reflect the actual risk involved in these contracts, which is a much smaller amount.

70. Frank Partnoy, *Infectious Greed: How Deceit and Risk Corrupted the Financial Markets* (New York: Times Books, 2003), 9–83.

71. Sarah Bartlett, "Bankers Trust Restatement Tied to Trading Style," *New York Times*, 22 July 1988, sec. D, p. 2.

72. In 1992, Congress gave the commissioner that authority when it enacted the "Futures Trading Practices Act" (H.R. 707, 102nd Cong., 2nd sess.).

73. Jerry Knight, "Energy Firm Finds Ally, Director in CFTC Ex-Chief," *Washington Post*, 17 April 1993, sec. B, p. 1.

74. Wendy Gramm, "In Defense of Derivatives," *Wall Street Journal*, 8 September 1993, sec. A, p. 12.

75. Public Citizen, "Blind Faith," 14–15.

76. David Ivanovich, "Sen. Gramm Could Face Conflict of Interest if His Wife Is Questioned on Enron," *Houston Chronicle*, 23 January 2002, sec. A, p. 12.

77. Roger Lowenstein, *When Genius Failed: The Rise and Fall of Long-Term Capital Management* (New York: Random House, 2000).

78. President's Working Group on Financial Markets, "Report on the Over-the-Counter Derivatives Markets and the Commodity Exchange Act," Washington, D.C., 1999.

79. Public Citizen, "Blind Faith," 16.

80. Senate Committee on Agriculture, Nutrition and Forestry, "CFTC Regulation and Oversight of Derivatives," 107th Congress, 2nd sess., 10 July 2002, 9.

81. Public Citizen, "Blind Faith," 19.

82. Senate Committee on Agriculture, "CTFC Regulation," 5.

83. Karen Masterson, "Big Energy Quashes Regulation Bid," *Houston Chronicle*, 11 April 2002, sec. A, p. 1.

84. Richard Stevenson and Jeff Gerth, "Web of Safeguards Failed as Enron Failed," *New York Times*, 20 January 2002, sec. A, p. 1.

85. Richard Stevenson, "Enron Sought Aid of Treasury Dept. to Get Bank Loans," *New York Times*, 12 January 2002, sec. A, p. 1.

86. Institute for Policy Studies, *Enron's Pawns: How Public Institutions Bankrolled Enron's Globalization Game* (Washington, D.C.: Institute for Policy Studies, 2002), 3–14.

87. Rebecca Smith and John Emshwiller, "Enron Faces Collapse, as Dynegy Bolts and Stock Price, Credit Standing Dive," *Wall Street Journal*, 19 November 2001, sec. A, p. 1.

88. One has to be careful, however, in interpreting these figures on losses too literally. As Alex Berenson has pointed out, they are "paper losses"; that is, they reflect the hypothetical losses sustained by shareholders had they sold their shares when Enron peaked as opposed to the value of their stocks at the end of the period. They do not reflect the actual difference between what investors paid for their stocks and the value of those stocks when they sold them (Alex Berenson, *The Number* [New York: Random House, 2003], 121).

89. Bethany McLean and Peter Elkind, *The Smartest Guys in the Room: The Amazing Rise and Scandalous Fall of Enron* (New York: Portfolio, 2003), 92–93. As an example of the philosophy that Enron's compensation committee used in rewarding senior executives, consider the following statement from an SEC filing in 1997:

> The Committee and the Board of Directors believe that Mr. Lay is the top CEO in the industry, as evidenced by the fact that stockholder value increased by 371 percent from 1989 to 1996. In order to retain him, the Com-

mittee entered into contract renewal discussions with Mr. Lay during 1996. The Committee is pleased to announce that effective December 9, 1996, Mr. Lay entered into a new five-year employment contract that will expire on December 31, 2001. The Committee and Board of Directors agree that retaining and motivating Mr. Lay is critical if Enron is to achieve or exceed its stated goals of at least double digit earnings per share growth annually and long-term average growth in earnings per share of 15 percent per year. On January 1, 1997, Mr. Lay received a $210,000 increase in his base salary to $1,200,000 to reflect the accomplishment of objectives, top quartile performance relative to general industry companies similar in size to Enron, and the fact that his last base salary increase was almost four years ago. Also, to ensure that Mr. Lay's interests remain properly aligned with stockholder interests, the Committee granted a total of 1,275,000 stock options, 50 percent granted in December, 1996 and 50 percent granted in January, 1997, at market value on each date of grant. The stock options will be fully vested on November 1, 2003. However, the vesting schedule may be accelerated if Enron's total stockholder return equals or exceeds 120 percent of the S&P 500 in calendar years 1997, 1998 and 1999. The Committee believes these stock options and vesting provisions provide the necessary linkage between stockholder returns and management rewards (Enron Corporation, "Proxy Statement, Schedule 14A," filed with the Securities and Exchange Commission, 24 March 1997, 16).

90. Enron Corporation, *Enron Annual Report, 1996*, 5.
91. Gretchen Morgenson, "How 287 Turned Into 7: Lessons in Fuzzy Math," *New York Times*, 20 January 2002, sec. 3, p. 1.
92. Jonathan Weil, "Energy Traders Cite Gains, But Some Math Is Missing," *Wall Street Journal*, 20 September 2000, sec. T, p. 1.
93. Ibid.
94. Dynegy, Inc., *Dynegy 2000 Annual Report* (Houston, Tex.: Dynegy, Inc., 2001), 2.
95. *Securities and Exchange Commission v. Dynegy Inc.*, Case No. Cv–H02–3623 (S.D. Tex. 2002).
96. John Emshwiller and Rebecca Smith, "Enron Jolt: Investments, Assets Generate Big Loss—Part of Charge Tied to 2 Partnerships Interests Wall Street," *Wall Street Journal*, 17 October 2001, sec. C, p. 1.
97. John Emshwiller, Rebecca Smith, Robin Sidel, and Jonathan Weil, "Enron Reduces Profit for 4 Years, by 20%, Citing Dealings with Officers' Partnerships," *Wall Street Journal*, 9 November 2001, sec. A, p. 3.
98. *In re: Enron Corp., et al.* Case No. 01–16034 (Bankr. S.D. N.Y. 2001) ("Second Interim Report of Neal Batson, Court Appointed Examiner," 21 January 2002), 48.
99. John Emshwiller and Rebecca Smith, "Murky Waters: A Primer on Enron Partnerships," *Wall Street Journal*, 21 January 2002, sec. C, p. 1.
100. Senate Committee on Governmental Affairs, Permanent Subcommittee on Investigations, "The Role of Financial Institutions in Enron's Collapse—Volume I," 107th Cong., 2nd sess., 23 and 30 July 2002, 6. Hereafter, in this chapter, this document will be cited in the text as *SC*.
101. "Enron's Enablers," *Wall Street Journal*, 29 July 2002, sec. A, p. 14.
102. Charles Gasparino and Randall Smith, "Merrill Executives Invested Their Money in Enron Partnership That the Firm Sold," *Wall Street Journal*, 30 January 2002, sec. C, p. 1.
103. McLean and Elkind, *The Smartest Guys in the Room*, 209.

104. *United States Securities and Exchange Commission v. Merrill Lynch & Co., et al.*, Case No. Cv–H–03–0946 (S.D. Tex. 2003) ("Complaint").

105. *United States v. Bayley, et al.*, Case No. Cr–H–03–363 (S.D. Tex. 2003) ("Superseding Indictment").

106. McLean and Elkind, *The Smartest Guys in the Room*, 59, 122.

107. Joint Committee on Taxation, "Report of Investigation of Enron Corporation and Related Entities Regarding Federal Tax and Compensation Issues and Policy Recommendations, Vol. 1," JCS–3–03, February 2003, 562.

108. Ibid., 561.

109. Ibid., 659.

110. These figures are from *Amalgamated Bank v. Lay, et al.*, Case No. 01–Cv–4198 (S.D. Tex. 2001) ("Complaint").

111. *Bullock, et al. v. Arthur Andersen*, Cause No. 32,716 (21st Judicial District, Texas, 2002).

112. Michael Musuraca (American Federation of State, County, and Municipal Employees), "Testimony on Examining Enron: The Consumer Impact of Enron's Influence on State Pension Funds before the U.S. Senate, Committee on Commerce, Science, and Transportation, Subcommittee on Consumer Affairs, Foreign Commerce and Tourism," 16 May 2002, text from: Federal Information System Federal News Service, available from: *LexisNexis Congressional* (online service) (Bethesda, Md.: Congressional Information Service, 2002); Associated Press, "Florida Drops Inquiry of Firm That Put State Funds in Enron," *New York Times*, 5 January 2003, sec. 1, p. 19; Mary Flood, "Enron-Related Lawsuit Set for Alabama Court," *Houston Chronicle*, 1 June 2002, sec. A, p. 8; U.S. Senate Committee on Governmental Affairs, "The Fall of Enron: How Could It Have Happened?" 107th Cong., 2nd sess., 24 January 2002, 22; New York State Office of the Comptroller, "Impact of the Corporate Scandals on New York State" (Albany, N.Y.: New York State Office of the Comptroller, 2003), 21.

113. *Chao v. Enron Corp., et al.*, Case No. Cv–03–02257 (S.D. Tex. 2003) ("Complaint"), 11–12.

114. U.S. Department of Labor, "Secretary of Labor Chao's Lawsuit Involving Enron Retirement Plans," press release, Washington, D.C., 26 June 3002.

115. *Chao. v. Enron*, 11–32.

116. Mimi Swartz and Sherron Watkins, *Power Failure: The Inside Story of the Collapse of Enron* (New York: Doubleday, 2003), 294.

117. NBC News Transcripts, "Latest on Enron Collapse and Tape of Meeting in Which Ken Lay First Told Employees Enron Was in Trouble," transcript of *Today* show, 30 January 2002.

118. *Chao v. Enron*, 17–18.

119. Senate Committee on the Judiciary, Subcommittee on Crime and Drugs, "Penalties for White Collar Crime," 107th Congress, 2nd sess., 19 June 2002, 5–6.

120. Ibid., 6.

121. Nelson Schwartz, "Is Energy Trading a Big Scam?" *Fortune*, 10 June 2002, 126.

122. Jerry Hirsch and Dan Morain, "Calif. Reaches Settlement with Power Provider," *Los Angeles Times*, 12 November 2002, sec. C, p. 1; Nancy Brooks, "Reliant to Pay up to $50 Million," *Los Angeles Times*, 3 October 2003, sec. C, p. 1; Alex Barrionuevo and Rebecca Smith, "El Paso Reaches Pact to Settle California Case," *Wall Street Journal*, 21 March 2003, sec. B, p. 3.

123. Federal Energy Regulatory Commission, "Commission Issues Sweeping Show Cause Orders to Companies Alleged to Have Gamed Western Energy Markets," press release, Washington, D.C., 25 June 2003.

124. California Attorney General's Office, "Attorney General's Energy White Paper" (Sacramento: California Attorney General's Office, 2004), 34.

125. Jonathan Peterson, "Two Power Sellers Agree to Settle Charges Related to State's Energy Crisis," *Los Angeles Times,* 1 November 2003, sec. C, p. 1.

126. Jonathan Peterson and Elizabeth Douglass, "Regulators Press Energy Firms but Uphold Disputed Contracts," *Los Angeles Times,* 26 June 2003, sec. A, p. 1.

127. Krugman, "Another Friday Outrage"; Federal Energy Regulatory Commission, "Commission Upholds Western Power Contracts, Connecticut Contract," press release, Washington, D.C., 25 June 2003.

128. Peterson and Douglass, "Regulators Press."

129. Rebecca Smith, "Dynegy, Venture Settle U.S. Case on Manipulation of Gas Indexes," *Wall Street Journal,* 20 December 2002, sec. B, p. 2.

130. Russell Gold, "El Paso Corp. to Pay $20 Million in Settlement," *Wall Street Journal,* 27 March 2003, sec. C, p. 3.

131. Rebecca Smith "Dynegy Ex-Trader Is Indicted on Criminal Fraud Charges," *Wall Street Journal,* 26 January 2003, sec. A, p. 6.

132. *U.S. v. Jamie Olis, et al.,* Case No. Cr–03–217 (S.D. Tex. 2003) ("Indictment").

133. Securities and Exchange Commission, "Dynegy Settles Securities Fraud Charges Involving SPE's, Round-Trip Energy Trades," press release, Washington, D.C., 24 September 2002.

134. Federal Energy Regulatory Commission, "Final Report," VI-35.

135. Corporate Fraud Task Force, "First Year Report to the President," Washington, D.C., 22 July 2003, 13.

136. The exception to this pattern (as of March 2005) was the indictment of Reliant Energy Services, a subsidiary of Reliant Resources, Inc., and four of its employees in April 2004 on charges related to the manipulation of energy prices in California (*United States v. Reliant Energy Services, et al.,* Case No. Cr–04–0125 [N.D. Cal. 2004]).

137. For a discussion of the legal status of round-trip trades, see, Katrina Miltich, "A Slap on the Wrist: Dynegy, Inc. v. Securities and Exchange Commission," *North Carolina Journal of International Law & Commercial Regulation* 28 (2003): 983.

Chapter 3. Too Much of a Good Thing

Epigraph source: Seth Schiesel, "In MCI-WorldCom Theory, New View of Competition," *New York Times,* 12 November 1997, p. 1.

1. Joseph E. Stiglitz, *The Roaring Nineties: A New History of the World's Most Prosperous Decade* (New York: Norton, 2003), 92–93.

2. Alessandra Petlin, "What Became of the Workers of WorldCom," *New York Times Magazine,* 6 June 2004, 72.

3. Kurt Eichenwald, "For WorldCom, Acquisitions Were Behind Its Rise and Fall," *New York Times,* 8 August, 2002, sec. A, p. 1.

4. Ibid.

5. Steve Lohr, "A Long-Distance Visionary," *New York Times,* 2 October 1997, sec. D, p. 4.

6. Frank Partnoy, *Infectious Greed: How Deceit and Risk Corrupted the Financial Markets* (New York: Times Books, 2003), 367–368.

7. Patricia Aufderheide, *Communications Policy and the Public Interest: The Telecommunications Act of 1996* (New York: Guilford Press, 1999), 13.

8. Ibid., 32.

9. Ibid., 41.
10. Ibid., 89.
11. Stiglitz, *The Roaring Nineties*, 53.
12. Esther Dyson, George Gilder, George Keysworth, and Alvin Toffler, "Cyberspace and the American Dream: A Magna Carta for the Knowledge Age," Appendix E in Aufderheide, *Communications Policy and the Public Interest*, 247.
13. Ibid., 242.
14. Ibid., 256.
15. Catherine Arnst, "This Is the Official Day the Telecom Wars Began," *Business Week*, 13 October 1997, 32
16. Stiglitz, *The Roaring Nineties*, 92.
17. *In re: WorldCom, Inc., et al.*, Case No. 02–15533 (Bankr. S.D. N.Y. 2002) ("First Interim Report of Dick Thornburgh, Bankruptcy Court Examiner"), 11–17. Hereafter, in this chapter, references to this document will be cited in the text as *T.*
18. Peter Elstrom, "The New World Order," *Business Week*, 13 October 1997, 28.
19. Mark Landler, "Upstart Offering $30 Billion to Buy MCI, Using Stock," *New York Times*, 2 October 1997, sec. A, p. 4.
20. Ibid.
21. Elstrom, "The New World Order."
22. Ibid.
23. Landler, "Upstart Offering $30 Billion to Buy MCI, Using Stock."
24. Arnst, "This Is the Official Day the Telecom Wars Began."
25. Elstrom, "The New World Order."
26. Ibid.
27. Schiesel, "In MCI-WorldCom Theory, New View of Competition."
28. Ibid.
29. Elstrom, "The New World Order."
30. Ibid.
31. Stephanie N. Mehta, "Is There Any Way Out of the Telecom Mess?" *Fortune*, 22 July 2002, 83.
32. Eichenwald, "For WorldCom."
33. Ibid.
34. Ibid.
35. Ibid.
36. Rebecca Blumenstien and Susan Pulliam, "Report Says Ebbers and Others Conspired in WorldCom Fraud," *Wall Street Journal.com*, 10 June 2003, 2 (accessed 15 June 2003).
37. Ibid.
38. At the peak, Ebbers was worth over $1 billion based on the value of the 19 million WorldCom shares he owned. He made personal investments in shipyards, timber farms, a minor league hockey team, and a six hundred thousand–acre ranch in Canada using loans that were secured with his WorldCom stock. As the value of the stock plummeted in the summer of 2000, Ebbers not only found his personal worth plunging (to $658 million) but also faced "margin debt" of $380 million (Gretchen Morgenson and Timothy O'Brien, "When Citigroup Met WorldCom," *New York Times*, 16 May 2004, sec. 3, p. 9).
39. Blumenstein and Pulliam, "Report Says Ebbers," 1.
40. Peter Elstrom, "The Big Promise in Little Telecoms," *Business Week*, 13 October 1997, 34.
41. Mehta, "Is There Any Way Out."

42. Steve Rosenbush, "Inside the Telecom Game," *Business Week,* 5 August 2002, 34.

43. Ibid.

44. Ibid.

45. Ibid.

46. Laura M. Holson, "The Battle for US West and Frontier Shows How Difficult the Sector Has Become to Analyze," *New York Times,* 21 June 1999, sec. C, p. 2.

47. Mehta, "Is There Any Way Out."

48. Rosenbush, "Inside the Telecom Game."

49. Julie Creswell and Nomi Prin, "The Emperor of Greed," *Fortune,* 24 June 2002, 6.

50. Partnoy, *Infectious Greed,* 356.

51. Cresewll and Prin, "The Emperor of Greed," p. 6.

52. Ibid.

53. Partnoy, *Infectious Greed,* 360–361.

54. Simon Romero, "Adding to Claims Against Global Crossing," *New York Times,* 30 January 2003, sec C, p. 4.

55. Partnoy, *Infectious Greed,* 357.

56. Bloomberg News, "Global Crossing Suit Allowed to Proceed," *New York Times,* 24 June 2004, sec. C, p. 8.

57. Mark Gimein, "Qwest: What Did Joe Know?" *Fortune.com,* 28 April 2003, 3 (accessed 1 May 2003).

58. Ibid.

59. Ibid.

60. Dennis Berman and Deborah Solomon, "Optical Illusion?: Accounting Questions Swirl Around Pioneers in the Telecom World," *Wall Street Journal,* 13 February 2002, sec. A, p. 12.

61. David Barboza and Barnaby J. Feder, "Enron's Swap with Qwest Is Questioned," *New York Times,* 29 March 2002, sec. C, p. 1.

62. *Securities and Exchange Commission v. Joel Arnold, et al.,* Case No. Cv–03–Z–0328 (D. Col. 2003) ("Complaint").

63. Barnaby J. Feder, "U.S. Takes Dual Actions in Qwest Case," *New York Times,* 26 February 2003, sec. C, p. 1; Christopher Palmeri, "Are Qwest Honchos Off the Hook?" *Business Week,* 24 May 2004, 86, 88.

64. Feder, "U.S. Takes Dual Action."

65. David Leonhardt, "Qwest Officials Made Millions in Stock Sales," *New York Times,* 30 July 2002, sec. C, p. 1.

66. Sandy Share, "Judge OKs Settlement of 5 Qwest Lawsuits," *phillyburbs.com,* 15 June 2004, p. 1 (accessed 1 July 2004).

67. Securities and Exchange Commission, press release, "SEC Sues Former and Current Qwest Employees for Fraud," 25 February 2002.

68. Bethany McLean and Peter Elkind, *The Smartest Guys in the Room: The Amazing Rise and Scandalous Fall of Enron* (New York: Portfolio, 2003), 299. Hereafter, in this chapter, this book will be cited in the text as *ME.*

69. Kurt Eichenwald and John Markoff, "Deception, or Just Disarray, at Enron?" *New York Times,* 8 June, 2003, sec. 3, p. 10.

70. Ibid.

71. Bruno Latour, *We Have Never Been Modern* (Cambridge, Mass.: Harvard Univ. Press, 1993).

72. Eichenwald and Markoff, "Deception, or Just Disarray, at Enron?"

73. Ibid.

74. Kris Hudson, "Montana's Power Failure," *Denver Post,* 10 August 2003, sec. A, p. 1.

75. Montana Power Company, *Montana Power/Touch America, 2000 Annual Report,* (Butte, Mont.: Montana Power Company, 2001), 10.
76. Bill Mann, "A High Tech Company You Never Heard Of," *The Motley Fool,* 29 September 1999, www.fool.com (accessed 15 February 2003).
77. Harlan Byrne, "Big Sky Telecom," *Barron's,* 9 October 2000, 20.
78. Quoted in Kate Thomas, "Montana Power," *Energy Markets,* June 1999, 44.
79. Hudson, "Montana's Power Failure."
80. *Margaret McGreevey, et al. v. Montana Power Company, et al.,* Case No. Cv–03–01 (D. Mont. 2003) ("Fourth Amended Complaint"), 16–18.
81. Jim Robbins, "As Power Prices Surge, Montana, Too, Asks Why?" *New York Times,* 13 May 2001, sec. A, p. 3. In November 2003, Montana Resources was able, with a $2 million loan from the state, to hire 350 workers to resume mining in Butte (Jim Robbins, "Mining Again in a Montana Town That's Fallen on Hard Times," *New York Times,* 8 November 2003, sec. A, p. 10).
82. Bill Richards, "Power Outage," *Wall Street Journal,* 22 August 2001, sec. A, p. 1.
83. Ibid.
84. Senate Committee on Energy and Natural Resources, "Electricity Rates," 107th Cong., 1st sess., 15 March 2001, 76.
85. Richards, "Power Outage."
86. Judy Pasternak, "Bush's Energy Plan Bares Industry Clout," *Los Angeles Times,* 26 August 2001, sec. A, p. 1.
87. Charles Lewis, "The GOP's New Lobbyist in Chief," *Washington Post,* 20 December 2001, sec. A, p. 43.
88. And there is the case of Thomas White, who retired from the U.S. Army in 1990 as a brigadier general to become vice president of Enron Energy Services, a unit that was directly involved in gaming the California market, and then became secretary of the Army under President George W. Bush. Regarding Mr. Thomas's involvement in the California scandal, Senator Ron Wyden of Oregon bluntly told a Senate panel: "There is substantial evidence that while Mr. White served as vice chairman, his former company was directly involved in Enron's trading schemes to manipulate West Coast energy markets, which has been devastating to my constituents" (Ron Wyden [senator from Oregon], "Opening Remarks on Enron's Role in the Western States Electricity Crisis before the Senate Committee on Commerce, Science and Transportation," 18 July 2002, text from *Federal News Service,* available from *LexisNexis Congressional* (online service) (Bethesda, Md.: Congressional Information Service, 2002).
89. Nick Ehli, "'How to Really Shaft Your Workers,' by Bob Gannon," *Bozeman (Mont.) Daily Chronicle,* 14 July 2003, http://bozemandailychronicle.com/article/2003/07/14/business/02nick.txt (accessed 9 April 2004).
90. Online response to Ed Kimmick, "Gannon's Ailment Diagnosed," *Billings (Mont.) Gazette,* 21 September 2003, www.billingsgazette.com/citylights (accessed 1 May 2004).
91. Stephen Labaton, "Telecom Crisis? Take 2 Aspirin and No One Will Call You in the Morning," *New York Times,* 25 July 2002, sec. C, p. 8.
92. Stephen Labaton, "Telecommunications: Lament But Little Repair," *New York Times,* 31 July 2002, sec. C, p. 5.
93. Stiglitz, *The Roaring Nineties,* 104.
94. Ibid., 91–99.
95. Gretchen Morgenson, "Deals within Telcom Deals," *New York Times,* 25 August 2002, sec. 3, p. 10.

96. Mark Gimein, "You Bought. They Sold," *Fortune*, 2 September 2002, 66.
97. David Leonhardt, "Qwest Officials Made Million in Stock Sales," *New York Times*, 30 July 2002, sec. C, p. 4.
98. Simon Romero, "5 Years and $15 Billion Later, a Fiber Optic Venture Fails," *New York Times*, 29 January 2002, sec. C, p. 10.
99. Ibid.
100. Geraldine Fabrikant and Simon Romero, "How Executives Prospered as Global Crossing Collapsed," *New York Times*, 11 February 2002, sec. C, p. 6.
101. Ibid.
102. Morgenson and O'Brien, "When Citigroup Met WorldCom."

Chapter 4. The Webs They Weave

1. Charles Tilly, *Big Structures, Large Processes, Huge Comparisons* (New York: Russell Sage Foundation, 1984), 54, 29.
2. Michael Indergaard. *Silicon Alley: The Rise and Fall of a New Media District* (New York: Routledge, 2004). Hereafter, in this chapter, references to this work will be cited in the text as *I*.
3. Jason McCabe Calacanis, "Star Gazing: SAR Talks Business with StarMedia's Million-Dollar Man," *Silicon Alley Reporter* 3, no. 8 (1999): 128–134.
4. StarMedia Networks, *Prospectus for Initial Public Offering* (New York: StarMedia Networks, Inc., 1999), 47–48.
5. Jennifer Rich, "StarMedia Faces New Challenges in Latin America," *New York Times*, 29 May 2000, sec. C, p. 34.
6. Calacanis, "Star Gazing."
7. Mark Walsh, "Star Attraction in Latin America," *Crain's New York Business* 10 August 1998, p. 14.
8. Flatiron started up in 1996 with a $50 million investment from Softbank (Japan) and Chase Manhattan; Chase added another $300 million stake in 1998 and $500 million more in 2000.
9. StarMedia, *Prospectus for Initial Public Offering*.
10. Ibid.
11. Calacanis, "Star Gazing."
12. Larry Kanter and Judith Messina, "Unexpected Riches Remake the City," *Crain's New York Business*, 29 November 1999, p. 47.
13. StarMedia, *Annual Report for Fiscal Year 2001* (New York: Star Media Networks, Inc., 2002).
14. StarMedia, *Annual Report for Fiscal Year 1999, 2000* (New York: Star Media Networks, Inc., 2000, 2001).
15. Calacanis, "Star Gazing," 28.
16. Alexia Vargas, "Star or Supernova? StarMedia Bets on Hitting Profitability Alone," *Crain's New York Business*, 5 February 2001, pp. 3, 46.
17. Rafat Ali, "Bad Things Come in Threes," *Silicon Alley Daily*, 19 November 2001, p. 3.
18. John Motavalli, *Bamboozled at the Revolution: How Big Media Lost Billions in the Battle for the Internet* (New York: Viking, 2002), 304.
19. Indergaard, *Silicon Alley*, 60.
20. Viviana Zelizer defines "circuits" as "networks of restricted exchange" where people make distinctive use of money (or some other medium of exchange). They

often do so when they are engaging in some delicate task, such as creating ties, dealing with risk, or controlling others. See Vivianna Zelizor, *The Social Meaning of Money* (New York: Basic Books, 1994).

21. Wolf Heydebrand and Annalisa Miron, "Constructing Innovativeness in New Media Start-Up Firms," *Environment and Planning* 34 (2003): 1951–84.

22. See, for example, Andy Pratt, "New Media," *Geoforum* 31 (2000): 425–436; Monique Girard and David Stark, "Distributing Intelligence and Organizing Diversity in New Media Projects," working paper (Institute for Social and Economic Research and Policy, Columbia University, 2001); Andrew Ross, *No-Collar: The Humane Workplace and Its Hidden Costs* (New York: Basic Books, 2003).

23. Jeff Madrick, "Devotion to Free-Market, Laissez-Faire Dogma Makes for Ineffectual Policy," *New York Times*, 5 September 2000, sec. C, p. 2.

24. Kara Scannell, "Bid to Dismiss IPO-Market Suits Is Denied by Judge," *Wall Street Journal*, 20 February 2002, sec. C, p. 5.

25. Gretchen Morgenson and Jonathan D. Glater, "$1 Billion Offered to Settle Suits on IPOs," *New York Times*, 27 June 2003, sec. C, p. 10.

26. John Cassidy, *Dot.con: How America Lost Its Mind and Money in the Internet Era* (New York: Perennial, 2002), 31.

27. Ibid., 83–88.

28. David Bell, "Unearthing an IPO Success," *Silicon Alley Reporter* 3, no. 22 (1999): 46.

29. Ibid.

30. Hengyi Feng, Julie Froud, Sukhdeve Johal, Colin Haslam, and Karel Williams, "A New Business Model? The Capital Market and the New Economy," *Economy and Society* 30 (2002): 486.

31. Jerry Colonna, "For Internet Stocks, the Fall of Overvalued Companies Can Hurt Strong Companies," *New York Times*, 1 June 1998, sec. D, p. 25.

32. Saul Hansell, "Gold Rush in Silicon Alley," *New York Times*, 7 February 2000, sec. C, p. 13.

33. Doug Mintz, "Flatiron's Future," *Silicon Alley Reporter* 5, no. 42 (2001): 28.

34. Frank Partnoy, *Infectious Greed: How Deceit and Risk Corrupted the Financial Markets* (New York: Times Books, 2003), 192.

35. Gretchen Morgenson, "Before Enron, There Was Cendant," *New York Times*, 9 May 2004, sec. 3, p. 1.

36. Jeremy Kahn, "Presto Chango! Sales are HUGE!" *Fortune*, 20 March 2000, 90.

37. Ibid.

38. Ibid.

39. Ibid.

40. *In re Homestore.com*, Master File No. 01–Cv–11115 MJP (E.D. Cal. 2001) ("First Amended Consolidated Complaint"), 27. Hereafter, in this chapter, references to this document will be cited in the text as *H*.

41. Daniel Gross, "Round-Tripping: How Enron and Qwest Ruined a Smart New Economy Business Practice," *Slate*, 21 August 2002, http://slate.msn.com (accessed 26 January 2003).

42. Susan Pulliam and Rebecca Blumenstein, "SEC Broadens Its Investigation into Revenue-Boosting Tricks," *Wall Street Journal*, 16 May 2002, sec. A, p. 1.

43. Securities and Exchange Commission, "SEC and United States Attorney Charge Former Homestore Executives with Scheme to Inflate Advertising Revenue," press release, Washington, D.C., 18 September 2003.

44. David D. Kirkpatrick, "Guilty Pleas in Securities Case Widen AOL Inquiry," *New York Times*, 24 September 2003, sec. C, p. 4.

45. James Ledbetter, "A New Media World Order," *Thestandard.com*, 14 January, 2000, p. 1 (accessed 1 February 2000).

46. Michael Wolf, "You Got Nailed," *New York Magazine*, 29 July 2002, 20.

47. *State of Alaska v. AOL, Inc., et al.*, Case No. 1JU–04–503 (Super. Ct. of Alaska, 1st District) ("Complaint"), 12.

48. Carol J. Loomis, "Why AOL's Accounting Problems Keep Popping Up," *Fortune .com*, 14 April 2003, 3 (accessed 15 April 2003).

49. David. D. Kirkpatrick, "Lawsuits Say AOL Investors Were Misled," *New York Times*, 15 April, 2003, sec. C, p. 13.

50. Loomis, "Why AOL's Accounting Problems Keep Popping Up."

51. Ibid.

52. David. D. Kirkpatrick, "AOL Says S.E.C. Is Questioning Its Accounting of $400 Million," *New York Times*, 29 March 2003, sec. C, p. 1.

53. David. D. Kirkpatrick, "AOL to Restate Troubled Unit's Revenue Again, Vexing Wall Street," *New York Times*, 24 October 2002, sec. C., p. 1.

54. Andrew Ross Sorkin and David D. Kirkpatrick, "AOL Time Warner Drops the 'AOL,'" *New York Times*, 19 September 2003, sec. C, p. 4.

55. Jerry Knight, "A Worse-Case Scenario for AOL?" *Washingtonpost.com*, 20 January 2003, p. 1 (accessed 1 February 2003).

56. Kirkpatrick, "Lawsuits Say AOL Investors Were Misled."

57. Knight, "A Worse-Case Scenario for AOL?"

58. *State of Alaska v. AOL, Inc., et al.* ("Complaint"), 16–18.

59. Ibid., 18.

60. Ibid., 21–22.

61. Ibid., 23–24.

62. Ibid., 26.

63. Ibid., 28.

64. Kirkpatrick, "Lawsuits Say AOL Investors Were Misled."

65. Knight, "A Worse-Case Scenario for AOL."

66. David A. Vise, "Time Warner Shareholder Suit Will Proceed," *Washingtonpost.com*, 6 May 2004, p. 1 (accessed 15 May 2004).

67. Ibid.

68. David D. Kirkpatrick and Jim Rutenberg, "AOL Reporting Further Losses; Turner Resigns," *New York Times*, 30 January 2003, sec. C, p. 6.

69. Wolf, "You Got Nailed."

70. Kirkpatrick, "Lawsuits Say AOL Investors Were Misled."

71. *State of Alaska v. AOL, Inc., et al.* ("Complaint").

72. *In re: Initial Public Offering Securities Litigation* (S.D. N.Y. 2003) ("Opinion and Order").

73. Gretchen Morgenson and Jonathan D. Glater, "$1 Billion Offered to Settle Suits on I.P.O.'s," *New York Times*, 27 June 2003, sec. C, p. 1.

74. *In re: Initial Public Offering Securities Litigation* ("Opinion and Order"), 7.

75. Ibid., 16.

76. Securities and Exchange Commission, *Report of the Special Study of Securities Markets of the Securities and Exchange Commission*, H.R. Doc. No. 88–95, pt. 1, at 553 (1st sess., 1963).

77. Securities and Exchange Commission, *Report of the Securities and Exchange Commission Concerning the Hot Issues Markets*, August 1984, 61–62.

78. *In re: Initial Public Offering Securities Litigation* ("Opinion and Order"), 18.

79. Ibid.

Chapter 5. Professional Pumpsters and Financial Engineers

Epigraph source: Steve Rosenbush, "Inside the Telecom Game," *Business Week,* 5 August 2002, 34.

1. Andrew Ross Sorkin, "Banker's Trial Gives Glimpse into Close Ties of Tech Boom," *New York Times,* 13 October 2003, sec. C, p. 1.
2. Linda Himelstein, "Inside Frank Quattrone's Money Machine," *Business Week,* 13 October 2003, 104.
3. Justin Lahart, "Bracing for an Earnings Hit," CNN/Money, 17 July 2002, www.money.com/2002/11/news/options (accessed 1 August 2003).
4. Bethany McLean, "Weighing ebay's Options," *Fortune,* 31 May 2004, 35.
5. John Judis, "Option Play: What W. Didn't Learn from Enron," *New Republic,* 6 May 2002, 19.
6. This practice is described by Joseph Blasi, Douglas Kruse, and Aaron Bernstein as no less than a new form of capitalism that they refer to as "partnership capitalism" (Joseph Blasi, Douglas Kruse, and Aaron Bernstein, *In the Company of Owners: The Truth About Stock Options* [New York: Basic Books, 2003]).
7. Public Broadcasting System, *Frontline: Bigger Than Enron* (originally broadcast on 20 June 2002).
8. Arthur Louis, "Companies Don't Want Their Options Limited," *San Francisco Chronicle,* 25 May 1994, sec. B, p. 1.
9. Public Broadcasting System, *Frontline: Bigger Than Enron.*
10. Ibid.
11. Sarah Teslik, Executive Director of the Council of the Institutional Investors, transcript of interview, on *Frontline: Bigger Than Enron* website, http://www.pbs .org/wgbh/pages/frontline/shows/regulation/congress/ (accessed 30 June 2003).
12. *Central Bank of Denver v. First Interstate Bank of Denver,* 511 U.S. 164 1994.
13. Frank Partnoy, *Infectious Greed: How Deceit and Risk Corrupted the Financial Markets* (New York: Times Books, 2003), 172.
14. Jane Bryant Quinn, "Making It Easier to Mislead Investors," *Washington Post,* 18 June 1995, sec. H, p. 2.
15. Jeri Mellon, "Keating's Revenge," *New York Times,* 15 December 1995, sec. A, p. 43.
16. President William J. Clinton, "Message to the House of Representatives Returning without Approval the Private Securities Litigation Reform Act of 1995," 19 December 1995, *Weekly Compilation of Presidential Documents* 31, no. 51 (1995): 2210
17. Stephen Labaton, "Now Who, Exactly, Got Us into This?" *New York Times,* 3 February 2002, sec. A, p. 1.
18. Ed Gillespie and Bob Schellhas, eds., *Contract with America* (New York: Random House, 1994), 150.
19. Mark Hoffman, "Rule of Law: Why Class Action Attorneys Stalk High-Tech Companies," *Wall Street Journal,* 18 January 1995, sec. A, p. 15.
20. Carolyn Lochhead, "Shareholder Lawsuits Defended by Lawyer at House Hearing," *San Francisco Chronicle,* 20 January 1995, sec. A, p. 4.
21. House Committee on Energy and Commerce, Subcommittee on Telecommunications and Finance, "Securities Litigation Reform," 103rd Cong., 2nd sess., 22 July 1994, 193.
22. Ibid., 2.
23. For example, in January 2002, Representative Markey sponsored legislation that

would have overturned many of the elements of the 1995 act, stating: "This ill-advised law has directly contributed to a rising tide of accounting failures, culminating in the Enron-Arthur Andersen fiasco. The checks and balances that a healthy concern about litigation risk create within each accounting firm have been undermined, and the pressure to look the other way at 'cooked books' of audient clients that also are big clients for consulting and other non-audit services can be intense" (Office of Congressman Ed Markey, "Markey Introduces 'Accountability for Accountants Act,'" press release, Washington, D.C., 23 January 2002).

24. Patrick Moynihan, "Defining Deviancy Down," *American Scholar* 62, no. 1 (1993): 17–30.

25. Public Broadcasting System, *Now with Bill Moyers*, "Interview with Eliot Spitzer," 12 December 2003, www.pbs.org/now/transcript/transcript246_full.html (accessed 16 November 2004).

26. Lynn Turner, former SEC chief accountant, transcript of interview, on *Frontline: Bigger Than Enron* website, http://www.pbs.org/wgbh/pages/frontline/shows/regulation/congress/ (accessed 30 June 2003).

27. Joseph E. Stiglitz, *The Roaring Nineties: A New History of the World's Most Prosperous Decade* (New York: Norton, 2003).

28. Partnoy, *Infectious Greed,* 151.

29. Ibid., 161.

30. Wendy Gramm, "In Defense of Derivatives," *Wall Street Journal,* 8 September 1993, sec. A, p. 12.

31. Partnoy, *Infectious Greed,* 150.

32. Ibid., 229.

33. Gretchen Morgensen, "The Fall of a Wall Street Ward Boss," *New York Times,* 19 October 2003, sec. 3, p. 1.

34. Ibid.

35. Ibid.

36. Ibid.

37. Gary Weiss, "The $140,000,000 Man," *Business Week,* 15 September 2003, 86.

38. Morgensen, "The Fall of a Wall Street Ward Boss."

39. Floyd Norris, "More Changes in Store for the Big Board," *New York Times,* 18 September 2003, sec. C, p. 4.

40. Morgenson, "The Fall of a Wall Street Ward Boss," p. 1.

41. Ibid.

42. Ibid.

43. *People of the State of New York, by Eliot Spitzer, the Attorney General of New York, against Richard A. Grasso, et al.,* Index No. 401620–04 (Supreme Ct., New York County, N.Y., 2004) ("Complaint"), 7.

44. Ibid., 9

45. Ibid.

46. Landon Thomas Jr., "The Man Behind Grasso's Payday," *New York Times,* 14 March 2004, sec. 3, p. 1.

47. Ibid.

48. Ibid.

49. Johnathan D. Glater, "Hurt by Slump, a Consulting Giant Looks Inward," *New York Times,* 30 June 2002, sec. C, p. 4.

50. Michael Indergaard, *Silicon Alley: The Rise and Fall of a New Media District* (New York: Routledge, 2004).

51. Ibid., 66.

52. Ibid., 75.
53. Marcia Vickers and Gary Weiss, "Wall Street's Hype Machine," *Business Week,* 3 April 2000, 120.
54. Indergaard, *Silicon Alley,* 75.
55. Mike France, "What About the Lawyers?" *Business Week,* 23 December 2002, 60.
56. Himelstein, "Inside Frank Quattrone's Money Machine."
57. Ibid.
58. Ibid.
59. Ibid.
60. Randall Smith and Susan Pullman, "U.S. Probes Inflated Commission for Hot IPOs," *Wall Street Journal,* 7 December 2000, sec. C, p. 1.
61. Himmelstein, "Inside Frank Quattrone's Money Machine."
62. Ann Grimes, "Quattrone Case Aired '90s Excesses," *Wallstreetjournal.com,* 27 October 2003, p. 2 (accessed 1 November 2003).
63. Himmelstein, "Inside Frank Quattrone's Money Machine."
64. Ibid.
65. In July 2004, the House passed a bill—strongly supported by tech giants, such as Intel and Cisco Systems—that would have severely limited a FASB proposal to require all companies to expense stock options (Bloomberg News, "House Passes Industry-Backed Stock Option Bill," *New York Times,* 21 July 2004, sec. C, p. 11).
66. *United States v. Frank Quattrone,* Case No. 03–Cr–00582 (S.D. N.Y. 2003).
67. John Cassidy, *Dot.con: How America Lost Its Mind and Money in the Internet Era* (New York: Perennial, 2002), 94.
68. Ibid., 95–96.
69. Stephen Gandel, "Analysts Get Downgraded," *Crain's New York Business,* 27 May 2002, pp. 1, 51.
70. Cassidy, *Dot.con,* 216.
71. Gandel, "Analysts Get Downgraded."
72. Duff McDonald, "The First Annual Target Price Awards," *Red Herring,* May 2000, 384, 386.
73. Ibid., 384.
74. Eric Dinallo, Assistant Attorney General, State of New York, *Affidavit in Support of Application for an Order Pursuant to General Business Law Section 354 with Regard to the Actions and Practices of Merrill Lynch & Co, Inc, Henry Blodget et al.* (8 April 2002), p. 13, http://www.oag.state.ny.us/press/2002/apr/MerrillL.pdf (accessed 10 December 2004).
75. *Spitzer v. Merrill Lynch,* Index No. 02/401522 (Supreme Ct., New York County, N.Y., 2002) ("In the Matter of Jack Grubman"), 27 April 2003, 3–15.
76. Peter Elkind, "Can We Ever Trust Wall Street Again?: Where Did Mary Meeker Go Wrong?" *Fortune,* 14 May 2001, 68.
77. Gretchen Morgensen and Timothy L. O'Brien, "When Citigroup Met World-Com," *New York Times,* 16 May 2004, sec. 3, pp. 1, 9.
78. Kurt Eichenwald, "For WorldCom, Acquisitions Were Behind Its Rise and Fall," *New York Times,* 8 August 2002, sec. C, p. 6.
79. Morgenson and O'Brien, "When Citigroup Met WorldCom," sec. 3, p. 9.
80. *In re: WorldCom, Inc., et al.,* Case No. 02–15533 (Bankr. S.D. N.Y. 2002) ("First Interim Report of Dick Thornburgh, Bankruptcy Court Examiner"), 112. Hereafter, in this chapter, references to this document will be cited in the text as *T.*
81. Citibank took over a $11 million loan Morgan Keegan had made to Ebbers; in return, SSB guaranteed Citibank against any loss on the Morgan Keegan loan and on Citibank's own loan to Ebbers—a total of $55 million. SSB agreed to let

part of the loan go unsecured—meaning that the stock held as collateral could fall as much as $10 million in value before it would start selling it. Citibank and SSB were also prepared to make a similar arrangement to take over a PaineWebber loan to Ebbers of $49 million, but the transaction was never implemented. Ibid.

82. Morgenson and O'Brien, "When Citigroup Met WorldCom."
83. Ibid.
84. Ibid.
85. *Spitzer v. Merrill Lynch* ("In the Matter of Jack Grubman").
86. Bethany McLean and Peter Elkind, "Partners in Crime," *Fortune*, 27 October 2000, 80.
87. Ibid.
88. Ibid.
89. Ibid.
90. Ibid.

Chapter 6. Counting on the Upside

Epigraph source: The video was for Arthur Andersen. Bethany McLean and Peter Elkind, *The Smartest Guys in the Room: The Amazing Rise and Scandalous Fall of Enron* (New York: Portfolio, 2003), 146. Hereafter, in this chapter, references to this work will be cited in the text as *ME*.

1. Edmund L. Andrews, Neela Bonerjee, and Andrew Ross Sorkin, "'99 Deal Failed After Scrutiny of Enron Books," *New York Times*, 27 January 2002, sec. A, p. 32.
2. Felicity Barringer, "10 Months Ago, Questions on Enron Came and Went with Little Notice," *New York Times*, 28 January 2002, sec. A, p. 11.
3. Ibid.
4. John A. Byrne, "Fall From Grace," *Business Week*, 12 August 2002, 55.
5. Alex Berenson, *The Number* (New York: Random House, 2003), 125.
6. Ibid., 127.
7. Ibid.
8. Jeremy Kahn, "One Plus One Makes What?" *Fortune*, 7 January 2002, 89.
9. Joseph E. Stiglitz, *The Roaring Nineties: A New History of the World's Most Prosperous Decade* (New York: Norton, 2003), 136.
10. Ibid., 27.
11. "Too Creative by 50%?" *Economist*, 6 July 2002, 58.
12. Barabara Ley Toffler, *Final Accounting* (New York: Broadway, 2003).
13. William J. Holstein, "Lessons of a Fallen Rival for Accounting's Big 4," *New York Times*, 23 February 2003, sec. C, p. 6.
14. Gary Hamel and Peter Skarzynski, "Innovation: The New Route to Wealth," *Journal of Accountancy* 192, no. 5 (November 2001): 67.
15. Tim Hallett, "Symbolic Power and Organizational Culture," *Sociological Theory* 21, no. 2 (2003): 139.
16. Melody Petersen, "Consulting by Auditors Stirs Concern," *New York Times*, 13 July 1998, sec. D, p. 1.
17. Floyd Norris, "Big Auditing Firm Gets 6-Month Ban on New Business," *New York Times*, 17 April 2004, sec. A, p. 1.
18. Kahn, "One Plus One Makes What?"
19. Janice Revell, "The Fires That Won't Go Out," *Fortune.com*, 29 September 2003, 5 (accessed 1 October 2003).

20. Rebecca Blumenstein and Susan Pulliam, "Report Says Ebbers and Others Conspired in WorldCom Fraud," *Wall Street Journal*, 10 June 2003, sec. A, p. 2.

21. Kurt Eichenwald, "Auditing Woes at WorldCom Were Noted Two Years Ago," *New York Times*, 15 July 2002, sec. C, p. 1.

22. Mark Gimein, "Qwest: What Did Joe Know?" *Fortune.com*, 28 April 2003 (accessed May 2003).

23. Simon Romero and Seth Schiesel, "The Fiber Optic Fantasy Slips Away," *New York Times*, 17 February 2002, sec. 3, p. 7.

24. Dennis K. Berman, Julia Angwin, and Chip Cummins, "As the Bubble Neared Its End, Bogus Swaps Padded the Books," *Wall Street Journal*, 23 December 2002, sec. A, p. 5.

25. Mike France, "The Rise of the Wall Street Tax Machine," *Business Week*, 31 March 2003, 84.

26. *In re: WorldCom, Inc., et al.*, Case No. 02–15533 (Bankr. S.D. N.Y. 2002) ("First Interim Report of Dick Thornburgh, Bankruptcy Court Examiner"), 12

27. Ibid., 13.

28. Nanette Byrnes and Louis Lavelle, "The Corporate Tax Game," *Business Week*, 31 March 2003, 80.

29. Cassell Bryan-Low, "KPMG Boosted Its Profits, Selling Intricate Strategies; Now It Faces U.S. Problems," *Wall Street Journal*, 25 February 2004, sec. A, p. 1.

30. David Cay Johnston, "Wall St. Firms Are Faulted in Report on Enron's Taxes," *New York Times*, 14 February 2003, sec. C, p. 6.

31. David Cay Johnston, "Tax Moves by Enron Said to Mystify the I.R.S.," *New York Times*, 13 February 2003, sec. C, p. 1.

32. Byrnes and Lavelle, "The Corporate Tax Game."

33. Johnston, "Tax Moves by Enron Said to Mystify the I.R.S."

34. Ibid.

35. Byrnes and Lavelle, "The Corporate Tax Game."

36. Ibid.

37. Jeremy Kahn, "Do Accountants Have a Future?" *Fortune.com*, 18 February 2003, 3 (accessed 20 February 2003).

38. General Accounting Office, "Internal Revenue Service: Challenges Remain in Combating Abusive Tax Shelters," GAO–04–104T, 21 October 2003, Washington, D.C., 11.

39. Bryan-Low, "KPMG Boosted Its Profits, Selling Intricate Strategies."

40. Ibid.

41. Ibid.

42. David Cay Johnston, "Skeptical Hearing for Audit Firm," *New York Times*, 19 November 2003, sec. C, p. 3.

43. David Cay Johnston, "Changes at KPMG After Criticism of Its Tax Shelter," *New York Times*, 13 January 2003, sec. C, p. 11.

44. Ibid.

45. Hallett, "Symbolic Power and Organizational Culture," 143.

46. Byrne, "Fall From Grace," 52.

47. Mike France, "What About the Lawyers?" *Business Week*, 23 December 2002, 60.

48. Ibid.

49. Kurt Eichenwald, "Andersen Misreads Depths of the Government's Anger," *New York Times*, 18 March 2002, sec. A, p. 1.

50. Richard A. Oppel Jr., "Inquiry on Andersen Lawyer Is Urged by House Committee," *New York Times*, 18 December 2002, sec. C, p. 7.

51. Bruce M. Price, "Changing Roles and Relationships of Lawyers in Silicon Valley," paper prepared for presentation at the 2nd Annual Program on the Corporation as a Social Institution, Berkeley, Calif., 18 May 2001.

52. Mike France, "Close the Lawyer Loophole," *Business Week,* 2 February 2004, 70.

53. Tommy Fernandez, "Tax Shelter Crackdown Hits Law Firms," *Crain's New York Business,* 14 June 2003, 32.

54. David Cay Johnson, "I.R.S. Unit Will Focus on Lawyers and Accountants," *New York Times,* 29 December 2003, sec. C, p. 2.

55. Fernandez, "Tax Shelter Crackdown Hits Law Firms."

56. Jonathan D. Glater, "Lawyers Are Warned on Mutual Fund Roles," *New York Times,* 5 December 2003, sec. C, p. 6.

57. France, "What About the Lawyers?"

58. John Schwartz, "As Enron Purged Its Ranks, Dissent Was Swept Away," *New York Times,* 4 February 2002, sec. C, p. 2.

59. Ibid.

60. Ibid.

61. Ibid.

62. Ibid.

63. Blake E. Ashforth and Vikas Anand, "The Normalization of Corruption in Organizations," *Research in Organizational Behavior* 25 (2003): 1–51.

64. Frank Partnoy, *Infectious Greed: How Deceit and Risk Corrupted the Financial Markets* (New York: Times Books, 2003); Maggie Mahar, *Bull! A History of the Boom, 1982–1999* (New York: Harper Business, 2004).

65. Lyn Spillman, "Introduction: Culture and Cultural Sociology," in *Cultural Sociology,* edited by Lyn Spillman (Malden, Mass.: Blackwell, 2002), 1–15.

66. Neil Fligstein, *The Architecture of Markets: An Economic Sociology of Twenty-First-Century Capitalist Societies* (Princeton, N.J.: Princeton Univ. Press, 2001).

67. Hallett, "Symbolic Power and Organizational Culture."

68. Simon Romero, "Internal Notes Questioned Qwest's Swaps," *New York Times,* 25 September 2002, sec. C, p. 4.

69. *In re: WorldCom, Inc., et al.,* Case No. 02–15533 (Bankr. S.D. N.Y. 2002) ("First Interim Report of Dick Thornburgh, Bankruptcy Court Examiner"), 6.

70. Ibid., 12.

71. Michael Indergaard, *Silicon Alley: The Rise and Fall of a New Media District* (New York: Routledge, 2004).

72. After Skilling became COO, he reconfigured offices in Enron's corporate tower to resemble a dot-com workplace. He said he wanted "to get rid of all the walls" so that "people will talk and throw things at each other and get all excited and creative." When the building managers objected, Skilling commented, the "building Gestapo didn't get it" (Schwartz, "As Enron Purged Its Ranks").

73. *In re: WorldCom, Inc., et al.,* Case No. 02–15533 (Bankr. S.D. N.Y. 2002) ("First Interim Report of Dick Thornburgh, Bankruptcy Court Examiner"), 22.

74. Kurt Eichenwald, "Auditing Woes at WorldCom," sec. C, p. 9.

75. France, "What About the Lawyers?"

76. Julie Creswell and Nomi Prim, "The Emperor of Greed," *Fortune,* 24 June 2002, 2.

77. *In re: WorldCom, Inc., et al.,* Case No. 02–15533 (Bankr. S.D. N.Y. 2002) ("First Interim Report of Dick Thornburgh, Bankruptcy Court Examiner"), 91–94.

78. Ibid.

79. Gretchen Morgenson, "Analyst Coached WorldCom Chief on His Script," *New York Times,* 27 February 2003, sec. A, p. 1.

80. Partnoy, *Infectious Greed,* 363.

81. France, "What About the Lawyers?"

82. Schwartz, "As Enron Purged Its Ranks."

83. Reed Abelson and Milt Freudenheim, "The Scrushy Mix: Strict and So Lenient," *New York Times,* 20 April 2003, sec. 3, p. 1.

84. Ibid.

85. Mark Gimein, "Qwest: What Did Joe Know?" *Fortune.com,* 28 April 2003, 4 (accessed 1 May 2003).

86. Ibid.

87. Charles Haddad, "How Ebbers Kept the Board in His Pocket," *Business Week,* 14 October 2002, 139.

88. *In re: WorldCom, Inc., et al.,* Case No. 02–15533 (Bankr. S.D. N.Y. 2002) ("First Interim Report of Dick Thornburgh, Bankruptcy Court Examiner"), 242.

89. Blumenstein and Pulliam, "Report Says Ebbers and Others Conspired," 2.

90. An actor that can broker ties between parties that otherwise are not connected has an information advantage and may be able to exert considerable influence on the impressions of those they link up. See Ronald Burt, *Structural Holes: The Social Structure of Competition* (Cambridge, Mass.: Harvard Univ. Press, 1992); Robert Tillman and Michael Indergaard, "Field of Schemes: Employee Health Insurance Fraud in the Small Firm Segment," *Social Problems* 46, no. 4 (November 1999): 572–591.

91. Jeremy Kahn, "Presto Chango! Sales are HUGE!" *Fortune,* 20 March 2000, 90.

92. Linda Himmelstein, "Frank's Life in the Rough," *Business Week,* 31 March 2003, 89.

93. Gretchen Morgenson and Timothy L. O'Brien, "When Citigroup Met World-Com," *New York Times,* 16 May 2004, sec. 3, p. 9.

94. Steve Rosenbush, "Inside the Telecom Game," *Business Week,* 5 August 2002, 36.

95. Simon Romero, "Internal Notes Questioned Qwest Swaps," 4.

96. Richard A. Oppel Jr., "Merrill Replaced Research Analyst Who Upset Enron," *New York Times,* 30 July 2002, sec. A, p. 1.

97. Richard A. Oppel Jr., "The Man Who Paid the Price for Sizing up Enron," *New York Times,* 27 March 2002, sec. C, p. 1.

98. Byrne, "Fall From Grace."

99. Richard A. Oppel Jr. and Kurt Eichenwald, "Arthur Andersen Fires an Executive for Enron Orders," *New York Times,* 16 January 2002, sec. C, p. 7.

100. Kurt Eichenwald, "Criminal Indictment Against Skilling of Enron Is Said to Be in the Works," *New York Times,* 14 February 2004, sec. C, p. 1.

101. Kurt Eichenwald, "Crimes of Other Wrecked Enron, Ex-Chief Says," *New York Times,* 27 June 2004, sec. 1, p. 1.

102. France, "What About the Lawyers?"

103. Partnoy, *Infectious Greed.* A somewhat similar argument was made by journalist and former prosecutor Jeffrey Toobin, who concluded, "[I]t may not be possible to divide up the systemic corruption within the company into easily understood portions of wrongdoing that can be served up to a jury of ordinary people" (Jeffrey Toobin, "End Run at Enron," *New Yorker,* 27 October 2003, 55).

104. Riva D. Atlas, "A Law Firm's 2 Roles Risk Suit by Enron, Experts Say," *New York Times,* 29 January 2002, sec. C, p. 1.

105. Gimein, "Qwest: What Did Joe Know?"

106. *U.S. v. Causey, et al.* Case No. Cr.–H–04–25 (S.D. Tex. 2004) ("Indictment"), 7–12.

Chapter 7. Forgive and Forget

1. Democratic Policy Committee, "How Do President Bush and Vice President Cheney Measure Up Against Their Own New Ethic of Corporate Responsibility Proposal?" 2002, www.democrats.senate.gov (accessed 26 January 2004); Jeff Gerth and Richard Stevenson, "Bush Calls for an End of Loans of a Type He Once Received," *New York Times,* 11 July 2002, sec. A, p. 1; Paul Krugman, "The Insider Game," *New York Times,* 12 July 2002, sec. A, p. 19; Joe Conason, "Notes on a Native Son," *Harper's,* February 2000, 39; Elisabeth Bumiller and Richard Oppel, "Bush Defends Sale of Stock and Vows to Enhance S.E.C," *New York Times,* 9 July 2002, sec. A, p. 1.
2. Alex Berenson and Lloyd Bergman, "Under Cheney, Halliburton Altered Policy on Accounting," *New York Times,* 22 May 2002, sec. C, p. 1.
3. President George W. Bush, "Exchange with Reporters in Belle, West Virginia," *Weekly Compilation of Presidential Documents* 38, no. 4 (2002): 102.
4. Michael Hedges, "Center of the Storm," *Houston Chronicle,* 20 January 2002, sec. A, p. 1.
5. David Ivanovich, "New Twists in Enron Fall," *Houston Chronicle,* 11 January 2002, sec. A, p. 1.
6. Janet Elliott, "Cornyn Recuses Self from State Probe of Enron," *Houston Chronicle,* 12 January 2002, sec. A, 20.
7. President George W. Bush, "Remarks on Corporate Responsibility in New York City," *Weekly Compilation of Presidential Documents* 38, no. 28 (2002): 1158.
8. Chuck Squatrigia, "Questions on Corporate Crime Cop," *San Francisco Chronicle,* 13 July 2002, sec. A, p. 13.
9. John Lancaster, "Lieberman Placed in Awkward Spot," *Washington Post,* 2 February 2002, sec. A, p. 4.
10. "Fighting Mr. Biggs," *Wall Street Journal,* 4 October 2002, sec. A, p. 12; David Hilzenrath, Jonathan Weisman, and Jim VandeHei, "How Congress Rode a 'Storm' to Corporate Reform," *Washington Post,* 28 July 2002, sec. A, p. 1.
11. "Corporate and Auditing Accountability, Responsibility, and Transparency Act of 2002," H.R. 3763, Introduced in House, 14 February 2002.
12. Hilzenrath et al., "How Congress."
13. President George W. Bush, "Remarks on Signing the Sarbanes-Oxley Act of 2002," *Weekly Compilation of Presidential Documents* 38, no. 31 (2002): 1283.
14. Mike Allen, "Bush Signs Corporate Reforms into Law," *Washington Post,* 31 July 2004, sec. A, p. 4.
15. Sarbanes-Oxley Act of 2002, Public Law 107–204, 107th Cong., 116 Stat. 745.
16. President George W. Bush, "Remarks on Signing the Sarbanes-Oxley Act of 2002."
17. Stephen Labaton, "Will Reforms with Few Teeth Be Able to Bite?" *New York Times,* 22 September 2002, sec. D, p. 3.
18. John Judis, "Option Play: What W. Didn't Learn from Enron," *New Republic,* 6 May 2002, 19.
19. Jeffrey Skilling (president and COO, Enron Corp.), "Testimony on Financial Collapse of Enron before the Senate Committee on Commerce, Science and Transportation" (26 February 2002), text from *Federal News Service* (online service) (Bethesda, Md.: Congressional Information Service, 2002).
20. Senate Committee on Governmental Affairs, "The Watchdogs Didn't Bark: Enron and the Wall Street Analysts," 107th Cong., 2nd sess., 27 February 2002, 2.

21. "Returning Civil Law to the 19th Century," *San Francisco Chronicle*, 9 March 1995, sec. A, p. 24.

22. House Committee on Energy and Commerce, Subcommittee on Oversight and Investigations, "Destruction of Enron-Related Documents by Andersen Personnel," 107th Congress, 2nd sess., 24 January 2002.

23. Arthur Levitt, former chairman of the SEC, transcript of interview on *Frontline: Bigger Than Enron* website, http://www.pbs.org/wgbh/pages/frontline/shows/regulation/congress/ (accessed 30 June 2003).

24. Center for Responsive Politics, www.opensecrets.org (accessed 10 February 2004).

25. Public Broadcasting System, *Frontline: Bigger Than Enron* (originally broadcast on 20 June 2002).

26. David Hilzenrath, "SEC Chief: 'Gentler' Agency," *Washington Post*, 31 October 2001, sec. E., p. 1.

27. Securities and Exchange Commission, "Speech by SEC Chairman: Remarks before the New York Financial Writers Association," 13 June 2002, http://www.sec.gov/news/speech/spch567.htm (accessed 12 December 2002).

28. Senate Committee on Banking, Housing and Urban Affairs, "Accounting and Investor Protection Issues Raised by Enron and Other Public Companies. V. II," 107th Cong., 2nd sess., 21 March 2002, 1071, 1088.

29. "Fighting Mr. Biggs," 12.

30. Ibid.; Joann Lubin, "TIAA-CREF Wants Options Seen as Expense," *Washington Post*, 24 July 2002, sec. A, p. 3.

31 General Accounting Office, "Securities and Exchange Commission: Actions Needed to Improve Public Accounting Oversight Board Selection," GAO–03–339, Washington, D.C., 2002.

32. Ron Suskind, *The Price of Loyalty* (New York: Simon and Schuster, 2004), 226–230.

33. Dana Milbank, "Enron's Influence Reached Deep into the Administration," *Washington Post*, 18 January 2002, sec. A, p. 1.

34. Suskind, *Price of Loyalty*, 234.

35. George W. Bush, "Remarks on Corporate Responsibility."

36. White House, "President's Corporate Fraud Task Force Compiles Strong Record," press release, Washington, D.C., 22 July 2002.

37. These data were produced by the Executive Office of the U.S. Attorneys, and, as reproduced here, were assembled by the Transactional Records Access Clearinghouse at Syracuse University.

38. In 2003, a new category, "corporate fraud," was added. The data show 322 prosecutions for the category in that year. However, since there is no comparable category for previous years, it is impossible to determine a trend.

39. U.S. Department of Justice, *FY 2003 Performance and Accountability Report*, Washington, D.C., 2004, II–63.

40. These trends are mirrored in the data on white-collar cases referred to prosecutors by the FBI. White-collar crime referrals declined from 13,720 in 1998 to 9,826 in 2003—a drop of 25 percent (Transactional Records Access Clearinghouse).

41. U.S. Department of Justice, Office of the Inspector General, "The Internal Effects of the Federal Bureau of Investigation's Reprioritization," Washington, D.C., 2004.

42. Securities and Exchange Commission, *Annual Reports*, 1997–2003.

43. Some of these individuals may have been charged in other criminal cases (John

Emshwiller, "Skilling Seeks to Name Names," *Wall Street Journal,* 10 December 2004, sec. C, p. 1).

44. Public Broadcasting System, *Now with Bill Moyers,* "Interview with Eliot Spitzer," 12 December 2003, www.pbs.org/now/transcript/transcript246_full.html (accessed 16 November 2004).

45. Columbia Broadcasting System, *60 Minutes: Sheriff of Wall Street* (originally broadcast on 25 May 2003), cbsnews.com/stories/2003/05/23/60minutes/main555310.shtml (accessed 22 February 2004).

46. General Accounting Office, *Investment Banks: The Role of Firms and Their Analysts with Enron and Global Crossing,* GAO–03–511, Washington, D.C., 2003, 13. However, the SEC apparently felt that it could overcome this legal obstacle when it charged Merrill Lynch and four of its executives with "aiding and abetting" Enron.

47. Public Broadcasting System, *Frontline: The Wall Street Fix,* "Interview, Eliot Spitzer," http://www.pbs.org/wgbh/pages/frontline/shows/wallstreet/interviews/spitzer.html (accessed 22 February 2004).

48. Jeffrey Skilling's lawyers, for example, told the media after his client was indicted: "They are trying to put on trial business practices that are common in lots of different companies and trying to hold my client responsible because he was COO and then CEO" (Lisa Girion, "Leading Skilling's Defense: A Lawyer of 'Enormous Talent,'" *Los Angeles Times,* 20 February 2004, sec. C, p. 1).

49. Business reporter Gretchen Morgenson observed that the $100 million penalty imposed on Merrill Lynch by the attorney general's office was less than a third of the $349 million the firm had spent on postage the previous year (Gretchen Morgenson, "Investors Want Cops on the Street," *New York Times,* 26 May 2002, sec. 3, p. 31).

50. Columbia Broadcasting System, *60 Minutes, Sheriff of Wall Street.*

51. Roger Lowenstein, *When Genius Failed: The Rise and Fall of Long-Term Capital Management* (New York: Random House, 2000).

52. Ari Weinberg, "The Rule Makers: Too Big to Fail?" *Forbes Online,* 15 October 2002, www.forbes.com (accessed 14 January 2004).

53. Kitty Calavita, Henry N. Pontell, and Robert H. Tillman, *Big Money Crime: Fraud and Politics in the Savings and Loan Crisis* (Berkeley: Univ. of California Press, 1997), 136.

54. The government's philosophy was hinted at in a speech by Larry Thompson, then head of the Corporate Fraud Task Force, in which he stated, "[W]here corporations are cooperating, we will exercise appropriate prosecutorial discretion in perhaps deciding not to charge or to bring lesser charges. We are always mindful of the real world consequences of a decision to indict a corporation—especially disproportionate harm to innocent employees, communities and shareholders" (Larry D. Thompson, "Remarks of Deputy Attorney General Larry D. Thompson," Ninth Judicial Conference, Kau'i, Hawaii, 25 June 2003).

55. Gerald Seib, "Insider Bailouts: Can They Feed Populist Politics?" *Wall Street Journal,* 30 September 1998, sec. A, p. 1.

56. Peter Elkin, "NYSE Pay Scandal: The Trials of Eliot Spitzer," *Fortune.com,* 1 June, 2004, 2 (accessed 15 June 2004).

57. Joseph Nocera, "Wall Street on the Run," *Fortune.com,* 1 June 2004, 6 (accessed 15 June 2004).

58. Ibid.

59. Gretchen Morgenson, "A Wall St. Push to Water Down Securities Laws," *New York Times,* 18 June 2002, sec. C, p. 19.
60. George W. Bush, "Remarks on Corporate Responsibility."
61. Rick Santorum, "Toward a Christian Free Market," *Crisis: Politics, Culture and the Church,* 1 January 2003, http://www.crisismagazine.com/january2003/hill.htm (accessed 20 Febrary 2004).
62. "Enron's Sins," *Wall Street Journal,* 18 January 2002, sec. A, p. 10.
63. Gloria Borger, "Don't Blame Bubba," *U.S. News & World Report,* 29 July 2002, 23.
64. Michael Lewis, "In Defense of the Boom," *New York Times Magazine,* 27 October 2002, 44.
65. Gary Becker, "Enron Was Mostly Right About One Thing: Deregulation," *Business Week,* 18 March 2002, 26.
66. Christopher Culp and Steve Hanke, "Empire of the Sun: An Economic Interpretation of Enron's Energy Business," *Policy Analysis* 470 (2003): 17.
67. George Gilder, "The Confidence Game," *Forbes,* 23 December 2002, 233.
68. The idea of criminals as "innovators," of course, has a long history in sociology, beginning with Durkheim's classic observation that the conditions that allow for individual creativity and social change also allow for criminality (Emile Durkheim, *The Rules of the Sociological Method,* translated by Sarah Solovay and John Mueller, edited by George Catlin [New York: Free Press, 1965], 71). Later, Robert Merton famously argued that lower-class individuals facing blocked opportunities for attaining success through legitimate means would turn to crime as an alternative avenue (Robert Merton, "Social Structure and Anomie," *American Sociological Review* 3, no. 5 [1938]: 672–682). More recently, Diane Vaughan applied the idea of innovation to corporate criminals (Diane Vaughn, *Controlling Unlawful Organizational Behavior* [Chicago: Univ. of Chicago Press, 1983]).
69. See, for example, Daniel Fischel, *Payback: The Conspiracy to Destroy Michael Milken and His Financial Revolution* (New York: HarperCollins, 1995). White-collar criminals themselves have also used the "economic innovator" argument to rationalize their illegal behavior. In a jailhouse interview, the Colbert brothers, who in the 1980s ran a profitable business exporting toxic waste to third-world countries, declared: "We were, in a sense, innovators ahead of the times. . . . We're basically pioneers in the surplus chemical business, which is something that's a necessary business for society" (Center for Investigative Reporting, *Global Dumping Ground* [Washington, D.C.: Seven Locks Press, 1990], 37).
70. Irwin Stelzer, "The Rise and Fall of Enron," *Weekly Standard,* 26 November 2001, 16.
71. Thurman Arnold, *The Folklore of Capitalism* (1937; reprint, New Haven, Conn.: Yale Univ. Press, 1964), 263.
72. Stan O'Neal, "Risky Business," *Wall Street Journal,* 24 April 2003, sec. A, p. 16.
73. Thomas Donahue (president and CEO, U.S. Chamber of Commerce), "Strengthening Our Capital Markets—The Role of Investors, Businesses, and Regulators," speech given in Washington, D.C., 12 November 2003; Andrew Hill, "CEOs Hit Back Over Reforms," *Financial Times,* 3 October 2002, p. 1. William Donaldson, Harvey Pitt's successor at the SEC, who had a reputation for being a tough-minded regulator, told an interviewer:

> Corporate America's got to move on. . . . I worry about the loss of risk-taking zeal. People are confusing business risk-taking with legal risk-taking, which is a mistake. . . . Sarbanes-Oxley unleashed batteries of lawyers across the country [resulting in] a huge preoccupation with the dangers and risks

of making the slightest mistake, as opposed to a reasonable approach to legitimate business risk (Adrian Michaels, "Comment and Analysis," *Financial Times,* 24 July 2003, p. 15).

74. PricewatercouseCoopers, *Managing Risk: An Assessment of CEO Preparedness,* 2004, 16, www.pwc.com (accessed 25 January 2004).
75. Tally Goldstein, Andrew Hill, and Peter Spiegel, "Feeling the Heat," *Financial Times,* 8 March 2002, p. 18.
76. John C. Danforth, "When Enforcement Becomes Harassment," *New York Times,* 6 May 2003, sec. A, p. 31.
77. Amy Borrus and Mike McNamee, "SEC Reforms: Big Biz Says Enough Already," *Business Week,* 2 February 2004, 43.
78. Paul Craig Roberts, "Wary of Fallout . . . and Funk," *Washington Times,* 16 July 2002, sec. A, p. 17.
79. Neil Weinberg, "Criminalizing Capitalism," *Forbes,* 12 May 2003, 74; William Norman Grigg, "Criminalizing Capitalism," *New American,* 26 August 2002, 10.
80. Grigg, "Criminalizing Capitalism."
81. Ayn Rand, "America's Persecuted Minority," in *Capitalism: The Unknown Ideal,* edited by Ayn Rand (New York: New American Library, 1966), 37. In this same volume, which was devoted to propounding Rand's philosophy of "objectivism," an essay appears by Alan Greenspan, an early acolyte of Rand's who would later become head of the Federal Reserve, in which he wrote: "[T]he major victim of 'protective' regulation is the producer: the businessman. Businessmen are being subjected to governmental coercion prior to the commission of any crime" (Alan Greenspan, "The Assault on Integrity," in Rand, ed., *Capitalism: The Unknown Ideal,* 115).
82. Friedrich Hayek, "The Mysterious World of Trade and Money," in *The Fatal Conceit: The Errors of Socialism,* edited by W. W. Bartley (Chicago: Univ. of Chicago Press, 1988), 89–105.
83. Lewis, "In Defense of the Boom."
84. Jennifer Steinhauer, "Mayor Says Careless Investors Share Blame for Stock Losses," *New York Times,* 29 June 2002, sec. B, p. 2.
85. 273 F. Supp. 2d 351; 2003 U.S. Dist. LEXIS 11005; Fed. Sec. L. Rep. (CCH) P92, 480.
86. Kenneth Lay, "Deregulation Done Right This Time—No State Control—Is the Answer to California's Energy Woes," *San Francisco Chronicle,* 1 March 2001, sec. A, p. 23.
87. Becker, "Enron Was Mostly Right."
88. Benjamin Zycher, *Power to the People: An Economic Analysis of California's Electricity Crisis and Its Lessons for Legislators* (San Francisco: Pacific Research Institute, 2002), 1, 16.
89. This view was well-summarized in a 1992 article in *Forbes* magazine that analogized policies that combined thrift deregulation with deposit insurance to a parent giving a fourteen-year-old a credit card. "This is the S&L crisis . . . the federal government in effect lent out its own capital by providing an all but unlimited guarantee of deposits and allowing the deposit takers to speculate with the money. As it turned out, this was equivalent to giving your 14-year-old kid your American Express card and telling him to go out and have a good time" (Gretchen Morgenson, "What Did Pop Expect to Happen When He Gave the Kid His Credit Card," *Forbes,* 28 September 1992, 95).
90. Don Dixon quoted in Daniel Fischel, *Payback,* 253.

91. Gordon Crovitz, "Fraud, the .05% Cause of the Thrift Crisis," *Wall Street Journal,* 10 April 1991, sec. A, p. 23.
92. Edwin Sutherland, who coined the term "white-collar crime," pointed this out in his seminal discussion of the issue in 1949 when he argued that "[white collar criminals] are not arrested by uniformed policemen, are not tried in criminal courts, and are not committed to prisons; this illegal behavior receives the attention of administrative commissions and of courts operating under civil or equity jurisdiction" (Edwin H. Sutherland, *White-Collar Crime: The Uncut Version* [1949; reprint, New Haven, Conn.: Yale Univ. Press, 1983], 7). Law professor Christopher Stone described the limitations faced by the law in controlling corporate behavior in his book *Where the Law Ends* (New York: Harper and Row, 1978).

Conclusions

1. John Byrne, "After Enron," *Business Week,* 26 August 2002, 68.
2. See, for example, Gary Becker, "What the Scandals Reveal: A Strong Economy," *Business Week,* 30 December 2002, 30. This view was also expressed by Alan Greenspan—the former Ayn Rand acolyte and longtime regulation foe—in March 2002, when he noted that "corporate governance has doubtless already measurably improved as result of this greater market discipline in the wake of recent events" and cautioned that "we have to be careful, however, not to look to a significant expansion of regulation as the solution to current problems" (Alan Greenspan, "Corporate Governance," speech delivered at the Stern School of Business, New York University, New York, N.Y., 26 March 2002). Yet, just a few months later he appeared to be rethinking his position, telling a Senate committee: "[M]y view was always that accountants basically knew or had to know that the market value of their companies rested on the integrity of their operations . . . and that, therefore, their self-interest is so strongly directed at making certain that their reputation was unimpeachable, that regulation by Government was utterly unnecessary and, indeed, most inappropriate. *I was wrong*" (emphasis added). Senate Committee on Banking, Housing, and Urban Affairs, "Federal Reserve's Second Monetary Policy Report for 2002," 107th Cong., 2nd sess., 16 July 2002, 32.
3. Senate Committee on Banking, "Federal Reserve's Second Monetary Policy," 11.
4. Huron Consulting Group, "2004 Annual Review of Financial Reporting Matters," www.huronconsultinggroup.com (accessed 2 March 2005).
5. Securities Class Action Clearinghouse, "Securities Class Action Case Filings: 2004: A Year in Review," http://securities.stanford.edu/clearinghouse_research/2004 _YIR/2004010305.pdf (accessed 30 June 2004).
6. Alessandra Galloni and Varoslaw Trofimov, "Behind Parmalat Chief's Rise," *Wall Street Journal,* 8 May 2004, sec. A, p. 1; Alessandra Galloni, David Reilly, and Carrick Mollenkamp, "Italian Officials Seek Charges Against Firms in Parmalat Case," *Wall Street Journal,* 19 March 2004, sec. A, p. 3.
7. Chip Cummins and Alexei Barrionuevo, "Shell Estimate Ignored Warnings," *Wall Street Journal,* 1 April 2004, sec. A, p. 3; Jeff Gerth and Stephen Labaton, "Shell Withheld Reserves Data to Aid Nigeria," *New York Times,* 19 May 2004, sec. A, p. 1.
8. In February 2004, the beleaguered El Paso Corp. announced that it was cutting its proven reserve estimates by 41 percent (Laura Goldberg, "Oil, Gas Firm El

Paso Corp. Reduces Reserve Estimates by 41 Percent," *Houston Chronicle,* 18 February 2004, sec. A, p. 1). A study by investment bank UBS found that in 2003 oil and gas companies reported 34 percent of their holdings to be "proved" reserves, as compared with 26 percent in 1994, reflecting "the companies' desires to post attractive reserve growth in an industry that has not been capable of generating production growth" (Stella Farrington, "Energy-Reserve Data Viewed as Aggressive," *Wall Street Journal,* 11 May 2004, sec. A, p. 1).

9. New York State Attorney General's Office, "State Investigation Reveals Mutual Fund Fraud," press release, Albany, N.Y., 3 September 2003.

10. Testimony of Stephen Cutler before the Senate Committee on Governmental Affairs, Subcommittee on Financial Management, "Mutual Funds: Trading Practices and Abuses That Harm Investors," 108th Cong., 2nd sess., 3 November 2003.

11. "Mutual Funds Scandal Scorecard," *Wall Street Journal Online,* http://online.wsj.com/documents/wsj-scandalscore010504.pdf (accessed 2 March 2005).

12. Randall Dodd, "Overview of Mutual Fund Scandal: 'A Gauntlet of Fraud,'" *Financial Policy Forum,* www.financialpolicy.org/fpfspb13.pdf (accessed 4 August 2004).

13. John Coffee, quoted in Joseph Treaster, "An Inquiry into Insurance Payments and Conflicts," *New York Times,* 28 April 2004, sec. C, p. 1.

14. Joseph Treaster, "Broker Accused of Rigging Bids for Insurance," *New York Times,* 15 October 2004, sec. A, p. 1.

15. Senate Committee on Government Affairs, Permanent Subcommittee on Investigations, Minority Staff, "U.S. Tax Shelter Industry: The Role of Accountants, Lawyers and Financial Professionals: Four KPMG Case Studies: FLIP, OPIS, BLIPS, and SC2," S. Prt. 108–34, 18 November 2003, 22.

16. Subcommittee investigators noted: "The dispute over whether KPMG sells benign 'tax solutions' or illegal 'tax shelters' is more than a linguistic difference; it goes to the heart of whether respected institutions like this one have crossed the line of acceptable conduct" (ibid., 26).

17. Public Broadcasting System, *Frontline: Tax Me If You Can* (originally broadcast on 19 February 2004).

18. General Accounting Office, "Internal Revenue Service: Challenges Remain in Combating Abusive Tax Shelters," GAO–04–104T, Washington, D.C., 21 October 2003, 11.

19. Mitchell Powelle, Alessandra Gailoni, and David Reily, "Fed Ties the Hands of Citigroup," *Wall Street Journal,* 18 March 2005, sec. C, 1, 5.

20. Geraldine Fabrikant, "Time Warner and S.E.C. Settle for $300 Million," *New York Times,* 22 March 2005, sec. C, 1, 8.

21. The IRS has stated that it will litigate "vigorously" against some six hundred individuals who did not join the settlement. "IRS Recoups $3.2 B from Abusive Shelter," CNN.com, 24 March 2005, 2. http://money.cnn.com/2005/03/24/pf/taxes/tax_shelter.reut/ (accessed 25 March 2005).

22. The five largest individual settlements by the banks involved are Citigroup ($2.58 billion), J. P. Morgan ($2 billion), Bank of America ($460.5 million), Deutsche Bank ($325 million) and ABN Amro ($278.4 million). Robin Sidel, "J.P. Morgan to Pay $2 Billion As Street's Bill for Bubble Soars," *Wall Street Journal,* 17 March 2005, sec. A, 1.

23. Ken Belson, "Ex-Chief of WorldCom Is Found Guilty in $11 Billion Fraud," *New York Times,* 16 March 2005, sec. C, 8.

24. Simon Romero, "Satisfaction and Sadness at the Sight of Handcuffs," *New York Times,* 9 July 2004, sec. C, p. 4.

25. Paul Krugman, "Enron and the System," *New York Times,* 9 January 2004, sec. A, p. 19.
26. Stephen Labton, "Hedge Fund Plan Fractures Civility of Republicans," *New York Times,* 16 July 2004, sec. C, p. 3.
27. Ibid.
28. Frank Rich, "Enron: Patron Saint of Bush's Fake News," *New York Times,* 20 March 2005, sec. 2, 1.
29. Richard Sandomir, "At (Your Name Here) Arena, Money Talks," *New York Times,* 30 May 2004, sec. 3, p. 1.
30. Ameet Sachdev, "What's a School to Do When Fallen CEO's Name Is on Wall?" *Chicago Tribune,* 23 October 2004, p. 1; John Byrne, "Seton Hall's Hall of Shame," *Business Week,* 30 September 2002, 14.
31. Sachdev, "What's a School to Do."
32. Alex Berenson, "A Patriarch's Shadow at Troubled Software Maker," *New York Times,* 23 April 2004, sec. C, p. 1.
33. Merrill Goozner, "Blinded by the Boom: What's Missing in the Coverage of the New Economy?" *Columbia Journalism Review* 39, no. 4 (November/December 2000): 23.
34. Arthur Levitt Jr., "The 'Numbers Game,'" speech given at New York University, 28 September 1998.
35. "Enron: Let Us Count the Culprits," *Business Week,* 17 December 2001, 154.
36. Anthony Trollope, *The Way We Live Now* (Oxford: Oxford Univ. Press, 1999).
37. Trollope describes the allure of Melmotte and his scheme to one of the novel's main characters, Paul Montague, in the following passage: "Mr. Melmotte was indeed so great a reality, such a fact in the commercial world of London, that it was no longer possible for such a one as Montague to refuse to believe in the scheme. Melmotte had the telegraph at his command, and had been able to make as close inquiries as though San Francisco and Salt Lake City had been suburbs of London" (ibid., 84).
38. Ibid., 89–90.
39. David Denby, *American Sucker* (New York: Little, Brown, 2004), 7, 85, 279.
40. Ibid., 319.
41. David Callahan, *The Cheating Culture: Why More Americans Are Doing Wrong to Get Ahead* (New York: Harcourt, 2004), 126.

INDEX

criminogenic conditions: in corporate
economy, 4; in energy trading industry, 100; flexible organizations and,
146; free market ideology and, 171; in
institutional environment, 24; neoliberalism as a cause, 14, 20, 171; New
Economy doctrine as a cause, 14, 20;
soft corruption of politics and, 171
CSFB. *See* Credit Suisse First Boston
culture: of cheating, 279–280; co-
optation of media and, 275–276; corporate domination of, 273–276; corporate symbolic power in, 276; of
corruption in Victorian England,
277–278; of fear, 222; of greed, 222;
as meaning-making, 223; New Economy conformist, 224; New Economy
icons, 273–276; New Economy mobilization of, 144–146; normalized corruption and, 222–231; power and,
222–231
cyberlibertarian rhetoric, Gingrich-
sponsored manifesto, 106

D'Amato, Sen. Alfonse: and inquiry
into Stratton Oakmont investments,
287n36; as investor in Stratton Oakmont, 35; as member of Computer
Associates auditing committee, 45; as
member of Senate Banking Committee, 44
Danforth, Sen. John, on oppressive law
enforcement, 259
Darr, Asaf, on moral economy, 285n34
Davis, Gov. Gray: criticism of FERC, 98;
on deregulation as causing energy crisis, 54
Davis, Tom (House Republican campaign chairman), blames Clinton culture of dishonesty, 255–256
Dell, Michael (Dell Computers
founder): Corvis IPO allocations to,
169–170; vetting of analyst, 170; woo-
ing by Quattrone, 169–170
Denby, David: belief in Blodget, 277–
278; need to believe, 278
Department of Justice, on FBI shift away
from white-collar cases, 247
deregulation: of California energy market, 54, 58–60; as cause of fraud, 280;
as disaster for consumers and taxpay-

ers, 280; as force for change, 129;
leaves subordinates vulnerable to coercion, 227; as natural and inevitable,
100; policing discourse on, 178; role
of campaign contributions in, 242–
243; role of influence peddling in,
100; World Bank funds for Enron, 83
derivatives: Bankers Trust scandal involving, 80; complexity problem of,
13; as core of Enron business, 80;
Enron efforts to keep unregulated,
79–81; Gramms' efforts to keep unregulated, 80–82; industry lobby
against regulation, 177; Long-Term
Capital Credit crisis and, 81; Orange
County bankruptcy and, 81, 177; regulatory exemption of energy, 82; report recommending regulation of energy, 81–82
deviancy: defined down, 175–176;
Durkheim on, 175; Moynihan on,
175–176; Spitzer on corporate tolerance of, 176. *See also* corporate
crime; corporate scandals; normalized corruption
DiMaggio, Paul, on shareholder value
model, 16
Dingell, Rep. John, Baby Bells ally, 106
Dixon, Don (former savings and loan
owner), on regulators as villains, 263
Dodd, Sen. Christopher: accounting industry contributions to, 242–243; role
in passing PSLRA, 242–243
Donaldson, William (former SEC chairman), hedge fund proposal, 272
dot-com industry, 137–168; feeding IPO
market, 138; firm reorganizations in,
146; fluidity of character in, 146;
frauds in, 146; importing Silicon Valley norms, 138, 144–146; IPO class action suit against, 143, 167–168; IPO
process in, 146–152; networks in, 146;
proposed settlement of class action
suit, 167; turning stock into currency,
138; rationality of founders, 142; revenue manipulation in, 153–156; role
in immoral economies, 138; reinvention in, 146; role in New Economy,
138; start-ups in, 144–152; stock option rallies by, 173; web of fraud in,
152, 166–168

ABOUT THE AUTHORS

Robert H. Tillman is a professor of sociology at St. John's University in New York City. He is the author of a number of recent books on white-collar crime, including *Big-Money Crime: Fraud and Politics in the Savings and Loan Crisis* (University of California Press), which received the Albert J. Reiss Award for Distinguished Scholarship from the American Sociological Association in 2001.

Michael L. Indergaard is an associate professor of sociology at St. John's University. He is the author of *Silicon Alley: The Rise and Fall of a New Media District* (Routledge) and has published in *Urban Studies, Urban Affairs Review, Social Problems,* and *Economic Development Quarterly.*